New World Disorder

New World Disorder

The Leninist Extinction

KEN JOWITT

UNIVERSITY OF CALIFORNIA PRESS
Berkeley   Los Angeles   Oxford

University of California Press
Berkeley and Los Angeles, California

University of California Press, Ltd.
Oxford, England

© 1992 by
The Regents of the University of California

Library of Congress Cataloging-in-Publication Data

Jowitt, Ken.
    New world disorder : the Leninist extinction / Ken Jowitt.
        p.   cm.
    Includes bibliographical references and index.
    ISBN 0-520-07762-8 (permanent paper)
    1. Communist state.   2. Political culture—Communist countries.
3. Communism—1945–   I. Title.
JC474.J69   1992   91-28260
321.9′2—dc20   CIP

Printed in the United States of America

9 8 7 6 5 4 3 2 1

The paper used in this publication meets the minimum requirements
of American National Standard for Information Sciences—Permanence
of Paper for Printed Library Materials, ANSI Z39.48-1984. ⊚

Contents

Preface

The phenomenon of Leninism should be seen in world-historical terms. For the most part, history is "protestant," characterized by highly diverse political, cultural, social, and economic institutions. Its "catholic" moments, when the intrinsic diversity of social life is subordinated to an authoritative and standard institutional format like Islam, Christianity, liberal capitalism, or Soviet Leninism, are few, highly consequential, and thus of particular significance. But does Leninism qualify for membership in this select historical group? After all, as an internationally and institutionally bounded entity with a continuously recognizable identity, Leninism lasted less than a century.

The Leninist phenomenon embraces the temporal, geographical, and developmental diversity of the October Revolution, Béla Kun's short-lived regime in Hungary, Stalin's "socialism in one country," Mao's Great Proletarian Cultural Revolution, Castro's Leninist conversion, Khrushchev and Deng Xiaoping's "Aquinian" reforms of Stalinist "Augustinianism," Pol Pot's Nazi-like movement of rage, "Eurocommunism," and the facade Leninism of Benin, Mozambique, and Ethiopia. It includes heroic revolutionary figures of Homeric stature like Trotsky, and the cruel pedestrian despotism of a Ceauşescu; heroic opposition to the Nazi assault, and hysterically genocidal attacks on Soviet and Chinese society. It offers instances of "Rubashov"-like self-sacrifice for "the cause," and vulgar "Rashidov"-like acts of personal and organizational corruption. But the strongest argument in favor of Leninism's status as a world-historical phenomenon was the transformation of ideological word into institutional flesh across developmental time and cultural space. For all the genuine diversity—historical, social, economic, cultural, political—in the areas subject to Leninist rule, an authoritative, standardized institu-

tional format was extended from the Soviet Union to Central
Europe, the Balkans, Northeast Asia, Southeast Asia, and Latin
America. In less than half a century, a set of Soviet replica
regimes was created in the most diverse settings: Albania, East
Germany, Vietnam, Cuba, and Czechoslovakia.

My intellectual passion has been to characterize Leninism's
novel institutional identity and developmental history.

EITHER . . . OR

Theory and comparative historical study never became central
features of communist studies. There are many reasons: one is
the difficulty of theorizing; a second is the bias in favor of
country or area study, one facilitated by the overwhelming centrality of the Soviet and, to a lesser extent, Chinese regimes.
The result has been a compartmentalized and largely atheoret-
ical set of case studies, with brilliant exceptions like Robert
Tucker's *The Soviet Political Mind* and Franz Schurmann's
Ideology and Organization in Communist China. Ironically, most
studies of Leninist regimes can be described in good Stalinist
fashion as "either . . . or" studies. Western studies of the Soviet
Union and Leninism imagine their subject as *either* completely
alien to *or* eventually convergent with Western institutional
forms. The longest standing paradigm—totalitarianism—conflated the ethical designation *evil* with the institutional definition *alien,* while those who speak of convergence see a gradual
dilution of the differences between liberalism and Leninism in
favor of liberalism. The emphasis on Leninism's alien quality
favored a polemically robust, but more often than not analytically anemic, grasp of the phenomenon, while the emphasis on
convergence erred in the direction of analytically assimilating
the unfamiliar to the familiar.

One can identify very few approaches to the Leninist phenomenon whose thrust is comparison, not assimilation or alienation of the subject. To characterize Leninism's historical and
institutional novelty, one needs a theoretical perspective and
conceptual language that takes Lenin's contention that he had
created a "party of a new type" seriously, and situates the Leninist phenomenon in comparative historical terms.

The essays in this book do that.

As an inertial political reality, Leninist regimes still exist in a minimally recognizable, *though still quite powerful,* form in a number of countries, including the Soviet Union and China. But as a bounded institutional form with a strategic purpose and unique claim and effect on members' identity, Leninism is extinct. In 1973 I wrote an (unpublished) paper titled "State, National, and Civic Development in Eastern Europe" for a conference at Berkeley. It began with this sentence: "The critical problem confronting communist regimes today is citizenship." Seven years later, Solidarity, the harbinger and, in good measure, instrument of Leninism's extinction, transformed theory into historical reality. Solidarity signaled the origination of the individual national citizen and the extinction of the party cadre; but, it may be hoped, not the end of our intellectual engagement with Leninism.

These essays express my engagement with one of history's most remarkable political phenomena: with the character, development, extinction, and legacy of the Leninist phenomenon.

1

THE LENINIST PHENOMENON

THE LENINIST RESPONSE

In both liberal and Leninist regimes (in contrast to peasant-status societies), social action is primarily oriented to impersonal norms.[1] What is particular about Leninist regimes is that impersonality is not expressed in procedural values and rules (i.e., due process), but rather in the charismatic impersonality of the party organization. The novelty of Leninism as an organization is its substitution of charismatic impersonality for the procedural impersonality dominant in the West.

The concept of charismatic impersonality is not readily digested, because it seems to be a contradiction in terms. The reaction to it is likely to be simple rejection, or a redefinition in terms that are more familiar, such as the routinization of charisma. But routinization is not what I am talking about. My focus (at least at this point) is on the unit designated as having extraordinary powers and being "worthy" of loyalty and sacrifice. In Leninism, that unit is THE Party.

As a means of demonstrating that the Leninist party is novel

This essay originally appeared in 1978 in *The Leninist Response to National Dependency,* Institute of International Studies Research Series, no. 37 (Berkeley: Institute of International Studies, University of California, 1978). It is reprinted here in slightly edited form.

1. This does not mean that liberal and Leninist regimes are the only conceivable means of establishing impersonal norms as authoritative action referents and determinants. However, I am impressed by the lack of success most other types of regimes in peasant societies have had in attempting to create a nationally effective set of institutions based on impersonal norms. To argue that Leninist regimes have been successful in this direction is not to argue that all spheres of social life are influenced to the same extent by these norms, that informal behavior based on personalistic norms does not exist, or that the definition and efficacy of such norms is not subject to developmental considerations.

in character, I shall offer a new and operational definition of charisma, contrast Leninism with Nazism, and develop the notion of the "correct line" as a character-defining feature of Leninist organization.

Charisma is not a concept that has suffered benign or any other kind of neglect. Nor should it. Discussion of it continues because it is a central feature of behaviors that recur and are seen as politically and socially significant.

For me there is one striking and defining quality of charismatic leaders. A charismatic leader dramatically reconciles incompatible commitments and orientations. It is in this sense that the charismatic is a revolutionary agent—someone who is able in certain social circumstances institutionally to combine (with varying degrees of success for varying degrees of time) orientations and commitments that until then were seen as mutally exclusive. It is the extraordinary and inspirational quality of such a leader that makes possible the recasting of previously incompatible elements into a new unit of personal identity and organizational membership, and the recommitment of (some) social groups to that unit.

Christ created a new unit—the Church—through his recasting of elements that had before been mutually exclusive— namely, commitment to Judaism as a corporate and parochial ethnic identity and incorporation of the Gentile world. For a significant range of social groups, Christ recast the terms of personal identity and organizational membership. To argue this is not to suggest that historical events did not play a critical role in the evolution of this doctrine and organization. Events after Christ's death make the importance of historical contingency quite clear.[2] One does not have to slight history or sociology in order to make the central point: for the comparativist (in contrast to the theologian), Christ's innovation was to combine in an inspirational fashion elements that had previously been mutually exclusive. He created a new unit of membership.

Hitler did with German nationalism and "Aryanism" what Christ did with Jews and Gentiles. The tension between Hitler's

2. See, for example, Hugh J. Schonfield, *The Pentecost Revolution* (London: Macdonald and Jane's St. Giles House, 1974), passim.

commitment to German nationalism and "Aryanism" is a defining quality of his movement. Hitler's orientation was not simply or exclusively to the German nation. Rather, he brought together in ideology and organization (e.g., in the SS) orientations and commitments that had been in critical respects and under different auspices highly conflictual—the exclusivity of ethnic nationalism and racial, supra-ethnic exclusivity.

If this conception of the defining quality of a charismatic leader is correct, one would predict that upon such a leader's death, his movement would be subject to splits representing the individual conflicting elements the leader had been able to unite. Thus, on Christ's death, his movement should have split into "Jewish" and "Gentile" factions. It did. The circumstances of Hitler's death make a parallel observation difficult. But even during his lifetime, one could observe some groupings more oriented to German nationalism (e.g., army factions) and others to a transnational "Aryan" line (e.g., SS members).

Lenin took the fundamentally conflicting notions of individual heroism and organizational impersonalism and recast them in the form of an organizational hero—the Bolshevik Party. His "party of a new type" was just that: a recasting of orientations that remained conflictual but were no longer mutally exclusive.[3] Lenin's innovation was to create an organization and membership effectively committed to conflicting practices—command and obedience with debate and discussion; belief in inexorable laws of historical change with empirical investigation of social development; heroic action with a persistent concern for the scientific and sober operation of an economy and society; and an emphasis on individual revolutionary heroism with an emphasis on the superordinate impersonal authority of the Party, itself the central heroic actor and focus of emotional commitment.

The manner and extent to which these different elements have been institutionally combined have varied significantly in the developmental history of the Soviet and Soviet-type re-

---

3. "Democratic Centralism" was for Lenin what "Nazi Germanism" was for Hitler and "Gentile Messiah" for Christ—i.e., a recasting of mutually exclusive elements into a conflictually based but practically effective new paradigm of membership and action.

gimes.[4] Yet crucial as the variations are, any attempt to grasp their significance depends on an appreciation of the central element in Lenin's innovation: the conflictual but effective recasting of charismatic-heroic and organizational-impersonal orientations in the form of a party in which heroism is defined in organizational, not individual, terms.

To argue that the novelty of Leninism as a political form is that it effectively recasts the mutually exclusive elements of individual heroism and organizational impersonalism is not to say there have not been historical precedents; nor is it to say that such an institutional amalgam of charismatic and modern orientations is constantly weighted in the same fashion. Religious organizations such as the Jesuits and Benedictines and military organizations such as the U.S. Marines are in certain respects instances of charismatic impersonalism. And as I have suggested at several points, Leninist regimes weigh and define charismatic and modern orientations quite differently over time. What is distinctive about Leninism as an instance of charismatic impersonalism— that is, as an institutional amalgam of charismatic and modern orientations—is that both these orientations are central to its definition. This contrasts with religious organizations whose secular-empirical orientations are ideally subordinate to nonmaterial, supernatural rationales. This argument obviously does not apply to a military organization, such as the Marines, that combines heroic orientations and technical-secular ones. However, the central place of war as a defining orientation for such an organization differentiates it from a Leninist party. To be sure, the revolutionary commitments of a Leninist party can be seen as comparable—and at certain points identical—to a war orientation. However, the Party's equally strong commitments to industrialization, scientific development, and economic planning as more than adjuncts to a war mission suggest an organization of a different order.

The difference among these types of charismatic-impersonal organizations, then, is by no means absolute, but it is significant.

---

4. I outline a model with static and dynamic features to account for the variations in chapters 3 and 5.

As suggested, it lies in the greater consistency that characterizes the place and role of modern elements in the Leninist amalgam. In ideal terms, these elements are less ad hoc, less instrumental, and more central to Leninism as a form of charismatic impersonalism.

To sustain an argument that Lenin's innovation as a charismatic leader was to create a political organization whose defining feature was charismatic impersonalism, one must come to grips with two outstanding and central "challenges" from Soviet history. The most obvious challenge to the argument presented here is Stalin's personal charismatic role from the time of the Seventeenth Congress in 1934 through 1953. However, there is a prior challenge, and that is the personal charisma Lenin possessed vis-à-vis his Bolshevik followers.

More than anyone, Robert Tucker has convincingly outlined the features of Lenin's personal charisma. In Tucker's words, "to be a Bolshevik in the early years was not so much to accept a particular set of beliefs as it was to gravitate into the orbit of Lenin as a political mentor, revolutionary strategist, and personality."[5] The Bolshevik colony in Geneva "proved to be a group of people who regarded themselves as Lenin's disciples and were worshipful in their attitude towards him. Although he was then only 33 years old, they habitually referred to him as the 'Old Man' (*starik*), thereby expressing profound respect for his Marxist erudition and his wisdom in all matters pertaining to revolution."[6] Lenin's charismatic status was, of course, enhanced and confirmed by his personal role in the October Revolution. Tucker makes a very strong case for what he terms the "leader-centered movement."

Without denying the significance of Lenin's personal charisma or the extent to which Leninism was and remains a movement with a strong leader orientation, I feel Tucker's argument is somewhat misleading. This is not because he fails to recognize elements in Lenin's behavior that are inconsistent with personal charisma, but rather because Tucker does not system-

---

5. Robert C. Tucker, ed., *The Lenin Anthology* (New York: Norton, 1975), p. xiv.
    6. Ibid.

atically relate Lenin's personal qualities to the defining features of the party he created.

In contrast, in a study entitled "The Great Headmaster," Edmund Wilson describes Lenin in terms that are quite literally coincident with those I have used to describe his Party. The core of Wilson's description is contained in the following passage:

> Though he [Lenin] was susceptible . . . to very strong personal attachments which survived political differences . . . [he] could no more allow these feelings to influence his political action than the headmaster can allow himself to be influenced in the matter of grades or discipline by his affection for a favorite pupil.[7]

In a society where personal attachments were an integral part of social organization, Lenin's detachment was culturally revolutionary. Furthermore, this personal detachment was placed in the service of a political organization designed to mirror his own qualities. In this light, Tucker's comments on Lenin's actions as Party leader and in response to the growing cult of his person take on added meaning. According to Tucker, "As supreme leader, [Lenin] did not simply issue commands to the ruling group; he did not rule by arbitrary Diktat. Automatic acquiescence in his position was not expected."[8] And when Lenin became aware that he was being made the object of a personality cult, he responded negatively. He summoned one of his aides in the Council of People's Commissars and asked:

> What is this? How could one permit it? . . . They write that I'm such and such, exaggerate everything, call me a genius, a special kind of man. Why, this is horrible. . . . All our lives we have carried on an ideological struggle against the glorification of personality, of the individual. We long ago solved the question of heroes.[9]

Lenin's reference to the "question of heroes" should not be treated casually. There is a sense in which both Leninism and Nazism emphasize the heroic ethic. It is not in the appreciation of heroism that Leninism differs from Nazism; it is in the des-

---

7. Edmund Wilson, *To the Finland Station* (Garden City, N.Y.: Doubleday, 1953), p. 391.
8. Tucker, *Lenin Anthology*, p. lvi.
9. Ibid., p. lx.

ignation of the heroic agent. For Lenin, the Party is hero[10]—
not the individual leader. The fact that Lenin possessed personal charisma is not as significant as the way in which he defined charisma and related it to the organization he created. As
an individual, he combined forceful charismatic certainty with
a genuine and persistent emphasis on empirical and impersonal modes of investigation and interaction. His party was
created (so to speak) in his own image. And that image was
distinctive in its novel recasting of elements—heroism, arbitrariness, and absolute certainty, along with impersonal discipline, planning, and empirical investigation.

One might well remark that perhaps there was a novel recasting of such elements during Lenin's lifetime, but certainly
not afterwards—not during the period of "high" Stalinism
from the 17th Party Congress in 1934 through 1953. As an
observation, this remark is valuable; as a conclusion, it is superficial. In fact, an examination of Stalinism is the best way to
point out the differences between Nazism and Leninism and
single out the defining features of Leninism.

Certainly the formal similarities between Stalinism and the
Nazi regime are striking and by no means all superficial. The
cult of personality that surrounded Stalin (and that has at times
surrounded other Leninist leaders) was in a basic respect every
bit as intense as that surrounding Hitler. Even more significant
than the cult of personality was the Stalinist "cult of cadres,"
captured in the saying "The cadres decide everything." Under
Stalinism, the Party and regime organization might be viewed
as no more than an aggregation of hierarchically ordered heroes—again quite like Nazi organization. These consequential
similarities do indeed allow for and call for comparison. However, the comparison itself reveals a character-defining difference between Stalinist Leninism and Nazism that is more important than the similarities.

In a relatively (and inexplicably) ignored article on factionalism in the Nazi Party, Joseph Nyomarkey has spelled out the

---

10. A study examining heroism as an integral component of Leninism's
conception of the cadre, the Party itself, the idealized character of the working class, and its images of postcapitalist society would be of great value.

difference between Stalinist Leninism and Nazism quite well. Nyomarkey is intrigued by the fact that in Nazism there does not appear to have been the same incidence or type of factionalism that appears in Leninism. His explanation is that there are two types of movements—charismatic and ideological. In a charismatic movement (i.e., Nazism), "the leader claims authority because he incorporates the idea in his person," while in an ideological movement (i.e., Stalinist Leninism), "the leaders will claim authority on the basis of the dogma, and will always represent themselves as its representatives."[11] Nyomarkey goes on to argue that in an ideological movement, it is the "dogma which ultimately holds the group together and which lends authority to the leader . . . [and] the dogma which can give rise to various interpretations which can in turn become the bases of factional conflicts."[12]

The point is crucial. It suggests that even under Stalin, the formal or ideal basis of Leninist party organization, membership definition, and policy formulation was independent from his personal insight. Can it be shown to have mattered? In several ways. First, Stalin had difficulty in establishing a führer position, whereas Nazism was defined precisely in terms of the *Führerprinzip*. Second, there is potentially within the Leninist party a legitimate basis for someone like Khrushchev to attack both the "cult of personality" and the notion that "the cadres decide everything."[13] A third and even more telling piece of evidence has to do with a character-defining feature of Stalinism itself: the idea of a "correct line." An appreciation of the place and meaning of this notion in Leninism (and Stalinism as one expression of Leninism) goes a long way in helping to delineate the novelty of Leninism as a distinctive amalgam of charismatic and modern (i.e., impersonal, analytic, and empirical) elements.

At the 16th Party Congress in 1930, Stalin addressed himself

11. Joseph Nyomarkey, "Factionalism in the National Socialist German Workers' Party, 1925–1926: The Myth and Reality of the 'Northern Faction,'" *Political Science Quarterly* 80, no. 1 (March 1965): 45.

12. Ibid.

13. George Breslauer emphasizes Khrushchev's critical stance toward the party cadres (apparatchiks) in "Khruschchev Reconsidered," *Problems of Communism* 25, no. 5 (September–October 1976): 18–34.

to the question of leadership. What—he asked—guaranteed that the Party would be an effective political organization? Was it the presence of a great leader? Someone privileged in his insight into the working of history? Stalin answered no. "For correct leadership by the Party it is necessary, apart from everything else, that the Party should have a correct line."[14] However, in 1930 Stalin had not yet attained the "sultanist" leadership that was to be his after 1934.[15] His comments at the 18th Party Congress in 1939—at a time when his personal mastery of the Party was well established—thus have added importance. Stalin once again turned to the question of leadership and made the following critical statement: "After a correct political line has been worked out and tested in practice, the Party cadres become the decisive force in the leadership. . . . A correct political line is of course the primary and most important thing."[16]

Let us now draw some conclusions about Leninist organization as a novel form of charisma—an instance of charismatic impersonality.

1. Both Leninism and Nazism are in crucial respects instances of heroically oriented responses to the class order developments of Western Europe.

2. Both Lenin and Stalin possessed personal charisma, and, particularly during Stalin's rule, the leader threatened the Party as the primary locus of charisma.

3. Even under Stalin the emphasis on the leader and cadres— at least in formal and ideal terms—always remained subordinate to the Party as the agent capable of formulating a

14. J. V. Stalin, "Political Report of the Central Committee to the Sixteenth Congress of the Communist Party of the Soviet Union (CPSU) (Bolshevik), June 27, 1930," in J. V. Stalin, *Works*, vol. 12 (April 1929–June 1930) (Moscow: Foreign Languages Publishing House, 1955; reprinted by Red Star Press, London, n.d.).

15. More properly, "neo-sultanism," a variant of a neopatrimonial political order in which the leader's personal (political) discretion is the political system's defining feature. Max Weber discusses the sultanist variant of patrimonialism in *Economy and Society*, (New York: Bedminster Press, 1968), 1: 231–32.

16. J. V. Stalin, "Report to the Eighteenth Congress of the CPSU (Bolshevik) On the Work of the Central Committee," in *The Essential Stalin*, ed. Bruce Franklin (Garden City, N.Y.: Doubleday, 1972), pp. 373–74.

correct line, a program separate from the personal insight of the leader.

4. The emphasis on the primacy of a correct line strongly suggests that even when minor or latent, the charismatic impersonalism of the Party is an integral/defining component of Leninism that is constantly available in a formal sense—and intermittently available in a political sense—as a legitimate basis for countering tendencies toward führerism. The 20th Party Congress is the most striking, but by no means the only, illustration of this point.

5. It is misleading to distinguish between charismatic and ideological movements à la Nyomarkey. Rather, one can distinguish different types of charismatic movements, with Leninism being one and Nazism another. The leader is charismatic in Nazism; the program and (possibly) the leader are charismatic in Leninism.[17]

The importance of the notion of the correct line in Leninism is that it is not a typical Party program. Instead, it parallels the organizational character of the Party, itself an amalgam of modern and charismatic elements. The "correct line" is simultaneously an analytic and empirical statement of the stages of national and international development, a set of policy guides, and an authoritatively compelling and exclusive ideological-political statement that must be adopted and adhered to.

In the "correct line," one has a striking contemporary instance of a modern program encompassed and understood in neosacral terms. Clearly, at different points in the developmental history of Leninist regimes, the empirical-impersonal elements have been severely constrained. Gulag, Lysenko, and "Dizzy with Success" cannot, should not, and do not have to be

17. There is a constant tendency in Leninism toward strong executive leaders. This is not the same as a constant tendency toward the emergence of a charismatic leader, as in the case in Nazism, fascism, or war bands. I would argue that it is possible to specify the developmental points at which the emergence of charismatic leadership in Leninist regimes is likely and when there is likely to be an attempt on the part of the Party elite to create a charismatic aura around a leader (a related but different phenomenon than the emergence of a charismatic leader).

ignored to sustain the argument that Leninism is a conflictual, but effective, amalgam of charismatic impersonalism.

Lenin recast the mutually exclusive elements of individual heroism and impersonal modern organization in creating a "party of a new type." This party combined heroism and impersonalism, charismatic arbitrariness (i.e., antipathy toward rational procedures and calculations) and sober empirical examination of social change. No better formal expression of this novel amalgam can be found than the notion of the "correct line." However, the striking differences in the weighting and definition of charismatic and modern elements in the Lenin, Stalin, Khrushchev, and Brezhnev regimes make clear the need for a synthetic statement of the constants and variables in the syndrome of Leninist charismatic organization.

One can identify charismatic and modern imperatives in Leninist parties and regimes. These imperatives are constant and conflictual. They provide for a continuously recognizable identity alongside the historically varying and developmentally related features of Leninist organization.[18] On the charismatic side, there is the concept of the working class, cadres, and Party as heroic elements. In particular, the Party is called on to sacrifice, struggle, and exercise continual vigilance to maintain its purpose and commitment to the realization of historical laws of social development that are conceived in teleological and universal terms. On the modern side, there is a materialist orientation that (with varying degrees of effectiveness but undeniable persistence) calls for an empirical, undogmatic examination of social change and organization, as well as for the collective discussion of social issues.

In contrast to the constant elements of Leninism, there are variables whose identification can explain the changes in the

18. To suggest the existence of organizational constants in Leninism is not to assert their "Platonic" imperviousness to the national and international environments with which Leninist regimes interact. Rather, the emphasis on the existence of organizationally constant imperatives directs one's attention to the types of situations Leninist regimes are likely to avoid, resist, and/or be unwilling/unable to adapt to. For a most impressive analysis of a nation's adaptation within the framework of ideological constants, see Louis Hartz, *The Liberal Tradition in America* (New York: Harcourt, Brace & World, 1955), passim.

institutional facade, policies, and ideological emphases that
mark the developmental profile of Leninist regimes. Two are of
particular importance. The first I term *developmental tasks*. For
current purposes, it is crucial to understand that a Leninist
elite's adoption of a specific task causes particular types of political uncertainties and, consequently, particular types of regime structures to manage those uncertainties.[19] These regime
structures vary in terms of the relative power held by the Party
leader and by the Party's central organs, the relative status of
the Party vis-à-vis police and military institutions, the distinctive
competence of the cadres recruited (i.e., in risk-taking, coercion, or social management), and the status of ideology, from
that of partisan empirical instrument to that of a stereotyped or
dogmatic conception of reality.

The second variable is the *sociocultural milieu* within which a
Leninist party and regime operates. Whether, to what extent,
and in which areas a society is primarily status- or class-oriented
and organized will significantly shape the way in which Leninist
leadership is expressed, policies are implemented, authority is
interpreted, and so on.

To summarize: The profile of a Leninist regime at any given
point reflects both the interplay of organizational constants—
charismatic (heroic) and modern (materialist) elements—and of
these constant conflictual imperatives with varying developmental tasks and changes in the sociocultural configuration of the
society being acted upon. To point out the complexity of this
relationship would be trite. Whether a phenomenon is simple or
complex is rarely the crucial consideration. It is whether we can
make the phenomenon intelligible. The terms and mode of
analysis presented here increase that possibility, if in no other
way than by not confusing organizationally constant with developmentally specific elements in the Leninist syndrome.[20]

19. See chapters 3 and 5.
20. While valuable in other respects, both Richard Lowenthal's "Development vs. Utopia in Communist Policy," in *Change in Communist Systems*, ed.
Chalmers Johnson (Stanford: Stanford University Press, 1970), pp. 83–117,
and Robert C. Tucker's "The Deradicalization of Marxist Movements," in
Tucker, *The Marxian Revolutionary Idea*, pp. 172–215, contribute to this confusion. (Along with my criticism of these two works, I very readily acknowl-

One highly signficant aspect of Leninism as a type of charismatic organization remains to be examined—that is, its status or traditional features. Once this is done, we shall have a more complete grasp of Leninism as an effective institutional substitute in some peasant countries with a nonfeudal legacy for the type of class organization and identification that emerged in nineteenth-century western Europe—a substitute that in certain respects "fits" and in others attacks the institutional and cultural profile of a status society.

To develop an argument about the status or traditional features of Leninist charismatic organization requires a summation and extension of Max Weber's observations about the relationship between tradition and charisma. According to Weber, charisma and tradition are fundamentally antithetical. Charisma calls for revolution; tradition, for conservation. However, in certain formal respects, traditional and charismatic orientations are similar, given their stress on personal (not abstract) and substantive (not formal) considerations. Both forms of social action are "hostile" to the impersonal-rational calculation that typifies modern organization. In Weber's words, "the two basically antagonistic forces of charisma and tradition regularly merge with one another; . . . the external forms of the two structures of domination are . . . often similar to the point of being identical."[21]

Identifying the formal overlap that exists between charismatic and status (or traditional) orientations is an important step in coming to grips with the ability of Leninism to operate effectively in a peasant-status milieu, but it is inadequate alone. Two other aspects of the charisma-tradition relationship—which to the best of my knowledge Weber did not develop—are

---

edge how much Lowenthal and Tucker have shaped my own interests.) Other influential studies in the field present a unidimensional or "collapsed" view of development in Soviet and Soviet-type regimes—for example, Samuel P. Huntington, "Social and Institutional Dynamics of One-Party Systems," in *Authoritarian Politics in Modern Society,* ed. S. P. Huntington and Clement H. Moore (New York: Basic Books, 1970), pp. 3–48, and Zbigniew Brzezinski, "The Soviet Political System: Transformation or Degeneration?" in *Dilemmas of Change in Soviet Politics,* ed. Brzezinski (New York: Columbia University Press, 1969), pp. 1–35.

21. Weber, *Economy and Society,* vol. 3, esp. p. 1122.

highly consequential for a charismatic leader's (or organization's) political effectiveness. First, charismatic leaders or organizations gain entry into the very societies they wish to destroy
and transform by possessing traditional features that are formally congruent with certain facets of a peasant-status society.
(I enumerate these features below.) A charismatic leader is unlikely to get the majority of a society to adhere to his vision for
the simple reason that, by definition, his vision is revolutionary
and entails fundamental revisions in the identity and organization of individuals and groups. Yet charismatic leaders have
adherents. The standard explanation from Weber through
Karl Deutsch has focused on social mobilization and turbulence.[22] A society subject to serious disruption, stress, and uncertainty creates a pool of persons available for recommitment.
This is a valuable and empirically confirmable point; however,
there is more to it. What makes the charismatic effective is not
only the availability of socially mobilized clusters, but also the
charismatic leader's (and/or organization's) possession of qualities that, at least in a formal or structural sense, are consistent
with the defining features of the society to be transformed. It is
the possession of these features that gives the charismatic entry
into the society he or she wishes to change.

Let us refer to the examples of charisma discussed earlier:
Christ lived at a time of great turmoil (i.e., social mobilization)
in Israel, but it was his status as a rabbi and student of Mosaic
law that made him intelligible to others, gained him an audience, and gave him a toehold in the society he wished to transform. It was Hitler's patriotic participation in the German army
in World War I and his credentials as a German nationalist and
supporter of the German army that provided him with a base in
a society that he wished to transform in ways that many a nationalist would come to rue.

Lenin's case would appear to be more difficult to interpret in
these terms. He was by no stretch of the imagination a Russian
nationalist (as, in a peculiar fashion, Stalin was). But he did
present himself in terms intelligible to a "mobilized" Russian

22. See Karl Deutsch, "Social Mobilization and Political Development,"
American Political Science Review 55, no. 3 (September 1961): 493–514.

audience. Not only was he considered "the old man" by his followers, but his self-presentation in critical respects obviously conformed to that role, as did his more general disposition, which Wilson captures with his notion of Lenin the headmaster. Wilson's comment that Lenin "had to have loyal adherents, with whom he could actually work . . . and [that] there appeared in his relation to his group something of the attitude of the older brother, carried over from his relation to his family, and a good deal of the inspired schoolmaster"[23] suggests that while Lenin was no Russian nationalist, he was—in identifiable sociocultural respects—a Russian.

Second, a charismatic's traditional features mediate between an organization with revolutionary commitments and its need to recruit members from a population that, even if socially mobilized, still culturally orients itself in terms of status (or traditional) orientations and expectations.[24] When Lenin said, "We can (and must) begin to build socialism, not with abstract human material, or with human material specially prepared by us, but with the human material bequeathed to us by capitalism,"[25] he might also have observed that the distinctiveness of his party's organization and orientation was its ability (under certain conditions) to offer itself as an intelligible medium for the recruitment and transformation of that "imperfect" material.

A case in point and one that can be used to demonstrate the utility of looking at the relationship between charisma and tradition in the terms we have devised is the success of the Chinese Communist Party in recruiting adherents during the Japanese invasion.

In his important works on peasant nationalism, Chalmers Johnson has argued that there was a direct relationship be-

23. Wilson, *To the Finland Station*, p. 390.

24. Too often it is uncritically assumed that to be uprooted from an institutional setting is to be stripped of one's cultural orientations. A distinction should be made between social and cultural mobilization. Typically, the latter lags behind the former. The difference in the extent of social and cultural mobilization within a given group may have a direct bearing on the types of organizations and appeals that are politically effective with that group.

25. V. I. Lenin, "Left-Wing Communism—An Infantile Disorder," in V. I. Lenin, *Collected Works* (Moscow: Progress Publishers, 1966), vol. 31 (April–December 1920), p. 50.

tween the social mobilization of Chinese peasants and the consequent opportunity for the Chinese Communist Party to provide uprooted peasants with new national-political identities. I
suggest this relationship is stated a bit mechanically. In light of
my argument about the relationship between charisma and tradition, I would hypothesize that in a situation of intense social
disruption, the Chinese Communist Party was successful in recruiting large numbers of adherents in part because, as an organization, it contained a number of features at least formally
or structurally congruent with a number of the defining features of a peasant-status society. The formal status features of
the Chinese Communist Party's Leninist organization mediated
between its charismatic-revolutionary and national commitments and the status orientations of the socially mobilized mass
base from which it had to recruit.[26]

It is now possible to provide a final characterization of Leninism: The distinctive quality of Leninist organization is the
enmeshment of status (traditional) and class (modern) elements
in the framework of an impersonal-charismatic organization.

The statuslike features (that at times are so consequential as
mediating elements in the process of recruitment) include the
following: (a) a marked tendency to distinguish between insiders (i.e., members of the Party) and outsiders; (b) an emphasis
on the security and protection of belonging to a closed, well-
bounded group; and (c) a placement of power in the hands of
cadres whose central personal role is emphasized—particularly
during the initial developmental phases of Leninist regimes.

These statuslike features, I have hypothesized, make a Leninist party intelligible to some sectors of a peasant population.
They do not necessarily or automatically make it politically acceptable or influential. Its influence depends, not on the formal
correspondence of certain of its features with those of peasant

---

26. See Chalmers A. Johnson, *Peasant Nationalism and Communist Power*
(Stanford: Stanford University Press, 1962), passim, and "Peasant Nationalism Revisited: The Biography of a Book," *China Quarterly* 72 (December
1977), p. 774. Obviously, the Party's mediating role was more central to those
peasants who joined the Party than to the larger number of nonparty peasant
soldiers and followers, who probably held a more complicated view of national identity than Johnson suggests.

society, but on the level of social mobilization in a society, and on whether there exist rival radical organizations whose substantive commitments are more aligned with those of a peasant population. To take the Romanian case as one in point: nativist nationalist movements of a charismatic order, such as the Iron Guard, in addition to an organizational format consistent with peasant orientations, had a set of substantive (religious and cultural) commitments closely related to the peasants' own; thus membership in a group like the Iron Guard involved much less of an identity shift for a peasant than if he were to join the Communist Party, with its materialist (modern) emphases.[27]

This discussion leads us to a fundamental hypothesis: Leninism's novelty as a political organization lies in significant measure in the fact that its traditional features are more structural than substantive in nature. One test of this hypothesis is that peasants who are recruited into a Leninist party should initially find much of its organization and orientation intelligible rather than alien. But after joining, they should become aware of organizational features of a substantive order that not only do not coincide with peasant social organization and orientation, but also actively oppose them. As we shall see below, there is supportive evidence for this hypothesis.[28]

The organizational features of Leninism that oppose peasant social organization are the Party's class or modern commitments. They include an emphasis on the individual responsibility of members for the execution of tasks, achievement as a central criterion for mobility and recognition, and—consequent on the relationship between personal effort and organizational-social mobility—the development of a sense of personal-individual efficacy and control over events. The Party also emphasizes a more empirical, less magical appreciation of social and political problems. In fact, the argument can be made that in societies and cultures where personal, discrete, and ritualistic orientations predominate, the potential significance and power of "sci-

27. For those interested in the Romanian case, I develop this point in Jowitt, *Revolutionary Breakthroughs and National Development: The Case of Romania, 1944–65* (Berkeley: University of California Press, 1971), pp. 85–89.
28. For example, Lucian Pye's interviews with Malayan ex-guerrillas (Pye, *Guerilla Communism in Malaya* [Princeton: Princeton University Press, 1956]).

entific socialism" are precisely in the emphasis it places on empirical, abstract, and critical modes of investigation of and orientation to social phenomena. Thus Constantin Dobrogeanu-Gherea's repeated emphasis that neo-serfdom was a systemic phenomenon—not the result of individually evil landlords—was a cultural break of epistemological and ontological proportions insufficient to bring about a social revolution but a significant component of such.

To stop at the point where one identifies a set of modern action orientations in the Leninist concept of organization and membership would be premature, misleading, and inconsistent with the theoretical approach of this work, however. To capture the distinctive quality of the class or modern features of Leninist parties and regimes, one has to specify their definition at an institutional—not social-action—level. It is the enmeshment of modern (and traditional) orientations in a novel type of charismatic framework that detemines the manner in which these modern action orientations express themselves. The charismatically impersonal features of Leninist organization are not simply neutral auspices under which modern developments of a Western liberal order occur. Rather, they constrain and shape the modes of modern or class developments. Thus individualism is expressed in the neocorporate unit of the collective (i.e., Party cell, work collective); achievement as a premise and imperative is in continual tension with the charismatic premise of Party membership as a heroic intrinsic quality; and scientific socialism as an emphasis on empirical, abstract, and critical orientations conflicts with the conception of scientific socialism as a grasp of inexorable, universal, and unilinear historical laws.

The Leninist Party and regime constitute a novel package of charismatic, traditional, and modern elements, a recasting of the definition and relation of these three elements in such a way that the Party combines impersonal and affective elements[29]

29. In this sense, the Leninist party can be seen as the formal organizational equivalent of Japanese social organization. As spelled out by Nakane, the distinctiveness of Japanese social organization rests on the fusion of affective and hierarchical-organizational elements. Unlike other peasant societies, in traditional Japanese society, the organization, not the family, has

and appeals effectively, if not logically, to some persons and groups in a turbulent society who themselves are a composite of heroic, status, and secular orientations.[30]

Is there any empirical support for the argument that Leninism's novelty lies in its recasting of status and class elements under impersonal-charismatic auspices? At the elite level, support for this argument comes from an examination of Ho Chi Minh's attraction to Leninism. At the mass level, there are interview data from Lucian Pye's seminal (and for some reason largely forgotten) study of Malayan ex-guerrillas.

From Ho Chi Minh's various statements about Leninism, one can identify a set of central perceptions. First, one is struck by Ho's admiration for Lenin.[31] This admiration is significant in two respects. To begin with, there was the traditional—and in this case mediating—dimension of Ho's seeing Lenin as a political "elder" and hero. Subsequently, Ho's personal admiration of Lenin developed into an appreciation of the novel quality of heroism in Leninism—its incorporation of impersonal and empirical orientations. In an article for *Pravda* entitled "Leninism and the Liberation of Oppressed Peoples," Ho identified Lenin's contribution as twofold:

> Lenin helped the working people . . . to realize in a more comprehensive manner the laws of social development, the requirements

---

been the object of identity and loyalty (see Chie Nakane, *Japanese Society* [Berkeley: University of California Press, 1970], esp. pp. 1–7 and 40–63).

30. Three considerations are relevant in connection with the reference to "some persons and groups": (1) The number of people in a peasant society both institutionally uprooted and (for whatever reasons) oriented to empirical, analytic, and impersonal conceptions and practices is likely to be relatively small. (2) These people are not simply peasants, but rather "composites" of status, charismatic, and secular orientations. In most cases they are the products of a peasant milieu, and (with exceptions) they are less mobilized culturally than socially. (3) The majority of those adhering to the Party at any given time is unlikely to be the "composite" type I refer to. For the majority, the decision to join the Party is likely to be based more on the absence of alternatives, decisions made by "significant others," career considerations, and so on. "Composite" types are more likely to be found within the influential cadre stratum. Pye, Hinton (*Fanshen* [New York: Vintage Books, 1966]), and Burks (*The Dynamics of Communism in Eastern Europe* [Princeton: Princeton University Press, 1961]) provide data that support this suggestion.

31. Bernard B. Fall, ed., *Ho Chi Minh on Revolution: Selected Writings, 1920–66* (New York: Praeger, 1967), pp. 23–24, 39–40, 61–62.

and objective conditions of the political struggle in every stage of the . . . revolution. . . . He gave [the oppressed masses] the miraculous weapon to fight for their emancipation—the theory and tactics of Bolshevism.[32]

In Ho's eyes, Lenin had created an organization—the Bolshevik party—that combined the heroic (i.e., the "miraculous weapon") and the scientific (i.e., the "laws of social development"). It was this novel recasting of familiar appeals in substantively new formats and of unfamiliar appeals in formally familiar guises that distinguished Leninism. For example, heroism (a familiar appeal) was related to an impersonal-formal organization (an unfamiliar format), while ideological support of anticolonialism, national equality, and political activism for the masses (unfamiliar appeals) were related to an authoritarian organization with a charismatic leader (a familiar format). It was this novel recasting that appealed to those like Ho who were themselves composites of status, charismatic, and secular orientations.

Ho saw Lenin as the "great leader [who] after having liberated his own people wanted to liberate other peoples, too." But he also saw that Lenin, unlike a traditional "big man," had "mapped out a definite program" to reach his goals.[33] And this program was ideally based as much on empirical analysis and critical theory as on conventional observation or inspiration. In short, for Ho, Lenin was a "big man," but a "big man of a new type."

To be sure, this is not an exhaustive explanation of Ho Chi Minh's commitment to Leninism, and it is a single case. But it is a highly significant case, and the fit between my identification of what is novel in Leninism and Ho's perception of Leninism's distinctiveness is not forced.

At the mass level, Pye's interview data from Malayan exguerrillas are remarkably consistent with my argument about Leninism. (That these findings have not been given the sustained attention they deserve is probably in part because of the absence of a conceptual statement about Leninism that would indicate their general significance.) According to Pye:

32. Ibid., pp. 255–56.
33. Ibid., p. 39.

In contrast to the impersonal relations of the . . . competitive labor market that had threatened [the ex-guerrillas'] sense of security before they joined the party, they felt that they had discovered in Communism the highly personal relations they craved, [but] they learned that behind the facade of personal intimacy lay the impersonal rationale of the party. . . . They discovered that in actual fact they were socially isolated within the party.[34]

In his very interesting discussion of comradeship and friendship in China, Ezra Vogel also supports my notion of the Party as a substitute form of impersonality—a charismatic impersonalism of discipline and affectivity.[35] Vogel's purpose is "to explore the decline of friendliness and the rise of comradeship."[36] The exploration comes up with the following discoveries. First, comradeship as a form of social interaction is more limited than friendship, engaging less of the total personality. It is more impersonal and formal—that is, ideally it is oriented to impersonal roles, not their incumbents. It involves the creation of a standardized public mode of interaction between equals, in contrast to unique relations among bounded groups of friends. In short, comradeship is a form of social market where the "goods"—that is, persons (rather than commodities)—are interchangeable, thereby increasing the combinatorial freedom and level of power available to the Party and state.

Second, the means used by the Chinese Communist Party to foster comradeship over friendship were to increase the fear of confiding too closely in one's friends; the Party did so by creating mutual distrust and consequent social distance. Emotion and affect were to be redirected toward the Party and away from one's social acquaintances and personal friends. How different this sounds from the descriptions by Western social scientists of the capacity for mutual trust that was supposedly such

34. Pye, *Guerilla Communism*, pp. 279–80; see also pp. 311–14.
35. Ezra Vogel, "From Friendship to Comradeship: The Change in Personal Relations in Communist China," *China Quarterly* 21 (January–March 1965): 1–28.
36. Ibid., p. 46. The language used below in summarizing Vogel's argument is my own. Vogel does not refer to a "standarized public mode of interaction," "social markets," or "combinatorial power." However, I do not think this language is inconsistent with the meaning of his argument.

an integral part of the West's unique developmental accomplishments! But was it? Certainly if one gives some weight to the
role of Calvinism as a mode of social organization and orientation in the development of Western capitalism, one has to
think twice. Calvinism argues adamantly for trust in God
(equivalent to the Leninist party), but according to Max Weber,
"especially in the English Puritan literature [Calvinism argues]
against any trust in the aid or friendship of men."[37] In both the
English and Chinese cases, the significance of such a social orientation in a status society based on corporate identity is clear
and revolutionary. It creates "isolated" individuals, undermines
the integrity of corporate social organization, and substitutes
impersonal frames of reference that coordinate and standardize
the actions of diverse people. Not trust, but impersonal, common organizational frames of reference are integral parts of
modern development.[38] The Leninist and liberal modes differ
significantly precisely with respect to the auspices under which
the new mode of impersonalism developed. In the English case,
impersonalism as an authoritative public norm developed in
good measure (though by no means exclusively) through an
internalized voluntary charismatic ideology, while in the Chinese and other Leninist cases, it has developed through the
authoritative imposition of a charismatic organization.[39]

There is additional information from Pye's Malayan study

37. Max Weber, *The Protestant Ethic and the Spirit of Capitalism* (New York:
Scribner's, 1958), p. 106.

38. There is some empirical support for this contention. In *Becoming Modern* (Cambridge, Mass.: Harvard University Press, 1974), Alex Inkeles notes
that "there were some personal attributes which the theory . . . had identified
as presumably part of the syndrome of individual modernity, but which nevertheless failed to legitimate their claim in our empirical investigation. . . . For
example, modern men evidently are not outstanding in trust" (p. 117).

39. As Max Weber noted about the creation of industries, "The mercan-
tilistic regulations of the State might develop industries, but not, or certainly
not alone, the spirit of capitalism; where they assumed a despotic authoritarian character, they to a large extent directly hindered it. . . . Thus a similar
effect might well have resulted from ecclesiastical regimentation when it became excessively despotic. It enforced a particular type of external conformity, but in some cases weakened the subjective motives of rational conduct"
(*Protestant Ethic*, p. 152). Analogously, there are different routes to a class
society based on the individual and impersonal norms of action, but different
routes ensure that class societies will vary in ethos and operation.

about the combining and recasting within the Party of traditional and modern elements under the auspices of a charismatic-heroic organization. Pye's interviews suggested to him
that for many ex-guerrillas, the Party was a route (the first in
their experience) to mobility based on personal achievement, a
route that gave them a sense of individual efficacy.[40] At the
same time, they found the hierarchical organization of the
Party quite consistent with their previous social and cultural
experiences. However, they ran into confusion when they came
up against the distinctive features of Leninist organization—
charismatic impersonalism. The ex-guerrillas responded to the
personal authority of leading cadres in quite traditional terms,
but they were often perplexed when cadres with whom they
had formed what they thought to be typical status-personal
relations criticized them for not having achieved certain organizational goals and even purged them on this basis.

While no comparable empirical studies of the Romanian
Communist Party (RCP) have been undertaken, a partial "substitute" for such may be found in an organizational comparison
with the other Romanian revolutionary movement during the
interwar period—the Iron Guard. Both the Guard and the
Party emphasized hierarchy and discipline of cadres. Both attempted to insulate their cadres from the contaminating effects
of society. Both had supranational referents—one religious,
the other ideological. Both argued the need for fundamental
cultural transformation, not simply elite change.

Eugen Weber, who has written the most sophisticated analyses
of interwar Romania, has suggested that for both the right and
the left, "the sources of dissatisfaction were similar, the radical
conclusions were similar, only the directions in which people
follow their conclusions were different, and even these were
essentially a combination of populism and sectarian elitism."[41]
Similarities between the Iron Guard and the Party did exist;
however, what Weber describes as "only the directions" is exactly

40. Pye, *Guerilla Communism*, pp. 316, 318.
41. Eugen Weber: "The Men of the Archangel," *Journal of Contemporary History* 1, no. 1 (1966): 124; and see id., "Romania," in *The European Right*, ed. Hans Rogger and Eugen Weber (Berkeley: University of California Press, 1966), pp. 501–75.

where the qualitative differences between the Guard and Party
lay.

For the Guard, a charismatic leader was the central ideological feature, both in theory and in practice; not so for the Party.
In the Guard, songs were favored over speeches—that is, the
Guard's emphasis was on form, externality, ritual, and magic,
while the Party's was a more analytic orientation to social issues.
In the Guard, men counted and programs were disdained; in
the Party, the emphasis on cadres was integrally related to the
formulation of a "correct line."[42] The Guard's symbolic references were the king and people—an almost paradigmatic status
relationship (personal and hierarchical).[43] The Party's major

42. As is well known, the line was anything but "correct" in many respects.
The Romanian Party's line was authoritatively set by Stalin, often in ignorance of Romanian conditions and without regard for the Romanian Party's
own political interests. While significant for certain issues, this point is relevant at a different level of analysis and does not contradict the one I am
making in my comparison of the Romanian CP and the Iron Guard.

43. The usual comparative reference for the Iron Guard movement has
been European fascism (though Eugen Weber has suggestively pointed to the
millenarian-syncretist movements of sub-Saharan Africa for comparison). I
suggest that the Guard might be more fruitfully compared with the Moslem
Brotherhood movement in Egypt during the interwar period. The points of
similarity are impressive. Both movements were dependent on a charismatic
leader (Codreanu for the Guard and al-Banna for the Brotherhood), and
neither ever really recovered after that leader's death. Both movements were
embedded in religious idioms and frameworks, each reflecting the different
content of the respective religions; for example, one does not find in the
Brotherhood the emphasis on death that there was in the Guard. Both emphasized absolute discipline and obedience without any pretext of criticism/
self-criticism or "debate before obedience." Both demonstrated a reluctance
to take power (at least until Codreanu's death in the case of the Guard), and
never effectively resolved their "educative" orientation with that of programmatic leadership. The revolutionary thrust of both movements was deflected
by their allegiance to the king, and both were consequently disarmed quite
easily. Both defined membership and organization in a fashion that emphasized affective-personal allegiances rather than affective-impersonal ones—a
limited but interesting indication being the Brotherhood's designation of its
membership units as *usra,* a term highly congruent with the Guard's use of
the term *nest.* In the composition of both movements, one sees the predominance of the same social types—particularly at the elite-activist levels. Students, clerks, civil servants, and teachers are found in large numbers—"those
who had passed through varying degrees of Westernization and had already
accepted some of its premises," but who for material and ideal reasons were
still attached to traditional religious and cultural frames of reference. Similarities in the respective positions and roles of Premier Brătianu in Romania

referent was class. Even the terms for the basic membership units in each organization highlight the parties' different characters (ethos as much as structure): in the Guard, the basic unit was the "nest"; in the Party, the "cell."

What emerges from these contrasts between the Guard and the Party is the difference in quality—not degree—that characterizes Leninism as a "direction" or response to conditions in a dependent peasant country.

There is another major element of Leninism, along with its substitution of charismatic for procedural impersonalism and its recasting of status and class features under charismatic organizational auspices. Leninism as a mode of analysis and strategy is based on an "ingenious error."

In his *General Economic History*, Max Weber refers to the "old truth . . . that an ingenious error is more fruitful for science than stupid accuracy."[44] With due modification, one could argue that Leninism as a particular approach to social change in a peasant country is founded on an "ingenious error." This error is the incorrect extrapolation of certain social distinctions from the economic differentiation Leninists observe in peasant society.

It was Joseph Schumpeter who pointed out the reductionist synthesis in Marxism of social and economic elements. Schumpeter argued for the autonomy of the social dimension and for recognizing the social character of classes. For him, classes were made up of families, not atomized individuals whose life chances were determined by their relation to the means of production.[45]

Teodor Shanin's study of the Russian peasant village extends and confirms, so to speak, Schumpeter's conception of social organization. Shanin found that Russian villages at the time of

---

and Zaghlul in Egypt, the Liberal Party and Wafd, the position of the monarchy in each country, the role of the army and that of the Great Powers—all add structural plausibility to a comparative study. (On the Moslem Brotherhood, see in particular Richard P. Mitchell, *The Society of the Muslim Brothers* [London: Oxford University Press, 1969], passim. On the Guard, see the references in E. Weber: "The Men of the Archangel" and "Romania.")

44. Max Weber, *General Economic History* (Glencoe, Ill.: Free Press, 1950), p. 30.

45. Joseph A. Schumpeter, *Capitalism, Socialism and Democracy* (New York: Harper & Row, 1962), pp. 9–20.

collectivization were vertically integrated units in which economic differentials existed but were not the primary dimension
along which a community was organized.[46] Rather, a village
community was made up of peasant family households that
experienced generational cyclical mobility—a phenomenon
that favored vertical integration rather than class antagonism.
Shanin's description of Russian villagers united around the village kulaks in opposition to the *kombedy* and Red Army very
much resembles the recent solidary village responses to efforts
at *vijijini ujamaa* (collectivization) in Tanzania.[47]

In short, theoretical argument and empirical investigation
seem to support the populist-nationalist idea that in peasant
society, economic differences do not signify that class is the
primary basis of identification and conflict. The Leninist analysis of village organization is in error—not in pointing to social
distinctions, but in conceiving them to be class (rather than

46. Teodor Shanin, *The Awkward Class* (Oxford: Clarendon Press, 1972),
passim.
47. *Kombedy* were committees of poor peasants. The original *kombedy*
movement occurred during the Russian Civil War. The committees were
revitalized during collectivization. In *Smolensk under Soviet Rule* (New York:
Vintage Russian Library, 1958), Merle Fainsod provides some data on the
tendency of poor and middle peasants to unite with kulaks against the regime's collectivization efforts: "Of the 122 persons who were apprehended in
October (1929, the Western Oblast) for committing 'terrorist' acts, approximately half were kulaks and well to do peasants, and another 45% were
middle and poor peasants. The latter group, observed the procurator, was
closely allied with the kulak elements by 'family and economic ties' and still
manifested a 'petty-bourgeois' ideology" (p. 241). On the response to collectivization in Dodoma, Tanzania, see Frances Hill, "Ujamaa: African Socialist
Productionism in Tanzania," in *Socialism in the Third World*, eds. Helen Des-
fosses and Jacques Levesque (New York: Praeger, 1975), esp. pp. 237–45.
Hill stresses that "those with little land were as insistent [i.e., opposed to
collectivization] as those with more to lose" (p. 241). On the other hand, Issa
G. Shivji, a Leninist, holds to the expected position that in Iringa, another
region in Tanzania where collectivization was opposed, "the poor and the
middle peasants remain politically dominated and economically exploited"
(*Class Struggles in Tanzania* [New York: Monthly Review Press, 1976], p. 108).
It is true that Iringa is economically more developed than Dodoma. However,
I remain skeptical that even in Iringa the peasants see themselves primarily in
economic class and exploitation terms. That there are tensions and conflicts in
Iringa and Dodoma and in every peasant region is obvious to anyone who has
had occasion to observe village life. To invariably interpret them in economic
class terms can be misleading.

status) distinctions. But the error—murderous in the Soviet case for several reasons, including the fact that much time had elapsed between land reform and collectivization, and the fact that land reform itself had not been accomplished by a regime with a strong rural Party apparatus (as in China)[48]—is "ingenious." The ideological-conceptual map with which Leninists work leads them to see economic differences as evidence of social polarization and the existence of "class allies" in the villages, and it enables them to do politically what nationalists can do only analytically—that is, distinguish and oppose competing social bases and conceptions of the nation-state (e.g., working-class versus middle-class nation). Working with such a paradigm, Leninists attack the institutional bases, not simply the elite organization, of peasant society.

The Leninist "error" leads to collectivization—an attack on the sociocultural bases of peasant institutional life, not (simply) to land reform—an attack on the political economy of elite organization in a peasant society.[49] The "right" targets are attacked for the "wrong" reasons. Not simply elites, but the basic institutions of a status society—the peasant corporate household and the village community—are broken through—not eliminated, but decisively transformed and given new roles in the social, economic, and political order.

An attack on institutions is the condition for breaking out of the pattern of "arrested development" characteristic of peasant countries.[50] In communist countries, the attack has typically

48. On China's land reform, Thomas P. Bernstein, "Leadership and Mass Mobilization in the Soviet and Chinese Collectivization Campaigns of 1929–1930 and 1955–1956: A Comparison," *China Quarterly* 31 (July–September 1967): 1–47.

49. David Mitrany's *Marx against the Peasant: A Study in Social Dogmatism* (New York: Collier Books, 1961) has long been considered a classic analysis of Leninism's relation to the peasantry. Yet in light of our discussion of the Leninist response to agrarian society, Mitrany's observations take on quite different meanings from those he assigns to his remarks about Leninism's artificial relationship to the revolutionary process in China and Eastern Europe and from what he considers to be Marxism's unnecessary and misguided opposition to the peasants.

50. My thesis is that any successful attempt decisively to change the structure and ethos of a peasant-status society depends on institutional, not simply elite, change. Leninism is one ideological-organizational and strategic means

taken the form of substituting organizational for social elites and formal organizations (e.g., the collectives) for social modes of economic production (e.g., the peasant village household). Organizational cadres do not necessarily displace village status figures ("big men," "patrons," "patriarchs") from affective and informal roles, but they do replace them in authoritative (political and economic) roles. Similarly, the collectives undermine the peasant households and village communities as institutions and models of social, economic, and political power more than as work units or informal social referents. The kulak is not an alien in the village who is seen primarily as an economic exploiter; he is a key figure in the corporate household and village system of social identification, organization, and power. Leninism errs in its understanding of his character and role, but it does so in a way that leads to strategies and policies that undermine the kulak, the peasant household, and the village community as defining institutions in a peasant-status society.

In historical retrospect, it might well be argued that, taken on a grand scale, the distinctive feature of Leninist programs of social change has been the substitution of the individual for the corporate group as the social and cultural base of social action and identification, and that this feat was accomplished by replacing the peasant household with the peasant nuclear family through collectivization (and accompanying industrialization and education).

That in communist countries the institutional expression of individualism differs significantly from its Western counterpart is predictable in terms of our analysis. The point here is that collectivization as the strategic manifestation of Lenin's "ingenious error" has a sociocultural as well as an economic significance.

The proverbial wisdom about collectivization is well illustrated by a comment by Zbigniew Brzezinski that Leninism is inapplicable to African conditions. According to Brzezinski, "a continuing Communist problem is the universal Communist failure in the agricultural sector, a failure that becomes espe-

---

of doing this in peasant societies at certain levels of social and economic development.

cially embarrassing in dealing with a continent that is primarily agrarian."[51] Brzezinski's error is far from ingenious. He has confused agricultural and agrarian problems—or, in the terms used in this analysis, political-economic with sociocultural problems.[52]

Collectivization is more than an effort to undermine landlords and kulaks economically and politically; it is more than an effort to industrialize. It is an attack on the social institutions and cultural orientations of peasant society. To quote Henry Roberts on the Romanian land reform of 1945: "The Communists undoubtedly exaggerated the economic importance of the boyars and the extent of their holdings. Nevertheless, a certain boyar spirit still prevailed in Rumania and the fact of land ownership continued to be a mark of prestige."[53]

Nothing that has been said thus far is meant to imply that Leninism and collectivization (industrialization) are the only means of bringing about significant changes in a peasant country. The reformist political economy analyses and strategies of Nikolai Bukharin, Kemal Atatürk, Indira Gandhi, or the Ford Foundation *do* significantly alter the social organization of a peasant country. Reformist strategies *do* seriously modify the character of the peasant household through commercialization and *do* bring about major revisions in the state's role.[54] However, these strategies tend to be more sectoral than national in application (if not in rhetoric) and generally more oriented to changes in elite than in institutional patterns.[55] The neomer-

51. Zbigniew Brzezinski, "Conclusion: The African Challenge," in *Africa and the Communist World*, ed. Brzezinski (Stanford: Stanford University Press, 1965), p. 210.

52. Interestingly enough, a Danish expert called to Romania in the interwar period to review its rural problems emphasized that the problems were agrarian rather than agricultural (see Henry Roberts, *Rumania: Political Problems of an Agrarian State* [New Haven: Yale University Press, 1951], p. 63).

53. Ibid., p. 299.

54. In this connection, see Colin Leys, *Underdevelopment in Kenya: The Political Economy of Neo-Colonialism* (Berkeley: University of California Press, 1974), chs. 5–8. The example of India is even more striking.

55. The difference between regimes that initiate some type of land reform and those that follow collectivization-industrialization is quite striking with regard to the effective penetration and integration of the rural areas with the

cantilist state-society that emerges from such changes continues to be based on a highly personalistic, stereotyped, and fragmented division of labor. Because of the absence of a nationally effective framework of impersonal norms that institutionally standardize human and economic resources, thereby allowing for their greater mobility and interchange, there is a high degree of (social) resource immobilization and fragmentation.

It is important to recognize that with Leninist modes of development there are also stereotyping and immobilization of certain types of resources at points in their developmental history, and in some respects unintentional reinforcement of certain status orientations among the population.[56] The differences between a reformist political-economy approach and a revolutionary sociocultural one are not absolute. But an observation of this order tends to be more placating than discriminating: while the differences are not absolute, they are basic. The two types of strategies differ in their impact on the central units of a peasant society—the extended household and village. Specifically, they differ in their ability to incorporate these units into a national political framework effectively based on impersonal norms of social action. The accomplishment of Leninism in a peasant society is that it authoritatively establishes a charismatic (not legal) type of impersonal institutional framework at all levels and in all sectors of society.

Developments during the NEP period in the Soviet Union highlight the relative incapacity of a reformist political-economy approach decisively to recast a status society into a class society.

Bukharin, the leading proponent of what is here referred to as a reformist or political-economy view, failed to see (as Robert Pethybridge has so correctly noted) that under the auspices of the NEP, Nepmen, kulaks, and *kustarnyi*, far from "growing into" socialism, were successfully using the new organizational formats introduced by the Party to expand and protect the social and cultural features of a kin-based, notable-ruled, corporately

---

urban (see Jowitt, *Revolutionary Breakthroughs and National Development*, pp. 7–69).

56. I examine this process in Romania and attempt to conceptualize it in chapter 2.

organized social order.[57] Bukharin held that owing to the changes in the rural elite brought about by land reform, the urban sector (the cities) could act as "commanding heights" for the rural areas; this notion was put to the test and came up short.

Gregory Massell's study of Soviet transformation efforts in Central Asia during the 1920s provides striking evidence of the Sisyphus-like quality of social-change strategies in a peasant country that emphasizes elite reorganization more than institutional transformation. According to Massell, "it would appear that the separation of traditional leaders from their followers, even when successfully carried out . . . did not . . . automatically lead to a community's dissolution."[58] Massell relates this observation to the segmentary character of social organization in the area, and goes on to note that under the circumstances

> valued lines of kin could serve as vehicles to fill whatever gaps there were. In effect, it is probable that ANY locally respected and strategically connected patriarch . . . could step into the place of lost traditional leaders. . . . It is also likely that heads of extended families or their eldest sons were able to form new, informally operating communal councils as quickly as members of old ones were removed.[59]

Still, pointing to the weaknesses of a reformist political-economy strategy is not the same as demonstrating the effectiveness of a revolutionary sociocultural strategy as a means of creating a type of class-based society. To that end, I shall now

57. See Robert Pethybridge, *The Social Prelude to Stalinism* (London: Macmillan, 1974), pp. 196–242, for an acute appraisal of the shortcomings of Bukharin's reformist policy. In China, also prior to collectivization, there was a tendency for local cadres to withdraw from the Party, attempt to become local social-economic notables, and influence Party policy and organizations in pursuit of personal-social interests (see T. P. Bernstein, "Problems of Village Leadership after Land Reform," *China Quarterly* 36 [October–December 1968], esp. the section on the "threat from below," pp. 1–23). In this connection, see too Ilya Harik, "The Single Party as a Subordinate Movement: The Case of Egypt," *World Politics* 26, no. 1 (October 1973): 80–106, on the distinction between collaboration and mobilization movements.

58. Gregory Massell, *The Surrogate Proletariat* (Princeton: Princeton University Press, 1974), p. 83.

59. Ibid.

examine collectivization in Romania, China, and the Soviet Union. This should allow me to scrutinize and develop my argument about Leninism's "ingenious error."

COLLECTIVIZATION

It would be erroneous to say that students of Leninist regimes have neglected collectivization. Especially in recent years, with the works of M. Lewin, Thomas Bernstein, James Millar, and others, collectivization has received a good deal of sophisticated attention.[60] However, it would not be erroneous to say that students of communist countries have given the greater part of their attention to industrialization, and that when collectivization has been studied, it has been from an economic- or political-control perspective.[61]

My thesis is twofold: collectivization may be the most distinctive feature of Leninist regime strategies, and its significance rests as much in its social as in its economic impact, and perhaps more. Expanding on this:

1. The neglect of the social dimensions of collectivization is extraordinary.
2. The distinctiveness of Leninist strategy may lie in collectivization as a particular means of undermining the peasant extended household and village—not so much as work units or social references, but rather as units and models of social, economic, and political power.
3. The effectiveness of collectivization as an attack on the status character of social organization is integrally related to a comprehensive policy of industrialization and education.
4. The collective farm may be viewed as a major instance of the neotraditional organization of Leninist regimes.

60. See M. Lewin, *Russian Peasants and Soviet Power: A Study of Collectivization* (Evanston, Ill.: Northwestern University Press, 1968); James R. Millar, ed., *The Soviet Rural Community* (Urbana: University of Illinois Press, 1971); references to Bernstein's works have already been made.

61. See, for example, J. R. Millar and Alec Nove, "Was Stalin Really Necessary? A Debate on Collectivization," *Problems of Communism* 25, no. 4 (July–August 1976): 49–63. Nove's argument is the more insightful.

5. An argument about the significance of collectivization as a defining feature of Leninist strategy does not depend on every Leninist regime implementing collectivization with the same urgency or in the same fashion.

Fortunately, there are some studies of the social impact of collectivization that can be examined in terms of these arguments. I shall approach these studies with the following questions: Do they provide evidence that collectivization undermines the peasant-status quality of social and cultural life, favors the emergence of nuclear families and the individual over the peasant extended household, and not only supports but also entails the effective introduction of authoritative and superordinate impersonal norms of action and organization?

Several studies about the impact of collectivization have been undertaken in Romania. Without doubt the most valuable has been that of the Romanian rural sociologist Mihail Cernea, who emphasizes that in precommunist Romania, the family was the organizational matrix in both the social and economic realms. According to Cernea, commercialization and the consequent development of supra- and extra-familial associations did not remove the extended family as either the model of organization or as an integral component of socioeconomic (and political) organization and action.[62]

The centrality of the extended family household as the basic unit of identity and action in precommunist Romania also comes out quite clearly in Katherine Verdery's study of a Transylvanian village that had a German and Romanian population. She found that Germans and Romanians measured prestige in radically different ways. Germans "assessed one another's position by a set of ideas about individual character, capabilities, and personal traits. . . . Rich Germans whose character was found wanting were simply not esteemed." In contrast, the unit ranked by the Romanians was not the individual; it was the household.[63]

62. Mihail Cernea, *Sociologia cooperativa agricole de productie* [The sociology of collective farms] (Bucharest, 1974), pp. 420–58.
63. Katherine Verdery, "Ethnic Stratification in the European Periphery: The Historical Sociology of a Transylvanian Village" (Ph.D. diss., Stanford University, 1976), pp. 256–57.

How did collectivization affect this situation? Cernea argues that collectivization has created new types of organization, which are formal rather than social. It has removed "familialism" as the fundamental organizing principle of agricultural organization. The brigade and team replaced the peasant family as the basic work units. The brigade made the individual the core production unit and (to a greater or lesser extent) detached him or her from familial ties. At the same time, it subordinated the individual to nonfamilial hierarchies and authorities based on impersonal orientations. This substitution of formal organization based on impersonal norms and the individual for social organization based on personal norms and the extended household was reinforced by a new system of remuneration based on the individual's work day.[64] The brigade system, which operated for twenty years, can be seen as an assault on the status organization of the village and peasant extended household.

But how effective was the brigade system in Romania (or China and the Soviet Union?)—and what do we mean by effective? These questions are crucial in light of two phenomena: (a) in communist countries, the family's role as a locus of trust and a unit of mutual help and gain has in certain respects been reinforced;[65] and (b) in recent times, the extended family has reappeared as the basic work unit on some collective farms. The meaning of these two phenomena is by no means self-evident. "Plus ça change, plus c'est la même chose" may appeal to some as a conclusion about social change under Leninist auspices. It certainly does not tax one intellectually or, in many cases, ideologically. But "economical" as such a conclusion might be, it is extremely misleading.

The discovery by some observers that the extended family is still a prominent feature of the Romanian (and Chinese) land-

---

64. Cernea, *Sociologia*, p. 199.
65. In response to periods of terror and provocation, the family became in some respects even more closely bound. In this connection, see A. Inkeles and Raymond A. Bauer, *The Soviet Citizen* (Cambridge, Mass.: Harvard University Press, 1961), pp. 210–33, and H. Kent Geiger, *The Family in Soviet Russia* (Cambridge, Mass.: Harvard University Press, 1968), pts. 3, 4, and 5.

scape is important but somewhat superficial. As a corrective to notions that social change can be conceived of in absolute terms, it is useful, but that is the extent of its usefulness. The question is not whether the peasant extended patriarchal household has been completely eliminated, but whether it has maintained or lost its integrity as the institution providing personal identity, exercising social, economic, and political influence, and acting as the cultural model of authority and interpersonal relations.

To observe that the peasant extended household still functions is not nearly as important as knowing *how* it functions and in what setting. To establish the meaning and significance of the extended family's continued presence in communist countries like Romania and China, one must examine the present internal organization of the "extended" household, look at the political institutional context in which such a family operates, and identify the types of norms that effectively shape the behavior of its members. Viewed in this contextual light, John Cole's findings in Romania and William Parrish's in China have very different meanings from those the authors argue.

Cole's interesting discovery that the extended family still functions in the industrialized country of Brasov (Romania) does not present much of a challenge to my thesis that collectivization (*cum* industrialization and education) undermines the integrity of the peasant extended household.[66] Parrish has examined the impact of collectivization on the Chinese village. Among his conclusions are the following: the production team in the collective is "somewhat traditional / somewhat modern"; one of the reasons agricultural transformation was comparatively easy and rapid in the mid 1950s was that collectivization relied heavily on natural communities; there seem to have been shifts in social patterns in the countryside, which in some ways made certain types of villages more "encysted" than they were even twenty years before; new collectives and subsequent brigade and team units tended simply to enclose old villages and

66. John Cole, "Familial Dynamics in a Romanian Worker Village," *Dialectical Anthropology* 1, no. 3 (May 1976): 251–67. My critique of Cole's conclusions is balanced by my appreciation of the very valuable empirical work he and his students have done.

surname groups.[67] Evidently, there is not much support here for the recasting or transformatory power of Leninist collectivization. However, Parrish has more to say about the Chinese village since collectivization. It seems that "today there is less need to mobilize kinsmen outside the village simply because the cooperation of fellow villagers is guaranteed by the collective interest everyone has in the success of the year's harvest. To an extent . . . the narrow administrative circle has replaced the wider network of kinship."[68]

Since collectivization, the village may in certain respects be more self-contained, but not "encysted." Parrish's use of the terms *narrow* and *wider* misleads as much as informs. That village neighbors rather than kin from several villages now cooperate economically may well signify a dramatic shift and broadening of social organization. The "narrowness" of kin cooperation has been broadened to include "strangers"—in this case, village neighbors. In similar fashion, neighbors now marry inside the village rather than going outside, and villages have their own schools. What appears to Parrish to be a narrowing appears to me to be a broadening process, one that decompartmentalizes the status-kinship divisions in a corporate-familial society. Furthermore, that interactions between individuals at the higher commune level are more formal, impersonal, and limited in scope is not necessarily a weakness of the rural system. Insofar as this development entails the breakup of status-familial organization at the level of the "standard marketing area" without removing the family as a source of private solidarity or work at various levels, it may in fact be an element of strength.[69]

The decisive change in China, Romania, the Soviet Union, and other communist countries has been the imposition—in the rural as well as urban areas—of authoritative and effective frameworks of action and organization neither modeled after

67. See William L. Parrish, "China—Team, Brigade, or Commune?" *Problems of Communism* 25, no. 2 (March–April 1976): 51–66; also see the same author's "Socialism and the Chinese Peasant Family," *Journal of Asian Studies* 34, no. 3 (May 1975): 613–30.

68. Parrish, "China—Team, Brigade, or Commune?" p. 54.

69. Insofar as a structurally multidimensional society is more adaptive than a society all of whose institutions and realms of social action are predicated on the same principle of orientation and organization.

nor based on the extended family. This does not mean status practices and orientations have been eliminated; it means they have effectively and regularly been subordinated to the regime's formal institutions and goals. The critical issue is not whether one can find instances of nepotism, corruption, and familialism in communist countries. It is whether these practices are informal responses in the context of authoritative institutions that limit their incidence and ensure to a great extent that they add to, rather than take away from, the regime's effective pursuit of its goals, or whether these practices are founded on largely intact status institutions that effectively compete with and subvert the operation of the regime's formal institutions and goals. To date, the difference between Leninist and "Third World" regimes is precisely in the greater success the former have had in subordinating status practices and orientations to the level of informal (not insignificant) behavior.[70]

To reiterate: the discovery of the continued existence of the extended family, the "narrowing" of the village, and corruption cannot uncritically be assumed to imply a lack of fundamental social change. One must ask: In what context do these practices and institutions exist, and consequently what systemic weight and character do they possess?

In his study of collectivization, Cernea notes the reappearance of the family as a strategic work unit on the collective farm. He goes on to ask the appropriate question: Does the reappearance of the family as the basic work unit on the collective farm mean the cooptation of the collective by the family? His answer is that the family unit has been incorporated at only one level of action—that of task execution. The system of *acord global*, one that recognizes the family as the contractual unit of work, utilizes "familialism" only where it proves functional—in work execution.[71] This functional recognition does not favor the reappearance of the (peasant) corporate patriarchal family as much as it favors an instrumentally oriented family made up of members with supplementary incomes and diverse careers,

---

70. This achievement is subject to developmental challenges, some of which Leninist regimes may be less successful in handling.

71. Cernea, *Sociologia*, pp. 208–9.

oriented as much to contracts as to connections, and to individual interests as to corporate ones.

In fact, the reappearance of the family as an important unit on the Romanian collective farm is possible in good measure precisely because of the prior developmental phase during which the peasant extended household and village were divested of their model and power qualities. The family that currently participates in the Romanian *acord global,* the Russian "link" system, and the Chinese production team is not the pre-collectivization family. Collectivization has not eliminated the family; rather, in conjunction with education, industrialization, and Party organization, it has recast the family's internal definition and its place in the social system. Leninist regimes have transformed their societies to the point where phenomena that once were public are now primarily private in standing and character. An example of this is Verdery's finding in the village collective she studied that former rich peasants and priests still receive more deference than either the Party secretary or the chairman of the collective.[72] But this deference has no direct political-economic significance. It is a private-social matter rather than (as in the past) an integral component and reflection of a particular type of sociopolitical order.

There is further evidence of institutional change in the Soviet case. Ian Hill, in his judicious and valuable examination of the ways in which the Russian rural population remains peasant, concludes with the following:

> Whilst, as I have indicated, certain groups still retain economic, social, and cultural peasant characteristics, in view of the depth and extent of cultural change it seems doubtful whether these characteristics are sufficient for us to continue applying the term peasant to members of the rural population. . . . The bulk of the rural population have learned to act within the confines of socialized agriculture and it seems that their peasant characteristics are a small element in their total cultural and behavioural makeup.[73]

72. Verdery, "Ethnic Stratification," pp. 271 and 277.
73. Ian H. Hill, "The End of the Russian Peasantry? The Social Structure and Culture of the Contemporary Soviet Agricultural Population," *Soviet Studies* 27, no. 1 (January 1975): 127.

Through the effective imposition of institutions (e.g., collective farms) that are neither modeled nor based primarily on personal norms of action and organization, and through the effective introduction of industrial and education policies, Leninist regimes have, to varying extents, successfully created societies that allow greater social mobility for the individual and resource mobility for the regime. They have created a neocorporate variant of class society, a charismatic "substitute" for the procedural type of class society that developed in the West.

"FAMILIALISM" IN COMMUNIST COUNTRIES

Though not to be understood as the persistence of the peasant corporate family, "familialism" may indeed be a current issue for Leninist regimes. There may well be new forms of "familialism" in communist countries, related to the routinization of the Party and the rationalization of society.

As I stressed earlier, the auspices of social change shape the organization and meaning of change. To use a familiar example, the West did not simply experience industrialism and national development. Entrepreneurial capitalism and feudalism have given a particular cast to the pattern of economic, social, and political development in the West.

In communist countries, a charismatic political organization acting as the purposive and dominant agent of change has generated a neotraditional ethos and institutional pattern at both the social and regime levels. In communist countries, status organization has not given way to the individual entrepreneur and citizen acting in market and public arenas. It has given way to a comprehensive set of neocorporate institutions (e.g., unity fronts, official unions, collective farms) with official-political status. The deliberate preemption by the Party of any potential political arena or role not coterminous with its own organization and membership—that is, its collapsing of the official and political realms—more than anything else determines the character of sociopolitical developments and the manner in which sociopolitical conflicts in communist countries are manifested and resolved.

At the regime level, the collapsing of the official and political realms favors Party familialization—that is, the routinization of a charismatic organization in a traditional direction.[74] This tendency is not unprecedented in Leninist regimes. The "new class" phenomenon has been observed over and over again. The difference today is the absence of a secret police–permanent purge mechanism able to ensure that the Party-apparatchik monopoly of political power does not become the monopoly of certain families who are in the Party.

Viewed in this light, Khrushchev's attempts at educational reforms can be seen more as attacks on the development of a ruling class of cadre families than as attacks on the development of a ruling class of Party cadres.[75] Certainly, Susan Shirk's study of Chinese middle schools suggests that the children of cadres have many of the attitudes and styles one associates with an established elite of interconnected families, convinced of their "right to rule" and basing that conviction on ascriptive characteristics such as family origin and official position more than on achievement considerations.[76] In Romania, recent criticisms of Party cadres acting as baptismal sponsors in return for deference and material goods, as patrons of clients engaged in semilegal and illegal business transactions (*nasul afaceristilor*), and as sponsors of (often unqualified) aspirants to Party or governmental offices point in the same direction.[77] Intermarriage at the Party elite level, "closing off" mobility at certain levels to nonelite families, and the development of a "right to rule" mentality within elite families (both Party and Party-connected) are phenomena that warrant empirical investigation in light of my conjecture about the direction Party traditionalization may be taking.

74. For Max Weber's comments on the traditionalization of charisma, see Weber, *Economy and Society*, 1:246–54.
75. See Jeremy Azrael, "Soviet Union," in *Education and Political Development*, ed. James S. Coleman (Princeton: Princeton University Press, 1965), pp. 233–72.
76. Susan L. Shirk, "Schoolcraft in China: Political Culture as Strategic Behavior" (manuscript, 1977). I am most grateful to Professor Shirk for having sent me her article before its publication.
77. See *Scînteia* (Bucharest) September 24, 1977, pp. 2–3.

The tendency toward "Party familialization" at the regime level has a counterpart at the social level. There also one encounters a phenomenon that can be approached in terms of a "familialism" different in character from what existed prior to the developmental efforts of Leninist regimes.[78] The efforts have succeeded noticeably in changing the occupational and educational profiles of communist countries. One striking manifestation is the emergence of a broad stratum oriented to achievement norms, calculable rules, and the nuclear family as the locus of affection and individual effort. However, the ethos and orientation of this stratum has a distinctive cast, one that often escapes those whose major interest is changes in social stratification. This ethos and orientation may be seen as a defensive response to the preemption of public political life by the Party-official stratum.

What one finds in communist countries today in some ways fits as well as any nineteenth-century Western example the picture of bourgeois society Marx drew in "On the Jewish Question."[79] One can point to a growing stratum of families whose achievement orientations and emphasis on individual effort and responsibility are suffused with an overriding concern with private life, private gain, self-interest, and career advancement. The political manifestation of this "selfish" individualism is the highly instrumental conception of regime legitimacy one finds within this stratum.[80] If we define as legitimate a regime able to assume the voluntary provision of private resources for official or public purposes, then in basic (not all) respects, regimes in communist countries are not very legitimate.[81] In some respects, Edward Banfield's image of peasant amoral society can

78. By "developmental efforts," I mean the collectivization, industrialization, and educational efforts of the Party.

79. Karl Marx, "On the Jewish Question," in *The Marx-Engels Reader,* ed. Robert C. Tucker (New York: Norton, 1972), pp. 24–52.

80. This observation is based on the author's experience and the observations of other students of Leninist regimes. Unfortunately, it does not have the support of survey data that would provide a more disaggregated and differentiated picture of political attitudes in these societies.

81. This statement should not preclude an appreciation of the extent to which a given regime's legitimacy varies over time and with respect to different facets of national life—e.g., participation, national defense capacity, or social welfare measures.

be transferred to communist countries under the label of urban amoral society.[82]

Ironically, the tendency at the regime level toward routinization of a Party based on charismatic impersonalism into a syncretic organizational-familial status group has been paralleled at the social level by the relative demise of status and the crystallization of a type of class orientation and family organization.

To be sure, this brief discussion of "familialism" at the regime and social levels in communist countries is speculative and schematic—and deliberately so. The motive is to identify those sociopolitical tendencies likely to define the field within which all politically conflictual forces in these countries interact. Among these forces, one should include the following: (1) the continued existence in Leninist regimes of leadership cadres committed to a conception of the Party as an impersonal-heroic organization and opposed to its routinization into a syncretic organizational-familial status group; (2) the widespread existence and persistence of statuslike attitudes among the peasantry, working class, the professional strata concerned with (job) security and maintenance of personal connections with those of elite status; and (3) the pressure on these regimes to respond positively to classlike developments in their own orders—pressures that come from increasing ties with Western economies and societies and that probably support those sectors within Leninist regimes more oriented to class than status or charismatic modes of action and organization.

An identification of contrasting regime and social developments is not a sufficient base for deducing the timing or specific content of particular crises, however. Nor can one deduce from a conceptual statement of this order—one that attempts synthetically to portray the distinctive quality of Leninist sociopolitical organization and analytically to identify the basic conflict points in that organization—the inevitability of political "degeneration" or cataclysm. To deal with the timing and content of crises, the formulations offered here must be complemented by empirical studies of particular Leninist regimes.

82. Edward C. Banfield, *The Moral Basis of a Backward Society* (New York: Free Press, 1958), passim.

My effort in this essay has had a different purpose. I have tried conceptually to specify the novelty of Leninism as political organization and strategy. I have proceeded on the assumption that the meaning of organization, strategy, and conflict in communist countries is not self-evident and that an adequate understanding of the developmental history and institutional profile of these regimes depends on more adequate conceptualization. Nowhere is this need more evident than in the relation between the national and international development of Leninist regimes.

COMBINED SUBSTITUTION

My analysis of Leninism as a particular response to the status organization of peasant society and the related phenomenon of dependency has been primarily national in focus.[83] The value of such a perspective, even if not fully realized in this essay, justifies such a study. However, simple observation strongly suggests that a historical and organizational phenomenon like the Soviet bloc was an integral—not marginal—part of the Leninist "response." For practically all Leninist regimes, dependence on the Soviet Union has been a defining feature of their developmental efforts for a greater or lesser part of their existence. The implication is that any attempt to specify the distinctiveness of Leninism as a response to the status organization of peasant society and dependency must include and explain the relationship between national and international levels of action and organization. I shall attempt to do so in this chapter.

In addressing this task, I shall introduce the notion of "combined substitution"—a concept that speaks both to the distinctiveness of Leninism as a national/international response to dependency and to the general need for concepts that systematically relate the national and international dimensions of sociopolitical change.

So far, three features of Leninism as a novel and effective (if

83. I address the "fit" between the internal ordering of a status society and the organization of international relations in "The Sociocultural Bases of Natural Dependency in Peasant Countries," in *Social Change in Romania, 1860–1940*, ed. Ken Jowitt (Berkeley: Institute of International Studies, University of California, 1978), pp. 1–30.

not highly efficient or legitimate)[84] mode of social change in a peasant country have been identified: the substitution of charismatic for procedural impersonalism; the recasting of status and the development of class features under charismatic organizational auspices; and Leninism's "ingenious error" of analysis, with an accompanying emphasis on institutional, not just elite, transformation of the agrarian sector.

A glance at the international position of most communist countries—at least during their initial phases of development—appears to complicate this view seriously, however. For a country like Romania (and in this case Romania typifies the greater number of Leninist regimes), one might argue that under the auspices of this novel Leninist organization, it simply shifted its "neocolonial" referent from France (or Germany) to the Soviet Union. In fact, *neocolonial* is too charitable a term. For more than a decade, most communist countries were more colonies than neocolonies of the Soviet Union. The presence of Soviet troops, advisers, and secret police officials; economic plans establishing the priority of Soviet interests; and the imposition of Soviet political and economic models meant direct Soviet domination, with a significant impact on a whole range of immediate- and long-term conflicts, from intra- and inter-Party conflicts to issues of national legitimacy for each of these regimes. Important as this dimension of Soviet colonialism is, however, it in no way exhausts its significance, for in a major respect, Soviet colonialism under Stalin was "colonialism of a new type."

For approximately a decade, the organization of the Soviet bloc was strictly analogous to the organization of a Leninist party. The relationship between the Communist Party of the Soviet Union (CPSU) and non-Soviet ruling parties was based on status and class features recast and shaped by charismatic impersonalism. As for status features, just as a Leninist party is based on the neotraditional insider-outsider distinction, so under the aegis of the Soviet Union, the Soviet bloc was a political

84. To be useful, the notions of "efficient" and "legitimate" must be related to the central ideological and situational features of an elite and society that are involved in a revolutionary process. I have made some observations on the issue of legitimacy in a revolutionary situation in Jowitt, *Revolutionary Breakthroughs and National Development*, pp. 115–20.

entity of insiders versus outsiders. Just as each local Party provided some sense of security for its members, so the Soviet regime provided political and military security for each of its member regimes.[85] Just as each party was led by a figure readily intelligible in traditional terms (i.e., Mao Tse-tung, Tito, Gheorghiu-Dej, Ho Chi Minh), so the regime bloc was led by a "big man," Stalin, a leader whose heroic feats—collectivization, industrialization, and defeat of the Nazis—created awe and inspired the conviction that "socialism in one country" could be generalized outside the Soviet setting.

This conviction was underwritten by Soviet insistence that each Leninist regime could and must replicate the Soviet industrial-rural breakthrough. As David Granick and, even more so, Paul Shoup have argued, this insistence that the "colonies" engage in rapid and comprehensive industrialization and rural transformation was a unique form of colonialism.[86] This colonialism insisted on the creation of engineers and agronomists, the building of factories and heavy industry, and the creation of an educational network and opportunities for social mobility on a scale that no other modern form of colonialism has come close to matching. These priorities reflected the class-order commitments and goals of each Leninist regime and the superordinate Soviet regime. That they were conceived of and organized as a rapid, intense, and often irrational assault was due to the heroic-charismatic ethos and orientation of those regimes.[87] The bloc was organized in the same terms and fashion as individual Leninist parties, but it was an international unit, and as

85. Furthermore, within the bloc, as within each party, security was threatened by the leadership's peremptory-arbitrary actions (i.e., purges)—in the former by the Soviet leadership, in the latter by the leadership of each party vis-à-vis its internal membership.

86. See David Granick, "The Pattern of Foreign Trade in Eastern Europe and Its Relation to Economic Development Policy," *Quarterly Journal of Economics* 68, no. 3 (August 1954): 377–401, and Paul Shoup, "Communism, Nationalism, and the Growth of the Communist Community of Nations after World War II," *American Political Science Review* 56, no. 4 (December 1962): 886–98.

87. One must be careful not to confuse the popular use of the terms *hero* and *heroism* with the concept of heroism. The former imply something good, a positively valued individual or action. The latter refers to a distinguishable type of behavior in which risk, prowess, and disdain for a rational calculus of cost and benefits are defining (though not the only) features.

such it added a crucial dimension to the efforts of its individual members to break through a "neocolonial" dependency pattern.

To break through dependency in a peasant country, a political organization with a paradigm antithetical to that of a social order based on status must simultaneously insulate itself from and recast the institutions of a peasant society AND insulate the country itself from international ties that constrain, shape, and reinforce domestic institutional patterns.

I call the dual process of insulation-transformation at the national/international level *combined substitution.*[88] The Soviet bloc in its initial phases is one historical instance of this phenomenon. Under the aegis of the Soviet Union, the bloc acted as an international organizational substitute for the international membership and reference groupings that shaped elite self-conceptions in these countries before Leninist parties took power. While the local parties substituted domestically for the social elites and institutions of a peasant-status society, the Soviet regime provided them with the models, resources, resolution, and "space" to act on their shared programmatic-ideological commitments.

There are a number of things to be said about Leninism as a

88. *Combined substitution* is an ideal-typical construct. Applied to the Soviet bloc phenomenon, it selects and emphasizes the distinctive ideological and strategic tendencies and actions of Leninist elites organized in a particular national and international fashion. It is not an inexorable law, familiarity with which allows an analyst to ignore the level of contingent political action. The analyst must operate at two levels in order to explain particular developments. For example, the fact that in 1948 the Soviet Union called for the implementation of social transformation in Eastern Europe should not be seen as an automatic consequence of its ideological commitments and organizational character, but rather as the coincidence of those two elements and the definition of its political interests in a particular set of environments (domestic, regional, international). In a quite different setting, Outer Mongolia, social transformations were in good part put off by the Soviet Union for some thirty years; insulation was achieved, but transformation was in many respects delayed. The reasons for the delay are to be found at the level of political contingency—in this case, the Soviet Union's absorption in the 1930s with its own social transformation and its concern over the role of Japan in Northeast Asia. The critical link between the level of politically contingent actions and ideological-organizational imperatives is an elite's definition of political interests. Presumably such definitions reflect ideological-organizational constants and environmental variables.

historical-organizational instance of combined substitution. First, we must come to grips with a fundamental distinction in the field of communist studies between independent and "derivative" regimes. This distinction between regimes such as the Chinese and Bulgarian or Yugoslav and Romanian is accurate and useful—but not equally so for all questions.

Although different countries and parties have had significantly different ties with the Soviet Union, and these ties have changed significantly over time,[89] even independent regimes like the Chinese, Yugoslav, and Vietnamese have recognized an ideological, military, and/or organizational debt to the Soviet Union in their initial efforts to establish a new domestic and international position.[90] This observation should be seen as an addition, not an alternative, to the independent-derivative formulation. The conclusion to be drawn is that even the relationship between the independent regimes and the Soviet Union has been in certain important respects and at particular times closer than the typical relationship between even allied sovereign states.

Second, there would appear to be a rather glaring anomaly to my argument that combined substitution is a necessary condition for avoiding or terminating a dependent domestic/international pattern. That anomaly is the Soviet case itself. The Soviet Union developed without the aid of a "bloc" substitute acting at the international level. Furthermore, of course, there are striking instances of non-Leninist countries avoiding dependency. In the nineteenth century, Japan and the United States provide two examples, as does Israel in the twentieth. All three underline a very important point—namely, although the Soviet bloc postwar pattern is an extremely important historical

89. I have tried to identify these changes in three works: "The Romanian Communist Party and the World Socialist System: A Redefinition of Unity," *World Politics* 23, no. 1 (October 1970): 38–61; "Inclusion and Mobilization in European Leninist Systems," *World Politics* 28, no. 1 (October 1975): 69–97 (see chapter 3); and *Images of Détente and the Soviet Political Order* (Berkeley: Institute of International Studies, University of California, 1977).

90. At later dates, these and other Leninist regimes have emphasized the negative contributions of the Soviet regime and their own "self-reliance"; while significant for the analyst, such declarations should not be viewed uncritically.

instance of combined substitution, it should not be confused with the concept itself.

The exhaustion of the western nations after World War I, the potential within the Soviet Union to build "socialism in one country," and the initial and sustaining faith in revolutionary support from western Europe are the components of the Soviet pattern of combined substitution. In the American case, the de facto international insulation provided by the British Navy and the absence of a peasantry domestically constituted another instance of combined substitution. I am not familiar with the Japanese case, but surely the role of the British Empire in the nineteenth century and the peculiar social-organizational domestic order that Chie Nakane has so insightfully described were central to Japan's avoidance of dependency.[91] What distinguishes the Soviet bloc pattern (not to be confused with the Soviet case per se) as an instance of combined substitution is that a set of regimes transformed their domestic social order and international position under the deliberate organizational auspices of a great power with which they shared an ideological affinity.

As already suggested, the particular Soviet bloc pattern of combined substitution is not the only one that has historically "worked." But it is worth noting that the domestic and international situation of most contemporary "Third World" peasant countries attempting to create sovereign national and modern social orders is closer to that of prewar Romania or Bulgaria than to the United States or Japan in the nineteenth century or the Soviet Union or Israel in the twentieth. Regardless of what similarities there may be, however, the particular Leninist pattern of combined substitution that was applied to the postwar period is no longer available to most of the "Third World" for the following reasons. First, there is no single leader in the Soviet bloc able to elicit the kind of awe and exercise the kind of power/authority that Stalin could. Second, Soviet Leninism, which after World War I was viewed by some activists in the colonies as revolutionary and liberating, is now seen by many as the conservative system of a powerful and potentially

91. Nakane, *Japanese Society*.

threatening state—the Soviet Union. Third, the emphasis (misplaced to an extent, if this analysis is correct) contemporary "Third World" regimes place on national "self-reliance" works against the creation of a bloc comparable to the Soviet postwar phenomenon.

For all these reasons, I suggest that Leninism is best seen as a historical as well as organizational syndrome, consisting of a political organization based on charismatic impersonalism; a strategy based on an "ingenious error" leading to collectivization-industrialization; and an international bloc led by a dominant regime, with the same definition as its constituent parts, acting as leader, model, and support. In this light, the Cuban revolution and Cuba's relationship to the Soviet Union are watersheds calling for careful examination and formulation.

One of the more intriguing questions of the latter part of the twentieth century is whether new combined substitution patterns of national development will emerge in the "Third World" or elsewhere.

2
POLITICAL CULTURE IN LENINIST REGIMES

THEORETICAL AND
METHODOLOGICAL CONSIDERATIONS

For at least some students of Leninist regimes, political culture is becoming a salient analytic and research perspective.[1] There are several reasons for this development. First, there is the question of intellectual and theoretical stance. Those students of revolutionary change who define revolution as involving decisive, but not absolute, change tend to be sensitive to the role of cultural elements in contributing to the character of political systems. This understanding of revolutionary change is one that accepts the assertion that revolution involves "fundamental and even abrupt ruptures with the past in many areas of life" but that "for good or ill, revolutions never shut the door to the

This essay was originally published in 1974 as "An Organizational Approach to the Study of Political Culture in Marxist-Leninist Systems," *American Political Science Review* 68, no. 3 (September 1974): 1171–91. It is reprinted here in slightly edited form. The author wishes to thank the Romanian Academy of Social and Political Science, IREX, the Institute of International Studies, and the Department of Political Science at the University of California, Berkeley.

1. I have in mind Frederick Barghoorn's *Politics in the USSR* (Boston: Little, Brown, 1966); Zbigniew Brzezinski and Samuel Huntington's chapter on "The Political System and the Individual," in *Political Power: USA/USSR* (New York: Viking Press, 1963); Richard Fagen's *The Transformation of Political Culture in Cuba* (Stanford: Stanford University Press, 1969); Richard Solomon's *Mao's Revolution and the Chinese Political Culture* (Berkeley: University of California Press, 1971); Lucian Pye's *The Spirit of Chinese Politics* (Cambridge, Mass.: MIT Press, 1968); and Robert Tucker's "Culture, Political Culture, Communism," *Newsletter on Comparative Studies of Communism* 4 (May 1971): 3–12.

past."[2] Political culture also recommends itself to those who approach the phenomenon of social change by focusing on personality factors.

Second, recognition of diversity seems to be closely related to an appreciation of political culture as a research focus. It is interesting to note that during the period of Stalinism and the hegemony of the totalitarian thesis in the West, the major analytic approach to Leninist regimes was a rather crude form of social-systems analysis.[3] Approaches of this order tended to discount or neglect the role of culture, largely because the relationship between regime and society was viewed simply as a pattern of domination-subordination. Similarly, during the reign of the "end of ideology" thesis in the West, structural-functional models dominated the analytic field. Only with the recognition of diversity does the analytic focus tend to expand and include cultural considerations.[4] The particular expression of diversity that has prompted consideration of foci that are complementary to a systems approach has to do with the visible and systematic impact society has on the character, quality, and

2. Benjamin I. Schwartz, "Continuity and Discontinuity in Contemporary China: Some Methodological Questions," *Bucknell Review* 19 (Spring 1971): 115–24, at p. 121.

3. An exception to this was the study by Raymond Bauer, Alex Inkeles, and Clyde Kluckhohn, *How the Soviet System Works* (New York: Vintage Books, 1956). In certain respects the argument to be presented in this essay consciously builds on the work initiated in that volume.

4. It is not surprising that the first formulations of the political-culture approach preserved the existing and rather crude paradigmatic distinctions made between totalitarian and liberal democratic regimes. Just as the "system theorists" responded to the changes after Stalin with the fallback concept of "rational totalitarianism," so students of political culture came up with the distinction between pragmatic and ideological cultures. (See Brzezinski and Huntington's contrasting of Soviet ideology and American political beliefs in "The Political System and the Individual," and S. Verba, "Conclusion: Comparative Political Culture," in *Political Culture and Political Development*, ed., Lucian W. Pye and Sydney Verba (Princeton: Princeton University Press, 1965), pp. 544–50. There are a number of problems connected with this type of distinction: (a) it is ethnocentric and obstructs through definition a concern with the complexities of all cultures; (b) it is unnecessarily static (it might for example prove more useful to consider both the United States in 1776 and the Soviet Union in 1917 as ideological and both in 1972 as pragmatic), (c) it fails to sensitize the analyst adequately to comparison of different ideological cultures, i.e., the United States in 1776 and in 1948, the Soviet Union in 1917, 1928, and 1957.

style of political life. One expression of this impact is the systematic discrepancy that occurs between statements about the ideal operation of a political system and its actual operation.

Third, political culture assumes greater salience as an analytic and research perspective as: (a) Leninist regimes themselves redefine their task priorities from transformation and consolidation to modernization, (b) the inter-regime community of ruling parties loses its cohesiveness and power as a membership group and identity referent,[5] (c) the social composition of the parties themselves changes, and (d) their posture toward the non-Leninist world changes.

For a variety of reasons, then, political culture is currently becoming a salient analytic-research focus for certain students and a research-policy focus for certain Leninist regimes.[6]

Political Culture and How to Study It

As conceived in this study, political culture is a complementary perspective, not a substitute for other approaches or a single-factor explanation. This understanding of its role is related to the assumption that social reality is complex and that the function of theory is not to deny this complexity but to make it more intelligible. The definition of political culture used here ideally sensitizes the observer to certain relationships between regime

5. On this point, see Kenneth Jowitt, "Political Integration and Political Identity in Eastern Europe," in *East Central Europe in the Seventies,* ed. Sylvia Sinanian, Istvan Deak, and Peter C. Ludz (New York: Praeger, 1972), pp. 180–84.

6. In recent years the Romanian, Bulgarian, Chinese, Hungarian, and Albanian regimes have all directed their attention, in the form of Central Committee discussions and resolutions, to the realms of education, ideology, and culture. The Chinese case is clear to all in the form of the Great Proletarian Cultural Revolution; for the Romanians, see *Scînteia* July 7, 13, November 4, 1971; for Bulgaria, see the article by Marin V. Pundeff, "Bulgaria under Zhivkov," and for Albania the article by Nicholas C. Pano, "Albania in the Sixties," both in *The Changing Face of Communism in Eastern Europe,* ed. Peter A. Toma (Tucson: University of Arizona Press, 1970), pp. 89–121 and 243–81. For Hungary, see the comments of Barnabas Racz in "Political Changes in Hungary after the Soviet Invasion of Czechoslovakia," *Slavic Review* 29 (December 1970): 638–39; and Bennett Kovrig, *The Hungarian People's Republic* (Baltimore: Johns Hopkins Press, 1970), pp. 131–83.

and society and allows him or her to approach these relationships in a way that contributes to our understanding of the
multifaceted reality characterizing these social systems.

Drawing an analogy with organizational theories, one can
note at least three ways of studying Leninist social systems. Both
in the study of American factories and in the study of the Soviet
Union, the first major analytic statements were primarily structural. In the first case, this took the form of Taylorism; in the
second, of totalitarianism. In each instance the range of phenomena generated by structural relationships, but not clearly
consistent with them, was perceived on the one hand by executives of Western business organizations as "anomalous" and on
the other by Leninist elites as "bourgeois remnants." Analysts
viewed such phenomena as either inconsequential and humor-
ous or, when it came to Soviet-type regimes, as indicative that
efforts to change these societies had been superficial. Whether
in an American factory or a Soviet-type regime, the informal,
cultural, and covert aspects of the system were inadequately
integrated into the theory used to explain the unit's character.

In organization theory, the reaction against this structural,
formal organization bias came with Mayo's human relations
school. Mayo shifted the emphasis to an appreciation of human
sentiment, of the factory culture, and of the significance of
informal groupings. In recognizing the significance of the human factor, Mayo failed, however, to attend adequately to critical considerations such as the power structure of the factory. I
would argue that within the field of comparative communism,
a development that parallels the Mayo school in organization
theory is Richard Solomon's work on China. Solomon also emphasizes the cultural dimension at the expense of the structural
dimension. At least two major costs are associated with this
failure. First, the terms of his analysis do not readily lend themselves to a discriminating comparative analysis of other Leninist
systems, largely because of his pursuit of the "unique" elements
of Chinese political culture. Second, rather ironically, much of
what Solomon perceives as uniquely Chinese turns out to be
something else. For example, the "uniquely" Chinese ambivalence toward authority and tendency to avoid conflict are, according to Michel Crozier, distinctive and basic features of con-

temporary French political culture.[7] The outcome of this "exceptionalist" approach to political culture may very well create more obstacles in the way of comparative analysis and consequently in the way of establishing what is truly distinctive about individual Leninist political structures and cultures.

A third approach to the study of organizations is that suggested by Crozier. Crozier suggests that organizations should be analyzed in terms of the interaction of formal structure and informal relationships. In his terms, these two elements should not be opposed. "They interpenetrate and complete each other. If one wants to understand them, one must study them together along with the system of power relationships that helps integrate them."[8] It is in this vein that I approach the study of political culture in Leninist systems. Political culture will be studied in conjunction with political structure; structure and culture will be viewed as establishing mutual, though not necessarily equal, limits for one another. Approaching the concept of political culture from this perspective allows us to (a) take explicit account of the cognitive element of political culture and to see political culture as largely a response to a regime with a given organizational format,[9] (b) avoid limiting the notion of political culture to the level of individual psychology as most students of the concept have done, (c) perceive the systemic significance of what is currently seen as either anomalous or unique in certain Leninist political cultures, and (d) generate hypotheses dealing with questions of conflict, change, and system identity. In short, the attempt here is to devise an analytic understanding of political culture that facilitates comparison of Leninist regimes in light of the interaction between formal-structural and informal-cultural elements,

7. See Solomon, *Mao's Revolution,* id., "Mao's Effort to Reintegrate the Chinese Polity: Problems of Authority and Conflict in Chinese Social Processes," in *Chinese Communist Politics in Action,* ed. A. Doak Barnett (Seattle: University of Washington Press, 1969), pp. 271–365; and Michel Crozier, *The Bureaucratic Phenomenon* (Chicago: University of Chicago Press, 1964), chs. 8 and 9.

8. Crozier, *Bureaucratic Phenomenon,* p. 164.

9. With regard to (a) see Carole Pateman, "Political Culture, Political Structure and Political Change," *British Journal of Political Science* 1, no. 3 (July 1971): 291–305.

thereby avoiding, on the one hand, the exceptionalist or uniqueness pitfall and, on the other, the tendency to assert through definition that structure alone is necessarily decisive in shaping the political character of Leninist regimes.

The relationship of political culture and political structure may be compared to the relationship that exists between the formal and informal organization of a factory. According to Chester Barnard, "when formal organizations come into operation, they create and require informal organizations . . . they are interdependent aspects of the same phenomena—a society is structured by formal organizations, formal organizations are vitalized and conditioned by informal organization . . . there cannot be one without the other."[10] Barnard argues that informal organization may be "regarded as a shapeless mass of quite varied densities, the variations in density being a result . . . of formal purposes which bring [people] specially into contact for conscious joint accomplishments. . . . Thus there is an informal organization of a community, of a state."[11] It is the informal organization of the state that I shall refer to as political culture. More precisely, political culture refers to the set of informal, adaptive postures—behavioral and attitudinal—that emerge in response to and interact with the set of formal definitions—ideological, policy, and institutional—that characterize a given level of society.

Perceiving the different levels of society, one can differentiate three types of political culture: elite, regime, and community political culture.[12] *Elite political culture* refers to the set of

10. Chester Barnard, *The Functions of the Executive* (Cambridge, Mass.: Harvard University Press, 1962), p. 120.
11. Ibid., p. 115.
12. To date most studies of political culture have been made at the community level. Robert Dahl has commented that "although students of political culture call attention to differences between elite and mass political cultures . . . up to now they have paid a good deal less attention to the beliefs of political elites" (*Polyarchy* [New Haven: Yale University Press, 1971], p. 167). For a perceptive analysis of elite culture, see Robert Putnam's "Studying Elite Political Culture: The Case of Ideology," *American Political Science Review* 65, no. 3 (September 1971), 651–82. To date, however, no one has argued for or analyzed a third arena, that of the regime in contrast to the elite and community levels. Among system-oriented studies, there is, of course, David Easton, *A Systems Analysis of Political Life* (New York: Wiley, 1965), pp. 154–247.

informal adaptive (behavioral and attitudinal) postures that emerge as a response to and consequence of a given elite's identity-forming experiences. One might for example analyze the Romanian and Chinese elite political cultures in terms of the difference between a conspiratorial-prison experience and a guerrilla-partisan experience.

Regime political culture refers to the set of informal adaptive (behavioral and attitudinal) postures that emerge in response to the institutional definition of social, economic, and political life. One would expect Leninist regime cultures to vary according to whether a given regime structure was predicated on a command or semi-market principle and whether it emphasized the participatory or command component of democratic centralism.

Community political culture refers to the set of informal adaptive (behavioral and attitudinal) postures that emerge in response to the historical relationships between regime and community. For example, one would expect very different community political cultures to emerge from a society in which organized religion stresses ritual and a mediated relation to God and one in which organized religion minimizes ritual and argues for a direct relation to God; similarly, the community political culture of a society in which state and society are related on the basis of an effectively institutionalized citizen-role should differ considerably from a society in which the mass of society has historically been excluded from political recognition and participation.

Having dealt with the basic orientations, concerns, and definitions, I should outline the basic analytic framework I shall employ to study political culture in Leninist regimes. Reflecting the contention that the study of political culture is most fruitful in connection with the study of political structure, my two independent variables will be structural. It is my thesis that all Leninist regimes are oriented to certain core tasks that are crucial in shaping the organizational character of the regime and its relationship to society. These tasks include: (1) transformation—the attempt decisively to alter or destroy values, structures, and behavior a revolutionary elite perceives as comprising or contributing to the actual or potential existence of alternative centers of political power;[13] (2) consolidation—the attempt to create the nucleus of a new political community in a setting that ideally prevents existing social forces from exercising any uncontrolled and undesired influence over the development and definition of the new community; and (3) modernization—the regime's attempt to develop more empirical and less dogmatic definitions of problems and policy, a formal, procedural approach rather than a substantive, arbitrary approach to the solution of problems, and an understanding of the executive function that stresses leadership rather than command competences.[14] Each of these tasks has organizational or structural corollaries. Transformation involves a confrontation between the regime and the "unreconstructed" society. Consolidation yields a structure of domination, as the politically defeated but "hostile" society must be prevented from "contaminating" the nuclei of the new socialist society. Modernization, however, requires a rather significant redefinition of the relationship between regime and society from mutual hostility and avoidance to the regime's selective recognition and managed acceptance of society.[15] Depending on the core task, then, the

13. See Kenneth Jowitt, *Revolutionary Breakthroughs and National Development: The Case of Romania, 1944–65* (Berkeley: University of California Press, 1971), pp. 8–9, 107–8.

14. Leadership competences refer to an elite's ideological acceptance of the political membership credentials of the mass of society. Nonparty members are considered bona fide participants rather than unreconstructed inhabitants of the national community. Tenets such as "state of the whole people" and "party of the whole people" are illustrative of this shift (which of course can be reversed or modified). Structurally, the shift from command to leadership competences involves the shift from coercive to manipulative skills, from a pattern of regime exclusivity to one of greater complementarity vis-à-vis society. Such a shift is illustrated by the decreased role of the secret police and at least formal attempts to upgrade Party activists in comparison to full-time Party functionaries (apparatchiks). Behaviorally, the shift in competence is reflected in new styles of leadership, greater emphasis on leadership visibility (i.e., Khrushchev versus Stalin, Gierek versus Gomulka, Dubček versus Novotny), direct contact with diverse social constituencies, and attempts to elicit social response to and confirmation of policy initiatives before the latter are given official status by the party.

15. *Selective recognition* refers to the regime's willingness to expand power by allowing greater functional autonomy in various organizational settings; *managed acceptance* refers to the regime's organizational preemption of social strata with recognition of aspirations or demands. An instance of managed

regime will be structured differently both internally and in relation to society. It is to be expected therefore that (a) the character of political culture will vary with changes in tasks or task mixes and (b) the introduction of a new task and regime structure will confront an already-existing set (elite, regime, and community) of political cultures.

The second independent variable I use is central ideological tenets. Briefly stated, all Leninist regimes define themselves in terms of their commitment to certain ideological principles. I am interested in two: the dictatorship of the proletariat and democratic centralism. These are of particular significance precisely because they have explicit and direct structural implications for the organizational definition of the regime itself and for the organizational or structural relationship between regime and society. Core task and central ideological tenets, with their structural correlates, provide the boundary conditions for the organizational definition of the regime and its relations with society. It is assumed that they directly contribute to the type of political culture that develops at the elite, regime, and community levels. The framework, however, is still not complete. Organizations do not occupy vacuums, but are defined in opposition to already existing organizations that have themselves generated corresponding cultures. Consequently, the process of specifying and acting on the organizational correlates of core tasks and ideological tenets is in part shaped by existing cultural postures. Furthermore, once a Leninist regime has come to power and established itself organizationally, the political cultures it generates assume a certain integrity of their own and begin to reinforce the regime's structure. For both these reasons, it is useful to consider political culture in the terms suggested by Harry Eckstein—namely, as an intervening variable.[16] In this formulation, political culture provides some substance for the "black box" between the stimuli (independent variables), such as core task and central ideological tenet, and the responses (dependent variables), such as the ease with

---

acceptance in Romania is the Front for Socialist Unity; an instance of selective recognition is the emphasis on collegial decision making in factories.

16. Harry Eckstein, "Memorandum to Participants in Conference on Political Culture and Communist Studies," 1971.

which certain tasks are accomplished in contrast to others, the manner in which they are acted upon, and the ease or difficulty a regime has in redefining its core task (i.e., from consolidation to modernization).

We must now ascertain whether the Leninist international subsystem provides a recognizable and widespread structural format for dealing with the tasks of revolutionary transformation and political consolidation. Is there in the historical experience of some of these regimes a shared definition, a similar formal-organizational approach to the tasks of transformation and consolidation? And if there is, what are the elements that define the character of this format, what are the consequences of this regime format for the political culture of these systems, and what is the significance of the interaction of this culture with regime structure for political change?

System-Building and Political Culture

Although there are fourteen Leninist or communist states, it is a historical fact that the Soviet Union's mode of development under Stalin has usually been the authoritative model, especially for most Eastern European regimes. In addition, for regimes such as the Chinese and Yugoslav, the Stalinist model was either adopted and then later rejected or continues to be espoused as a model by certain elite members. The Stalinist mode of transformation and consolidation may be termed a system-building approach. It is this approach that has shaped the overall character of the Soviet regime and the majority of Leninist regimes. And it is the legacy of this approach that these regimes must deal with in their current efforts to modernize.

System-building contains three major related components. First, the dictatorship of the proletariat becomes the defining relationship for interactions both between regime and society and within the regime. One can specify three structurally significant aspects of this political principle: (a) the explicit and sustained policy of separating the elite and regime sectors from and opposing them to the rest of society, (b) the explicit utilization of widespread coercion and violence and the subordinate role of persuasion in the initial phases of "constructing socialism," and (c) the tendency of Leninist parties to monopolize the public sector through their assumption of comprehensive and direct responsibility for social developments and the corresponding concentration of decision-making powers within the Party. What is involved here is the denial of any integrity to the public realm as distinct from the official realm.

Second, system-building regimes are concerned with the rapid development of their societies and the sustained mobilization of resources. What is structurally significant is that relations between regime and society are organized along elite-designated priorities. In Leninist terms, this is a "commanding heights" strategy, an approach to development that I choose to label "revolutionary laissez-faire." In such a system, the emphasis is on controlling decisive points and sectors in a given social subsystem and on structuring a society on the basis of tacit trade-offs or exchanges. In return for performance in priority sectors, and with respect to priority items, members of society are "allowed" to manipulate nonpriority sectors for their private benefit.[17] A variety of causal factors underlie this type of development strategy; some, such as the inadequate number of cadres, are historical, while others, such as the concern with rate of development,[18] are more ideological. Of interest here, however, is the type of regime organization and regime-society relations produced by this "commanding heights" or priority strategy. As Herbert Simon has noted, any formal organization "will always differ from the organization as it actually operates in several important respects. First, there will be many omissions in it."[19] As Simon goes on to note, what is decisive is whether or not the formal organization sets limits to the infor-

17. For a vivid description of this exchange relationship, see Merle Fainsod, *Smolensk under Soviet Rule* (1958; New York: Vintage Books, 1963), pp. 85, 151. While there are variations in the format over time and between countries, the essentials of this relationship persist in many Soviet-type systems.

18. See Kenneth Jowitt, "Time and Development under Communism: The Case of the Soviet Union," in *Temporal Dimensions of Development Administration*, ed. Dwight Waldo (Durham, N.C.: Duke University Press, 1970), pp. 233–64.

19. Herbert Simon, *Administrative Behavior* (New York: Macmillan, 1961), p. 148.

mal relations that develop within it. Mobilization in a system-building regime means that while all social areas are provided with political limits, several areas do not receive the kind of attention that characterizes priority areas. To emphasize the distinction, nonpriority areas are controlled rather than transformed. In this sense, they are "omitted" by the regime.

Third, system-building regimes are led by elites with "production mentalities." The Stalinist approach to socialist construction has been one of "walking on one leg"—that is, of defining success in constructing socialism as a function of political, economic, and social breakthroughs, while viewing cultural transformation as basically a derivative accomplishment. The predominance of the production mentality in system-building regimes manifests itself in the following ways: (a) as an "island-hopping strategy" whose premise is that with the redefinition of the economic, political, and social domains, the cultural domain can be effectively circumscribed, transformed, and the few "remnants" of bourgeois origin gradually "mopped up"; and (b) as an instrumental approach to culture and individuals that attends to such areas when they directly affect the regime's ability to act effectively on its priorities—social and economic change.

The significance of these major aspects of the system-building approach is twofold. First, a system-building approach to the tasks of transformation and consolidation unintentionally reinforces certain features of the existing (non-Leninist) community political culture that are considered negative by Leninist parties. This reinforcement occurs largely because of the congruence between major elements in the ideological and organizational format of system-building regimes and major elements in the community political cultures of the various societies that have become Leninist. Second, as these societies develop under Leninist auspices, they characteristically generate challenges to existing structural and cultural definitions and postures at the elite, regime, and community levels.

One implication of this analysis is that the current challenges faced by most Soviet-type regimes are not simply threats to power and efficiency. Rather, the current crises in these systems involve the confrontation of different structural-cultural sets, and what is at stake is not only power and efficiency but the character of political authority and social relations. This dimension of current developments has not been adequately examined, and the study of political culture can greatly enhance our understanding of the complexity and relatedness of developments within these regimes.

THE PARADOXICAL CHARACTER OF SYSTEM-BUILDING

It is paradoxical that in their attempt to redefine society critically, Leninist regimes simultaneously achieve basic, far-reaching, and decisive change in certain areas, allow for the maintenance of prerevolutionary behavioral and attitudinal political postures in others, and unintentionally strengthen many traditional postures in what, for the regime, are often priority areas. How and why are the obvious questions. In order to answer them, to deal with the substantive as well as formal dimensions of political culture in Leninist systems, an empirical referent is required. For that purpose, I shall focus primarily on a single political culture—that of the Romanian Socialist Republic—and on the interaction between its regime and society. The analytic results of this exercise should ideally be a greater appreciation of the partially contradictory character of Romanian development since 1948 and a heightened appreciation of the character of development and developmental problems in other system-building regimes.

The Dictatorship of the Proletariat and Political Culture

I have already stated that as a structural or organizational principle, the dictatorship of the proletariat involves the separation of the elite and regime sectors from the rest of society. This separation has occurred in Romania and has also occurred in similar regimes. Its rationale was twofold. Initially, it was predicated on the need to minimize regime commitments to a politically unreconstructed and hostile society. After the achievement of a decisive political breakthrough, the posture of avoidance was still maintained, adhering to the Soviet thesis that even after the political defeat of the old regime, its influence still threatens the construction and consolidation of new institutions, roles, and values.[20]

In at least two respects, the separation or dichotomization of regime and society had a critical impact on the cultural orientation of both elite and nonelite segments of the Romanian population toward the political realm. The first is the reinforcement of a status ordering of regime and society. In an article signaling a campaign against *bakshish,* its author noted that such a practice properly belonged to a period in the past, to a time when "our [Romanian] society experienced domination by a stratum of rulers or boyars," and he asked how a practice associated with such a political structure could survive in a socialist society.[21] The answer to this question can be found in the structural similarity between the dictatorship of the proletariat and the historic relationship of state and society in Romania. During the period of the dictatorship of the proletariat,[22] the Romanian Communist Party was in effect a corporate, privileged status group that asserted its identity and perquisites in opposition to the rest of society. My purpose here is not to deny the significant social, economic, and cultural transformations initiated during the Gheorghiu-Dej period, but rather to focus on a feature of this period that has not been examined by Western scholars or understood by the Romanian Party itself.

Given its goals of transformation and consolidation and its perception of how to achieve those goals, the Romanian elite created a political structure that in certain basic respects not only allowed for maintaining, but even reinforced, certain traditional political attitudes and behavior in both elite and non-

20. See J. V. Stalin, *The Foundations of Leninism* (Peking: Foreign Languages Press, 1965), pp. 42–43. "The bourgeoisie has its grounds for making attempts at restoration, because for a long time after its overthrow it remains stronger than the proletariat which has overthrown it." See also the passages from Lenin that Stalin quotes.

21. *Scînteia,* July 23, 1971. The title of this article translates as "Let us wipe out Bakshish: A practice incompatible with the ethical climate of our society."

22. While the dictatorship of the proletariat is still an operative concept in Romania, the current regime's structure and policy in many respects depart from my working definition of this principle. When I use the term *dictatorship of the proletariat,* I am referring primarily to the period 1948–64.

elite members of the population. Just as *boiar* (nobleman) and subject had historically been mutually exclusive statuses, so cadre and citizen became mutually exclusive statuses rather than complementary roles. The structure of the regime made it possible for cadres to "consider a public office a source of personal income and those in their charge as serfs."[23] The *nomenclatura*[24] became the equivalent of the legal underpinnings of nobility, an organizational statement that a certain category of the population was subject to special considerations. Thus, Mihai Gere, a member of the Romanian Party's secretariat, has noted that "sometimes those [cadres] who damage [*aduc prejudicii*] our society [i.e., through corrupt behavior] are shifted to another position or even promoted instead of being removed from their work."[25] Such behavior is not unnoticed by those who are lower in the political and social hierarchy. In contrast to the ideal regime criterion of worth based on social discipline, responsibility, and political maturity, the popular understanding of what is actually the criterion of worth reflects the dichotomous status ordering of regime-society relations. Reporting on an organization's failure to punish an accountant for proved offenses, a correspondent for the party newspaper *Scînteia* concluded that the incident involved "the removal of our principle criteria for appreciating men and their deeds [and their replacement] with subjective criteria." What were these subjective criteria? It seems that the prosecution of offenders depended on whether or not the individuals involved were *cei cu funcţie sau fără funcţie* (those with official positions or those without); in short, the effective criterion was membership in the *categorie de privilegiaţi* (privileged category).[26]

There is some evidence that the posture of nonelite members of society toward the political realm is based on this dichotomous structure of privileged versus unprivileged. In another

23. *Scînteia*, July 23, 1971.
24. The *nomenclatura* is a party listing of politically critical posts and the personnel eligible for them.
25. *Scînteia*, November 5, 1971. See in this connection Steven J. Staats, "Corruption in the Soviet System," *Problems of Communism* 21, no. 1 (January–February 1972): 40–48.
26. *Scînteia*, November 13, 1971.

report about the use of public resources for private ends, the Party correspondent noted that when the culprits were faced with their offenses, they without exception adopted a lamentable position, admitting only to the crime of not occupying a prominent enough position (*suficient nivel*).[27] Another example of the understanding elite members have of their position, perquisites, role, and relation to political life is found in an article that discusses the phenomenon of *răzgîndirii*, or rethinking of a verdict.[28] Although the reasons behind this phenomenon vary, depending on the case, it appears that local Party units often act much like other corporate privileged groups in trying to protect "their own."

It is significant that the tendency to dichotomize elite and nonelite membership during the dictatorship of the proletariat has reinforced the political culture that existed prior to the rule of the Communist Party, a political culture in which the elite sector was distinct in character and prerogative, not simply in role. We have examined some instances of this perspective at the elite level; let us now turn again to the mass level.

It is striking that system-building regimes based on the dictatorship of the proletariat have reinforced many pre-Leninist political cultural dispositions (attitudinal and behavioral) at the community level. By responding adaptively to the political reality of a status-based relationship between regime and society, many members of Romanian society continue to behave in partially traditional modes. For example, it is often necessary for the ordinary citizen to *stimula atenţie*, or gain the attention of those with a regime position, a doctor, bureaucrat, or party cadre, and many individuals with such positions demand *mica atenţie*, a little attention (i.e., money) before the performance of a public service.[29] The terms themselves are revealing. In a society based on explicit and authoritative status differences, it is rational for nonelite members to act on the premises enforced by the elite sector. As one of the "mass," the ordinary citizen must distinguish himself from other nonelite subjects if

27. *Scînteia*, November 30, 1971.
28. *Scînteia*, November 10, 1971.
29. *Scînteia*, November 17, 1971.

he is to get a response; he must "stimulate" the attention of a superior. Doing this is simultaneously a means of gaining the superior's attention, recognizing the superior's elite status, and often a means of decreasing the uncertainty and anxiety of the encounter.[30]

The widespread phenomenon of *pile* ("pull," or "connections") may also be viewed as a continuation of pre-Leninist political culture and as an informal adaptive response to a political structure that devalues adherence to legal-rational rules. The dictatorship of the proletariat is, after all, defined by Lenin as the "rule—unrestricted by law and based on force—of the proletariat over the bourgeoisie."[31] *Pile* at the community level and in the interaction between community and regime is the informal, covert equivalent of the *nomenclatura* at the official level; both are mechanisms for dealing with a structure based on status, not on rule considerations.

The most important point, then, is that from the perspective of the structural dichotomization it generated, the dictatorship of the proletariat supported certain pre-Leninist political cultural dispositions at both the elite and nonelite levels of the new Leninist regime. Ironically, these dispositions are essentially antithetical to the appearance of a Leninist nation-state in which legal-rational (though not necessarily liberal democratic) norms and institutions have a major role.[32]

30. In this connection see Robert Price, "The Social Basis of Administrative Behavior in a Transitional Polity: The Case of Ghana" (Ph.D. diss., University of California, Berkeley, 1971), particularly chs. 1 and 5.

31. Stalin, *Foundations of Leninism,* pp. 45–46.

32. One can, of course, argue that a Leninist regime cannot simultaneously maintain its political identity and incorporate legal-rational norms and institutions. In fact, this assertion is one of the "proverbs" in the field of communist studies. It may be a correct one but has not been demonstrated convincingly. Arguments about the incompatibility of Leninism and modernity often fail to recognize that all modern political communities are to varying degrees characterized by a conflict between several of the imperatives associated with modernity and the imperatives associated with the particular ideology of a given regime. Viewed in this light, liberal as well as Leninist communities are characterizied by persistent conflict between ideological commitments and commitment to a legal-rational ethos. One can identify one ideology (i.e., liberalism) with a particular ethos (modernity) and then conclude by definition that because Leninists aren't liberal, they cannot be modern, or can only be modern if they become liberal; but it would be more

It was asserted earlier that, in at least two ways, the dichotomous and oppositional relationship of regime and society contributes to the maintenance of a pre-Leninist political culture. We have examined the first, the reinforcement of a status ordering of regime and society. The second pertains to the basic cultural ethos of a peasant-traditional society, an ethos captured in George Foster's brilliant notion of "limited good." According to Foster, "broad areas of peasant behavior are patterned in such fashion as to suggest that peasants view their social, economic, and natural universes—their total environment—as one in which all of the desired things in life such as . . . friendship . . . honor, respect, status, power, influence, security, and safety, exist in finite *quantity* and *are always in short supply* . . . hence it follows that *an individual or a family can improve a position only at the expense of others.*"[33] In short, peasants tend to define relationships in zero-sum terms and to conceive of values rigidly and concretely. What is so striking in this instance is the high degree of congruence between the traditional cultural ethos of a peasant society and several Leninist-Stalinist precepts. Just as for the peasant, social relationships are zero-sum, so for Lenin and Stalin many of the relationships between the Party and society were also zero-sum. Examples include the basic political question raised by Leninists, *kto-kovo?* or who-whom?—which political force will triumph? The outcome is seen as precluding long-term sharing of power: that is, either the bourgeoisie or the proletariat gains power—not both.

Similarly, the rigid Stalinist conception of the Party's leading role and of the unitary nature of leadership has made those whose political identities were formed during the Stalinist period fearful that a shift to collegial leadership would "dilute" the Party's power, place, and effectiveness. Finally, there is the

---

productive analytically (a) to establish the range and type of conflicts that are typical of modern or modernizing societies with different ideologies, (b) to scrutinize more critically the varying dimensions of modernity and then attempt to establish what aspects of modernity different regimes are likely to stress and what institutional definitions of modernity they are likely to posit.

33. George M. Foster, "Peasant Society and the Image of Limited Good," *American Anthropologist* 65, no. 2 (April 1965): 293–315; see pp. 296–97. My emphasis.

Leninist-Stalinist aversion to faction; differences of opinion are often seen as a threat, as "weakening" the regime's unity.[34] It is remarkable how formally compatible these Leninist-Stalinist "limited good" interpretations of basic structural considerations have been with the "limited good" interpretations of value and structural considerations in a peasant society. Consequently, it is not surprising that the "limited good" conception of the dictatorship of the proletariat held by Lenin, Stalin, and their emulators in Eastern Europe could enhance the traditional cultural postures of a peasant society and in turn be reinforced by them. As in the case of the hierarchical status relationship between regime and society, a major link between the regime's conception and definition of its organizational character and the society's response to it was that society's social composition. Romania was approximately 80 percent peasant in the late 1940s. Peasants provided the regime not only with its major constituency but also with a large proportion of its membership. If one realizes that the urban population of Romania, particularly the industrial population, basically consisted of peasants recently turned workers, one can better appreciate how easy it was for the large numbers of party cadres drawn from the ranks of the peasantry or peasant-worker stratum to understand, accept, and operate with the Party's "limited good" conception of its own identity, tasks, and prerogatives.[35] Here was a classic instance of the Party partially defeating its own purposes and not recognizing it. In its effort to recruit and socialize cadres, to create "new men," its very ideological images and organizational definitions unintentionally acted in part to reinforce the traditional view of the rela-

34. One index of the modification of a Leninist regime's character is its approach to internal party criticism. It is significant that after assuming power Ceauşescu repeatedly stated that criticism is not tantamount to disloyalty; however, the resistance to implementing this nondogmatic (though authoritarian) and nonlimited good notion of criticism is still widespread. See Nicolae Ceauşescu, "Adunarea activului de partid al municipiului Bucureşti," in *România pe drumul desăvîrsirii construcţiei socialiste* (Bucharest: Editura Politică, 1969), 3:199–200.

35. See Zygmunt Bauman, "Social Dissent in the East European Political System," *European Journal of Sociology* 12, no. 1 (1971): 25–52, for a much needed and very useful discussion of the importance of the "peasant factor" in the development of Leninist regimes.

tionship between regime and society, a view that stressed the antagonistic, zero-sum character of that relationship. Once again the Party's attempts at transformation and consolidation produced a mixed set of outcomes.

Along with the separation or dichotomization of regime and society, an integral part of the dictatorship of the proletariat in Romania and elsewhere has been the regime's explicit and persistent use of coercion in relations with society and within the regime itself. This coercion had a major impact on the type of political culture that has developed within these systems.

In a very perceptive article, Emanuel Turczynski has pointed out the chasm that historically existed between state and society in Romania. The absence of an indigenous middle class, village-oriented cultural and social structure, and experience with foreign domination all contributed to a sharp difference between the private and social realms on the one hand and the public and official realms on the other. Turczynski suggests that this state of affairs was not conducive to the appearance of any effective popular identification with the state.[36] The coercive character of the dictatorship of the proletariat in certain respects (though not all) reinforced this separation of the private and public sectors of society, the antagonism between the two, and the perception of the public arena as a threatening, hostile, alien sector. The Leninist regime's employment of violence resulted in significant sectors of the population adopting a split posture, one of public compliance on the one hand and private avoidance, skepticism, or rejection on the other. A syndrome of this order is perfectly consistent with social psychological studies that have demonstrated, "if threatened punishment [for noncompliance] is very high, then compliance [public dependent influence] will occur without private acceptance. There is no dissonance since the high . . . punishment provides sufficient basis for the inconsistency between private belief or attitude and public behavior."[37]

36. Emanuel Turczynski, "The Background of Romanian Fascism," in *Native Fascism in the Successor States, 1918–1945*, ed. Peter F. Sugar (Santa Barbara, Calif.: ABC Clio), p. 109 and passim.

37. Barry E. Collins and Bertram H. Raven, "Group Structure: Attraction, Coalitions, Communication, and Power," in *The Handbook of Social Psy-*

And, in fact, it seems that the manner in which, and the extent to which, most Leninist regimes employed coercion reinforced a cultural disposition that was highly calculative toward the political realm, a posture of complying publicly in order to protect and preserve one's private domain. Robert Scalapino, for example, in a comprehensive study of North Korea, notes that "a number of persons appear to adjust to the demands of an authoritarian state by developing a series of external responses including an intricate series of participatory actions that differ from and provide some protection for internal or private responses."[38] Unlike "Third World" regimes in which coercion and rewards are too low to produce compliance with modern norms, and unlike regimes such as the Chinese, which appear to have employed coercion more judiciously,[39] in their formative stages, system-building regimes employed too much coercion and thereby reinforced what in certain respects might be termed a ghetto political culture. Before pursuing this point, let me emphasize that the dictatorship of the proletariat in Romania and elsewhere has done more than unintentionally reinforce and enhance pre-Leninist political cultural postures that were and remain antithetical to several of a Leninist regime's basic goals. One cannot, however, understand the current crises facing these regimes without analyzing the ways in which they did reinforce and enhance such postures.

Historically, Romanian political culture appears to have stressed the antagonistic relationship between public and private spheres. Experience with the basically coercive, extractive, and status-based rule of Turks, Russians, Austrians, Hungarians, native *boiars,* and native regimes stimulated the development of what often resembled the political culture of a ghetto. As in the past and as in a ghetto, under the dictatorship of the proletariat, the regime or official sphere represented "trouble,"

chology, vol. 4, ed. Gardner Lindzey and Elliot Aronson (Reading, Mass.: Addison-Wesley, 1969), p. 181.

38. Robert Scalapino and Chong-Sik Lee, *Communism in Korea,* vol. 2 (Berkeley: University of California Press, 1972), p. 847.

39. In this connection, see Thomas Bernstein, "Leadership and Mass Mobilization in the Soviet and Chinese Collectivisation Campaigns of 1929–1930 and 1955–1956: A Comparison," *China Quarterly* 31 (July–September 1967): 1–47.

being identified as the locus of demands and sanctions rather than of political support and recognition. The result was the adoption of a calculative, instrumental, and often dissimulative approach to the official or public sphere of life. In this respect, the similarity to ghetto culture is quite clear. Rather than identify with regime values, norms, and goals, such as disciplined work, the community developed a set of postures that in many instances were antithetical to the regime's expectations. Certainly from the Romanian Party's point of view, its social investigations have too often discovered individuals whose highest value is *trai usor* (the easy life) and who place too high a value on *timp liber* (free time.)[40] And yet each of these postures is an instance of an informal adaptive response to a political structure that has until very recently related to society in extractive and coercive terms, that failed to and in fact feared to identify with its society—a fear that may well be rational during the initial stages of a revolution but that produces mixed, unanticipated, and undesired consequences for a revolutionary elite.

Estrangement is the quality that unites the various postures I have referred to—the calculative, instrumental approach to social tasks and official priorities, the emphasis on free time and the easy life. If, as at least one student of the topic has argued, alienation "refers to an enduring sense of estrangement from salient objects in specified contexts," and denotes "the absence of basic attachments to and identifications with salient objects in a particular context,"[41] then it is plausible to conclude that during the period of the dictatorship of the proletariat (approximately 1948–64), the Romanian regime partially reinforced the alienated posture of large segments of the Romanian population. The use of coercion and the easily identifiable source of that coercion—easy precisely because of the dichotomy the Party created between itself and society and because of the con-

40. See Alexandru Ivasiuc, "Republica Muncii" (The republic of work), *Scînteia*, December 30, 1971; see also "Distracţii inofensive care afectează grav destinele unor tineri," *Scînteia*, September 18, 1971; "Parazitul cu blazon," *Scînteiă*, September 13, 1971; and "Acolo unde educaţia şi echitatea erau doar teme de şedinţă . . . ," *Scînteia*, December 14, 1971.

41. See Jack Citrin, "Political Disaffection in America, 1958–1968," (Ph.D. diss., University of California, Berkeley, 1972), pp. 66 and 73.

centration of decision-making power within its boundaries—in certain respects sustained and increased the community distrust of things official, public, and political, and created a major obstacle for the regime in its attempts to create a more positive relationship with society.

The third feature of the "dictatorship of the proletariat" component of system-building is the marked tendency of such a regime to fuse the official or elite sector with the public sectors of society.

In one of Petru Dumitriu's novels, *Incognito*, there is a passage describing a Party member's reaction to the criticism made of one of the higher party cadres at a social gathering. In response to the news of this occurrence, the Party member exclaims, "I can't understand *why it has been allowed*."[42] Phrased more formally, system-building regimes have tended to monopolize political discretion, initiative, and responsibility. Events do not occur, decisions are not made, and facts are often not recognized as facts until they are allowed to occur or to be recognized.

For such regimes, the absence of a public domain with an integrity separate from that of the official elite domain and the private social domain has several consequences. Lacking any substantial control over their own definition and role, public institutions in such a regime often fail to elicit identification from those who work within them. Given the absence of any autonomous public domain, the Party's demands that individuals identify with the public interest rather than with their private interest are unrealistic; the political reality is that only two discernible interests exist: the regime's and the individual's. Without a differentiated public domain capable of eliciting identification from large sectors of society, and with a regime that minimizes its commitments to society, it is not surprising to find so many instances of theft, pilfering, and lack of involvement with one's work. One could argue that given the fusion of official and public sectors and the low popular identification with these sectors, the public domain becomes the equivalent of a "treasure find" in a traditional peasant society. In such soci-

42. Petru Dumitriu, *Incognito* (New York: Macmillan, 1964), p. 53. Stress in the original.

eties based on the notion of "limited good," one can only afford
to appear more prosperous by attributing one's new wealth to
a source outside the local community—simply because in a
society based on an ethos in which resources are fixed, if one
person adds to his well-being, it means someone else has
become less well off. Now, given the political structure of a
system-building regime, specifically, its monopoly of all non-
private domains, the public domain (i.e., the commercial sector
of the economy) becomes for many the equivalent of a
"treasure find." Since public servants are prevented from effectively identifying as participants by the structure of the regime itself, and often left to their own devices to supplement
their income, the incidence of *ciupeli marunte* (petty pilfering) is
understandable. While regimes such as the Romanian still do
not recognize the causes of such behavior, they seem to be
aware of the ethos that informs it. One indication is the idiom
employed when such practices are criticized. In a recent attack
on theft, pilfering, and lack of work discipline, the author of an
article in *Scînteia* argued that "illicit gains are not gifts of chance
[i.e., a 'treasure find'], they are the fruit of repeated violations
of work discipline and of the law."[43] Apparently certain elite
members are sensitive to the persistence of semitraditional orientations to the public domain.

A second consequence of the regime's monopoly of the public domain, of its concentration of decision-making power, has
been that those who have positions within the regime, but not
necessarily elite positions within the Party, tend to separate the
status and role components of their position. In his work on the
social basis of administrative behavior in Ghana, Robert Price
discovered that Ghanaian bureaucrats tend to separate the status or prestige component from the role or behavioral component of their positions. His explanation is that the role demands
of positions in a modern organization are incongruent with
fundamental elements of traditional African culture, and that
consequently one would expect this separation to persist as long
as those traditionally prominent elements retain their impor-

43. *Scînteia*, September 15, 1971.

tance.[44] In Leninist countries, particularly in the rural areas, one can find a tendency to separate the prestige from the behavioral component of official positions, and it is often related to the Party's organizational weakness in such areas, the low level of ideological sophistication among the cadres, and the claims made on them by families and friends. Additional and distinctive factors, however, are at work in Leninist systems that lead officials to separate the prestige and role components of their positions. Given the sharp distinction made in the dictatorship of the proletariat between elite and nonelite positions, there is a corresponding tendency to emphasize the prestige component of one's position. The fact that historically the position of official was seen in terms of status and power rather than of functions and services has only made the bias toward the prestige component easier to sustain.

There is yet another reason, however, for the failure of many officials to act consistently with the formal definition of their position. In a system-building regime based on the dictatorship of the proletariat, where the Party places a premium on exercising a monopoly over politically relevant behavior, and where the definition of politically relevant behavior is deliberately diffuse rather than specific, an official who bases his behavior primarily on the formal role prescription of his position is in effect posing a challenge to that monopoly. For to base official behavior on the formal role prescriptions of a given position is to have as one's main referent a universalistic, impersonal set of action determinants. In the framework of the dictatorship of the proletariat, however, the Party does not accept the value of such impersonality or neutrality. In fact, the dictatorship of the proletariat is defined explicitly in substantive, not procedural, terms. The discrepancy between the concern of regime officials with status and their frequently poor performance in terms of the formal definition of their role is not primarily due, as in "Third World" settings, to the conflict and incongruence between modern role prescriptions (i.e., treat all clients equally) and traditional cultural elements (i.e., favor one's relatives) but to the political penalities that often accompany attention to role

44. Price, "Social Basis of Administrative Behavior," pp. 72–86.

prescriptions rather than to political cues. Because regimes interested in transforming an existing society and consolidating the nuclei of a new one are committed to controlling and defining the premises and substance of politically relevant behavior, any such behavior with a nonparty premise as its major referent is a potential challenge. What is routine behavior for an official in a nonrevolutionary context becomes an illegitimate initiative for one in a revolutionary setting. The consequence, one discovers, is that in such a regime, officials are reluctant to take the formal definitions of their positions seriously. In light of the structure of the regime and its political-ideological orientation, this is a quite rational stance to adopt. The net result of all of this is that in a "Third World" peasant society there are societal forces working against the integration of the status and role components of a position, and in a peasant society subject to the dictatorship of the proletariat, there are additional regime forces working in the same direction. Both forces work against an effective appreciation of what role- and rule-based behavior implies and support a political culture that views politically relevant behavior as dependent on permission by and familiarity with authoritative figures.

A final consequence of the regime's monopoly of the public domain is the premium often placed on withholding critical information from the purview of decision makers. Within system-building regimes, a particularly large number of events are hushed up (*muşamalizat*). It was argued earlier that intra-elite mutually protective behavior is partly a function of the Party's corporate group attitude of protecting "its own." However, mutual protection also occurs because the Party assumes responsibility for so much. Given the scope of the Party's responsibility, it is not surprising that cadres who were unaware of misdeeds in their sectors often work to prevent such deeds from becoming widely known, since exposure will result in their own punishment. Such behavior could be documented throughout Eastern Europe and the Soviet Union by a random search of Party newspapers. In his study of North Korea, Scalapino found a classic example of this phenomenon. There it was brought to the attention of a provincial secretary that a "half-won business" was operating. He was unfamiliar with this term, and it was explained that it referred to prostitution. The secretary and several other cadres carried out an investigation, identified the individuals involved, and concluded: "This was a serious problem for us, because if we reported this matter to higher offices of the Party, we would all be subject to disciplinary treatment, including the . . . Party secretary and myself, because we had allowed such a thing to develop. It was the season of the annual committee inspection and . . . we did everything to prevent them from reaching the hamlet. . . . Later [we] called on those implicated. . . . We could not implicate them in any case, however, or we would have been deeply involved."[45] Paradoxically, then, the Party's assumption of total responsibility for the public domain contributes in certain instances to collusion between elite and nonelite actors regarding illegal behavior, and to the withholding of important information, since its release may result in negative sanctions against regime members. The consequence of all of this is the development of a regime political culture composed in part of dissimulation and complicity. Monopolization of the public domain, the fusing of elite and public spheres, and the corresponding denial of institutional integrity to public institutions (economic, administrative, social, and political) have in some ways reinforced the traditional political culture that viewed all relationships in terms of their hierarchical rather than their complementary character and that defined responsibility as the avoidance of public initiative.

Mobilization and Political Culture

A second defining feature of all Leninist regimes is their preoccupation with the rate of social development. Communist governments emphasize the fulfillment of potentiality. "Structurally, the political community is the means of translating potentiality into some sort of reality."[46]

A major feature of this mobilization ethos and the corre-

---

45. Scalapino, *Communism in Korea*, 2:777.
46. David E. Apter, *The Politics of Modernization* (Chicago: University of Chicago Press, 1965), p. 31.

sponding relationship between regime and society are the targets and priorities authoritatively established by the elite and used to gauge both the regime's and society's performance. Joseph Berliner has analyzed the character and consequences of this political structure in the Soviet regime's economic sectors. Berliner related the existence of extremely ambitious targets, tight time constraints, scarce resources, and authoritative sanctions ("the plan is law") to a series of informal adaptive responses that included searching for a safety factor, hoarding, and dissimulation.[47] Though to date no study of this magnitude has been undertaken for other system-building regimes, one could, in fact, find similar informal adaptive responses in most Eastern European regimes.[48] What is most significant about Berliner's findings is that they can be generalized to other sectors of society.

In their effort to create an ethos of expanding good—an ethos that views resources and values as complementary and dynamic rather than mutually exclusive and static—mobilization regimes often unintentionally generate an understanding of resources and values based on "limited good." For example, just as families in traditional peasant societies jealously guard their own interests rather than cooperate extensively, so factory managers in a mobilization system are judged by their subordinates according to how successfully they defend their factory's interest in opposition to that of the ministry or trust. As one of Berliner's respondents commented: "We look to the director to promote our interests, to push through for us at the ministry and to defend the interests of the plant."[49] And just as a factory in such a system is always on the lookout for a safety factor and prone to hoard resources, so individuals in such a system tend to hoard "connections." Connections are as jealously guarded by individuals and families as material resources are by facto-

47. Joseph S. Berliner, *Factory and Manager in the USSR* (Cambridge, Mass.: Harvard University Press, 1957), pp. 318–29 and passim.

48. For a recent analysis pointing out differences between the Romanian and Soviet economic structures, see David Granick, "The Orthodox Model of the Soviet-Type Firm versus Romanian Experience" (International Development Research Center Working Paper, Indiana University, 1972).

49. Berliner, *Factory and Manager,* p. 230.

ries, and for similar reasons. Both the ethos and the structure of a mobilization regime are antagonistic to the routinization of tasks and the authority of impersonal stable rule. Striving to ensure that the potential of the society is completely realized, the regime defines targets, goals, and priorities substantively rather than procedurally, and rapidly redefines them. Thus a premium is placed on informal adaptive mechanisms (signified by the Russian term *blat*[50] and the Romanian term *pile*, or pull) that allow for some stability and certainty in response to what is often perceived as an arbitrary and threatening regime. Both *blat* and *pile* refer to relationships and dispositions that obstruct the development of a political culture based on overt, public, cooperative, and rule-based relationships. Instead, they reinforce the traditional community and regime political cultures with their stress on covert, personalized, hierarchical relationships involving complicity rather than public agreements.[51]

The ethos and structure of mobilization regimes influence the political culture of a society in a number of other ways. Along with the generation and reinforcement of a "limited good" perspective, mobilization regimes often unintentionally reinforce traditional conceptions of time. In an interesting book written in 1904, an insightful observer of Romanian society noted that Romanians at all levels of society worked in an "unregulated rhythm," and oscillated between periods of hard intense work and periods of prolonged inactivity. In Constantin Rădulescu-Motru's words, "We [Romanians] are capable of any virtue so long as it doesn't require too great a persistence on our part."[52] In 1972, Nicolae Ceauşescu noted that policies initiated at the National Party Conference in December 1967,

50. According to Berliner (ibid., p. 182), *blat* "implies the use of personal influence for obtaining certain favors to which a firm or individual is not legally or formally entitled."

51. A number of phrases in contemporary Romanian parlance refer to different forms of complicity. Recently in *Scînteia* an article dealing with certain illegal practices in a factory found "un spirit de 'amabilă,' ingăduinţă reciprocă, de 'binevoitoare' toleranţă, de 'delicată' închidere a ochilor" (November 30, 1971). All of these phrases refer to semilegal or illegal covert cooperation.

52. C. Rădulescu-Motru, *Cultura română şi politicianismul* (Bucharest: Cultura Naţională, 1904), p. 56.

"while leading to positive results are not being carried out consistently." He continued: "As a matter of fact, comrades, this [lack of measured persistence] is a habit of ours. We begin an action with a great deal of noise, obtain a series of results, but after a period of time we lose sight of segments of the policy . . . and we interest ourselves in other things."[53]

One could conclude that the changes in regime in Romania have been superficial and that although the form changes, the substance (i.e., cultural dispositions) remains. Such an argument would itself be superficial. The reality is more complex and intriguing as the character of the industrial production process in system-building regimes with a mobilization structure illustrates. A major characteristic of production in such a setting is the phenomenon of "storming," an uneven attention to tasks, varying intensity of job performance, and "campaign"-like resolution of tasks. These characteristics are a function of the regime structure itself and are highly congruent with traditional behavioral and attitudinal postures toward time and antithetical to modern notions of task performance based on scheduled—that is, measured, continuous—behavior. In this instance, one has an example of a regime concerned with and in some major respects succeeding in transforming the character of an entire social system and yet actually reinforcing certain cultural postures that are antithetical to its basic goal.

A third and highly significant consequence of the mobilization structure and ethos of a system-building regime is its connection with dissimulation as a modal behavioral posture in Leninist societies. Berliner discovered that managers who wish to maintain their positions systematically engage in the practice of dissimulation. In Russian the term is *ochkovtiratelstvo,* which literally refers to cheating at cardplaying by altering the character of a card. "In economic activity, it [*ochkovtiratelstvo*] signifies the simulation of a successful performance by some deceptive manipulation."[54] As with the case of hoarding, I should like to suggest that dissimulation is a general feature of a society and system based on a mobilization ethos and structure.

53. *Scînteia,* February 20, 1972, p. 2.
54. Berliner, *Factory and Manager,* p. 114.

Several things can be said about dissimulation as a form of behavior. To begin with, it should be differentiated from formalism, which refers to strict adherence to external forms, usually to inadequate and inflexible understanding of a role's meaning. As Price has suggested, formalism is often fostered by the conflict between established societal norms and official or regime norms.[55] Dissimulation refers to something related but quite distinct. What is involved is not simply rigid adherence to rules in order to reduce uncertainty, but also "deceptive manipulation," the conscious adoption of false appearances. This posture does not arise as much from the conflict between established traditional norms and newly initiated modern norms as from (a) the perceived need to deflect the regime's attention from possible or real underfulfillment of tasks, and (b) the general desire to minimize the scope of regime interference in one's private and social life. Dissimulation is based on fear and avoidance. It is an adaptive response to a regime that, in its concern for realizing the entire society's potential, periodically attempts to penetrate most areas within the society. As a political posture, dissimulation is hardly something foreign to the experience of the Romanian population, which in its history has had to develop informal adaptive postures in order to maintain a private zone of unofficial, covert attitudes and practices while publicly complying with the coercive, extractive demands of alien rulers. The demands of a system-building regime have reinforced the Romanian population's tendency to separate the public and private arenas sharply, and to perceive them in antagonistic rather than complementary terms. Dissimulation is the posture, response, and strategy that integrates the two arenas. In such a society, one often finds a highly calculative and selective recognition of regime authority. This stance takes the form, not so much of political opposition, as of a strong antipolitical privatism in which family and personal interests are emphasized at the expense of regime and societal interests.

Finally, system-building regimes with a mobilization ethos and structure are based on a "commanding heights" principle that entails the attempted transformation of certain areas,

55. Price, "Social Basis of Administrative Behavior," pp. 72–86.

roles, and values and the attempted control of nonpriority areas, roles, and values. What differentiates a revolutionary Leninist regime from a radical nationalist regime is not the Leninist regime's attempt substantively and simultaneously to transform all areas of a social system but its determination (a) to control and/or transform critical points at all levels of the social system and (b) to prevent existing social forces from defining their resentment and hostility in terms of political opposition at any point or level of the society.

This pattern of transformation and control, of revolutionary laissez-faire, contributes in the short run at least to a highly heterogeneous and often incompatible set of political cultures. One can distinguish at least three types of areas in a system-building regimes: (a) poor rural areas experiencing more political control than cultural transformation. In such areas, traditional peasant political culture probably persists to a great extent. A classic illustration is the investigation of a Romanian cooperative in which a number of illegal practices were discovered. Asked about why such practices were not criticized in the assembly, one member noted: "Here in this cooperative we are neighbors and relatives. There are too many relatives in the cooperative, and it isn't wise to get on the wrong side of them."[56] In nonpriority arenas, such as the rural, given the scarcity of their resources (i.e., time, cadres, goods) system-building regimes have emphasized political control more than cultural transformation. (b) Another area consists of modern industrial projects in urban settings. The likelihood is that in these instances there has been a greater transformation of general and political culture reflecting the work setting, nature of work, and the correlates of an industrial milieu. (c) There is also an intermediate area that combines modern forms and traditional practices.[57] The commercial and service sectors in system-building regimes provide a good deal of evidence for the argument that there is no simple demarcation between traditional and modern political cultures, between conceptions of authority based on

56. *Scînteia,* November 22, 1971.
57. In this "area" one can find many instances of what Fred Riggs has termed "prismatic behavior." See *Administration in Developing Countries* (Boston: Houghton Mifflin, 1964).

hierarchical, personalized, and command considerations, and conceptions of authority based on complementary, rule, and leadership considerations. As the Romanian regime itself has noted, the commercial and service sectors in urban as well as rural areas are major sites for the practice of *bakshish.* It is, in fact, noted that many individuals attempt to get jobs in these areas precisely because they are so lucrative. The incidence of corruption (or "behavior which deviates from the formal duties of a public role because of private-regarding [personal, close family, private clique] pecuniary or status gains")[58] in the service and commercial sectors provides another good example of regime and societal forces combining to produce behavior antithetical to official values. It is not accidental that the commercial and service realms are characterized by widespread corruption. In a traditional society, services are rendered not on the basis of impersonal rules but of personal recognition; in the commercial and service realms (in contrast to the industrial realm), personal encounter is the basis of exchange and productivity. If, in addition, one realizes that these are low-priority realms for system-building regimes, it is not surprising that corruption is so pervasive within them. Actors within these realms, while complying with the externally imposed quotas or targets, concentrate on maximizing their personal, private interests, much as cooperative farmers relate organizational tasks to their interest in their private plots. This propensity to deal instrumentally and calculatively with official responsibilities and ingeniously with personal interests characterizes many actors in all realms of the society, but given the low-priority status of the commercial and service sectors and their personal-encounter character, this propensity is less constrained here and consequently flourishes.

Production Mentality and Political Culture

The third and final aspect of a system-building regime to be considered here is its conception of tasks. I am particularly

58. J. S. Nye, "Corruption and Political Development: A Cost-Benefit Analysis," *American Political Science Review* 61, no. 2 (June 1967): 417–27; see p. 419.

interested in the way in which system-building regimes approach the task of cultural transformation, a task that all Leninist regimes assert as a major goal. System-building regimes tend to see the resolution of this task in derivative terms: it is assumed that as the consequence of constructing a new political, economic, and social system a new and congruent culture will emerge. Leninist leaders often quote Lenin to the effect that "the transformation of all customs and practices . . . is a work of decades."[59] I am, however, suggesting something slightly more complex: the way in which certain Leninist regimes deal with the task of cultural transformation is often contradictory and in part self-defeating. System-building regimes have tended to neglect the cultural realm in favor of other sectors of society and have been selective, often formalistic, in their efforts at transforming culture. The result has been an uneven, mixed developmental profile. The reasons behind this are varied and involve several elements: elements that are shared by certain elites (i.e., a Stalinist or neo-Stalinist conception and approach to the tasks of transformation and consolidation); elements specific to individual elites (i.e., their political identity-defining experiences); and elements specific to individual community cultures (i.e., the type of religious belief and organization that characterizes a given society). An analysis of the Gheorghiu-Dej regime in Romania will illustrate this argument.

Historically, formalism has been a noted and criticized component of the relationship between Romanian institutions and Romanian society. In observing a major Romanian institution, the Orthodox Church, Rădulescu-Motru noted that it differed from Protestant churches in the West in being more oriented to ritual and formalistic practices than to practical moral and political lessons.[60] In a similar vein, Adolf von Harnack noted that in Orthodoxy, "doctrine comes to be administered in stereotyped formulas accompanied by symbolic acts. . . . For ninety-nine per cent of these Christians, religion exists only as a cer-

59. See, e.g., D. Mazilu, "Socialismul—orînduirea cinstei şi dreptăţii," *Scînteia*, September 3, 1971.
60. Rădulescu-Motru, *Cultura română şi politicianismul,* p. 97.

emonious ritual, in which it is externalised."[61] At the community
level, then, a major defining experience for the mass of the
Romanian population involved uncritical adherence to a belief
system manifested in terms of symbol and ritual and a private
life that remained basically untouched by the formal ritualistic
components of that belief system. This separation of religious
ritual from private life characterized not only the mass of the
population but also many of the Orthodox clergy.[62] Such a
separation of spheres was not necessarily considered hypocrit-
ical, because the integrity of religious belief tended to be identified with the correct application of ritual. In short, ritual was
regarded as both substance and form. It was out of this milieu
that the faction headed by Gheorghiu-Dej came to power and
established the dictatorship of the proletariat. Under Dej, the
Party belief system was in some critical respects as dogmatic and
externalized as Orthodoxy's belief system had been.[63] This tendency to externalize and ritualize the structure and ethos of the
new regime was not simply a function of Dej's socialization in an
Orthodox milieu. One must relate this socialization (Dej's as
well as that of his followers and major sectors of Romanian
society) to two other elements: the identity-defining experiences of the Romanian Communist Party (RCP), and the adoption of a Stalinist approach to social transformation and political consolidation.

The Romanian Party did not have a mass base or following
before assuming power and was consequently highly concerned
with identity questions. Its adoption of a very rigid interpretation of Leninism was a response to its isolation during the interwar period from effective and sustained interaction with a

61. Adolf von Harnack, "On Eastern and Western Christianity," in Tal-
cott Parsons et al., *Theories of Society* (New York: Free Press, 1961), 2:1114–15
and passim.
62. In novels such as Zaharia Stancu's *Barefoot* (New York: Twayne, 1971)
one can find very insightful portrayals of the clergy's place in the community,
and the community's perception of the clergy.
63. To suggest that Dej was influenced by the Orthodox milieu of his
society does not imply that he was religious or accepted the substantive tenets
of Orthodoxy; only that certain formal attributes of Orthodoxy were important in shaping the way in which he approached and interpreted his own
beliefs.

mass following, insecurity over its "proletarian character" in the midst of a peasant society, and conflicts with parties whose ideology was primarily oriented to national culture and the peasantry. The Romanian leadership lacked the historical experience, political confidence, and consequently the ideological sophistication that enabled the Chinese Communist Party to approach the basic social force in a traditional society—the peasantry—in a flexible rather than dogmatic, repressive fashion. As suggested, the third element behind the Romanian Party's formal and dogmatic approach to cultural transformation was its adoption of a Stalinist strategy in dealing with the tasks of transformation and consolidation. This strategy consists of "walking on one leg," of stressing the organizational and instrumental components of development at the expense of a direct concern with multiple forms of political education and participation.[64] The interaction of these three elements—a community culture shaped by Orthodoxy, a party whose historic experience made it reluctant to engage rather than repress the peasantry and its culture, and a Stalinist conception of its political tasks—contributed to a dogmatic, ritualistic, and formalistic approach to the task of cultural transformation. A striking illustration of the uneven development that has resulted was discussed in the Party paper, *Scînteia,* under the heading "Any Work Is Clean, Only Laziness Is Dirty." Correspondents reported that several high school graduates were demanding office positions and refusing skilled-labor positions in a factory. Interviewing the family of one graduate, the correspondents quickly discovered that the father and mother had successfully socialized their son in a highly traditional fashion.

64. The Chinese model of transformation and consolidation differs from the Stalinist precisely in giving less weight to the production mentality. Some scholars in effect combine the Leninist-Stalinist models and view Chinese development as a deviant case. I would view both Stalin and Mao as Leninists who have emphasized and partially revised the major elements of the Leninist political-ideological paradigm. As these revisions have drawn on different elements of the paradigm, the resulting models do differ in significant respects. One can still argue, however (though for various reasons an argument of that order is not feasible at this point) that both models are in the political tradition of Lenin (just as Bendix and Parsons, with all their real differences, may be said to be in the intellectual tradition of Weber).

Both they and their son were shocked to think that anyone who had been educated and who "spoke so beautifully" (*Ce frumos vorbeste!*) could be considered for a laborer's position.[65] This is not an isolated incident. The Romanian (and other) regimes are beginning to reap a harvest that is plentiful but unexpected and certainly undesired. While the regime has been quite successful in its attempts to increase the education and skill of many individuals, the corresponding and expected changes in cultural dispositions have not occurred as consistently or as widely as was hoped. Instead, traditional expectations of status, defined as prestige, have persisted in the face of formalistic demands that they disappear.

The restrictive understanding that characterizes a production-mentality approach to cultural transformation appears to complement the selective character of a "commanding heights" approach to social change. Both the commanding heights and the production-mentality orientations neglect critical elements in the units they are dealing with. The commanding heights or "revolutionary laissez faire" approach places a relatively low priority on the rural-agricultural areas, and in certain respects on the private arenas of society as well; the production-mentality approach fails to appreciate adequately or to come to terms with the expressive dimension of human behavior. The combination of a commanding heights mobilization effort and a production mentality creates a milieu in societies and regimes such as the Romanian in which individuals are in effect rewarded for attending simply to their own interests both at work and in private settings. In such a context, those individuals who are *puşi pe capătuială* (stimulated by the prospect of gain) and functionaries who *nu-şi văd decît interesele lor* (don't see anything but their own interest) are reacting rationally and predictably to the regime's structure and ethos.

Through their organization and ethos, then, system-building regimes have stimulated a series of informal adaptive responses—behavioral and attitudinal—that are in many respects consistent with and supportive of certain basic elements of the

65. *Scînteia*, September 29, 1971.

traditional political culture in these societies. These elements in turn are antithetical to the appearance of a regime and society with an ethos and structure predicated on a complementary relationship between the public and private realms, on the viability of impersonal rules and norms, and on the value of egalitarianism expressed in the role of effective participant.

3

INCLUSION

In the history of Leninist regimes one can identify at least three elite-designated core tasks and stages of development.[1] The first is transformation of the old society; the second is consolidation of the revolutionary regime; the third and current task is inclusion: attempts by the Party elite to expand the internal boundaries of the regime's political, productive, and decision-making systems, to integrate itself with the unofficial (i.e., non-apparatchik) sectors of society rather than insulate itself from them.

Typically, designation of a core task has two major, related consequences. It specifies a particular locus of political uncertainty and generates a particular regime structure, one that simultaneously reflects the task at hand and the corresponding locus of uncertainty. To expand and illustrate these points: the transformation task refers to a Leninist party's attempt decisively to eliminate the political and military capacity of opposition elites. The defining characteristic of the social and political environment during this period is turbulence. The existence of a highly turbulent environment has very specific political im-

This essay was originally published in 1975 as "Inclusion and Mobilization in European Leninist Regimes," *World Politics* 28, no. 1 (October 1975): 69–97. It appears here in slightly edited form.

1. The term *Leninist regimes* will be used throughout in a generic sense. Distinctions of a developmental nature will be referred to in terms of specific syndromes of tasks, uncertainties, and structures (i.e., transformation, consolidation, and inclusion regimes). Thus, in reference to the period of Stalin's rule in the Soviet Union, the term *Leninist regime* does not reflect a lack of appreciation of the differences between 1935 and 1925, or between Stalin and Lenin as individual leaders. The term *Leninist* refers to the existence of an organization-ideology that, although changing in significant respects over time, remains identifiable as a particular type of charismatic institution.

plications for regime organization, power distribution, and, consequently, regime-society relations. In such circumstances, Leninist parties are faced with a set of conflicting imperatives within the Party and in the Party's relations to society. Within the Party, the imperatives of obedience to central directives and the need for discretion "in the field" compete with one another; in Party-society relations, the imperatives of gaining sociopolitical support and controlling that support partially conflict with one another. In short, acting on the task of transformation engenders social and organizational turbulence, which in turn makes it difficult for the regime simply to command support from social groups and obedience at all levels of the Party. The need to bargain with "heroic" local cadres and to persuade social strata who are essential in the battle against the class enemy produces a particular type of Party organization and regime-society relationship.

With the achievement of a political and military breakthrough, the self-perceived task of a Leninist regime changes from transformation to consolidation. The Party's efforts shift to creating the nucleus of a new political system and community in a setting designed to prevent existing, "unreconstructed" social and cultural forces from exercising any uncontrolled and undesired influence over the development and definition of the institutions, values, and practices favored by the Party. With the adoption of the consolidation task, the locus of political uncertainty shifts. Instead of searching for "risk-taking cadres" and demonstrating a capacity to attract political support, the Party elite (or a section thereof) attempts to maximize its insulation from society, to secure the undivided commitment of its cadres by reducing the reference groups for those cadres to one—the Party as represented by its leadership. The task of consolidation and the corresponding uncertainty surrounding the issue of cadre insulation bias the distribution of power and the definition of the regime in favor of those individuals and institutions most likely to depersonalize the Party's contacts with the society and to maximize obedience within the Party.

Just as success with the task of transformation redefines the regime's internal and external environments by creating a less turbulent situation, thereby depriving local cadres and social groups of control over a major locus of uncertainty and power,[2] so success with consolidation—creation of an articulate socialist intelligentsia, elaboration of an industrial base, and the development of military power—has made it increasingly difficult to sustain the rationale for and format of a consolidation regime.

With the achievement of consolidation, these regimes complemented the political-military destruction of traditional elites with the social and economic destruction of traditional institutions; they achieved a decisive breakthrough.[3] The locus of political uncertainty has shifted once again, reflecting a change in the sociopolitical environment and a corresponding attempt by certain components of the Party leadership to redefine the regime's core task in light of this change and the Party's concern with self-maintenance. The locus of political uncertainty has shifted from protecting the precarious values of a newly established revolutionary regime with charismatic qualities to ensuring that the social products of its developmental efforts identify themselves in terms consistent with the Party's ideological self-image and organizational definition. Uncertainty involves the possibility that the increasing social heterogeneity of socialist society, in the form of an increasing range of articulate social audiences,[4] might express itself as an articulated plurality of political-ideological definitions.[5] Inclusion is an attempt to

2. There is no longer a need for the regime to depend on "heroic" local cadres to secure the political support of local social constituencies against the "class enemy"; neither is there any longer the disruption that prevented the extension of central party control.

3. Revolutionary regimes differ from reformist regimes in their attempts to attack tradition comprehensively at two levels. Reformist regimes are more likely to limit their efforts at social change to changes in elite structure. Revolutionary regimes attack traditional institutions as well as traditional elites. Collectivization in contrast to land reform is a striking instance.

4. I would like to suggest the notion of "articulate audiences" in place of both "masses" and "publics" to describe a diverse set of social groups in contemporary Leninist regimes. Unlike masses, these groups are politically knowledgeable and oriented. Consequently they are capable of offering the regime support of a more differentiated and sophisticated character. Unlike publics—i.e., citizens who voluntarily organize themselves around major political issues—these "audiences" are restricted in their political behavior to those roles and actions prescribed by the regime itself.

5. For one Leninist regime's attempts to move in this direction, see Jowitt, "Political Innovation in Romania," *Survey* 20, no. 4 (Autumn 1974): 132–52.

prevent that plurality by revising the regime's format and its relationship to society from insulation to integration. The argument to be presented here attempts to explicate this situation, the defining situation for the majority of Leninist regimes. It is hoped that the perspective expressed will enable students of these regimes to get beyond analyses that (a) posit a unilinear de-radicalization or de-utopianization of Leninist regimes,[6] (b) effectively reduce social change in its broadest sense to the proposition that socioeconomic change determines political change[7] or (c) juxtapose, in a Manichean variant, a series of social changes that are described as progressive and political responses, which, if not "adaptive" in the sense of becoming more liberal, are seen as resulting in "arrested" development.[8]

INCLUSION

The task of inclusion refers to a ruling Leninist party's perception that the major condition for its continued development as an institutionalized charismatic organization is to integrate itself with, rather than insulate itself from, its host society. More specifically, it involves a Leninist party's attempt to devise a new role and set of institutions that allow for a more effective mediation between the status of Party apparatchik and formal Party membership or nonparty status. It refers above all to an attempt to expand membership in the regime in a way that allows politically coopted social elites or activists to maintain their social-occupational identity,[9] *and* the party apparatus to

6. See Robert C. Tucker, "The Deradicalization of Marxist Movements," in *The Marxian Revolutionary Idea* (New York: Norton, 1969), pp. 172–215; and Richard Lowenthal, "Development vs. Utopia in Communist Policy," in Chalmers Johnson, ed., *Change in Communist Systems* (Stanford: Stanford University Press, 1970), pp. 33–117.

7. See Samuel P. Huntington, "Social and Institutional Dynamics of One-Party Systems," in Samuel P. Huntington and Clement H. Moore, eds., *Authoritarian Politics in Modern Society* (New York: Basic Books, 1970), pp. 3–48.

8. See Zbigniew Brzezinski, "The Soviet Political System: Transformation or Degeneration?" in Brzezinski, ed., *Dilemmas of Change in Soviet Politics* (New York: Columbia University Press, 1969), pp. 1–35; for a restatement of this thesis, see Zvi Gitelman, "Beyond Leninism: Political Development in Eastern Europe," *Newsletter on Comparative Studies of Communism* 5 (May 1972): 18–44.

9. During the consolidation period, Leninist regimes typically attempt invidiously to distinguish regime supporters from nonsupporters and to iso-

maintain its institutionalized charismatic status. The process of expanding membership has typically included expanding the boundaries of the regime's productive and decision-making systems along with the internal boundaries of the political system itself. The most dramatic instance of the latter phenomenon has been the admission of a wide range of social elites to consultative status in sociopolitical activities.[10] Stable expansion of a political system's membership base indicates a political elite's recognition of the need to respond to previously excluded, distrusted sectors of the population. Such expansion often entails the development of leadership capacities within the regime that utilize relational skills of persuasion and manipulation in contrast to command capacities largely based on coercion; the latter typify regimes maximizing their insulation from (rather than integration with) their host society.

In the case of Leninist regimes, expansion of the decision-making system has taken the form of placing relatively greater emphasis on the weight of empirical premises (in contrast to ideological assumptions). Such an emphasis creates a more critical, less dogmatic orientation toward problem definition and problem resolution, in part through a greater appreciation of discussion, consultation, and experimentation. Finally, expansion of the productive system in these societies has resulted in placing greater emphasis on merit and procedural criteria. This emphasis indicates a heightened appreciation of formal rationalization as an efficiency- and resource-expanding process. Jointly, these boundary revisions of the political, productive, and decision-making systems reflect a perceived need to gauge and control the complexities of society more accurately, and a

---

late the former socially. In short, at the social level as well as in the relations between society and polity, insulation is the major characteristic at this stage of development. Social "elites" are forced to forsake their social-occupational identities in order to share in political status and responsibilities. Inclusion regimes are characterized by attempts to integrate social and political roles. On the "insulative" tendencies of consolidation regimes, see Reinhard Bendix, *Work and Authority in Industry* (New York: Wiley, 1956), pp. 400–434.

10. On this central point, see Peter C. Ludz, *The Changing Party Elite in East Germany* (Cambridge, Mass.: MIT Press, 1972), pp. 40–42, 126, 185; Alfred G. Meyer, *The Soviet Political System* (New York: Random House, 1965).

basic, if not thoroughgoing, confidence that past developmental efforts (social, political, and economic) have succeeded in creating a set of strategic groups that can serve as the social basis of a Leninist political community.

However, the adoption of inclusion as a defining or core task presents problems as well as opportunities for a Leninist regime. The opportunities consist primarily of an enhanced ability to control the potential political implications of an emerging set of articulate social audiences. The problems stem from the regime's intention to enhance its legitimacy without sacrificing the charismatic exclusiveness of its official (apparatchik) component. Insofar as inclusion becomes a defining task orientation, it adds complexity to the social system. Complexity increases, not simply through the arithmetical introduction of more elements (i.e., expert consultants), but also through the introduction of elements more resistant to elite fiat and arbitrariness (characteristics of routinized charismatic organizations as well as charismatic leaders). For example, to the extent that the Party's leadership is committed to a more rational decision-making process, it is constrained by the operation of empirically grounded premises. Also, if the Party leadership is committed to eliciting, rather than commanding, the support of different social audiences, it is again constrained—this time by the aspirations and concerns of those elements in the population whose support it desires. In addition, if the Party leadership tries to increase productivity by introducing and strengthening formal rules, it is somewhat constrained by their operation.

Throughout the 1950s, and early 1960s, consolidation was the predominant task orientation for the majority of Leninist regimes. However, beginning in the late 1950s and early 1960s, there is more than adequate evidence that attempts were made within several parties to either modify or redefine the priority of consolidation in favor of inclusion. Modification occurred in North Korea and Bulgaria in 1965–66. Redefinition of task and regime structure occurred in the Soviet Union in 1959–61, in Romania between 1965 and 1968, in Yugoslavia and Hungary in 1966, and in Czechoslovakia in 1967–68. There is a crucial difference between the modification and the redefinition of a regime's character. One must distinguish between the introduction of inclusive policies and the creation of a regime structure based on the task of inclusion. When the dominant faction of a party makes the authoritative ideological statement that the issue of "capitalist restoration" has been decisively resolved, and when social reality (both domestically and internationally) is no longer conceived, or related to, in dichotomic terms, it is appropriate to conclude that a change in regime character has occurred. The paradigmatic case is Khrushchev's Soviet regime. The ideological formulations of "state" and "party of the whole people" were announced at Party congresses and signified a new structural relationship between regime and society—one of reconciliation versus antagonism, integration versus insulation. Recognition of the "Third World" and the *obshchestvenniki*,[11] as well as of the intrinsic value of science, signified dramatic and character-defining breaks with the ideological-philosophical-organizational definitions and practices of the consolidation period.

However, regardless of whether the outcome was modification or redefinition of regime format, for over a decade the major feature of most Leninist regimes has been the conflict between and accommodation of individuals, policies, ideological formulations, and institutional definitions representing either an inclusion or a consolidation bias. This conflict-accommodation pattern is similar in many ways to the more general conflict-accommodation pattern one discovers between tradition and modernity. Consolidation regimes are obviously not identical with feudal, patrimonial, or tribal sociopolitical orders; however, in some respects they are comparable. It may even be suggested that the congruence between several of the defining premises of a consolidation regime and the defining premises of a traditional peasant society has been one stabilizing factor in many societies that have had consolidation

11. *Obshchestvenniki* are Party members who, while active as consultants and even as officeholders in the Party organization, are not full-time Party apparatus workers. I have attempted to analyze their significance in terms of national development in "State and National Development in Contemporary Eastern Europe" (unpublished paper, 1973).

regimes.[12] In examining the conflict-accommodation pattern of consolidation and inclusion policies, institutions, and norms, we are studying a variant of the more general encounter between tradition and modernity.

In ideal-typical terms, regime structure may be viewed as a set of political-organizational adaptations that emerge in response to specific developmental tasks and strategic political uncertainties (both external and internal). Any particular regime structure will reflect the pattern of conflict and accommodation (within a given ruling coalition) among factions with different task priorities.

Regime structure can be analyzed in terms of the organizational, ideological, and policy correlates of a given core task such as consolidation and inclusion. Specification of these correlates should enhance our grasp of the major political uncertainties, conflicting goals, and patterns of conflict and accommodation that characterize contemporary Leninist regimes.

PROFILE OF AN INCLUSION REGIME

To the extent that a Leninist regime shifts its core task from consolidation to inclusion, a series of adaptive changes tend to occur. To begin with, the Party develops its corporate character and leading role in opposition to those institutions whose distinctive competence is violence—the security and/or military forces. This institutional shift in influence toward the Party as a corporate organization is accompanied by a shift toward oligarchy, away from a neopatrimonial type of leadership. Within the Party, the political manager becomes the defining political actor in place of the political bureaucrat. There is a marked change in the social base of the regime as well, with the more professional, skilled, and articulate strata increasing their status vis-à-vis the "new class" of peasant-worker recruited officials. Power is expanded within the regime to allow for a more institutionalized mode of consultation with a variety of social groups. It must be stressed that consultation also occurred during the consolidation period, and consolidation regimes, like inclusion

12. See chapter 2.

regimes, depend(ed) on social support for their existence (despite a tendency in the literature prior to Stalin's death to assert "society's" nonexistence). However, the mode of consultation in the inclusion regime is distinguished by the regime's willingness and capacity to allow members of particular socio-occupational strata to complement their social and occupational identities with political-organizational responsibilities rather than exchanging them. For understandable reasons, regimes oriented not to inclusion but rather to consolidation typically define the relationship between socio-occupational status and political-organizational status in mutually exclusive terms. Society and regime are related in a strict hierarchy. A change in status in such a situation does not consist primarily of a change in role, but of a change in identity—a change from unofficial to official, or apparatchik, status. A structure of this order is predictable in a regime that equates effective political penetration with maximum organizational insulation from social claims. Such a regime will emphasize assimilation to a narrowly defined and exclusive political-ideological status—the quintessential expression of which is the member of the apparat.

The radical innovation of inclusion regimes is that, while cooptation remains the sole means of exercising political influence, it is no longer primarily based on the categoric separation and opposition of socio-occupational identity and political-organizational responsibilities in the Party.

Consistent with this change, when inclusion becomes the core task, manipulation, rather than domination, becomes the defining relationship between regime and society.[13] Policymaking is expressed more in terms of initiative based on critical scrutiny of problems and less in terms of an indiscriminate emulation of external references and/or dogmatic adherence to past policies. The legislative and representative organs of the state are ideologically and institutionally upgraded. This point warrants some elaboration. The proverbial wisdom is that during the consoli-

13. This formulation is inaccurate. In the inclusion stage of development, manipulation does not replace domination (i.e., the Party's politically exclusive and hierarchical rule). Rather, manipulation replaces terror as the primary expression and instrument of domination.—K.J. (1991).

dation stage (i.e., during Stalin's rule), the state was overwhelmingly powerful. In fact, the security forces were overwhelmingly powerful and in most cases effectively subordinated all other state functions and institutions. During the consolidation period, the state, as a set of institutions and symbols representing the political unity of the whole society, is afforded at best an ambivalent and more often a distinctly inferior status to those state institutions (such as the Ministry of the Interior) whose distinctive competence is vigilance rather than representation.

Inclusion regimes typically upgrade their ideological evaluation of the nation-state. This process is marked by ambivalence and selectivity and differs significantly from the way consolidation regimes deal with the nation-state. Finally, Leninist inclusion regimes define their international position in terms of a more extensive set of complementary membership groupings. At both the national and international levels, inclusion regimes typically adopt a more differentiated and less exclusive view of their political identity.

All of these revisions in regime definition involve a shift away from command, arbitrary, and dogmatic modes of action and organization, and a move toward leadership, procedural, and empirically oriented modes.

A. The movement to redevelop the integrity of the Party as *the* leading political institution may be viewed as an attempt to assert the primacy of an organization whose distinctive competence is sociopolitical rather than coercive, an organization with manipulative and persuasive capacities as well as coercive ones, an organization with a certain claim to social representativeness as well as political and ideological exclusiveness.

B. The restructuring of the Party's leadership from a neopatrimonial to a more oligarchic pattern has typically included a stress on performance, merit criteria, a more rational division of labor at various levels in the Party, stricter adherence to scheduled meetings, the regular publication of their results, and in some instances the elaboration of statutes that at least formally guarantee the right of individual dissent within the Party.[14] The

14. On the extent of rights of dissent in the Romanian Party, see *Statutul Partidului Communist Roman* (Bucharest, 1959), p. 40.

critical or empirical component of inclusion is evident in the
emphasis on collective leadership, which ideally allows for more
open inquiry, more diverse sources of information, and more
discussion within the leadership echelon. The stress on merit
criteria is a development with both procedural and empirical
dimensions, given the emphasis on impersonal standards of
recruitment and promotion as well as on achievement and observed performance. A measure such as the promulgation of
Party statutes formally guaranteeing the right of individual dissent within the Party simultaneously embodies procedural, empirical, and leadership dimensions, given its (at least formal)
specification of legal-rational rights, its support of more open
discussion, and its indirect contribution to interaction based
more on considerations of reciprocity and less on fear.

C. The appearance of a new type of cadre, the political manager, is of particular importance. Let me clarify what this cadre's defining features are. I am not suggesting that economic
cadres become dominant in Leninist regimes stressing the inclusion task. We should also not confuse the political manager
with the technocrat. This confusion is perhaps one of the greatest errors in the literature; namely, the identification of the
technocrat as the alternative to the apparatchik.

The managerial political cadre is distinguished by two competences: first, his relatively high level of technical expertise
and/or experience, and second, and perhaps more important,
his manipulative skills in sociopolitical settings. Unlike the
technocrat and the apparatchik, the manager is a political actor
sensitive to the social-personal dimensions of a situation and
possessed of a capacity and willingness to manipulate those
dimensions to achieve his goals. It is this competence, a leadership competence, that distinguishes the political manager
from both the command-oriented apparatchik and the rule-
oriented technocrat. For reasons that will become evident when
we discuss the policymaking process in an inclusion regime,
political managers tend to complement their leadership orientation with a reliance on empirical and procedural orientations.

D. The increasing recognition given to the professional-
skilled stratum in societies ruled by Leninist regimes is a telling
indication of the shift from a consolidation to an inclusion ori-

entation. The party's ideological upgrading of the "intelligentsia," the differentiation of wages, and the recruitment patterns of the various parties suggest that for varying periods of time and to different degrees, Leninist regimes during the 1960s began to orient themselves to the social products of their own mobilization-industrialization efforts. The New Class, with its dogmatic, arbitrary, and command orientation, is no longer the sole sociopolitical stratum that can represent itself as the legitimating base of a Leninist regime. In contrast to the New Class, the new, articulate, professionally skilled stratum is distinguished by its higher level of training and expertise, its preference for revised authority relations, and its various recognition aspirations. Its preferences seem to lean in the direction of a more rule-ordered system (not necessarily democratic), both as a condition for effective performance and as a guarantee of its status as the indigenous product of the regime's efforts at social-political transformation.

E. The expansion of power is reflected in a Leninist party's willingness to approach the question of power in a more complex fashion, to differentiate types of power, and to allow different elements in a society to exercise different forms of power. Specifically, the expansion of power refers to the Party's willingness to permit a significant degree of functional or expert autonomy in the performance of specific tasks. This tendency, one that has been noted by a number of analysts, is marked by leadership rather than command orientations inasmuch as it involves the Party's recognition, acceptance, and manipulation of skilled strata in the pursuit of regime goals. Its empirical component manifests itself as a greater appreciation of the need for debate and multiple types of information. Finally, the expansion of power contributes to the place of procedural norms in the social system insofar as the expansion of power reflects the Party's acceptance of distinct and differentiated areas of competence as well as the scheduled and coordinated discussion of specific topics.

F. Perhaps the most significant difference between consolidation and inclusion regimes involves the character of authority relations. The shift from a regime-society relationship based on domination through terror to one emphasizing domination through coercive manipulation is a shift from a sociopolitical order based almost exclusively on command and violence to one in which leadership skills of manipulation and persuasion are more significant than in the past. Manipulation, however, is not simply a more economical and clever mode of domination. It allows for a certain measure of recognition of and influence by aspiring social strata that have felt relatively deprived of status, influence, and economic well-being. To date, the discussion of manipulation in Leninist regimes has worked with the established sociological paired concept of real and felt influence.[15] I should elaborate this distinction to suggest that there are at least two forms of real influence and two types of felt influence. Real influence may be exerted over routine and defining issues, the latter being those that have a direct impact on the overall character of a social-political system.[16] Felt influence or manipulated participation may also be of two types, one that is characteristic of (but not limited to) consolidation regimes, the other of inclusion regimes. Consolidation regimes engage almost exclusively in symbolic manipulation; the most striking instance is the manipulation of nationalist symbols. Symbolic manipulation indicates the Party's perceived need to address imbalances between the regime and society in a context of continuing political distrust and avoidance of commitments to that society. Organizational manipulation—that is, the revitalization of national-front organizations, the upgrading of trade unions, and the emergence of peasant unions—is quite a different kind of manipulation. Organizational manipulation not only indicates the regime's recognition of an imbalance, but also allow social elements (i.e., professionals) real involvement in routine decisions.

G. In the policy sphere, regimes oriented to inclusion tend to stress policy initiation more than emulation as the basic premise of policymaking. The critical and empirical components of ini-

15. See, e.g., Thomas Baylis, "East Germany: In Quest of Legitimacy," *Problems of Communism* 21, no. 2 (March–April 1972): 46–56.

16. Influence over routine issues must not be confused with influence over insignificant issues. Routine issues may well be significant; they differ from defining issues in the order of significance. The resolution of defining issues has a direct impact on the basic character of the major institutions, values, and/or behavior that provide a social system with its distinct identity.

tiation in contrast to emulation as a policy stance are too clear to warrant extended comment here. Consolidation regimes are "traditional" in that major policies tend to become ritualized rather than being continually scrutinized—whether the commitment is to machine tractor stations, a reified dichotomic worldview, or a dogmatic conception of the party's "leading role."

Policy initiation in turn places a premium on leadership rather than command skills, and on procedural norms rather than political arbitrariness. Policy initiation assumes a degree of discretion by decision-making units. Discretion is an integral component of a decision-making style based on the critical-empirical examination of a problem. However, command orientations emphasize standardization of environments rather than their differentiation. Command orientations also typically emphasize the authority of superior ranks rather than the importance of a particular policy situation or environment. A leadership (rather than command) structure is thus a key element in ensuring the effective operation of a policymaking process marked by policy initiation.

If one views the nation as a decision- or policymaking unit, it is not accidental that independent communist regimes vociferously demand that international relations within the bloc be based on mutual, reciprocal adjustment among leaders, not on obedience to the commands of one set of leaders—those of the Soviet Union. The rationale behind this argument is at least partially that each leader is most familiar with his own policy environment and must have discretion in order to base policy on an adequate (empirical) relationship to that environment. Command structures focus attention on superiors; leadership structures focus attention on problems as well.

Policy initiation also depends on the upgrading of scheduled operations, of formal procedures over political arbitrariness. Formal procedures (i.e., contracts) are designed to ensure the effective coordination of distinct policymaking units and to minimize any interference with the regular and differentiated analysis of problems and solutions in particular policymaking environments.

H. All Leninist regimes attending to the task of inclusion

through necessity and/or choice tend to upgrade those state institutions and symbols that emphasize the representative and unifying quality of the state. The reverse of this is that such regimes typically downgrade those institutions (i.e., the Ministry of the Interior) and slogans (i.e., "vigilance") that during the consolidation period dominate and subvert all other state institutions and functions.

The state as a set of representative institutions and symbols is downgraded during the consolidation period precisely because the major concern of the Party during such a period is to deny the "whole people" representation and legitimation. The nation is precisely what has to be "reconstructed" and denied influence in the process of creating new socialist elites, institutions, and culture during the period of consolidation. The state at this time is upgraded only in one sense: its monopoly of organized violence is secured and enhanced. When Leninist regimes upgrade the state as a set of institutions and symbols emphasizing representative and reconciliatory functions, it is a sign that in their view the process of consolidation (as defined here) has been decisively effected, with the class enemy not only defeated but replaced by a new, more trustworthy set of social strata deserving ideological and organizational recognition. The upgrading of the state in this manner involves both the symbolic and organizational recognition of "society," and is predicated on a greater incidence of leadership rather than command orientations, and of political reconciliation rather than bureaucratic insulation. In turn, the added stress on more regular meetings of parliament, increased periods of debate, and greater specialization of committees is based on procedural and empirical premises.

I. Finally, to the extent that Leninist regimes orient themselves to the task of inclusion, they are more likely to demonstrate a positive ideological evaluation of the nation-state. This often involves a more sophisticated and critical attitude toward the country's pre-Leninist history and a more flexible political attitude toward sectors of its national constituency, rather than a "for us or against us" posture. Inclusion-oriented regimes are also likely to define themselves internationally in terms of multiple rather than exclusive membership groupings. The tendency of certain Leninist regimes to define their political identity on the basis of their complementary relationships with different membership groupings (i.e., the "Third World," Western Europe, the Warsaw Pact, the United States, or the "world socialist system") reflects a major disposition within such regimes to define themselves by consciously and critically appraising the relationship between their goals, resources, and environments. This disposition may legitimately be interpreted as having an empirical rather than dogmatic character. A critical-empirical posture of this order, one based on complementary memberships, may aptly be called universalistic in contrast to the neotraditional and particularistic definition of political identity adhered to by consolidation regimes. The latter define membership in exclusive terms; that is, being a member of the socialist bloc means *not* regarding one's country as a "Third World" or "small" nation. It must also be noted that a Leninist regime's expansion of the criteria and premises for deciding on its posture in the international arena has implications in other realms. The adoption of complementary and diverse memberships favors the development of leadership (rather than command) skills within the Party elite—skills that enable the regime to recognize and manage multiple international constituencies. Finally, the perceived need to relate to, but differentiate, memberships in different settings (i.e., all-European, Warsaw Pact) favors the appreciation of procedural norms such as sovereignty as a device for stabilizing a more complex environment.

One can find a fair amount of illustrative material to support the argument that during the 1960s the majority of Leninist regimes began to shift their priorities in the directions suggested here.

Beginning with the removal of Beria, and continuing with the condemnation of the neopatrimonial "cult of the personality" and Khrushchev's upgrading of the Party as a corporate institution in the late 1950s, up to the attacks within the Czechoslovak Party in 1967 on Novotny's mode of leadership, the reassertion of the Party's corporate integrity has been a visible and politically significant development. The greater emphasis on oligarchic leadership (or, in Leninist terms, collective leadership) was closely related to this reassertion of the Party's corporate integrity. Oligarchic leadership has been based on a greater specification of intra-elite responsibilities (one instance was the differentiation of the executive committee and presidium in Romania in the period 1965–74), the rationalization of structure (such as occurred during the mid 1960s in East Germany and Hungary), the stress on scheduled meetings (a characteristic of both the Gierek and Ceaușescu regimes), and an upgrading of the Party's regional and local units in regimes as diverse as the Soviet and Yugoslav.

The appearance of political managerial cadres can be documented in a number of regimes. Thomas Baylis and Peter Ludz have noted this development in the DDR and Ross Johnson has pointed out the managerial component in the Polish party and its conflict with the *apparatchiki*.[17] However, along with Ludz and Baylis, Johnson is disposed to label these cadres technocrats, thereby possibly obscuring their distinctive political skills and their greater sensitivity to social situations and capacity to manipulate them. The higher level of education among Central Committee members has been noted by a number of analysts.[18] Data on their operating style are harder to come by. We would suggest, however, that during the 1960s a style of leadership exemplified by Ceaușescu, Kádár, and most recently Gierek, appeared in Eastern Europe—one that sharply contrasted with that of leaders like Gomułka, Novotný, Gheorghiu-Dej, Chervenkov, and Stalin. In certain respects, the "model" for the political managerial cadre is the former U.S. Secretary of Defense Robert McNamara. In an article devoted to McNamara, David Halberstam points to a number of attributes that are also characteristic of the new Leninist political managers.[19] They

17. Baylis, "East Germany: In Quest of Legitimacy"; Peter C. Ludz, "Continuity and Change since Ulbricht," *Problems of Communism* 21, no. 2 (March–April 1972): 56–57; Ross Johnson, "Poland: End of an Era," *Problems of Communism* 19 (January–February 1970): 28–40. Ludz has provided an excellent and succinct analysis of development in the DDR in *The German Democratic Republic from the Sixties to the Seventies* (Occasional Papers in International Affairs, Center for International Affairs, Harvard University, November 1970).

18. See, e.g., Robert H. Donaldson, "The 1971 Soviet Central Committee: An Assessment of the New Elite," *World Politics* 24, no. 3 (April 1972): 382–409.

19. David Halberstam, "The Programming of Robert McNamara," *Harper's* 242 (February 1971): 7–21. The term *model* should not suggest that "managerial" cadres in Leninist regimes consciously have McNamara in mind.

are rationalists, men who are well-trained, authoritarian but still appreciative of the need to receive expert information and to structure situations so as to elicit that information and support. They are "win-oriented," not neutral pragmatists or technocrats. They tend to be sober individuals with a penchant toward the puritanical. They contrast with the rather hedonistic apparatchik New Class cadre in the way the modern bourgeoisie analyzed by Weber differed from the traditional capitalist.[20] It is a change from the Berias to the Katushevs, the Stoicas to the Winters.

As for the rise in prominence of the professional and skilled strata, a large number of examples can be provided to illustrate this phenomenon. The Czechoslovak Action Program of the late 1960s, with its stress on the intelligentsia, science,[21] and the need for merit-performance norms, provides a clear instance of one regime's ideological recognition of this stratum. The central places accorded to economic managers and skilled individuals in the economic reform the East Germans promulgated in 1963, and in the New Economic Management of the Hungarians in 1968, are additional instances.[22] The recruitment patterns of the Yugoslav, Polish, Hungarian, and Czech parties in the 1960s provide another illustration of the ascendance of this stratum.[23] In Romania the slogan *omul potrivit la locul potrivit* (the right man for the right job) reflects an increased emphasis on technical qualification and a heightened appreciation of the

20. For Weber's comparison, see *The Protestant Ethic* (New York: Scribner's, 1958), pp. 69–78.

21. Central Committee of the Communist Party of Czechoslovakia, "The Action Program of the Communist Party of Czechoslovakia," in Robin Alison Remington, ed., *Winter in Prague: Documents on Czechoslovak Communism in Crisis* (Cambridge, Mass.: MIT Press, 1969), pp. 88–137.

22. For the East German reform, see Baylis, "East Germany: In Quest of Legitimacy," and "Economic Reform as Ideology: East Germany's New Economic System," *Comparative Politics* 3, no. 2 (January 1971): 211–31. See also Bennet Kovrig, "Decompression in Hungary: Phase Two," in Peter A. Toma, ed., *The Changing Face of Communism in Eastern Europe* (Tucson: University of Arizona Press, 1970), pp. 196–202, for an analysis of the upgrading of economic-managerial personnel that attended the Hungarian reforms.

23. On recruitment patterns during the 1960s, see Frank Parkin, "Class Stratification in Socialist Societies," *British Journal of Sociology* 20, no. 4 (December 1969): 355–75.

professional strata created by twenty-five years of mobilization and industrialization.

Perhaps the most instructive example, however, can be found in the Soviet Union, where, during the 1960s, there was a struggle over the type of propaganda personnel the regime should employ. It seems that around 1965, "concrete proposals were advanced in the press to replace the traditional agitators with more sophisticated 'politinformators'—that is, information specialists capable of influencing knowledgeable mass audiences."[24] Note the characteristics of the "politinformators." They were drawn not from the ranks of workers and peasants but from those of officials, economic managers, scientists, engineers, agronomists; in short, the professional stratum. They specialized in differentiated forms of propaganda. Their skills seemed to be aimed at new types of audiences—audiences that were more articulate, educated, urban, and skilled. Their competence appears to be based on manipulating select audiences with specialized information rather than haranguing mass audiences with symbolic slogans. According to Aryeh Unger, they had emerged as a countrywide institution by 1967, and they may now number over two million.[25]

As with so many other aspects of the change from consolidation to inclusion, the expansion of power was initiated by Khrushchev with his practice of providing organizational fora for the participation of experts in policy discussions. The attention given to trade unions in Hungary,[26] the increased scope of public debates in the Soviet Union,[27] the creation and revitalization of expert organizations exemplified by the conferences of managers and engineers in Romania,[28] the rela-

24. Aryeh L. Unger, "Politinformator or Agitator: A Decision Blocked," *Problems of Communism* 19 (September–October 1970): 31.

25. Ibid.

26. See Kovrig, "Decompression in Hungary"; also Barnabas Racz, "Political Changes in Hungary after the Soviet Invasion of Czechoslovakia," *Slavic Review* 29 (December 1970): 633–51; and in particular William F. Robinson, *The Pattern of Reform in Hungary* (New York: Praeger, 1973), pp. 238–45, 326–42.

27. See Jerry Hough, "The Soviet System: Petrification or Pluralism?" *Problems of Communism* 21, no. 2 (March–April 1972): 25–46.

28. For a report of the meeting of economic managers, see *Scînteia*, February 18, 1972.

tive differentiation of social-scientific from strictly ideological studies evident in the growth of sociological institutes throughout most of Eastern Europe—all are instances of a tendency that emerged during the 1960s. It was a movement toward less rigid control and more differentiated appreciation of the social system.

I have already pointed out that the question of manipulation is very complex. It could be argued that all modern societies, regardless of political and ideological orientation, are primarily (though not exclusively) based on manipulative rather than command skills. The nation-state, itself the structural expression of modernity in the political realm, is partially based on the capacity to manipulate the allegiance and identification of millions of people. In this respect, the Leninist regimes' manipulation of society in the postconsolidation period can be seen as a variant of modern manipulation, not as a unique phenomenon. The relative shift from regime domination to regime manipulation of society in Leninist regimes depends on at least two developments: first, the appearance of urban, educated, and articulate strata that can make a legitimate claim to recognition as integral and trustworthy components of society; second, at least partial acceptance of this claim by managerial party cadres within the respective regimes. As a mode of control, manipulation indicates the emergence of a more "articulate society" in place of a "silent society," and of a political decision by the regime to organize rather than repress the heterogeneity that characterizes its environment in order to act effectively on its multiple goals.

Examples of organizational (rather than symbolic) manipulation include periodic visits by the first secretaries of the parties to various areas and constituencies. In this respect, Khrushchev, Gierek, Ceaușescu, and Kádár are quite different from Stalin, Gomułka, Gheorghiu-Dej, and Rákosi. A second instance can be found in the proliferation of what are termed representative and collective decision-making units, whether they are agricultural unions, workers' committees, upgraded youth organizations, or nationality organizations. It is not necessary to conclude that the recent attention and emphasis placed on these organizations by Leninist regimes signifies that they are now politically significant in their own right. However, this attention and emphasis do tell us something important about the perceptions of the elites in these regimes—about what new strategies they consider necessary and appropriate. In turn, these strategies indirectly provide us with an insight into the types of social (not just economic) uncertainties these elites see themselves facing. The attempt to control society "from within," as opposed to commanding it from an insulated position, is a major change that has character-defining implications for these regimes.

The development of sociology as a legitimate academic pursuit is also indicative of the shift from domination to manipulation. It is not surprising that the manipulation of statistics became a substitute for sociology during the period of consolidation; it was a period during which the regime distrusted the existing society and avoided empirical studies that might challenge its dogmatic beliefs about social reality. With the appearance and recognition of what in certain basic respects are new societies, the reappearance of sociology is not accidental. The system-quantity focus of statistics stands in contrast to the community-quality focus of sociology, a greater concern with the dynamics of social situations. The rise of sociology is a strong indication of the shift in regime tasks, and of significant changes in society and in regime-society relations.[29]

I have suggested that policy initiation is an integral aspect of the shift from consolidation to inclusion. The Romanian emphasis on the right to define internal and external policy independently;[30] the statement in the Czechoslovak Action Program that the "Czechoslovak people will formulate its own attitude toward the fundamental problems of world policy," and the criticism that in the past the Party had "not taken

29. The rapid and visible rise of sociological studies in Leninist political systems is easily documented. For an interesting analysis of this rise, see Alvin Gouldner, *The Coming Crisis of Western Sociology* (New York: Basic Books, 1970), pp. 447–78.

30. For the Romanian position, see "Statement on the Stand of the Rumanian Workers Party concerning the Problems of the International Communist and Working Class Movement (April 1964)" in William E. Griffith, *Sino-Soviet Relations, 1964–1965* (Cambridge, Mass.: MIT Press, 1967), pp. 269–97.

advantage of all opportunities for active work; it did not take the initiative"; the distinguishable initiatives of the Bulgarians in the areas of agriculture and of foreign policy in the Balkans during 1965–66;[31] the Hungarian approach to economic organization; and the Yugoslav approach to the questions of nationality, economic organization, and distribution of political power between 1965 and 1970—all are instances of Leninist regimes engaging in policy initiation rather than emulation, and of a differentiation process within the "world socialist system."

The upgrading of certain state institutions has occurred in a number of countries. The strengthening of the state council in Romania and Ceauşescu's assumption of the role of president of the state council; the suggestion at the 10th Congress of the Bulgarian Party that a state council replace the presidium of the National Assembly and have important executive and legislative functions;[32] the upgrading of the personnel attached to state functions in Romania; and the somewhat greater role played by legislative organs in most Eastern European nations and the Soviet Union signaled: (a) a regime shift from a "Calvinist" oppositional posture toward society to a "Lutheran" reconciliation posture;[33] (b) a move toward the institutionalization of distinct functions and values; and (c) the tentative construction of a "substitute" public arena distinguishable from both the official and private sectors of the social system.[34]

31. See Remington, ed., *Winter in Prague*, pp. 133–34. On Bulgaria, see J. F. Brown, *Bulgaria under Communist Rule* (New York: Praeger, 1970), pp. 173–301; Michael Costello, "Bulgaria," in Adam Bromke and Teresa Rakowska-Harmstone, eds., *The Communist States in Disarray 1965–1971* (Minneapolis: University of Minnesota Press, 1972), 135–58; Marin V. Pundeff, "Bulgaria under Zhivkov," in Toma, ed., *Changing Face of Communism*, pp. 89–121.

32. Costello, "Bulgaria," 155.

33. For the comparison of Calvinist and Lutheran attitudes toward man on which this image is based, see ch. 4 of Weber, *Protestant Ethic*, esp. pp. 137–38.

34. The character and role of publics in national development is a neglected topic in the field of comparative studies, particularly in the study of Leninist systems. The notion of publics and public domain has been bypassed, as has the more general and related focus of national development in the study of Leninist systems, in favor of attention to interest groups and the possibility of multiparty democratic systems. Such attention has in part re-

Concerning the adoption of a more positive attitude toward the nation-state, one must be careful to observe that during the consolidation period, Leninist regimes do not simply forget the nation-state. There are the examples of Stalin's manipulation of Great Russian national feeling, Gheorghiu-Dej's affair with the "Dacians," Moczar's posture in Poland, the Bulgarian and Albanian emphasis on national history, and Kim Il Sung's attention to nationalism. It is not the manipulation of nationalism that distinguishes (Leninist) inclusion regimes from consolidation regimes; it is the type of nationalism. Consolidation regimes typically manipulate national feelings and symbols in an attempt to generate cohesiveness and support for the regime in the absence of any concrete regime commitments to the society. The result is often the mobilization of traditional ethnic nationalism within the society and the somewhat unintentional adoption of chauvinist postures by the regimes. A prime example is the Gheorghiu-Dej regime in Romania.[35] Inclusion regimes tend to adopt a romantic nationalist rather than an integral or chauvinistic posture. The basis for this is the partial but significant reconciliation of "regime" and "society," and the assertion of Party sovereignty vis-à-vis the bloc. Thus, while the move toward Party sovereignty may not be initially predicated on nationalist premises (as Galia Golan correctly argues in the case of Czechoslovakia),[36] the assertion of Party sovereignty, and more generally the commitment to more empirical premises, lead to a reevaluation and redefinition of the Party's various membership groups. Inclusion regimes give some evidence of a balanced and integrated appreciation of the nation-state as a unit marked by continuities and decisive changes. There is support for this argument in the position of the Romanians between 1967 and 1970, and in the Action Program's comments

---

flected and in part contributed to the tendency implicitly to confuse national development in Leninist systems with movement toward liberal political orders.

35. For an analysis of a development of this order, see Jowitt, *Revolutionary Breakthroughs and National Development: The Case of Romania, 1944–65* (Berkeley: University of California Press, 1971), pp. 221–24, 280–82.

36. Galia Golan, "The Road to Reform," *Problems of Communism* 20, no. 3 (May–June 1971): 11–22.

on the nation.[37] One might expect similar tendencies under Gierek.

Finally, the argument that inclusion regimes tend to define their international position in terms of multiple rather than exclusive memberships is clearly demonstrated in the case of nonaligned Yugoslavia in contrast to Bulgaria, Romania in contrast to Albania, and Czechoslovakia under Dubček in contrast to the same country during Novotný's rule.

I am arguing that at various points during the 1960s, the majority of Leninist regimes responded to changes—intended as well as unintended—in the composition of society and regime in a manner distinct from the institutional, ideological, and policy syndrome that characterized them during the 1950s. I am not suggesting that social and political developments within the "world socialist system" inevitably led to the complete defeat of each consolidation regime, to the proportional elaboration of empirical, procedural, and leadership premises in the ideological, institutional, and policy domains of all Leninist regimes, to the appearance of fourteen regimes of a uniform political-social character, or to the elimination of all major elements of the preceding regimes. Rather, I see the interaction of consolidation and inclusion forces within Leninist regimes and the societies they rule as a conflict-accommodation process leading to the distinctiveness of each regime and society, much as the interaction of modernity and tradition has historically produced distinctive political, social, cultural, and economic amalgams. I do not define significant change as complete change. To argue that Leninist regimes significantly changed their character during the 1960s, it is not necessary to posit the removal of all Stalinists, any more than it is necessary to posit the complete removal of traditional elements in Japan after 1945 in order to call Japan modern. However, in almost all such regimes, issues were raised within the Party and problems were presented within society that challenged the existing consolidation format and demanded consideration and adoption of

37. See Miron Constantinescu, "Valorificarea critică a moştenirii culturale," in *Luceafărul*, May 6, 1972, and Remington, ed., *Winter in Prague*, pp. 131–32.

more inclusion-oriented postures and responses. It is important to point out that policy did not always match verbal intent
(as in Bulgaria), that development along inclusion lines was not
proportional in all domains (as in Romania), that certain regimes emphasized certain developments rather than others (as
in Hungary), and that the commitment lasted longer in some
countries than in others (Hungary in contrast to Bulgaria).
However, such observations do not invalidate the argument
that the 1960s witnessed major and relatively widespread
changes in the ethos, structure, and policy of many Leninist
regimes, in the direction of inclusion. This period was distinguished by the partial, but significant, replacement of consolidation with inclusion features, plus the development of conflict-accommodation patterns between the two.

INCLUSION AND MOBILIZATION

The most striking development in Leninist regimes in the late
1960s and early 1970s was the apparent reversal of the inclusion emphasis that had emerged with varying degrees of
strength in the 1960s. The pattern is not neat—no neater than
the initial shift from consolidation to inclusion—but it is discernible and significant, if thus far inadequately interpreted.
Developments in East Germany and Bulgaria in 1967–68,[38] the
Husák phenomenon in Czechoslovakia, and the reorientation
of the Romanian regime between June 1971 and July 1972
were reactions against the ethos, organization, and policies connected with the adoption of inclusion-oriented policies or inclusion as a core task. How can this apparent reversal be explained, and what is its content?

To begin with, the initial move by Leninist regimes to expand
the internal boundaries of their political, productive, and decision-making systems was predicated on the combination of
success and failure they had experienced during the consolidation period. However, movement toward or adoption of inclusion as a new core task and political posture revealed additional

38. See Baylis, "East Germany: In Quest of Legitimacy" and "Economic
Reform"; Costello, "Bulgaria."

problems of unsuspected magnitude and raised challenges to the Leninist conception of a socialist political community.

The shift by various regimes to the inclusion task and its correlates strikingly revealed the uneven nature of development that had occurred in the period of "socialist construction." This unevenness was by no means limited to the economic field, but was evident in the social and cultural fields as well. For all the talk in the West of a "postmobilization" period, the continuing impact of industrialization on many of these societies was, if anything, increasing in several senses during the 1960s. First of all, their social heterogeneity was growing, as working classes with an identity of their own began to crystallize.[39] Second, there was a growth in the whole range of problems associated with geographical and occupational mobility. A third problem involves the crystallization in social-psychological, if not social-political, terms of the professional and skilled strata, and their desire to become the primary support base of the regime—a development that presaged the replacement of the bifurcation of regime and society based on the "New Class" with one based on the professionally skilled class.[40] A fourth problem, the cynicism of the youth, became more apparent as a result of sociological studies and remains a highly salient issue and a persis-

39. As Neil Smelser has pointed out in "Mechanisms of Change and Adjustment to Change," in Bert F. Hoselitz and Wilbert E. Moore, eds., *Industrialization and Society* (Paris: UNESCO, Mouton, 1968), pp. 32–57, the process of differentiation places a premium on effective integrative processes. Social disturbances are often the result of discontinuities between differentiation and integration. One may view the reassertion of a mobilization posture in many Leninist regimes as the Party's attempt at an integrative response.

40. On this point, see the discussion in Frank Parkin, *Class Inequality and Political Order* (London: MacGibbon & Kee, 1971), pp. 137–86; on the conflict between workers and managers in Hungary and on the increasing status of managers under the New Economic Mechanism, see Kovrig, "Decompression in Hungary," and Racz, "Political Changes in Hungary." The place of China in all of this is complex. I would suggest that the Great Proletarian Cultural Revolution was both an attack on the "new class" (i.e., against a Stalinist consolidation structure) *and* an attack on a Soviet-type inclusion structure with its emphasis on "political" integration with a new professional class and exclusion of the mass of the population.

tent regime concern.[41] The ideological standing of the working class as well as its social and economic status also emerged as character-defining issues.[42]

However, the most dramatic questions have been raised about the organizational and ideological definition of the Party itself. The rejection of the consolidation model has not spontaneously provided models of organization and development immediately acceptable to Leninist elites.[43] Directly connected to the perceived challenge to the Party's institutionalized charismatic organization is the concern within these parties that social development not be equated with the emergence of a new political frame of reference that would jeopardize the Party's status as *the* political membership unit in the whole social system. At the international level, a related concern is that greater attention to the Party's domestic constituency must not jeopardize the existence of some form of international Leninist regime community.

The general response to these problems and challenges has been a reassertion of the mobilizational or charismatic character of Leninist regimes. This reassertion may be seen in part as an attempted elaboration of the expressive dimensions of human behavior evident in the stress on moral incentives, ethical standards, and ideological consciousness.[44] Evidence of such a

41. Kovrig has characterized the contemporary social ethos in Hungary as "collective and intergenerational alienation . . . obsessive materialism and a partial breakdown of traditional morality" ("Decompression in Hungary," p. 208). He notes that young people in Hungary "are reluctant to be transformed into obedient factors of production" (p. 21). There is evidence that young people in Bulgaria, Poland (under Gomułka), Romania, Yugoslavia, and the Soviet Union are estranged in many respects from the structure and ethos of Party rule.

42. This has been quite evident in Czechoslovakia in the discussions that have been going on since 1967, and in Romania since 1970. One can also find it, not unexpectedly, in consolidation-oriented regimes such as North Korea, with its ideological notion of "working-classizing" society, and in Albania.

43. In this light, the concern expressed by several Leninist regimes to develop studies of leadership, to create a "science of leadership" in order to analyze the dimensions of the leadership task in industrial societies can be seen as an adaptive (how successful is a question of a different order) response to the uncertainty over what is currently meant by the "leading role of the Party."

44. For example, see the Romanian Party's statement on November 4, 1971 (*Scînteia*); the emphasis on ideological preparation in Hungary mani-

stress and orientation is by no means evidence of its success. However, such efforts do indicate the continued institutional strength of charismatic orientations within these regimes. But it would be a mistake to conclude at this point that we have adequately defined the reaction of Leninist regimes to the inclusion task and process. What has been established is that this reaction has a mobilization thrust. It would be incorrect to assume that the nature and import of this thrust are identical to the mobilization efforts that characterized these regimes in the late 1940s and early 1950s. Yet, lacking a diversified perspective, many analysts appear to have fallen into this trap.

The chief explanation is that Western analysts of development in these regimes have typically adopted something of a Manichean perspective on the relationship between "regime" and "society." Although the power disparity between the two realms (often discussed as though they were real things) is recognized, there is little (if any) evidence of a multifaceted conception of the term *development* and the process to which it refers. In place of the assertion that during the consolidation period, society had no political impact, we have the new assertion that the Party is a stumbling block in the way of future "progress." In certain respects, the Party is just that. However, that observation does not exhaust or clarify the question of development and developmental patterns in Leninist regimes. Aside from the invitation such formulations offer for the confusion of political preference and analysis, they fail to extend our understanding of what is happening in these regimes.[45] To do so, a more "protestant" and analytical appreciation is called for. Such an approach would view the issues of regime development and social development as reciprocal processes and attempt to define the specifics of each set of dynamics and their relationships. Undifferentiated notions of de-radicalization, de-utopianization, or "postmobilization" obstruct the efforts of

---

fested in county-level "educational directorates" (Racz, "Political Changes in Hungary," p. 638); the thrust of the Chinese Great Proletarian Cultural Revolution; the emphasis in North Korea on the ideological revolution; the emphasis on *consciencia* in Cuba, and recent developments in Yugoslavia.

45. Gitelman's "Beyond Leninism" is a case in point.

the most qualified scholars. For example, in an impressive "devil's advocate" article, Jeremy Azrael correctly and succinctly points to the reappearance of mobilization efforts in several regimes.[46] The problem with his argument is that it relies on an undifferentiated pairing of the concepts mobilization/ postmobilization, which he is in one respect opposing. Although he correctly criticizes those who posit the linear de-radicalization of Leninist regimes, his conceptual formulation limits him to the assertion that continued political mobilization is still apparent. However, the major point concerning the most recent instances of mobilization is that they are not simply or even primarily the same type of mobilization that was manifest in the transformation or consolidation periods. It is crucial to note that the current mobilization efforts are partially constrained and shaped by the prior efforts and continued commitments to expanding the internal boundaries of the regimes' political, productive, and decision-making systems through greater reliance on empirical, procedural, and leadership premises—in short, by the commitment to the inclusion task.

The current emphasis on mobilization within individual Leninist systems has varied. But even those regimes that made the most limited changes in the direction of inclusion, reacted most strongly against it, and could be expected to limit their understanding of mobilization to that suggested by the Stalinist consolidation model—that is, the Bulgarian and North Korean regimes—have not rejected all the changes.[47] If this is true for regimes with the greatest commitment to the task of consolidation, it is even more true of regimes such as the East German, Hungarian, and Soviet. As an example, I refer once more to the issue of the "politinformator" in the Soviet Union: within a year or two there was a "mobilization" reaction against the "politinformator" in favor of the traditional "agitator"; it did not, how-

46. Jeremy Azrael, "Varieties of De-Stalinization," in Johnson, ed., *Change in Communist Systems*, pp. 135–53.

47. Though important, the changes in these regimes, particularly the North Korean, were quite limited. On Bulgaria, see Brown, *Bulgaria under Communist Rule;* on North Korea, see Joseph Sang-hoon Chung, "North Korea's Seven Year Plan (1961–1968): Economic Performance and Reforms," *Asian Survey* 12, no. 6 (June 1972): 527–45.

ever, result in the removal of the "politinformator" but did restore the agitator to a high-status position.[48] The point is that we are witnessing the appearance of amalgam regimes based on selective, tentative, and, to varying degrees, fragile combinations of inclusion and mobilization.

The developmental and leadership orientations of these regimes reflect a suspicion of strategies that reduce leadership to the tasks of aggregation and coordination and neglect mobilization. Given their continued charismatic bias, one that is organizationally supported, they seek to create Party activists and not simply citizens. They are in varying degrees committed to the maintenance of an international regime community as well as to their individual nations; to the deliberate preemption of any potential political arena or role not coterminous with the Party organization and Party membership; and to a philosophical stand stressing becoming over being, and potential over current performance. The question to be raised about these regimes is, In what sense do they continue to be radical, mobilizational, or utopian?—not, Are they or aren't they radical, utopian, or mobilizational? The issue can be stated at the most general level in this way: are inclusion and mobilization stances antithetical, or can they be seen as conflicting imperatives? Units may be defined as antithetical when the integrity of one is dependent on the subordination of the other.[49] A system made up of antithetical units is not viable until one of them is effectively subordinated to the other, or until they are effectively compartmentalized. Units (i.e., decision-making premises, social forces, or ideological tenets) may be viewed as con-

48. See Unger, "Politinformator or Agitator."
49. Thus, at the point of their initial encounter, tradition and modernity are antithetical. They can and do form amalgams, but their viability depends on one or the other establishing a de jure or de facto superordinate position. "The two things that cannot be combined at all are the best in traditional society and the best in modern society. Indeed before anything significantly traditional can be combined with anything significantly modern, a revolution must first have torn apart the closed system of tradition so that it may not merely add or substitute the new, but become capable of assimilating it" (Manfred Halpern, "The Revolution of Modernization in National and International Society," in Robert J. Jackson and Michael B. Stein, eds., *Issues in Comparative Politics* [New York: St. Martins Press, 1971], p. 52). See also Jowitt, *Revolutionary Breakthroughs*, pt. 1, esp. n. 5, pp. 63–64.

flicting imperatives when the integrity of one unit is dependent on the oppositional integrity of the other. An excellent example of the latter is provided by Max Weber in his discussion of the formal and substantive bases of legal-rational justice;[50] another example would be a functioning two-party system.

The answer requires a developmental perspective. To the extent that groups challenging the fundamental structure of the regime were denied access to resources that might have allowed them to translate their social dissent into political opposition, and to the extent that the regime has created a diverse set of strategic social-support groups, such a regime can engage in mobilization without terror and simultaneously allow for the partial expansion of its internal boundaries in the manner I have spoken of. To say, however, that mobilization and inclusion stances can at certain points in a developmental process stand in a partially complementary relationship to one another is NOT to deny the continual conflict between the two stances and underlying premises.[51] For although mobilization may in some respects be seen as a specific form of the inclusion process—ideally, mobilization expands the number of people, the amount of their time, the extent of their awareness, and their involvement with political tasks—mobilization is based on an approach to tasks that differs radically from that associated with inclusion. The inclusion process is one marked by the methodical consideration and management of tasks. Political mobilization is marked by controlled or elite-directed disruption. Disruption of established routines—social, personal, institutional, and psychological—is the defining element of mobilization. Let us be clear: no value judgment is being made to the

50. See Reinhard Bendix, *Max Weber: An Intellectual Portrait* (Garden City, N.Y.: Anchor Books, 1962), pp. 383–416.

51. Here, as in many other basic respects, my conception of development in Leninist regimes differs from that proposed by Huntington, who sees the current stage of development (which he terms "adaption") as one where the conflict between specialists and political generalists is "one between complements" ("Social and Institutional Dynamics of One-Party Systems," p. 33). I see the tension between the legal-rational thrusts of inclusion and the sustained charismatic preferences of the apparatus and leadership as much more consequential.

effect that inclusion is always and necessarily a "better" regime posture, or that mobilization occupies such a position. It may be that the viability of all regimes (as Jefferson and Mao suggested) is dependent on some mix of the two.

To return to our immediate concern, the mobilization stance adopted by postconsolidation Leninist regimes has several characteristics that in significant fashion do conflict with those associated with the inclusion task and process. The definitional tendency of Leninist regimes—their attempts to control and specify the substantive dimensions of social developments, not merely the framework within which such developments occur—does pose a challenge to the integrity and effectiveness of formal, procedural norms; the mobilization emphasis on potential and rate poses a challenge to any thorough critical and empirical evaluation of issues and policies; and the charismatic stress on unity poses a challenge to the still-fragile collegial orientations and relational competences of these elites. Not only do these stances—mobilization and inclusion—conflict with one another; there is no guarantee that Leninist regimes will effectively combine them. However, that their success is problematic and partial cannot automatically be taken as evidence that they "fall short" of modernity. They do indeed fall short of the liberal variant of modernity.[52] Still, one must consider the possibility that all variants of modernity, including the liberal one, are based on conflicting imperatives and are amalgams with distinctive characters. All modern societies appear to be based on conflicting imperatives of achievement and equality of performance and potential. In China, Liu Shao-ch'i and Mao represented these imperatives; in a different context, Madison and Paine represented them in the early history of

---

52. See Mark Field, "Soviet Society and Communist Party Controls: A Case of 'Constricted' Development," in Donald W. Treadgold, ed., *Soviet and Chinese Communism: Similarities and Differences* (Seattle: University of Washington Press, 1967), for an analysis that confuses liberal modernity with modernity. In spite of that, Field's analysis of regime-society relationships and developments is very acute. For a more complex appreciation of the character of Soviet development, see J. P. Nettl and Roland Robertson, "Industrialization, Development, or Modernization," *British Journal of Sociology* 17, no. 3 (September 1966): 274–91.

American development and modernization.[53] In fact, these two examples demonstrate the importance of recognizing and relating the universal attributes of modernization as well as the specific and distinctive historical expressions that provide them with sociopolitical substance. Viewed from this perspective, different modern or modernizing societies can be perceived in terms both of their similarities *and* their distinctiveness, thereby minimizing the danger of raising one historical variant to the position of the model itself. It then becomes possible to investigate in what respects certain societies are more modern than others, to compare the variety of problems that characterize different types of modern societies, and to differentiate modern societies in terms of the imperatives they stress and those they tend to neglect. In this light, the whole issue of convergence becomes more interesting, complex, and demanding. The focus can shift from a zero-sum perspective that defines development simply in terms of "them" becoming more like "us" or vice versa, to a perspective that appreciates and examines the "unprecedented" but bounded variety of modern amalgams that may emerge and persist. We must be prepared for unprecedented types of modern systems—such as might have emerged from Dubček's Czechoslovakia.[54]

53. For an excellent and insightful analysis of the conflicting emphases in the American tradition and the character of its resolution, see Norman Jacobson, "Political Science and Political Education," *American Political Science Review* 57, no. 3 (September 1963): 561–69; for the Mao-Liu conflict, see the revised edition of Franz Schurmann's *Ideology and Organization in Communist China* (Berkeley: University of California Press, 1968), pp. 501–93, as well as Benjamin Schwartz's "The Reign of Virtue: Some Broad Perspectives on Leader and Party in the Cultural Revolution," in John Wilson Lewis, ed., *Party Leadership and Revolutionary Power in China* (Cambridge, Mass.: Cambridge University Press, 1970), pp. 149–70.

54. The evidence suggests that Leninist regimes lack the adaptive capacity simultaneously to sustain their charismatic political exclusivity AND relativize their political "constitution." Party cadre and national citizen are mutually exclusive bases for a polity.—K.J. (1991).

4

NEOTRADITIONALISM

Past studies of the Soviet Union have identified and examined the informal practices pervading the Soviet polity and economy.[1] The characterization of these practices as informal testified (correctly, I think) to the Soviet regime's ability to ensure that for the most part they contributed to, rather than subverted, the Party's formal tasks and general interest(s). However, it seems that something substantially new has appeared in the Soviet (and many other Leninist) regimes. To put it a bit cryptically, informal practices have become corrupt practices, practices that subvert, rather than contribute to, the Party's formal goals and general interests; practices that directly threaten the Party's organizational integrity.

Organizational integrity refers to an organization's practical (not simply rhetorical) ability to sustain a specific competence by identifying sociopolitical tasks and enforcing strategies that subordinate particular members to general organizational interests. *Corruption* refers to an organization's loss of its specific competence through failure to identify a task and strategy that practically distinguish between, rather than equate or confuse, (particular) members with (general) organizational interests.[2]

This essay was originally published in 1983 as "Soviet Neotraditionalism: The Political Corruption of a Leninist Regime," *Soviet Studies* 35, no. 3 (July 1983): 275–97. It appears here in slightly edited form.

1. See Joseph S. Berliner, *Factory and Manager in the USSR* (Cambridge, Mass.: Harvard University Press, 1957), and Raymond A. Bauer, Alex Inkeles, and Clyde Kluckhohn, *How the Soviet System Works* (New York: Vintage Books, 1956).

2. This definition of corruption avoids a major weakness of current approaches to corruption that emphasize the difference between public and private aspects of social organization. Reliance on this difference makes it impossible to specify the existence and meaning of corruption in settings where no public-private distinction exists institutionally. The definition of

For a Leninist party, organizational integrity means the competence to sustain a combat ethos among political officeholders who act as disciplined, deployable agents.[3] Phrased somewhat differently, a Leninist party's organizational integrity rests on its regular ability to prevent both the ritualization of its combat ethos and the transformation of (deployable) Party agents into (undeployable) Party principals.

In this essay I analyze and characterize the process of political corruption in the Soviet regime. The focus is the Soviet Party's loss of organizational integrity—that is, regime corruption. Thus, a phenomenon like the "second economy" will not be viewed primarily as evidence of the increasing level and scope of personal corruption; nor will it be viewed primarily as an economic phenomenon. Rather, it will be understood as a central component in the neotraditionalization of a novel form of charismatic organization and rule—the Leninist Party regime, in this case the Soviet regime.[4]

CONCEPTUALIZATION

Some see the Soviet Union as a modern society. Richard Lowenthal, for example, argues that the long-run legitimacy of the Soviet Union "can only rest on the creation of effective institutional procedures by which rules are selected and decisions reached." This is so because "for modern societies there is

---

corruption offered here emphasizes the difference between general and particular interests in an organization or institution, with corruption referring to a situation in which organizational members confuse/equate their particular interests with the organization's general interests, and organization leaders fail in operationally establishing the difference between general and particular interests.

3. See the classic statement by Philip Selznick, *The Organizational Weapon* (New York: McGraw-Hill, 1952), pp. 18–25.

4. I disagree with Reinhard Bendix's suggestion that "Communist dictatorships" are "clearly outside Weber's tripartite division." Bendix goes on to say, "One may well ask whether the old terminology of charisma, tradition, and legality is applicable at all . . . ?" (*Work and Authority in Industry* [Berkeley: University of California Press, 1974], p. xli). I intend to demonstrate that Weber's 'tripartite division' when appropriately reformulated is, in fact, the most useful basis for understanding the organizational and developmental features of Leninist regimes.

no long-run alternative to legitimacy based on institutional procedures. Of the two other types of legitimacy listed by Max
Weber—traditional and charismatic—the first does not apply to
modern civilization and the second does not apply to the long
run."[5] There are two problems with this formulation. To begin
with, someone has failed to inform, or better convince, the
Roman Catholic Church about the relationships of charisma to
the long run. More important, Lowenthal reifies the notions of
modernity and tradition, so by definition the Soviet Union cannot be traditional in any meaningful sense. For Lowenthal, the
somewhat mechanical result is that of a "modern" society waiting on a truculent regime to recognize its "only" option: catch
up with society.[6]

Others, like Jerry Hough, seeing that scientific, technological, industrial, and secular processes and orientations are integral parts of Soviet social organization, erroneously conclude
that the Soviet Union is simply a variant of Western modernity.
"In some sense," according to Hough, "there may not be much
difference between stating that the Soviet Union is basically a
directed society with a number of pluralistic or semi-pluralistic
elements and stating that the Soviet Union is a kind of pluralist
society with certain types of restrictions. It is perhaps the difference between saying that the bottle is 55% full or that it is
55% empty: the difference in tone is greater than the difference in substance."[7] Hough's characterization of the Soviet polity parallels the position and duplicates the error made by M. I.
Rostovtzeff in the controversy over the "ancient economy."
Once it was recognized that during the Hellenistic and early
Roman periods the economy was far from primitive, the issue
of relating and differentiating ancient economy from modern
capitalist economy arose. According to Rostovtzeff, "the difference between the economic life of this (earlier) period and that

5. Richard Lowenthal, "On 'Established' Community Party Regimes,"
Studies in Comparative Communism 7, no. 4 (Winter 1974): 353.
6. This is the dominant formulation in Soviet studies. It absolutizes the
confrontation of a supposedly progressive "society" and a "regressive" regime
and practically rules out a conceptual grasp of regime-society amalgamations.
7. See Jerry F. Hough, *The Soviet Union and Social Science Theory* (Cambridge, Mass.: Harvard University Press, 1977), p. 14.

of the modern world is only quantitative, not qualitative."[8] In short, more a question of "half full or half empty" than of substance.

But for others in the debate, like M. I. Finley and Karl Polanyi, the issue was clearly one of substance. Recognizing the error of categorically juxtaposing primitive and modern economies, they understood that the organization and ethos of formally similar processes and phenomena are decisive in establishing their fundamental similarity or difference. As they have noted, it is both common and costly conceptually to confuse social forms and processes in non-Western settings with the substantive features they possess in Western settings; or in Trotsky's words, to "seek salvation from unfamiliar phenomena in familiar terms."[9] As examples, Finley points to studies of the ancient economy that confuse state noninterference in the economy with laissez-faire, or the state's concern with the "satisfaction of material wants" with the quite different notion of "needs of the economy."[10] The lesson is clear: "The social scientist who deals with cross-cultural problems is inevitably concerned with institutions and cannot use effectively a set of tools which deliberately abstracts from the institutional framework."[11] When he does, à la Rostovtzeff or Hough, the result is a "false account."

A "truer" account of the Soviet polity/economy begins with Alec Nove's formal recognition that "we may be facing a qualitatively new phenomenon for which our customary categories (whether derived from Marx or from Parsons) may require substantial modification";[12] and with Cornelius Castoriadis's

---

8. Harry W. Pearson, "The Secular Debate on Economic Primitivism," in Karl Polanyi, Conrad M. Arensberg, and Harry W. Pearson, eds., *Trade and Market in the Early Empire* (Chicago: Henry Regney, 1957), p. 9.

9. Leon Trotsky, *The Revolution Betrayed* (New York: Merit Publishers, 1965), p. 245.

10. M. I. Finley, *The Ancient Economy* (Berkeley: University of California Press, 1973), pp. 159–60.

11. Daniel B. Fusfeld, "Economic Theory Misplaced: Livelihood in Primitive Society," in *Trade and Market in the Early Empires*, p. 344.

12. Alec Nove, "Is There a Ruling Class in the USSR?" *Soviet Studies* 27, no. 4 (October 1975): 626.

observation that the Soviet economy "is not capitalist, it is not socialist, it is not even on its way to either of these two forms: the Soviet economy represents a historically new type and its name matters little if its essential features are understood."[13] However, names affect understanding. Fortunately, in Alexander Gerschenkron's notion of historical substitutes a conceptual base exists for moving beyond formal recognition of the Soviet polity/economy's novel quality to a more substantive characterization of the Leninist substitute for liberal capitalist modernity.[14] Leninism substitutes the Party's charismatic impersonalism for the procedural impersonalism dominant in the West. Lenin took the fundamentally conflicting notions of personal heroism and organizational impersonalism and recast them in the form of an organizational hero, the Party. What distinguishes the "party of a new type" is the enmeshment of modern features (e.g., the emphasis on empirical investigation, discussion, and individual efficacy) *and* traditional features (e.g., the definition of Party membership as a corporate, exclusive, superior status ideally embracing the whole of a person) in a novel form of charismatic organization.

That novelty expresses itself in the conception of the Party as an amalgam of bureaucratic discipline and charismatic correctness;[15] and as a heroic principal whose combat mission is more social than spiritual or military. Three features of this novel organizational amalgam should be emphasized. First, a Leninist party's charismatic features formally coincide with and unintentionally reinforce many cultural and social dispositions present in a traditional or status society.[16] Second, in a communist country, the Party's "organizational impersonalism" provides a regular basis for the generation of secular, empiri-

---

13. Ibid.; my emphasis.
14. See Alexander Gerschenkron, "Economic Backwardness in Historical Perspective," and "The Approach to European Industrialization: A Postscript," in Gerschenkron, *Economic Backwardness in Historical Perspective* (Cambridge, Mass.: Harvard University Press, 1966), pp. 5–31, 353–67.
15. For a more elaborate discussion of the institutional amalgamation of charisma, modernity, and tradition in Leninism, see chapter 1.
16. I have analyzed and conceptualized this process in chapter 2.

cal, and individual—that is, modern—orientations and practices. This means that modern social, cultural, and economic elements are integral elements of the Soviet polity/economy. At issue, however, is their significance—their weighting, meaning, and place in the Soviet order. Third, as charismatically conceived and organized units, Leninist parties require combat environments to preserve their organizational integrity. Formulating Leninism's basic features in this way emphasizes the integral place modern elements have in a Communist Party regime and how qualitatively different from the West the institutional matrix is within which they are generated, weighed, and understood.

To illustrate the very different meanings formally similar behavior can have in institutionally distinct contexts, let us take a shared Western and Soviet phenomenon—the rise in theft of social property. If one views the Soviet Union and Great Britain primarily as modern societies, one can, as Zygmunt Bauman has, interpret the theft of social property in Great Britain as a response to the shift from market to bureaucratic impersonalism,[17] presumably a more "soviet" form of organization. In this view, Western and Soviet variants of modernity are converging. However, if one views the Soviet Union as a novel form of charismatic organization, one places a very different meaning on theft of social property in Great Britain and the Soviet Union. To wit, what one sees in Great Britain are efforts by individuals to sustain their individuality in an increasingly bureaucratic, impersonal setting. Here corruption appears, only in part to be sure, as an adaptive response to a new type of impersonalism—bureaucratic rather than market. In contrast, in communist countries corruption testifies to the absence of either market or bureaucratic impersonalism. Corruption in a communist setting suggests something essentially different— namely, the party's inability to sustain cadre impersonalism: an amalgam of legal-rational impersonalism and heroic personalism. The growth of corruption in communist countries suggests

17. See Zygmunt Bauman's "Hidden Economy—East/West" (paper prepared for conference on "The Study of the Second Economy in Communist Countries," organized by Gregory Grossman, Washington, D.C., January 1980).

that the "Gletkins"[18] are being transformed in ever greater numbers into traditional-type patrons and "big men." In this view, the convergence occurring is more with the peasant-status societies of the "Third World" than with the class societies of the West.[19]

In summary, then, views of the Soviet polity/economy stressing its modern, Russian, or alien character all produce "false accounts." The Soviet regime is best seen as an institutionally novel form of charismatic political, social, and economic organization undergoing routinization in a neotraditional direction, one quite consistent with its political organization and ideological self-conception. Soviet regime corruption stems from the Party's refusal fundamentally to alter its view of itself as a heroic transforming principal and its corresponding claim to exclusive political status in a situation where it appears unable to identify an ideologically correct and strategically feasible social combat task.

THE CHARISMATIC ORGANIZATION AND ETHOS OF THE SOVIET "OIKOS"

The organization and ethos of Soviet institutions reflect the type of charismatic leadership a Leninist party imposes on the broad process of social development.[20] The result is an institutional pattern resembling Ralf Dahrendorf's description of Imperial Germany as a "peculiar combination of military and

18. Gletkin, of course, is the quintessential impersonal-cadre interrogator in Arthur Koestler's *Darkness at Noon* (New York: New American Library, 1961), pp. 92–97, and the section titled "The Third Hearing" provides very suggestive characterizations of what I refer to as cadre impersonalism.

19. For a typological contrast of status and class societies, see the author's *The Leninist Response to National Dependence*, Part 1.

20. The Greek term *oikos* refers to a social configuration in which the political, economic, and social dimensions of society are not institutionally differentiated or conceptually delineated in private/public terms. Obviously the Soviet Union is not literally organized as a "household." However, its political-economic organization does formally approximate that of an *oikos*. See in this connection Max Weber's discussion in *Economy and Society* (New York: Bedminster Press, 1968), 1:381–84. Also very useful is Finley's discussion in *The Ancient Economy*, particularly ch. 1.

industrial virtues."[21] The striking amalgam of charismatic, traditional, and modern features in Soviet institutions finds expression in the central place of "heroic" and "booty" orientations in the Soviet political economy, the centrality of *blat* in social transactions, the "arithmetical" conception of the Soviet industrial economy, the secretive quality of Soviet political life and the organization of sociopolitical life around the *kollektiv*. I shall examine each of these in turn.

According to Max Weber, pure charisma is foreign to economic considerations—but only in particular respects. Charisma does not "always demand a renunciation of property or even of acquisition. . . . The heroic warrior and his followers actively seek booty. . . . What is despised, so long as the genuinely charismatic type is adhered to, is traditional, or rational everyday economizing, the attainment of a regular income by continuous economic activity devoted to this end." In contrast, "support by gifts . . . involving donation, endowment, bribery, and honoraria . . . constitutes a voluntary type of support . . . [while] booty and extortion whether by force or by other means is the typical form of charismatic provision for needs."[22] The resemblance between Weber's characterization of the charismatic's typical mode of economic support and Konstantin Simis's description of how local Soviet Party and state cadres maintain themselves is remarkable. According to Simis, the local Party and apparat receive tribute in the form of the best produce from state and collective farms, reserved dining rooms in restaurants where bills, if presented, "in no sense reflect the value of what was consumed (or, even more important) imbibed," transport of all forms at their immediate disposal, housing costs borne by state or collective farms, and labor and building materials furnished by state construction organizations. Significantly, these "tributes are not for specific services [the local apparat] renders, but for [the local state and Party elite's] general benevolent attitude and protection."[23]

21. Ralf Dahrendorf, *Society and Democracy in Germany* (Garden City, N.Y.: Doubleday, 1969), p. 53.

22. Weber, *Economy and Society*, 1:244.

23. Konstantin Simis, "The Second Economy and Corruption at the District Level" (paper prepared for conference on "The Study of the Second

The charismatic's relationship to the economy, then, is not one of simple rejection. Rather, the charismatic, whether he be feudal noble or Party cadre, "rejects as undignified all methodical rational acquisition."[24] In the case of the feudal noble, Marc Bloch delineates this configuration perfectly. The noble's "very vocation prevented him from engaging in any direct economic activity. He was committed body and soul to his particular function—that of the warrior." For the noble, fighting was an essential part of his status identity, not simply a role attribute. Yet, "fighting was also, and perhaps above all, a source of profit—in fact, the nobleman's chief industry."[25] To juxtapose these two elements and argue that either the noble was a crude entrepreneur with a different "tone" than the bourgeois entrepreneur, or a romantic with no concern with his or his followers' economic welfare is a sterile exercise. What compels one's attention is precisely the manner in which economic pursuits are integrally enmeshed with, subordinated to, and supportive of what the noble saw as his raison d'être—combat.

The Party cadre's "noble" disposition toward economic pursuits is dramatically captured in a phrase by a commissar in Vladimir Maksimov's novel *Sem'dnei tvoreniya.* Speaking to a young worker-communist, the commissar responds to the worker's comment that the times are hard, goods and money short, with the assertion: "'*Den'gi dryan'* [Money is rubbish]. Power gives the right to everything. Now women come to me." Nove, who quotes this exchange, correctly observes that the phrase *den'gi dryan* reflects the contemptuous attitude to the market and to money-making typical of Party men of the period, who saw their power as opposed by the power of the market.[26] Evidence abounds that the attitude persists and not simply because an entrepreneurial system would challenge the cadres' material interests—that is, their political power. The attitude persists because the Party persists: one with a heroic

---

Economy in Communist Countries," organized by Gregory Grossman, Washington, D.C., January 1980).

24. Weber, *Economy and Society*, 3:1113.

25. Marc Bloch, *Feudal Society* (Chicago: University of Chicago Press, 1968), 2:289, 296.

26. Nove, "Is There a Ruling Class in the USSR?" pp. 623–24.

self-conception, with a heroic record, and with a definition of membership emphasizing the elite's superior status, not simply its function. Cadres oppose the ethos as well as the power of the market system as a source of contamination, as a mode of existence that is undignified, demeaning, and inappropriate. In short, ideal as well as material interests support the Party's charismatic orientation to economic action.

The imperative facing all charismatic status groups is to provide for their material wants without sacrificing their self-conception. To preserve their identity and power, they must devise and sustain political-economic arrangements guaranteeing them economic power and well-being and freeing them from "methodical rational acquisitive" pursuits. One way to solve the problem is to designate certain economic activities consistent with or even part of the heroic ethic. For example, in primitive societies, the hunt is considered a heroic undertaking suitable for warriors. In a communist country like the Soviet Union, heavy industry, machine-building, and construction of missiles and Kama trucks are equivalents. They are areas of endeavor worthy of "heroes of a new type"—that is, production heroes.[27] In contrast to these "heroic" activities stand "household" activities (e.g., areas of light industry; agriculture in many, though not all, respects; and service and trade occupations) and "pariah" activities (e.g., the whole gamut of black market and "second economy" pursuits).

Viewed in these terms, the relationship between "command economy" and "second economy" has much more than a functional dimension. Zev Katz is probably right that the "command economy is able to concentrate so heavily on regime selected targets and [be] successful not despite the private NEP economy but rather because the latter takes care of many needs not provided for . . . by the command economy."[28] But the division of labor between "command" and "second" economies is much

27. See Katerina Clark's nuanced appraisal of the "production hero" in her "Utopian Anthropology as a Context for Stalinist Literature," in Robert C. Tucker, ed., *Stalinism* (New York: Norton, 1977), pp. 180–99.
28. Zev Katz, "Insights from Emigres and Sociological Studies on the Soviet Economy," in *Soviet Economic Prospects for the Seventies* (Washington, D.C.: Government Printing Office, 1973), p. 89.

more than functional; it is an ingenious, not fully conscious, not fully accidental arrangement that sustains and reflects the invidious distinction between "heroic activities" and "household/ pariah activities"; between the privileged exclusivity of the cadre stratum, demesne, and style of life on the one hand and the dependent, privatized situation of the politically excluded on the other.

The prevalence of *blat* in social interactions is another expression of the charismatic-traditional quality of the Soviet polity/economy. *Blat* typically refers to ties of reciprocity, not to impersonal, strictly accountable, exchanges of standardized value. In this respect, Soviet social organization broadly resembles primitive economies where "reciprocity demands adequacy of response not mathematical equality,"[29] and traditional peasant communities where "reciprocal favours are so dissimilar in quality that accountancy is difficult."[30] Exchanges based more on reciprocity than standardized exchange indicate and sustain a polity based on mutually exclusive status—for example, nobles / serfs, big men / small boys, or Soviet cadres / Soviet citizens. *Blat* emphasizes the status and personal nature of exchanges, with deference, appreciation, generosity, and loyalty becoming defining parts of social transactions. Social exchanges associated with the term *blat* are not simply or primarily functional arrangements expediting the performance of economic tasks in situations of scarcity, urgency, and unpredictability. *Blat* relationships and exchanges are status-type substitutes for the impersonal/individuated predictability and standardization of a market economy and electoral polity.

The Soviet leadership's "arithmetical" approach to the economy is yet another example of the novel way in which modern orientations and practices are enmeshed in a charismatic-traditional framework. The Soviet "arithmetical" approach resembles that of the tsars in an important respect. According

29. See Karl Polanyi, "Aristotle Discovers the Economy," in *Trade and Market in the Early Empires*, p. 73.
30. J. K. Campbell, "Honour, Family and Patronage: A Study of Institutions and Moral Values in a Greek Mountain Community," in Steffan W. Schmidt, James C. Scott, Carl Landé, and Laura Guasti, eds., *Friends, Followers and Factions* (Berkeley: University of California Press, 1977), p. 254.

to Richard Pipes, "the administrative order of pre-1917 Russia rested on a peculiar system of farming out which resembled neither bureaucratic centralism nor self-government. Its prototype was the Muscovite institution of *kormlenie* (feeding) which gave the civil service virtually free rein to exploit the country, *demanding only that it turn over to the state its fixed share*."[31] In Catherine the Great's words: "So long as I am supplied exactly, in quantity and quality, with what I have ordered, and no one complains of neglect on the subject, I am satisfied; I think it of little consequence whether out of the fixed sum I am cheated through cunning or economy."[32]

Now listen to Kirill Alexeiev's tale about setting up and operating an *artel* in the Soviet Union: "Like every other Soviet economic undertaking, this artel had a plan, specifying a certain amount of production. It not only carried out but exceeded the plan by 50%. . . . But the planned output represented only 2% of the little workshop's productive capacity."[33] The difference between the tsarist and Soviet systems is apparent. The latter's emphasis is developmental—that is, it increases plan demands regularly. But the similarity is equally apparent. Both tsarist and Soviet leaderships work with a traditional, "arithmetical," conception of the economy. The state (communist or tsarist) expects a concrete, fixed amount in priority areas (e.g., court expenses for Catherine, missiles or heavy trucks for Brezhnev), and "the rest" is practically, if not ideally, "left over" for those who are cunning or "economical."

Arithmetic is defined as that branch of mathematics dealing with real numbers; mathematics is defined as the science of numbers and their operations, combinations, and abstractions. An "arithmetical" conception of the economy is consistent with a traditional ontology that stresses the discrete and physical quality of social reality; an ontology geared more to generalization than abstraction. Gregory Grossman's portrayal of the Soviet approach to planning dramatically underscores this

31. Richard Pipes, *Russia under the Old Regime* (New York: Scribner's, 1974), p. 282; my emphasis.
32. Ibid.
33. Kirill Alexeiev, "Russia's Underground Capitalism," *Plain Talk* 4 (December 1949): 20.

point. Planning's "chief daily task and chore is the maintenance of balance with regard to each economic good over the short term." The "crucial importance of balancing is the reason that planning in a command economy must be chiefly physical planning. The financial plans apart . . . Soviet plans are almost entirely either in physical units or in crypto-physical units." Finally, "coordinative planning as it is conducted in the Soviet Union does little by way of consciously steering the economy's development or finding efficient patterns of resource allocation. Its overwhelming concern is simply to equate both sides of each material balance by whatever procedure seems to be most expeditious. . . . The concepts of economic calculation, efficiency, and optimality have been virtually absent from Soviet economics until recently."[34]

Aron Katsenelinboigen also stresses the central (by no means exclusive) place the "arithmetical" approach occupies when he argues that even today, despite the revival of economics in the Khrushchev era, "the majority of Soviet economists lack [L. V.] Kantorovich's understanding of the role of prices as tools in the elaboration and realization of an economic plan."[35] According to Katsenelinboigen, the Soviet leadership and the majority of Soviet economists look upon the economic mechanism "as a bazaar; i.e. as a system where the producer displays his merchandise and sells it, depending on the demand for it. As a rule, there is no recognition of the fact that the market is a highly developed mechanism of horizontal relationships coordinated with a complex structure of institutions: banks, stock markets, etc."[36]

None of this is meant to deny the presence or even growth of modern "mathematical" approaches to the Soviet economy. In fact, both Grossman and Katsenelinboigen point to such—for example, the "discarding of the old 'gross value of output' success indicators for the individual enterprise . . . and replacement by such targets as gross sales and profit," the appearance

34. Gregory Grossman, "Notes for a Theory of the Command Economy," *Soviet Studies* 15, no. 2 (October 1963): 108–9.

35. Aron Katsenelinboigen, "Conflicting Trends in Soviet Economics in the Post-Stalin Era," *Russian Review* 35, no. 4 (October 1976): 377.

36. Ibid., p. 387.

of better-trained economists, and evidence of economic debates in elite circles.[37] The novelty of Soviet (and more generally of Leninist) institutions is that they do regularly generate modern elements and as regularly enmesh them with and subordinate them to charismatic-traditional frameworks. To take the case of "mathematical" developments in the Soviet economy, according to Katsenelinboigen, even among the new generation of economists, "the majority . . . to this day are not properly acquainted with the new trends in economics."[38] Second, the "mathematical" challenges to the dominant "arithmetical" approach appear to be supported more by situational factors (i.e., the existence of an oligarchical leadership) than ideological toleration and intellectual appreciation of competing approaches. Third, while the "mathematical" reformers and reforms occupy a significant intellectual, professional, and political place in the Soviet Union, they have not decisively altered the tenor, style, or pattern of economic action.

In short, while the "arithmetical" quality of Soviet planning and economic life is no more an exclusive feature of the Soviet polity/economy than are its "heroic," "booty," and *blat* features, all are dominant features integrally connected with the organization, operation, and ethos of the Soviet *"oikos."* Each is a substantial component and reflection of the peculiar amalgam and weighting of the charismatic, modern, and traditional features that make up the Soviet developmental and organizational framework. So is the persistently secretive quality of official political life in the Soviet Union.

One has only to note the variety of examples Hedrick Smith provides to get a sense of the scope and pervasiveness of secrecy in the Soviet Union. From airplane crashes to reporting Khrushchev's removal, from crime waves to Nixon's visit, from Aeroflot's refusal to inform passengers if its flights are delayed to the absence of substantial information about the mining of

37. Gregory Grossman, "The Solidary Society: A Philosophical Issue in Communist Economic Reforms," in Grossman, ed., *Essays in Socialism and Planning in Honor of Carl Landauer* (Englewood Cliffs, N.J.: Prentice-Hall, 1970), p. 207; and Katsenelinboigen, "Conflicting Trends," p. 396.
38. Katsenelinboigen, "Conflicting Trends," p. 389.

Haiphong, information is restricted and compartmentalized.[39] In fact, the most telling expression of the Soviet polity's neotraditional quality may be its peculiar combination of secrecy and publicity—one in which secrecy dominates.

More than anyone else, Georg Simmel examined secrecy sociologically and emphasized its significance in the contrast between traditional aristocratic and modern democratic polities. Simmel observed that as late "as the seventeenth and eighteenth centuries [western European] governments kept anxiously silent about the amounts of state debts, the tax situation, and the size of the army."[40] However, in the nineteenth century, something dramatic occurred in western Europe, "publicity invaded the affairs of state to such an extent that . . . government officials published facts without whose secrecy, prior to the nineteenth century, no regime seemed even possible."[41] Simply stated, democracies are prone to publicity; "aristocracies exploit the psychological fact that the unknown itself appears to be fearsome, mighty, threatening. In Sparta, the number of warriors was kept secret as much as possible,"[42] and in the Soviet Union so is the number of apparatchiks.

This suggests something general: secrecy is a constituent element of charismatic groups that see themselves as differing from others in character, not simply role. As Simmel noted "the secret gives one a position of exception . . . everything mysterious is also important and essential."[43] The secrecy pervading the Soviet polity is not because it is "Russian"; rather the Russian Empire and the Soviet Union, each in their different ways, are examples of a charismatic-traditional order. Nor is secrecy in the Soviet Union primarily a case of official bloody-mindedness or contempt.[44] Rather, secrecy is a defining feature of a charismatic status group (i.e., Soviet regime cadres) that views

39. See Hedrick Smith, *The Russians* (New York: Ballantine Books, 1976), pp. 459–501.

40. Kurt H. Wolff, trans. and ed., *The Sociology of Georg Simmel* (Glencoe, Ill.: Free Press, 1950), p. 336.

41. Ibid.

42. Ibid., p. 365.

43. Ibid., p. 332.

44. Hedrick Smith offers this as a major explanation of Soviet secrecy. See *The Russians*, p. 468.

itself and the political order in essential, not dimensional terms, is concerned more with public awe than public legitimacy, and sees the public dissemination of information independent of Party control as destabilizing, not demystifying, political life.

Lenin's claim to genius rests on his assertion that he had created a "party of a new type." Now, as many have recognized, the political party is the specifically modern political institution. In the West, it reflects and substantiates the differentiation of political power from state, social, economic, and religious power—that is, the existence of a public realm. Leninist party regimes are neotraditional in that while they extend political activity to previously excluded social forces, they oppose the emergence of an autonomous public realm. Leninist polities are neotraditional entities characterized by the extension of political activity but not the opposition of official and public realms.[45]

The phenomenon of "closed" lectures, of meetings "at which important state functionaries make information available on a confidential basis to a specially selected audience,"[46] illustrates the manner in which (modern) elements of publicity are enmeshed with and subordinated to (charismatic-traditional) elements of secrecy. In this instance, the formally modern process of disseminating information to strategic groups for the purpose of critical comments is assimilated to a charismatic format and culture. Those invited to the closed lecture are raised to a special status; they share the mysteries of political information and they thereby become separate from those who must content themselves with living in the "cave" of political rumor and jokes. Brezhnev himself unwittingly provided a superb example of the neotraditional quality of Soviet political life when he pointed to reports given by Party personnel to Soviet workers

45. See, in this connection, James R. Townsend, *Political Participation in Communist China* (Berkeley: University of California Press, 1967), and for a clear distinction between the expansion and distribution of power, see Frederick W. Frey, "Political Development, Power and Communications in Turkey," in Lucian W. Pye, ed., *Communications and Political Development* (Princeton: Princeton University Press, 1963), pp. 298–327.

46. This is Alexander Yanov's succinct description of a closed lecture (*The Russian New Right: Right-Wing Ideologies in the Contemporary USSR* [Berkeley: Institute of International Studies, University of California, 1978], p. 1). My emphasis.

on the substance of pre-election Party meetings as proof of Soviet democracy.[47] What he pointed to, in fact, was the novel Leninist amalgam of charisma and modernity, in this instance of official secretive deliberations followed by selective publicity for the "laity."

Finally, there is the Soviet *kollektiv*, an institution neither traditional, in the sense of a social or familial corporate group, nor modern, in the sense of individuals voluntarily associating either as interest groups or as publics.

Leninism's attitude toward the individual is ambivalent. The Party's ambivalence toward the individual expresses itself as positive evaluation of the individual's historical emergence and a negative evaluation of individual*ism*.[48] Trotsky, for example, could praise the "progressive side of individualism . . . (the expression of critical views, the development of one's own opinion, the cultivation of personal dignity),"[49] while rejecting the bourgeois institutional framework historically associated with it. However, what sets the Leninist *kollektiv* institutionally apart is its substitution for both Lockean *and* Marxist notions of individuality. Locke argued for individuality and Marx for "sociality,"[50] but both argued for individual organization and ac-

47. Leonid Brezhnev, "Report to the XXV Congress (CPSU)," Foreign Broadcast Information Service [FBIS], Sov-76-38, vol. 3, no. 38, supp. 16 (February 25, 1976), p. 47.

48. I believe the Party's invidious contrast of the individual and individualism rests on its confusion of individualism and personalism. By *personalism* I mean a social pattern in which traditional institutional authority has been breached but cultural orientations and actions remain largely intact. Individualism refers to something quite distinct, to a revolutionary and historically recent social and cultural gestalt; to a social order in which persons play roles making only partial (i.e., "Menshevik") claims on their identity rather than occupying mutually exclusive and identity-encompassing (i.e., "Bolshevik") status positions. *Individualism* refers then to a social pattern in which the basic units and frameworks of social action have been recast; *personalism* to a setting in which traditional orientations and behavior exist in the absence of (traditional) institutional restraint and purpose. As Tocqueville put it, "Individualism is a novel expression to which a novel idea has given birth. Our fathers were only acquainted with egoism (selfishness)" (Alexis de Tocqueville, *Democracy in America* [New York: Vintage Books, 1945], 2:104. More generally, see pp. 104–32.

49. Leon Trotsky, *Revolution Betrayed*, p. 176.

50. For a useful contrast of Locke's and Marx's notions of individuality, see Ellen Meiksins Wood, *Mind and Politics: An Approach to the Meaning of*

tion free of official sponsorship and control. In contrast, the *kollektiv* may be viewed as a logically contradictory, institutionally "faulted," way of stimulating individualist orientations and subordinating them to the imperatives of an intrusive charismatic official organization, the Party.[51]

A striking example of the Soviet regime's efforts to assign social and personal identity in neotraditional terms, to create a pattern of "official individuality," is the practice of awarding titles and medals. That this effort to encompass and define individuality in neotraditional frameworks and terms can succeed appears clearly in the following episode. It seems that Emmanuil Kaminka, a reciter, was about to appear at a variety concert in a factory club. "Kaminka asked the announcer not to mix up his titles, and several times before making his entrance repeated his request, explaining: first say, Lauriate, then Merited Artist of the Republic, and then Master of the Artistic Word." However, by the time Kaminka was to appear, the young and somewhat flustered announcer forgot the appropriate sequence of ritual status designations, and "not able to come up with anything, cried out in desperation—Emmanuil Shirinka. . . . The performance by the Master of the Artistic Word never took place. Deeply offended, Emmanuil Kaminka left the club immediately." In contrast, when Aleksandr Vertinsky returned to the Soviet Union to give a concert, his reaction to the master of ceremonies' inquiry as to his title was one of perplexity and surprise followed by the response, "I don't have a title, I have a name."[52]

What distinguishes the Soviet (Leninist) institutional gestalt then is the curious placement and definition of modern ele-

---

Liberal and Socialist Individualism (Berkeley: University of California Press, 1972), particularly pp. 126–87.

51. Three valuable studies of the party's "intrusive" efforts are Allen Kassof, *The Soviet Youth Program* (Cambridge, Mass.: Harvard University Press, 1965); Martin King White, *Small Groups and Political Rituals in China* (Berkeley: University of California Press, 1974); and Susan Shirk, *Communist Competition: Career Incentives and Student Behaviour in China* (Berkeley: University of California Press, 1981). In particular, see Fox Butterfield's comments on the *danwei* system in *China* (New York: Times Books, 1982), pp. 42–44, 322–24.

52. See Radio Liberty Background Report, September 24, 1979. "Text of a Talk by Vera Enyutina."

ments, their systemic generation, enmeshment, and subordination in a novel form of charismatic institutional framework. This framework recognizes methodical economic action but favors "heroic" storming; values professionals but subordinates them to tribute-demanding apparatchik "notables"; attempts to upgrade contract as a mode of economic predictability but debilitates its institutional integrity with *blat;* strives for a scientific industrial economy but approaches it "arithmetically"; emphasizes the mass scope of its democracy but operates it secretively; asserts it has substantively freed the individual but captures him in the *kollektiv.* What all this points to is the integral place modern orientations occupy in the Soviet "*oikos,*" as well as their conflict with and subordination to the charismatic-traditional features of Leninist institutions.

REGIME CORRUPTION AND
NEOTRADITIONALIZATION IN THE SOVIET UNION

A remarkable feature of the Soviet Communist Party is that over time it has sustained its organizational integrity as a novel institutional amalgam of charismatic, traditional, and modern feature despite a persistent tendency to organizational corruption—that is, for its members to equate their particular status interests with general organizational interests. This tendency is related to what Max Weber termed the routinization of charismatic movements.[53] In his dramatic phrasing, "every charisma is on the road from a turbulently emotional life that knows no economic rationality to a slow death by suffocation under the weight of material interests."[54] The similarity between what I have termed organizational corruption and routinization comes out clearly in Weber's suggestion that above all routinization means "making it possible to participate in normal family relationships, or at least to enjoy a secure social position in place of the kind of disciplesnip . . . cut off from ordinary worldly connections, notably in the family and in economic relationships."[55]

53. Max Weber, *Economy and Society,* 1:246–71; 3:1121–48.
54. Ibid., 3:1120.
55. Ibid., 1:246.

I use the term *corruption* as well as *routinization* because Weber does not adequately distinguish between routinization that stabilizes and secures the material well-being of a charismatic organization's officials while maintaining that organization's integrity, and routinization that stabilizes and secures the material well-being of officials at the expense of the organization's specific competence and integrity. Routinization of the first type consists of the transfer of personal charisma to office charisma, the best example being the papal office in the Catholic Church. The second type of routinization entails the subordination of office charisma to the incumbents' particular interests. This is corrupt routinization.

The tendency to "corrupt" routinization was pronounced during the NEP, at the time of the 17th Party Congress, and after World War II. But in each of those situations (different) leadership coalitions—under Stalin—succeeded in giving the Party a social combat task that subordinated particular interests to authoritative definitions of the Party's general task and interest. In contrast, today what impresses one about the Soviet Union is the Party leadership's inability and/or unwillingness to devise a credible and authoritative social combat task capable of sustaining a distinction between the regime elite's particular status interests and the Party's general competence and interest. Today the Party leadership appears unable to transform its elite members into deployable combat "agents," to prevent the routinization of a party based on charismatic impersonal discipline into a neotraditional status organization of cadres primarily oriented to personal, familial, and material concerns. Reading the literature about political and economic corruption in the Soviet Union today, I am reminded of a letter Saint Boniface wrote in the eighth century, in which he informed the archbishop of York that he was compelled to restore adulterous priests to their positions "because if all the guilty ones were punished as the canons demanded there would be no one to administer baptism and perform other rites of the Church."[56] The Soviet Party appears to face a similar crisis.

56. See Earl Evelyn Sperry, *An Outline of the History of Clerical Celibacy in Western Europe to the Council of Trent* (Syracuse, N.Y.: N.p., 1905), p. 18.

But why has it reached such proportions at this point in the Party's history? Put more generally, if all charismatic organizations are persistently threatened with the corruption of their extraordinary qualities—their sense of mission and ability to translate it into strategic terms—when does the persistent threat become a successful challenge? Like Weber, Marx noted the persistent threat to social types who rejected mundane material and familial concerns. His comments on the ascetic capitalist entrepreneur's fate have a formal bearing on the heroic communist cadre's fate: "Original sin is at work everywhere. . . . While the capitalist of the classical type brands individual consumption as a sin against his function and as 'abstinence' from accumulating, the modernized capitalist is capable of looking upon accumulation as 'abstinence' from pleasure." Paraphrasing Goethe, Marx pointed out that within the ascetic capitalist's breast "two souls do dwell . . . the one is ever parting from the other."[57] But when is the parting decisive? When does routinization become institutionally defining, not simply threatening?

The problem for organizations with charismatic definitions of elite membership (e.g., priest versus minister, cadre versus politician) is that having taken control of society and transformed it into a "Christian" or "socialist" entity, the combat tension so vital to their ability to subordinate elite particular interests to general organizational interests disappears. Routinization succeeds when a charismatic organization's leadership can no longer identify a compelling transformation task, define it strategically (not merely symbolically), and mobilize significant sections of the organization around both task and strategy.

With the defeat of the internal "class enemy," the ending of international encirclement, and the consolidation of the new socialist order, the Soviet leadership finds it increasingly difficult politically to establish and enforce a distinction between a general Party organizational interest and the elite membership's security and status demands. The result, as illustrated by the fate of Khrushchev's Party-State Control Commission, is a marked decrease in the Party's leadership ability and willingness to maintain its cadre deployability competence.

57. Karl Marx, *Capital: A Critique of Political Economy* (New York: Modern Library, 1960), p. 650.

With the denunciation of Stalin's "cult of personality" and the related practice of opposing the security police to the Party apparat, some of the Party leadership recognized the need for new means to prevent the Party losing its ability to deploy and discipline its members—that is, to prevent organizational corruption. Khrushchev proposed a Party-State Control Commission, whose task (ideally) was to maintain the distinction between general Party and Party staff interests. The results of his efforts were: a seven year intraparty conflict, opposition from the highest cadre level (e.g., Kozlov), the maintenance of a separate Party-Control Commission able to protect Party cadres accused by the Party-State Control Commission of corruption, the assignment of the most junior Party secretaries to head the Party-State Control units at lower levels, the failure to provide political substance to the "assistance groups" of rank-and-file Party members who were to act as support groups for these commissions, the overall weakness of the Party-State units at local levels, and Khrushchev's failure to make the Party-State Control Commission responsible to the Party Congress rather than the Central Committee.[58]

What was a tendency in 1934 became a reality in 1965. With Brezhnev, Kirov triumphed. The remarkable emphasis on cadre tenure signals the success of organizational corruption and political routinization in the Soviet Union. From the Stalinist injunction, "the cadres decide all," the situation has become one where the cadres are practically unremovable. According to Robert Blackwell, "in the post-Stalin era each successor has been more limited than his predecessor in choosing tactics for expanding his power vis-à-vis the collective. Khrushchev, for example, gained power in part on the premise that he would not use it to terrorize his colleagues. Besides this limitation, Brezhnev has not had a free hand in manipulation of cadres' assignment."[59] The contrast with the situation under Stalin is fundamental. Then, as now, the tendency to confuse particular

58. See Grey Hodnett's excellent study "Khrushchev and Party-State Control," in Alexander Dallin and Alan F. Westin, eds., *Politics in the Soviet Union* (New York: Harcourt, Brace & World, 1966), pp. 113–65.

59. Robert E. Blackwell, Jr., "Cadres Policy in the Brezhnev Era," *Problems of Communism* 28, no. 2 (March–April 1979), pp. 29–42. My emphasis.

cadre and general Party interests existed, the tendency, as Alexander Gerschenkron once put it, for the "khozyaistvennik to become a khozyain."[60] But in Stalin's time "the local apparatchiki were merely overseers, unquestioningly carrying out the economic will of the central administration. Their management and coordination function was restricted not only from above, but also horizontally by the local MVD agencies that held sway over them."[61] Under Stalin, cadres were political deputies, political agents. Now they are political principals.

Having rejected Stalinist patrimonial organization and thwarted Khrushchev's attempted plebescitarian alternative, the Party has become more patriarchal in political organization. What distinguishes patriarchal from both patrimonial and plebescitarian rule is that the leader's dominance "must be exercised as a joint right in the interest of all members, and is thus not freely appropriated by the incumbent."[62] The fit between this concept, the reality of cadre tenure, and the limits on Brezhnev's personal power is impressive. Apparently, the Soviet elite cadre has succeeded where the Soviet working class failed; it has become a group "in itself and for itself." It has successfully identified, or better confused, the Party's general interest with its particular status interests of career and personal security, privileged material, and superior political position. In doing so, it obstructs the emergence inside as well as outside the Party of any political force able to demonstrate the relativity of cadre interests. What appears to be well advanced in the Soviet Union is the "unionization" of the Party's elite cadre. If recently in the United States "the growth of police unions has made steady inroads on the discretion of police executives to employ various techniques for controlling the conduct of their subordinates . . . [so that] the major obstacles to the reform of corrupt police departments may no longer be a corrupting organizational environment, but rather the application of more than due process guarantees to police officers

60. Alexander Gerschenkron, *Economic Backwardness.*
61. Alexander Yanov, *Détente after Brezhnev: The Domestic Roots of Soviet Foreign Policy* (Berkeley: Institute of International Studies, University of California, 1977), pp. 32–33.
62. Max Weber, *Economy and Society*, 1:231.

acting through unionized strength,"[63] in the Soviet Union the regime's elite cadre has also made "steady inroads on the discretion of [party] executives."

It was Zbigniew Brzezinski who once asserted that "the need for the purge will not diminish with the growing stability of the totalitarian regime. . . . Measures to eliminate stagnation and corruption will always be needed."[64] Unfortunately, he confused the genetic and developmental aspects of Leninist organization. The Party may indeed "need" periodic purging to maintain its organizational integrity, but no metaphysical imperative exists to ensure that the motivation and means to meet the "need" will always exist. Stalin's power to purge and maintain cadre deployability rested on his ability to designate a general task and mission for the Party, one like rapid socio-industrial development that called for and was consistent with a combat setting and deployability competence, and then succeed in identifying that task and its imperatives with the particular interests of strategic Party sectors.[65]

The present Party leadership's inability and unwillingness to designate a politically compelling social combat task, assert its deployability powers, and thereby prevent the conflation of elite cadre and general organizational interests strongly indicates the ritualization of its combat qualities and the emergence of a neotraditional institutional pattern, one of the central components of which is the Soviet "second economy."

Today political, not entrepreneurial, capitalism is growing in the Soviet Union.[66] The sponsorship by cadre-patrons of quasi-

63. Lawrence Sherman, *Scandal and Reform* (Berkeley: University of California Press, 1978), p. 261.

64. Zbigniew Brzezinski, *The Permanent Purge: Politics in Soviet Totalitarianism* (Cambridge, Mass.: Harvard University Press, 1956), p. 170.

65. See Franz Schurmann, "Politics and Economics in Russia and China," in Donald W. Treadgold, ed., *Soviet and Chinese Communism: Similarities and Differences* (Seattle: University of Washington Press, 1967), pp. 297–327, particularly pp. 318–19, for a substantial treatment of this point.

66. Political capitalism differs ideally from entrepreneurial capitalism in at least three respects: the institutional framework within which economic activity takes place (i.e., administrative hierarchy versus market), the ethos of such activity (i.e., uncertainty caused by the arbitrariness of one's political sponsor versus the greater predictability of impersonal market regulations), and the primary agents (i.e., the fiscal oriented corporation versus the indi-

legal and illegal economic activities and the gratitude, deference, fear, and "tribute" they receive from those given the right
to engage in these activities suggest a variant of "Stuart," not
"Puritan," capitalism. The development of Soviet political capitalism signifies a major adaptation by a Leninist organization
lacking a combat task, seeking to preserve its political exclusivity and perquisites, and in a "state of the whole people," trying
to accommodate a wide range of social interests. Like the Roman senators who engaged in "political money-making" but
abhorred moneylenders (*faenatores*), the Party elite are "in-
hibited as a group" from becoming either businessmen or politicians. Like Ciceronian Rome, the Party will adapt to new
circumstances, but "in some directions, not in all."[67] The preferred direction is toward an elite pattern of socioeconomic
"concubinage," not the "methodical rational acquisition" of either goods or votes.

In organizations like the Party, where elite membership ideally enlists the whole of a person's identity,[68] where membership is more status than role, the organization typically attempts
to distinguish categorically between the elite member's commitments prior to occupying an elite position and after. Thus,
beginning in the fourth century, the Church argued that mar-
ried men who became priests should cease conjugal relations
with their wives.[69] Analogously, in the Soviet Union, Hedrick
Smith tells the story of a high-ranking Soviet scientific admin-
istrator who, on being promoted to deputy minister, was told he
would get a state dacha in Sovmin. "The man gracefully tried to
decline on grounds that he had purchased a nice dacha of his
own . . . and did not want either to move or to have to give up
his expensive piece of property. . . . He was sternly admon-

---

vidual entrepreneur). For a more extended set of comments, see Max Weber,
The Protestant Ethic and the Spirit of Capitalism (New York: Scribner's, 1958),
passim, but esp. ch. 5.

67. Finley, *Ancient Economy*, pp. 54–55, 60–61.

68. The Party is one example of what Coser has termed a "greedy institution," i.e., "one that seeks exclusive and undivided loyalty . . . [its] demands
are omnivorous" (Lewis A. Coser, *Greedy Institutions: Patterns of Undivided
Commitment* [New York: Free Press, 1974], pp. 1–21).

69. Sperry, *Outline of Clerical Celibacy*, p. 331.

ished: 'Are you trying to insult the system of nomenklatura? You must sell your private dacha and take the state dacha that goes with your position.' He complied."[70] However, if organizational corruption occurs when a charismatic organization can no longer strategically identify a compelling combat task, at that point the organization's ability to prevent the personalization of status should decrease. This is precisely what the "duplication phenomenon" in the Soviet Union suggests. Alexander Yanov reports that members of the Soviet elite who possess departmental dachas "prefer to duplicate them by acquiring their own."[71] This means the Party "victory" Smith reported may be harder and harder to repeat.

The "duplication phenomenon" points to an elite-ownership pattern that is neither institutionally nor ideologically based solely in the market, nor restricted to complete reliance on party benefices and largesse. It points to an elite-ownership pattern more analogous to concubinage than to either marriage or celibacy. An ownership pattern of this order appears ambiguous, transitional, and tenuous only if it is forced into a restrictively Western historical and conceptual framework. The major instance of this is the pervasive (almost obsessive) effort to study the Soviet elite in class terms.

"Has the Soviet ruling stratum become a ruling class?" Nove's answer to this recurrent question captures the frustration of those who approach the Soviet order in these terms. Nove says the Soviet ruling stratum "has some of the characteristics of a ruling class, *though not that of ownership,* except possibly in some collective sense."[72] Similarly, Roy Medvedev sees that "those in charge of Soviet society now constitute a definite stratum sharing certain customs and rules of conduct," that "this estate has passed beyond the control of society," and that "advancement is largely dependent on personal patronage" but "these groups do not constitute a class in the socio-economic sense of the word *. . . they do not own the means of production or the land . . .* and are

70. Smith, *The Russians,* p. 51.
71. Yanov, *Detente after Brezhnev,* p. 11.
72. Nove, "Is There a Ruling Class in the USSR?" p. 632. Nove's article is still a major contribution to breaking away from the very monotonous perspectives that define the Soviet field. My emphasis.

not able to bequeath their rights, privileges, or positions to their children."[73] However, the Soviet elite's "failure" to establish its private ownership of major social resources is perplexing only if one tries to assimilate Soviet institutions and practices conceptually to Western—that is, class and procedural—forms of organization and development. Viewed as substitutes for Western forms of modernity, Soviet institutions, practices, and elites appear less perplexing and "incomplete." Viewed as a variant, not of Western elite formation, but of charismatic status organization, the Soviet elite may be expected to disdain as well as fear a social order based on the skills and ethos of businessmen and politicians and to avoid the benefits and terms of private/market ownership; they are too threatening.[74] The current Soviet pattern of sociopolitical "concubinage"—with its mix of private and official perquisites and possessions, tenure of political position, physical security, and privileged stable access to careers—serves the interests of this organizationally corrupt status elite very well indeed.

Still, one might ask whether or not, in this type of regime, social and political corruption might act as solvents, with private wealth eventually replacing political status as the basis of social organization, the result being more a Soviet variant of than substitute for Western social organization. Walter Lippmann once observed that in England "corruption [was] the practical substitute for factional wars. In the eighteenth century the civil wars in England came to an end and the habit of political violence dissolved finally in the organization of a thoroughly corrupt but peaceable parliament."[75] Might not the political and economic corruption that has replaced the Soviet Terror (i.e., the "civil wars") be a step toward a Western outcome? Gregory Grossman speaks of this possibility when he argues that the

73. Roy A. Medvedev, *On Socialist Democracy* (New York: Knopf, 1975), pp. 299, 297. My emphasis.
74. I do not mean to deny the ambivalence many within the regime's elite cadre may feel toward private ownership; I mean to suggest that on balance its members appreciate the material and ideal dangers with which such a system would threaten them.
75. Walter Lippmann, "A Theory about Corruption," in Arnold A. Heidenheimer, ed., *Political Corruption: Readings in Comparative Analysis* (New York: Holt, Rinehart & Winston, 1970), p. 297.

"prevalence of economic illegalities and corruption elevates the power of money in [Soviet] society to rival that of the dictatorship itself, rendering the regime's implements of rule less effective and less certain." And he goes on to suggest that "the next logical step in the development of [Soviet] corruption would seem to be the capitalization of expected future streams of graft, and hence the purchase and sale of lucrative official positions."[76]

In seventeenth-century England, one sees the widespread sale of office, the absorption and accommodation of a new bourgeoisie into a framework of political capitalism and absolutism, and then in the eighteenth and nineteenth centuries the emergence of market capitalism and electoral democracy. The question again is might not money and corruption play a comparable role in the Soviet Union's future development. It is unlikely! To begin with, the accommodation of the bourgeoisie during the seventeenth century did not prevent a civil war in England.[77] Second, the dominance of entrepreneurial capitalism over mercantilism was the result of prolonged conflict between groups and institutions representing each, not a matter of peaceful evolution from one to the other.[78] Third, and more generally, England's social and political organization was hardly representative of western Europe, let alone of other parts of the world.

More representative of the impact social and financial corruption might have on a polity like the USSR is the historical experience of France and the contemporary experience of a country like Morocco. In France, corruption did open up access to office for a period of time. However, the ennobled bourgeoisie "gradually closed its ranks, making ennoblement increasingly less available as a channel of social mobility. . . . This restriction of [the bourgeoisie's] access to status and power in-

76. Gregory Grossman, "The 'Second Economy' of the USSR," *Problems of Communism* 26, no. 5 (September–October 1977): 37, 32.

77. James C. Scott suggests that this type of accommodation may, however, have made the Civil War less bloody (*Comparative Political Corruption* [Englewood Cliffs, N.J.: Prentice-Hall, 1972], p. 47).

78. See Max Weber, *General Economic History* (Glencoe, Ill.: Free Press, 1950), ch. 29, esp. pp. 350–51.

creased the likelihood that more radical means of redress would be sought."[79] Similarly, in Morocco, John Waterbury notes, "high level corruption may allow outsiders to buy their way into the circuit, but it is no easy task. Corruption in Morocco may have contributed to the stratification of resources within a particularist bourgeois elite."[80]

In short, historically in France and currently in Morocco, corruption directly contributed to the extension and then reinforcement, not demise, of a status ordering of political, economic, and social life. If my characterization of the Soviet regime's sociopolitical "constitution" has merit, corruption is likely to have a similar effect there.

That in the Soviet Union bribes "are being offered and taken for everything, ranging from certificates of place of residence, to apartments, to ministerial posts in the republics,"[81] does not mean the replacement of a closed political status group by entrepreneurial market elements. Rather, it speaks to the adoption of practices that on balance sustain the politically superior and economically privileged position of the elite cadre; to the emergence of a Leninist neotraditional variant of political capitalism. An excellent example of such a practice was the appearance in Hungary of semiprivate organizations led by private entrepreneurs run under the aegis of official agricultural collectives. On the surface this might be viewed as "creeping capitalism," and one might see this innovation as a "Western" development. All the more important then is Kalman Rupp's valuable study of these organizations.

According to Rupp, "full capital ownership (and accumulation) rights of Semi-Private Plant entrepreneurs were never completely accepted by the (agricultural) cooperatives, a notable limitation of administration protection for private venture." Also both cooperative leaders and entrepreneurs "viewed the possibility of establishing and running semi-private organizations as a short-run opportunity." Finally, when the interests of

79. Scott, *Comparative Political Corruption*, p. 47.

80. John Waterbury, "Endemic and Planning Corruption in a Monarchical Regime," *World Politics* 25, no. 4 (July 1973): 549–50.

81. Konstantin Simis, "The Machinery of Corruption in the Soviet Union," *Survey* 23, no. 4 (Autumn 1977–78): 39.

the official cooperatives had been served, the entrepreneurs were sacrificed. These observations, and Rupp's conclusion that the "administrative protection offered for entrepreneurs in Hungary did not result in stable and lasting protection: [that] uncertainty was an inherent part of the game,"[82] are perfectly consisteht with the institutional features and ethos of political capitalism.

Private entrepreneurship was accommodated, enmeshed, manipulated, and subordinated to the Hungarian Party's neo-traditional framework of political absolutism and political cap-italism. To argue this is not to deny the threat that money, corruption, and private entrepreneurship pose to the status ordering of political and economic life in a communist country. It does suggest there is an important difference between a threat and an effective rival. Money, corruption, the "second economy," and, most of all, the transformation of Party cadres from organizational agents to organizational principals are all significant elements and developments. The task is to under-stand their significance and not confuse it with that associated with formally similar developments in Western history.

If today one can "deduce that the purchase and sale of positions for large sums of money signifies the profound insti-tutionalization in the Soviet Union of a whole structure of brib-ery and graft, from the bottom to the top of the pyramid of power,"[83] in good measure this suggests how successful the Party has been in preserving its politically exclusive qualities while accommodating a diverse array of social interests and demands. However, one interest and latent demand is not com-patible with the Party's exclusive political status: political equal-ity between Party cadres and Soviet "citizens." The stability of

82. Kalman Rupp, "Private Entrepreneurs and the Communist Political Machine" (paper prepared for conference on "The Study of the Second Economy in Communist Countries," organized by Gregory Grossman, Wash-ington, D.C., January 1980), p. 34.

83. Gregory Grossman, "The 'Second Economy' of the USSR," p. 32. From all indications it would appear that Isa. 1:23, "Your very rulers are . . . confederate with thieves; every man of them loves a bribe and itches for a gift" (*The New English Bible with the Apocrypha* [Oxford University Press, Cam-bridge University Press, 1970], p. 810), describes a very central feature of the Soviet regime.

the Soviet neotraditional pattern of political evolution rests on the regime's continued ability to sidestep and displace this issue of political equality.

Here corruption in its manifold forms plays a central role. As Samuel Huntington has noted, "in the absence of agreement on public purpose, corruption substitutes agreement on private goals."[84] But the Soviet leadership's de facto toleration of and even reliance on corruption in the Party and Soviet society has serious costs. The Party risks the social anger of those excluded from the privileged access structure of Party patronage, and the political anger of "citizens" who resent its very existence.[85] The Party also risks responding inadequately to the mobility demands of lower-level cadres, and alienating cadres interested in restoring the Party's organizational integrity. However, any attempt to restore the Party's ability to create deployable agents means adopting a combat relationship with Soviet society, and this is a difficult and dangerous undertaking. It is a difficult because with socialism having triumphed "fully and conclusively in the country" a combat task is hard to locate and justify.[86] It is dangerous because a combat relationship would threaten the stability of the regime cadres' well-secured personal and familial interests.

---

84. Samuel P. Huntington, *Political Order in Changing Societies* (New Haven: Yale University Press, 1968), p. 64. Tocqueville's comment in *Democracy in America*, vol. 2, ch. 4, on how despotisms favor social and personal selfishness as a diversion from public affairs is pertinent here.

85. Like Trotsky, I do not believe that better living standards in a communist country will decisively lower the level of corruption, because the latter rests on the configuration of contemporary Leninist political organization. Trotsky put it this way: "The very existence of a greedy, lying, and cynical caste of rulers inevitably creates a hidden indignation. The improvement of the material situation of the workers does not reconcile them with the authorities; on the contrary, by increasing their self-respect and freeing their thoughts for general problems of politics, it prepares the way for an open conflict with the bureaucracy" (*Revolution Betrayed*, pp. 285–89). The fit between this evaluation and the actions of Polish workers in August 1980 is remarkable.

86. Not impossible. I shall discuss one possible scenario involving the emergence of a new combat setting and a new heroic regime agent—the Soviet Army.

THE REGIME'S FUTURE

The neotraditional direction taken by the Soviet regime since Khrushchev is an attempt to sustain a particular type of status elite in a changed political, societal, and international environment, and a stimulus for further political and socioeconomic developments. Three possible developments merit attention: the emergence of a Western-type regime, the emergence of a regime led by military-Party cadres, and the emergence of a regime much like the present one in which KGB personnel will assume a very prominent political role.

One of Leninism's novel features as a charismatic mode of organization and operation is the integral place modern elements and orientations occupy—for example, the emphasis on empirical investigation, on (organizational) impersonalism, and on science.

In the Soviet Union today, a wide array of social phenomena speak to the continued presence, even growth, of modern phenomena with Western liberal implications. There have been market experiments in the economy, at one point "consulting firms" appeared offering a private management service, a number of sophisticated economists work in the planning sectors, and at the philosophical level there has been movement from a dogmatic conception of shared interests to one in which the "existence of particular economic interests and aims is acknowledged." One finds intellectuals with empirical and technical dispositions entering the Central Committee's apparatus, and scientists like Fedoseev preferring "to buy his holiday *putevki* on the black market rather than getting them from authorities and establishing an obligation."[87] Finally one must note the existence and public actions of humanist liberals like Andrei Sakharov. From the idiosyncratic to the general, each of these examples testifies to the existence and persistence (in the Soviet *oikos*) of modern orientations and discrete practices with Western liberal implications. Does not the possibility, even the likelihood, exist that these orientations will continue to grow at the expense of the neotraditional institutions in which they are embedded and by which they are shaped and constrained? My

87. "Inside the CPSU Central Committee," interview by Mervyn Matthews, in *Survey* 20, no. 4 (Autumn 1974): 94–104.

answer is no. Institutions have a powerful advantage over orientations and discrete practices.

At no time has economic reform radically recast the neopatriarchal anti-market-system quality of Soviet (or for that matter Hungarian) economic organization.[88] The entrepreneurial "consulting firms" were treated by the Soviet authorities "with great suspicion and most of the firms were closed down and some of their managers imprisoned."[89] A middle class intellectual like "Pravdin" who joined the Central Committee apparat to help clean up corruption and embezzlement found the anti-individualism, anti-expert tenor of that organization as secure as it was offensive.[90] Fedoseev's preference for the black market over a patron-client dependence on political superiors offers dramatic testimony about the character and weight of the "Western" alternative. Fedoseev's "market individualism" found support in a sub rosa, illegal, "pariah" institution. As for the Soviet elite's philosophical admission of particular social and personal interests, their relationship to general social interests is still understood in substantive, not procedural terms. Consequently, no effective institutional provision exists in the Soviet Union for the juxtaposition of public and official interests, for governance rather than dominance. (One implication of this is that Merle Fainsod's title *How Russia Is Ruled* is conceptually accurate; Jerry Hough's title *How the Soviet Union Is Governed*, conceptually inaccurate.) But perhaps Sakharov's position more than anything else symbolizes the real, but limited, potential of Western-type liberal development in the Soviet *oikos*. Sakharov's ability to speak for so long rested on elite calculation,[91] not institutional toleration, and his exile symbolizes the existence and subordination of modern elements within a

88. On the limits of the very significant Hungarian reforms, see Edward A. Hewett, "The Hungarian Economy: Lessons of the 1970's and Prospects for the 1980's" (prepared for inclusion in U.S. Joint Economic Committee, *East European Assessment* [Washington, D.C.: Government Printing Office, 1981], pp. 483–525).

89. Dimitri K. Simes, "The Soviet Parallel Market," *Survey* 21, no. 3 (Summer 1975): 50.

90. "Inside the CPSU Central Committee," interview by Mervyn Matthews, in *Survey* 20, no. 4 (Autumn 1974): 94–104.

91. The regime elite cadre's corporate desire to protect itself creates a high threshold for punishing anyone who occupies generalized elite status.

historically new type of charismatic-traditional institutional framework.

If I may offer an analogy, modern liberal elements in the Soviet *oikos* occupy a position similar to that of contract in Western feudalism. There, contract was an integral part of the social order, distinguishing Western feudalism from patrimonialism.[92] However, contract was enmeshed and in basic respects subordinated to an institutional framework based on personal loyalty and heroic action. It took a series of civil and revolutionary wars, religious and political, to disembed the "contractual elements" from their subordinate position. It took a combination of Erasmian humanism, Calvinist intolerance, civil and military violence, and regional as well as national decentralization to "produce" Western liberalism.[93] The implication is clear. Liberal development of the Soviet Union is unlikely in the absence of intense social and military violence carrying with it only the possibility, not the certainty or even likelihood, of a Western outcome.[94] The Sakharovs are no more likely to succeed in their attempts to reform the Soviet institutional framework than their Erasmian predecessors were able basically to reform Catholicism.

A more likely development, should the Soviet polity experience a series of traumatic national and/or international shocks, would be the appearance of a Party-military regime. However, the Soviet regime's movement in that direction would also encounter strong internal resistance. Leninists have always viewed "Bonapartism" as a critical threat to the political and ideological integrity of the Party—with good reason. The military and the Party are "competing heroes," heroes with opposing competences. Historically, the Party has been oriented to heroic social

92. See Max Weber's comparison of feudalism and patrimonialism in *Economy and Society* 3:1070–1110.

93. The most impressive analysis I have seen of this historical process is in H. R. Trevor-Roper, *Religion, The Reformation, and Social Change* (London: Macmillan, 1972), ch. 4.

94. Such an outcome appeared to have greater possibilities in Poland, where a de facto situation of political toleration existed, and where for a brief time trade unions achieved a position reminiscent of "free cities" in West European history.

combat, the military to war. Ideally, the Party's competences are political and persuasive, the military's administrative and command. Materially, groups fearing a relative loss of power, privilege, and prestige would oppose a major growth in the military's political power, as would those who saw in such a development a threat to the regime's and/or world's existence. After all, the move to power of a military-Party group would probably signify a level of international tension that threatened world war.

Still, if a Western outcome is practically impossible in the Soviet Union, the military outcome is only improbable, and that for several reasons. To begin with, in its current developmental phase the Party operates with an "inclusive" but not democratic definition of political membership.[95] While viewed by the Party as politically benign, the Soviet population is not treated as politically equal. The military's close relationship to national symbols offers a way to square this circle by substituting national unity of elite and citizens for political equality of elite and citizens. Second, while the military's heroism is basically incompatible with the Party's, it is also true that the military is a Soviet institution, with a genuine heroic record.[96]

But the potentially decisive element favoring a Party-military outcome in the Soviet Union is the superimposition of intracommunist national conflicts (e.g., between China and the Soviet Union) on Soviet-American conflicts (e.g., in the Middle East and South-East Asia). In the absence of a compelling domestic combat task, the apparent corruption of the Party's organizational integrity, the perceived efforts at American-Chinese encirclement, and destabilization in the East European "territories," the Soviet military may be seen as the needed and appropriate heroic agent to deal with a proliferating number of ethnic-national combat tasks: domestically, in the bloc, and internationally.

Without dismissing a likely rise in the Soviet military's role

95. For a more elaborate consideration of this distinction see chapter 3.
96. However, the Soviet Army may lose prestige, morale, and influence should it be placed for long in a protracted Afghan (or Polish) conflict. Such an experience would also have a major impact on internal Soviet politics.

and stature, it may be predicted that the primary development in the Soviet Union, within the now existing neotraditional order, will most probably be the political upgrading of the KGB [this was written in April 1980]. In a perceptive passage about the relationship between Party officials and factory managers, Vera Dunham has observed that in the post-Stalin period, "something has changed. . . . It is the difference in role and function, in accountability and initiative between manager and party bosses. The partners have become more easily interchangeable."[97] I suggest the same thing has happened between Party and KGB officials. This changed relationship speaks to the movement of the Soviet polity from a consolidation to an inclusion stage, one characterized by a less than categoric and invidious distinction among organizational sectors within the elite. Today a generalized elite stratum exists in the Soviet Union, one not lacking functional or institutional distinctions or rivalries, but not limited to such. For this reason, I have repeatedly and deliberately used the general term *cadre*[98] rather than emphasize the different types of organizational and functional elites. The term *regime cadres* suggests an elite stratum in which organizational and functional distinctions *cum* rivalries persist but coexist within a more generalized elite status. In the case of the KGB, the point is not to deny its organizational distinctiveness; it is to argue that the KGB is not the NKVD.

The Soviet regime's move from consolidation to inclusion meant the elimination of the security forces' superiority over the Party, the destruction of their status as elite agents of a "sultanist" ruler, and their integration into a framework of Party-organizational control. These changes in status and role have made the KGB more a component than opponent of the

97. Vera S. Dunham, *In Stalin's Time* (Cambridge, Mass.: Cambridge University Press, 1979), p. 246.
98. Interestingly, in China cadres may not even be Party members. However, according to White, the ambiguity of the term in China has to do with the Chinese leadership's "continual effort to blur the leader-led distinction" (*Small Groups and Political Rituals in China,* pp. 58–59). I am suggesting a somewhat different basis for the generalized status implied by the term *cadre;* namely, the creation of an established officialdom characterized by social familiarity and ease, intermarriage, and interorganizational career mobility.

Party.[99] Additionally, in the Soviet polity, one oriented primarily to substantive, not procedural, rationality, the KGB with its image of organizational rectitude can readily be viewed as the appropriate sector of the Party regime to combat instances of regime and social corruption. Indeed, there are striking examples of this happening. Hedrick Smith notes that in the aftermath of the purge of corrupt Party officials in Georgia, "the Politburo picked a former cop (Interior Minister) Eduard Shevardnadze, a man of Cromwellian rectitude." Similarly, in Kirghizia and Azerbaijan, the KGB was used to restore Party morality.[100] These examples point to the existence within a neotraditional polity of a Party organization, the KGB, offering itself as the exemplar of official Party rectitude and morality, and using its coercive powers in a neopatriarchal fashion when social or elite abuse threatens to rouse the Soviet population's anger, and/or undermine the Party's leadership, to maintain organizational limits on personal aggrandizement.

In connection with its role as political moral exemplar and image of personal and organizational rectitude, the KGB probably enjoys selective, ambivalent, and real support from a number of social and elite sources. Within the Party, those concerned with maintaining the Party center's leverage over regional and local Party-state cliques may well support the "guardian" role of the KGB. Soviet professionals, from skilled workers to scientists, might find common (though ambivalent) ground with the KGB in the demand for social and official rectitude, honesty, and probity. Party ideologists concerned with the Party's organizational integrity are another possible source of support, as are cadres reluctant to see the military

99. Zbigniew Brzezinski's belief that the "ascension of Yuri Andropov . . . represents an unprecedented triumph of a coalition of the secret police and armed forces over the traditional Communist Party bureaucracy," and that "Andropov succeeded where Beria . . . failed," rests on an uncritical static projection of a past, not present, party-police relationship. The change in this relationship—as I have defined it—may be the single most significant political-organizational change in the post-Stalin period. For Brzezinski's comment, see Brzezinski, "A Deal for Andropov," *New Republic,* December 13, 1982, p. 11.

100. Smith, *The Russians,* p. 127; and see Konstantin Simis, "Machinery of Corruption," p. 47.

appear as the agent of renewed morality and political purpose. Support, then, for the political role of the KGB would be diverse, selective, wary and substantial. Opposition would also be diverse, but different in origin. It would originate more likely at the regional and local levels of Party leadership, from social groups benefiting most from the "second economy," from the organizational-personnel departments of the Party apparatus, and from those with good memories of the role played by the security forces in the pre-Khrushchev/Brezhnev periods.

As for the KGB itself, it probably has an approach/avoidance attitude to a more "public" political role. The probable attractions include the increased power (and perhaps prestige) that would accrue to KGB cadres, and the increased opportunity to enforce norms many of them consider necessary to contain or eradicate social and political corruption. The avoidance attitude has two sources. First, continuous executive responsibility for political and economic life will threaten the organizational insulation so closely connected with the relatively high degree of rectitude of the KGB. Second, the political use of the KGB in anticorruption activities reflects the degree to which it has become a trusted component of the Party regime. As such, KGB cadres themselves have a vital stake in the current regime's maintenance. They and their families benefit from the neotraditional political, economic, and social configuration that emerged under Brezhnev. For this and other reasons already dealt with, the anticorruption activities of the KGB are likely to be decidedly reformist, not radical. In the near future, what one may well see in the Soviet Union is a sort of Ottoman oscillation between periods of increasingly visible and "abusive" displays of cadre-familial aggrandizement, and efforts at organizational and moral revitalization in which the KGB plays a major role in reforming and maintaining Soviet neotraditionalism.

5

"MOSCOW CENTRE"

Existing explanations of the Soviet Union's international relations with other Leninist regimes and the West are inadequate. They can be grouped into two categories: "monotheist" and "polytheist."

"Monotheist" arguments rest on the claim that the Soviet Union's political character essentially differs from and opposes the West's. In this view, the West is at war, not with Soviet conduct, "but with [the USSR's] existence; convinced that its existence and its hostility [are] the same."[1] Such a view allows for variations in Soviet orientation while asserting essential continuity of Soviet organization and behavior. Charles Gati's assertion that, despite change in the Soviet Union's domestic and international environments, "Soviet leaders . . . have . . . continued to rely on the old historical mix of assertiveness and accommodation,"[2] is representative. Assertiveness and accommodation are attitudinal, not developmental, variations available to a regime that in this view has remained "platonically," or essentially, the same since 1917.

This essay was originally published in 1987 as "Moscow 'Centre,'" *Eastern European Politics and Societies* 1, no. 4 (Fall 1987): 296–348. It appears here in slightly different form. The author thanks the National Council for Soviet and East European Research for its support, as well as Jack Citrin, Gail Lapidus, Bob Price, Steve Krasner, Mel Croan, J. F. Brown, Ernie Haas, Mike Rogin, Zvi Gitelman, and Jacques Levesque for their critical enthusiasm, and John Le Carré for "suggesting" the title.

1. The phrase is Edmund Burke's and was directed at the "Jacobin system." Paul Seabury "makes it his own" with a simple substitution of *Soviet* for *Jacobin* in his "Reinspecting Containment," in Aaron Wildavsky, ed., *Beyond Containment* (San Francisco: Institute for Contemporary Studies Press, 1983), p. 43.

2. Charles Gati, "The Stalinist Legacy in Soviet Foreign Policy," in Erik P. Hoffman, ed., *The Soviet Union in the 1980's* (Montpelier: Capital City Press, 1984), p. 225.

Similar in conception though more nuanced in presentation is Henry Kissinger's description of the Soviet Union as an amalgam of "an ideology that cannot resist movement," a bureaucracy that "mixes caution with persistence," and a regime subject to environmental constraints—that is, difficulty in winning new ideological adherents. Kissinger subordinates this nuanced description of the Soviet regime to the "monotheist" conclusion that "the Soviet Union has not changed fundamentally."[3]

Those who conceive of the Soviet Union in "monotheist" terms typically conclude that variation over time in the Soviet regime's format is less important than the persistence of elements that provide the Soviet Union with a continuously recognizable and essentially unchanged identity. "Monotheists" see the Soviet regime's essential political features as more important than its developmental changes and, in fact, typically reduce the latter to changes in style and attitude.

In contrast to a "monotheist" interpretation of the Soviet Union as a "platonic" regime form that is essentially alien and permanently aggressive, the "polytheist" interpretation points to the existence of "many" Soviet Unions depending on the arena the Soviet elite acts in, the issues it confronts, the opponents it faces, the partners it aligns with, the divisions within its own elite, and the priority it sets on a given goal. For "polytheists," Soviet foreign policy and behavior are not viewed as inherently and permanently soft or hard. Instead, they are viewed as the "consequences of complex, intersecting, aggregate internal and external variables, and they can be expansionist, aggressive, assertive, moderate, defensive, or deferential depending upon circumstances and personalities."[4] Though it is not stated explicitly, "polytheists" seem to argue

3. "Summary of Kissinger Speech to U.S. Ambassadors," *New York Times*, April 7, 1976.
4. Vernon V. Aspaturian, "U.S. Perceptions of Soviet Behavior: Contending Approaches or Analytical Continuum?" in Robert E. Osgood, ed., *Containment, Soviet Behavior, and Grand Strategy* (Berkeley: Institute of International Studies, University of California, 1981), p. 21. As Haas has observed, "polytheist" or what he calls "mixed explanations . . . correct overly simple analyses of the [Soviet] mystery without giving us a satisfactory clarification of the mystery itself." See Ernst B. Haas, "On Hedging Our Bets," in Wildavsky, ed., *Beyond Containment*, p. 108.

that: (a) developmental changes in the post-Stalin period have produced a Soviet foreign policy essentially different from that of the Stalin era, or (b) that even under Stalin, Soviet foreign policy never fit the American "monotheist" interpretation. In contrast to the quasi-sacral conception of the "monotheists" who detect a more "genuine" reality of unchanging political essence underlying the "apparent" reality of a more politically sophisticated and confident post-Stalin Soviet leadership, the "polytheists" combine an analytically sophisticated disaggregation of the Soviet regime's behavior and a theoretically superficial statement about the Soviet regime's political character.

In place of "monotheist" conceptions and "polytheist" descriptions of the Soviet regime's political character, I propose a "trinitarian" theoretical framework to explain the Soviet Union's relations with other Leninist regimes (and the West). The "trinity" consists of the essential, developmental, and international elements that shape the Soviet regime's organization and action at given points in its political history. I argue that the Soviet Union's political character does differ essentially from the West's—it is not a variant but rather a "substitute," in Gerschenkronian terms, for Western liberal modernity.[5] However, the essential or permanent features of the Soviet regime that provide it with a continuously recognizable political identity have been substantially recast organizationally, ideologically, and behaviorally in the course of the Soviet Union's political development. As Hans Küng notes in his analysis of the Catholic Church: "There is not and never was in fact, an essence of the Church by itself, separate, chemically pure, distilled from the stream of historical forms."[6] More precisely, developmental changes in any organization involve more than shifts in style and attitude; they are substantial revisions of an

5. See Alexander Gerschenkron, "Economic Backwardness in Historical Perspective," in his *Economic Backwardness in Historical Perspective* (Cambridge, Mass.: Belknap Press, Harvard University Press, 1966), pp. 5–31. I have developed the notion of "substitute" for the Soviet case in *The Leninist Response to National Dependency* (Berkeley: Institute of International Studies, University of California, 1978).

6. Hans Küng, *The Church* (Garden City, N.Y.: Image Books, 1976), p. 23.

organization's epistemology, as well as the institutional format within which an organization's ideological tenets and leadership take on political expression, meaning, and consequence.

A third factor, the way in which the Soviet regime's international environments are organized, has affected the Soviet regime's character and behavior throughout its developmental history.

The Soviet Union's political character and the nature of its political relations with other Leninist regimes are shaped, then, by the interaction of three elements: the permanent features that provide the Soviet regime with a continuously recognizable identity; the developmental changes that periodically recast the institutional configuration of the regime's ideological, organizational, and behavioral features; and the impact the organization of international politics has on relations within the Leninist regime world.

THE ESSENTIAL

"Monotheists" assert correctly that the Soviet Union's political character differs essentially from the West's. That assertion should be understood as a conceptual and analytic challenge to specify the Soviet regime's political uniqueness. To argue like Zbigniew Brzezinski that the "expansion of the Soviet imperial system is a unique organic imperative produced by a sense of territorial insecurity of the system's Great Russian core,"[7] is more mystical than conceptual. I suggest we exorcise the demonological and emphasize a more anthropological approach to the genuine insight that the Soviet political order *is* alien to the West's political order.[8]

In this vein, George Modelski suggested that "the Soviet Union's status is not that of an alliance leader . . . it resembles more that of a head of a family or of a tribe, interested in and

7. Zbigniew Brzezinski, "The Soviet Union: World Power of a New Type," in Hoffman, ed., *Soviet Union,* p. 147.
8. As Louis Hartz once observed, "Russian development has turned its back on the Western concept of personality" (*The Liberal Tradition in America* [New York: Harcourt, Brace & World, 1955], p. 308).

responsible, in a sense, for all family or tribal affairs."[9] From a political anthropological viewpoint the Soviet-centered Leninist regime world—that group of regimes ruled by Leninist parties and primarily, if not exclusively, oriented to the Soviet Union—does essentially resemble an extended traditional family led by a "patriarchal" figure, the Soviet regime, whose degree of arbitrariness and command varies, but who uses substantive (not procedural) criteria, like the "Brezhnev Doctrine," for deciding when to interfere in related "households" (i.e., other Leninist regimes). The relative neglect by Leninist regimes of procedural norms helps explain Jerry Hough's observation that "developments within Eastern Europe are essentially treated [by the USSR] as domestic ones,"[10] and William Zimmerman's reflection: "Curiously, the relatively closed Soviet Union is probably potentially more subject to influence by members of its regional [Eastern European] system than is the United States."[11] This is anthropologically true. The West is a more regime-individuated political universe, with both the resources and dispositions to demand more regime "privacy," or sovereignty.

When Fidel Castro says, "I think proletarian internationalism is the most remarkable feature of Marxism-Leninism or socialism, and I could say the revolutionaries' most noble quality,"[12] he is not merely making an implicit claim on Soviet aid; he is making a political anthropological statement as a Leninist about an absolutely preferred mode of international and domestic political organization.

Similarly, when the USSR criticized the 1958 Yugoslav Draft Program for having "reduced proletarian internationalism to the principles of equality and non-interference in internal affairs," thereby failing to recognize that "under certain conditions proletarian internationalism demands the subordination of the interests of the . . . struggle in one country to the interests

9. George Modelski, *The Communist International System* (Princeton: Center of International Studies, 1960), p. 52.

10. Jerry Hough, "The World as Viewed from Moscow," *International Journal* 37, no. 2 (1982): 194.

11. William Zimmerman, "Hierarchical Regional Systems and the Politics of System Boundaries," *International Organization* 26, no. 1 (1972): 24.

12. F. Castro Ruz, "Marxism-Leninism and the Cuban Revolution," *World Marxist Review* 22, no. 1 (1979): 15.

of the struggle on a worldwide scale,"[13] it was doing more than demonstrating a penchant for political interference. The Soviet criticism of the Yugoslavs revealed a particular political ontology, an understanding of regime and inter-regime organization more charismatic and traditional than modern in conception. However, nothing captures the Soviet regime's traditional-charismatic political ontology more than the meaning and status it assigns the October Revolution.

According to Mircea Eliade, "every sacred place implies a hierophany, an irruption of the sacred that results in detaching a territory from the surrounding cosmic milieu and making it qualitatively different."[14] For the Soviet elite, the October Revolution remains a political hierophany and the Soviet Union the corresponding politically sacred space; the October Revolution is *the* historical event that split the world in two and gave the "whole of international life a single pivot; namely, the struggle of the world bourgeoisie against the Soviet state and its natural allies."[15] But the revolutionary eruption of a politically charismatic regime implied more for the Soviet leadership than simply the reorganization of international lines of conflict. To refer to Eliade again, where a sacred entity—in this instance a revolutionary regime viewed in quasi-sacral terms—appears, "we everywhere find the symbolism of the Center of the World";[16] precisely the status and definition every Soviet leadership since Lenin has given the Soviet Union in relation to all other Leninist parties and regimes.

On the first page of *Left-Wing Communism,* Lenin emphasized how Soviet experience "shows very definitely that certain fundamental features of our revolution have a significance that is not local . . . or Russian alone, but international." Lenin meant that this experience has an "international validity or the histor-

---

13. *Kommunist* (Moscow), 1958, no. 6 (April 19, 1958), in Robert Bass and Elizabeth Marbury, eds., *The Soviet-Yugoslav Controversy, 1948–1958* (New York: Prospect Books, 1959), pp. 158–59.

14. Mircea Eliade, *The Sacred and the Profane* (New York: Harcourt Brace Jovanovich, 1959), p. 26.

15. Konstantin Zarodov, "Leninism and Some Questions of Internationalism," *World Marxist Review* 25, no. 4 (1982): 10.

16. Eliade, *The Sacred and the Profane,* p. 37.

ical inevitability of a repetition, on an international scale."[17] Thus began a persistent tendency to conflate the October Revolution and the Soviet regime; to identify a revolutionary hierophany—the October Revolution—with a concrete "sacred" political center—the Soviet Union. Before the end of the civil war, Lenin was implicitly identifying the Soviet regime as the embodiment of the essential features of *the* charismatically correct revolution (in Clifford Geertz's terms, as an "exemplary center" or revolutionary *"negara"*),[18] and consequently laying claim for the Soviet regime—if only implicitly at first—to be the concrete criterion and exemplar of revolutionary authenticity.

Grigori Pyatakov's emotional enquiry, "What was the October Revolution . . . what indeed is the Communist Party but a miracle?"[19] captures the Soviet leadership's conception of the Soviet regime as a revolutionary hierophany. But the October Revolution's significance is not exhausted by recognizing that all Soviet leaderships (certainly since 1925) have seen the Soviet Union as *the* political center and criterion, not simply as *a* political reference for other revolutionary socialist regimes. That significance extends to a political historical fact: Soviet organization and practice have been the substantive basis for almost all Leninist regimes at crucial points in their political organization and development. The Soviet regime and experience have been the source of their primary institutional definition and can still be characterized as their "permanently decisive origin."

Vernon Aspaturian accurately observes: "As the original homeland of Marxism-Leninism the Soviet Union is the common inspiration and point of departure for all communist parties." It remains true that "the Soviet Union's pivotal significance in the system cannot be denied even if ambiguous and in

17. Lenin, *Left-Wing Communism—An Infantile Disorder,* in V. I. Lenin, *Collected Works,* vol. 31 (Moscow: Progress Publishers, 1966), p. 21.

18. For Geertz's use of the terms *negara* and *exemplary center,* see his *Negara: The Theatre State in Nineteenth Century Bali* (Princeton: Princeton University Press, 1980), pp. 4, 13, and 43. This is not the place to expand on Lenin's initial "embarrassment" at "usurping" Germany's presumed revolutionary role, or on the increasing acceptance of the central rather than anomalous state of the Soviet revolution.

19. See Robert Conquest, *The Great Terror: Stalin's Purges of the Thirties* (New York: Macmillan, 1968), p. 127.

a state of transition."[20] This pivotal significance has two components. First, all other Leninist regimes, including the Cuban, have modeled their institutions more rather than less on Soviet institutions.[21] Second, as the original revolutionary hierophanic center, the Soviet Union still considers itself the charismatic criterion of correctness and measures the authenticity of other Leninist, or "revolutionary," parties and regimes, by their institutional proximity to the Soviet regime, by their ideological fealty, and by the extent of their status deferral to the myth of the October Revolution.[22]

We have a remarkable bit of contemporary evidence to support this argument. In 1983 Richard Jacobs, the Grenadian ambassador to Moscow, wrote a long memorandum vividly illustrating the very practical international implications of the Soviet leadership's quasi-sacral conception of the October Revolution. Jacobs observed that "by itself, Grenada's distance from the USSR, and its small size, would mean that we would figure in a very minute way in the USSR's global relationships. Our revolution has to be viewed *as a world wide process with its original roots in the Great October Revolution.*"[23] Not, you will note, a continuation of the October Revolution, the Chinese Revolution, the Yugoslav Revolution . . . but rather the substantive

---

20. Vernon V. Aspaturian, *The Soviet Union in the World Communist System* (Stanford: Hoover Institution Press, 1966), pp. 15, 18.

21. The unique feature of Cuba's relation to the Soviet Union is that it drew on the Khrushchevian (inclusion) experience, not the Stalinist (consolidation) experience. Louis Hartz in an ingenious comparison of nations that emerge from the British experience has developed the notion of "fragments." Australia, for example, draws on the British labor fragment while the United States draws on the liberal middle-class fragment of the total British experience. It might be fruitful to compare Leninist regimes as "fragments" of the Soviet experience. Thus Hungary would be a Khrushchevian fragment, Albania a Stalinist fragment, and Husák's Czechoslovakia a Brezhnevian one. See Louis Hartz, *The Founding of New Societies* (New York: Harcourt, Brace & World, 1964), pp. 1–69.

22. *Myth* here has no negative connotation. I use it in its anthropological sense.

23. "Confidential Report by Grenadian Ambassador to Moscow, W. Richard Jacobs (dated July 11, 1983)," in Paul Seabury and Walter A. McDougall, eds., *The Grenada Papers* (San Francisco: Institute for Contemporary Studies Press, 1984), p. 207. The emphasis is mine.

extension and continuation of the original Soviet October Revolution.

The Khalq regime's obligatory recognition—even prior to the Soviet invasion—that the Saur revolution in Afghanistan "was a continuation of the Great October Revolution"[24] resembles the Grenadian genuflection. But the creation in 1976 of a Leninist party and corresponding institutions in Cuba provides an even more dramatic and substantive instance of political replication, one that prompted Jacques Levesque to make the following comment in his study of Cuban-Soviet relations:

> One of the themes that constantly recur in the many articles published in the Soviet Union during 1976 in celebration of the first Congress of the Cuban party was the fact that the documents of the Congress confirmed the validity of the "general laws of socialist development" tried and tested by the experience of the Soviet Union. . . . The fact that the Soviet Union attached so much importance to the Congress is a good illustration of its fetishism concerning political structures.[25]

Fetishism indeed! If, as I argue, the Soviet leadership operates with a charismatic conception of the October Revolution and the "sacred" space associated with the Soviet Union, then replication of its Party regime and acceptance of the Soviet Union's status as revolutionary origin and center become the ideal criteria of a "revolutionary" party or regime's authenticity.

However, this by no means exhausts the matter. To begin with, historically the Soviet regime has entered into substantial, and at times preferential, relations with non- and even anti-Leninist regimes. This has been true from the inception of the Soviet regime, when its relations with Weimar Germany were in crucial respects more substantial than those with the only other Leninist regime, Outer Mongolia. And it is true today, as a comparison of Soviet-Indian and Soviet-Chinese relations demonstrates. The Soviet regime has never acted like the Essenes

24. Anthony Arnold, *Afghanistan: The Soviet Invasion in Perspective* (Stanford: Hoover Institution Press, 1981), p. 87.

25. Jacques Levesque, *The USSR and the Cuban Revolution: Soviet Ideological and Strategical Perspectives, 1959–1977* (New York: Praeger, 1978), p. 186.

and absolutely refused to have contact with entities of an opposing or even different order.

Second, one must recognize the extent to which the Soviet
claim to be the authenticating center and leader of the Leninist
world has been challenged from within that very world. At one
point in the late 1960s, that challenge came from a majority of
Leninist regimes: China, Vietnam, North Korea, Albania, Yugoslavia, Romania, Cuba, and Czechoslovakia. And in some
instances the challenge was absolute, because it refused to recognize anything but the symbolic association of the October
Revolution with the Soviet regime.

Finally, one must appreciate the extent to which the Soviet
leaders themselves have, over "developmental" time, significantly revised what they understand to be their rights of revolutionary authentication and international leadership.

The question is: Do any or all of these observations undermine the contention that the Soviet Union assigns itself a
unique status in the Leninist world, one charismatic and traditional in nature, *and* one that has action, not simply symbolic,
implications? I do not think so.

Take the first observation: on occasion, Soviet relations with
some non- or anti-Leninist regimes are more forthcoming and
substantial than relations with some Leninist regimes. The "realist" explanation would be in terms of material interests or
necessity. "Capitalist" India and Nigeria are more important
materially—economically, strategically, and politically—than
"socialist" Burma and Benin. The "realist" explanation is inadequate but not incorrect. There is a distinction between material and ideal interests. Ideal interests have more to do with
actions and relations a regime considers appropriate and
proper, while material interests have more to do with actions
and relations a regime considers useful and expedient.[26] In
light of this distinction, I offer the following hypothesis: other
things being equal, the USSR will choose and develop relations

26. On material and ideal interests, see Ken Jowitt, "Scientific Socialist
Regimes in Africa: Political Differentiation, Avoidance, and Unawareness," in
Carl G. Rosberg and Thomas M. Callaghy, eds., *Socialism in Sub-Saharan Africa: A New Assessment* (Berkeley: Institute of International Studies, University
of California, 1979), pp. 148–49.

with regimes "made in its own image," but other things being unequal, it will establish relations with non- or even anti-Leninist regimes. As a rule, however, there is a much lower threshold for terminating these relations, and much less willingness to expose the USSR to risk for such a regime or come to its aid than would be true if it were Leninist.

In this context, one should also note that as soon as the Soviet Union presented itself as the concrete incarnation of Leninism, all Soviet political actions and international relations immediately became, by definition, ideologically principled. Ideology and power as motive forces and rationales in foreign policy could not, therefore, be mutually exclusive (as they are so monotonously presented in discussions of Soviet foreign policy).

As for the second observation, about critiques and even rejection by some Leninist regimes of the Soviet power to authenticate them as such, this does pose a serious challenge to the Soviet Union's preeminent political and ideological status among Leninist regimes. To be real, charisma must be recognized, not simply asserted. Negative responses within the Leninist regime world to Soviet authenticating and leadership claims have included criticism of Soviet leaders, opposition to Soviet policies, and condemnation of the Soviet Union's institutional integrity as Leninist. To grasp the meaning and consequences of Soviet claims, and the occasional, but persistent, opposition to them, one must appreciate the essential difference between the "West" and the Leninist regime world. The former locates its origins in many revolutions, the English, French, American, and others; the latter is based on one unique historical event, the October Revolution. The West legitimates itself in terms of a formal rationality, more exactly procedural institutions; the Leninists in terms of a substantive rationality, more exactly a charismatic institution, the Party. Two political consequences follow from these differences. First, while the Soviet regime can recognize on a de facto basis the existence of Leninist regimes that fail to emulate and defer to it, the Soviet leaders consider this a sufferable, not a natural or legitimate, condition. In such circumstances, a tension exists within the Leninist regime world for which there is no comparable base in the West. The second consequence of the charismatic nature of

Leninist organization and the specific charismatic claims to primary status of the Soviet Union is that opposition to the Soviet Union by another Leninist regime is typically a traumatic experience for that regime (or party), and as such a highly destabilizing event both within the opposing regime and within the Leninist regime world. However, to all of this, one must add that if the Soviet regime's charismatic claims to authenticating power and leadership status have periodically been challenged, they have rarely been denied completely. Rather, Soviet power and status have regularly been recognized by most Leninist regimes most of the time. While it is important to analyze the motives for that recognition, the balance between necessity and choice, it is equally important to recognize how historically impressive long-term ideological deferral to the uniqueness of the Soviet October Revolution and the political adoption and persistence of Soviet institutions within the Leninist regime world have been.

This brings us to the third "complicating" feature related to the Soviet Union's appropriation of a unique status in the Leninist world. The ideological conception and political expression of that status have been substantially recast in response to changes in the Soviet leadership's internal and external environments. To argue, as "monotheists" do, the Soviet regime's power to remain impervious to such changes, and survive, is to ascribe a magical power to the Soviet regime that has eluded all other historical entities. I propose now to identify and examine at some length the nature of the change in the Soviet self-conception and organization of the Leninist regime world. To do this, it is necessary to identify a predictable pattern of development in the political organization and action of the Soviet and other Leninist regimes, and consequently in their mutual relations with each other, with the West, and with the Third World.

THE DEVELOPMENTAL

One can identify two substantially different modes of political organization and action in the history of Soviet relations with other Leninist regimes and with the West. These modes correspond to the consolidation and inclusion stages of Soviet regime development. Both modes are essentially charismatic-traditional but vary substantially in their institutional definitions and political implications—internally and internationally.

During the Stalinist consolidation stage, the Soviet Union was viewed by Leninists as the incarnation of the October Revolution. The term *incarnation* refers to "the concrete or actual form of a quality or concept,"[27] and accurately evokes the Soviet Union's status during Stalin's rule. This development was more a response to a victorious regime's anxious political need to insulate its quasi-sacral identity from what were viewed as potentially "contaminating" domestic and international environments than the result of Stalin's personal pathology. The typical response of any organization relatively secure about power and insecure about identity is to adopt a dogmatically concrete definition of its essential features, to juxtapose that identity to its potentially contaminating environments, and to try to distance itself from and dominate those diffusely hostile environments. Organizations in the developmental stage of consolidation typically adopt "castle profiles." Under Stalin, the Soviet Union became a "castle regime."

The developmental imperative toward dogmatic concreteness manifested itself in the Soviet Union in several ways, but most expressively as "socialism in one country."[28] With that concept, Stalin concretely located the Revolution by dogmatically identifying it with a particular regime, the Soviet Union. "Socialism in one country" answered the anxious political and ideological need for a visible, specific revolutionary site and base. The Stalinist ideological claim that defense of the Revolution meant the defense of the Soviet Union, and the popular Party saying that "one Soviet tractor is worth ten foreign communists," signified the incarnation, not simply reification, of the October Revolution in the form of the Soviet Union. The Soviet Union was a particular type of organization, a regime

27. *Webster's Seventh New Collegiate Dictionary* (Springfield, Mass.: Merriam Co., 1971).

28. The most thorough examination of this concept and its evolution is by Elliot R. Goodman, *The Soviet Design for a World State* (New York: Columbia University Press, 1960), pp. 129–64.

understood by its members as heroic, charismatic, and historically extraordinary. For such a regime, the process of consolidation was a process of sacralization. In Robert Tucker's words,
the USSR became more than an instance of a phenomenon,
more than a symbol; it became the "repository of the socialist
idea," the object of "the cult of the USSR."[29] "Socialism in one
country" not only "located" the Revolution by identifying it
with a particular regime, it elevated that regime in an extraordinary way. From being a Marxist revolutionary anomaly, the
Soviet Union became a revolutionary incarnation. In the eyes
of Leninists, the October Revolution transformed "biblically
last" Russia into the "biblically first" Soviet Union. The periphery of the Western world became the nucleus of a "superior"
socialist one.

The "juxtaposition imperative" is an equally integral feature
of Leninist consolidation regimes. In his political autobiogra-
phy, Wolfgang Leonhard notes that "reality in the Soviet Union
was completely different from the picture presented in *Pravda*.
But somehow I dissociated these things. It was almost as if there
were two separate levels, one of everyday events and experiences which I found myself often criticising; the other that of
the great party line . . . which I still regarded as correct."[30]

This stark contrast has regularly been seen as an instance of
Soviet hypocrisy or a consequence of Stalin's peculiar psyche.
Tucker, for example, points to the existence of a "Potemkin
Russia" during Stalin's rule and asks, "For whom was the great
show staged?" According to Tucker, "the main spectator was
Stalin. It was he who imperatively needed the Potemkin
Russia. . . . The idealized Russia was a background panorama for
the figure of the idealized Stalin."[31] I prefer more anthropology
and less psychology to explain the Stalinist juxtaposition of
"sacral Soviet" reality and "profane Russian" reality. Leonhard
gets it anthropologically right when he contrasts the quasi-sacral
"correct," and therefore "essentially more real," not idealized,

29. Robert C. Tucker, *The Soviet Political Mind* (New York: Praeger,
1963), p. 173.

30. Wolfgang Leonhard, *Child of the Revolution* (Chicago: Henry Reg-
nery, 1958), p. 89.

31. Tucker, *Soviet Political Mind*, pp. 174–75.

Soviet reality, to the empirical, but ordinary, and therefore somehow "less real," life that contradicted it. Stalin's castle regime was very "Augustinian," a mix of the contaminating ordinary cultural and social reality of Russian society and the politically asserted "sacral" reality of the Party and its actions. For Stalinist "Augustinians," Potemkin Russia was sacrally real and as such had to be insulated from and dominant over its unreconstructed and potentially contaminating environments.

The distance and domination imperatives of consolidation manifested themselves in the creation of political, ideological, and coercive "moats" between the Soviet regime and its society on the one hand and the regime and the outside world on the other. In the former setting, secretiveness and a terror apparatus created both distance and domination, while internationally the so-called Iron Curtain quite graphically captured the imperative of cultural, political, and ideological "distance" from what was viewed as not simply a militarily hostile but also an ideologically polluting international environment.

Stalinist consolidation in the Soviet Union created a regime with three features: the dogmatically concrete identification of the Soviet regime's particular features with the general features of Leninism; the juxtaposition of the "sacral" features of regime organization with those of the "contaminating" and "profane" features of the surrounding society; and the coercive political-ideological separation of the two realms. By 1948 these three features also dominated the national organization of the newly created Leninist regimes in Eastern Europe as well as the international organization of the Soviet bloc.

The Soviet Bloc

The appearance after World War II of additional regimes ruled by Leninist parties created serious political and ideological problems for the Soviet elite. Ideologically, the Soviet leadership had to define the status of these new regimes in relation to the Soviet Union, while politically it had to decide on a mode of inter-regime organization. These were crucial issues. To incorporate Eastern Europe into the Soviet Union would risk the material interests of the Soviet regime should civil wars in Eastern Europe occur and possibly trigger a third world war. Incorporation would also challenge the material power of Soviet cadres by adding Eastern European cadres directly to the Soviet elite structure. But incorporation would challenge more than Soviet material interests. Soviet ideal interests would also have been jeopardized in two ways.

To incorporate Yugoslavia would have meant incorporating a competing charismatic leader and heroic Party. In light of Stalin's and the Soviet Union's absolute sacralization, the Soviet elite must have considered such a move ideologically unacceptable, even "sacrilegious." More generally, if I am right about the thrust of consolidation as a developmental stage, the Soviet leadership would have seen Eastern Europe's incorporation as a highly contaminating measure, particularly in light of the institutional disruption caused by the war in the Soviet Union itself.[32] To incorporate several "capitalist" Eastern European countries politically would have created a very hostile and "polluting countryside" around the militarily victorious, but institutionally disrupted and ideologically indecisive, Soviet "castle."[33] Stalin's solution to these material and ideal challenges was ingenious.

Stalin created a Soviet bloc that more than anything resembled Emile Durkheim's notion of a society based on mechanical solidarity. Replication and segmentation are the primary features of a mechanically solidary society, one in which individuality finds no support. According to Durkheim, mechanical solidarity "can grow only in inverse ratio to personality." The organization of such a society resembles the rings of an earthworm in its segmental replication of a central pattern.[34] Now consider Paul Shoup's description of the Soviet–Eastern European relationship after 1948. In that year, the Soviet leadership

32. See Susan J. Linz, ed., *The Impact of World War II On the Soviet Union* (Totowa: Rowman & Allenheld, 1985).

33. William O. McCagg, Jr., has studied the ideological and political debates within the Soviet leadership after World War II in terms that are very congruent with the perspective I employ in this piece. See his very valuable *Stalin Embattled, 1943–1948* (Detroit: Wayne State University Press, 1978), particularly pp. 97–167.

34. Emile Durkheim, *The Division of Labor in Society* (New York: Free Press, 1964), pp. 129, 177, 181.

began to apply the notion of "socialism in one country" to *each* of the Eastern European regimes. Shoup acutely observes that the Stalinist "pattern of development which was to lead to a world Communist state was therefore unique. *It was not integrative as much as it was reproductive.*"[35] Precisely.

The Soviet bloc was an international political organization based on political replication of the Soviet "sacred center" and political segmentation of its constituent "castle regimes." The Soviet bloc was a remarkable contemporary instance of autarkic, mutually isolated regimes linked to and through a center whose identity was replicated in detailed fashion at the expense of each non-Soviet regime's political "personality." This mode of organization did much more than reflect Stalin's desire for absolute control; it was a response to other and more fundamental imperatives. It satisfied the Soviet belief that its particular regime organization was *the* correct Leninist organization, that the Soviet regime was the incarnation, not simply a representation, of the October Revolution's universality. It satisfied the Soviet demand for political control of Eastern Europe without the risk of cultural contamination that incorporation would have created. It satisfied the charismatic, heroic aspiration of each Eastern European Leninist regime to "construct socialism"; for each Eastern European leadership was told it *could* replicate Soviet achievements. And it satisfied the ideological need of Eastern European and Asian regime leaders for definite reassurance that their political efforts to construct "socialism" would be "correct"—that is, would not inadvertently result in political or social backsliding.

Under Stalin, relations between individual Leninist regimes and between the Soviet bloc and the West were cast in consolidation terms. The marked tendency of a Leninist organization during consolidation to respond to its "contamination anxiety" by interpreting its political and ideological tenets dogmatically and concretely was a defining feature of the Soviet bloc. To begin with, all Leninist regimes were initially linked geograph-

---

35. Paul Shoup, "Communism, Nationalism and the Growth of the Communist Community of Nations after World War II." *American Political Science Review* 56, no. 4 (1962): 892. My emphasis.

ically to the Soviet Union. During the late Stalinist period, the Soviet Union was not simply the center but the middle of the Soviet bloc, if one appropriately includes Outer Mongolia, North Korea, China, and, after 1954, North Vietnam. Rudolph Arnheim's observation that only "in geometry is the center and middle always the same because geometry deals with the static aspect of things"[36] accurately captures the organization and ethos of the Stalinist political universe with its preference for geographically contiguous replica regimes.

Dogmatic concreteness also expressed itself in the detailed replication of the Soviet political order in the most diverse cultural settings. In a clear instance of mechanically solidary international organization, "little" Stalins created replica "socialisms in each country," with replicated steel industries and collective farms. The Soviet regime became a contemporary Klungkung or Ife,[37] an "exemplary regime-court" viewed as the incarnation of political development and ideological worth, institutional proximity to which established the authenticity and relative worth of all other related regimes. Concreteness also took the form of Soviet troops, advisers, secret police, and political personnel being physically present, powerful, and prestigious; the existence of joint-stock companies; the required teaching of Russian; and the unrequired but noticeable practice, at least in Eastern Europe, of marrying Russian wives. At times the concreteness of political definition and identification with the Soviet regime went to absurd lengths. Mao offers us a marvelous example. He reminded one audience that he, "couldn't have eggs or chicken soup for three years because an article appeared in the Soviet Union which said that one shouldn't eat them." As Mao pointed out: "It didn't matter whether the article was correct or not, the Chinese listened all the same and respectfully obeyed. In short, the Soviet Union

36. Rudoph Arnheim, *The Power of the Center: A Study of Composition in the Visual Arts* (Berkeley: University of California Press, 1982), p. 1.

37. Geertz discusses the "exemplary center" status of Klungkung in Bali in *Negara;* Ife occupied a comparable position among the kingdoms of the Yoruba. See Robert S. Smith, *Kingdoms of the Yoruba* (London: Methuen, 1969), pp. 15–51. See especially Smith's description of the court at Oyo on pp. 113–15.

was tops."[38] More than "tops," the Soviet Union was the source
of dogmatic wisdom; more than powerful, authoritative; more
than authoritative, awesome.

The second feature of the Soviet bloc was the stark juxtaposition and distancing of the "sacral" and "profane." Within
each Leninist regime, this took the form of an invidious separation and tension between regime members and nonmembers.
George Heltai describes it best: "The post-capitalist period of
Eastern European history has witnessed the establishment not
only of a 'new class,' but of a new micro-society—a 'master
society'—above the destructured old society."[39] I would say that
there was a new "castle society"[40] insulated from and dominating
the destructured but still diffusely hostile and potentially "contaminating" old society, protected from it by a secret police
"moat." Within the bloc, the same juxtaposition of "sacral" and
"profane" elements played a central role in inter-regime relations. A major expression was the invidious contrast between
Party-to-Party and state-to-state relations, and a good example
occurred in connection with the Soviet-Yugoslav rapprochement in the mid 1950s. According to the Yugoslav ambassador
to Moscow, Veljko Mičunović, the Soviet leaders were unhappy
with the Belgrade Declaration. They considered it a weak doc-
ument "because it bears a state not a Party character."[41] During
the consolidation stage, the Party is considered the exclusive
bearer of charisma. Consistent with the argument that during
consolidation one sees a pronounced tendency toward concreteness, Party charisma is typically appropriated by the (physically
concrete) leader. The state apparatus, though practically more

38. "Talks at the Chengtu Conference, March 1958," in Stuart Schram,
ed., *Chairman Mao Talks to the People* (New York: Pantheon Books, 1974), p. 98.
39. George G. Heltai, "Changes in the Social Structure of the East Central European Countries," *Journal of International Affairs* 20, no. 1 (1966): 169.
40. "Of castles two things must be said. The first is that they are, if we
seek to define them, the fortified residences or residential fortresses of
lords. . . . The second is that the military role of the castle was at least as much
offensive as defensive" (R. Allen Brown, *The Normans* [New York: St. Martin's
Press, 1984], p. 39). Consolidation regimes are not simply state-coercive organizations; they are "residential fortresses," not of lords but of the Party and
its New Class social base.
41. Veljko Mičunović, *Moscow Diary*, trans. David Floyd (Garden City,
N.Y.: Doubleday, 1980), p. 7.

powerful than the Party apparatus, is ideologically cast as the necessary, coercive, and "ordinary" agent suitable for dealings with non-Leninist "stranger" regimes, but not other Leninist "hero" regimes.

Distancing and juxtaposition within the bloc also took the form of keeping to a minimum lateral relations between Leninist regimes. As Władysław Gomułka's former interpreter noted, "The men in power in the Eastern bloc talk constantly of 'internationalism,' but . . . no friendly neighbour relationship of the type that has developed since the end of the war between the French and the Germans has ever linked the Poles with the Russians or the Czechs or even the people of the DDR. They have remained 'stranger[s] to each other'";[42] and, one might add, strangers to their own national populations. Bloc organization rested on the juxtaposition and distancing of Leninist rulers from the ruled. Eastern European leaders identified more with the "sacrally" real Soviet regime than with the "profanely" real nations they ruled.[43]

Relations between the Soviet bloc and the West rested on a similar base of juxtaposition and distancing. Zhdanov's postwar notion of two opposed camps[44] and the purge of the American communist leader Earl Browder for thinking that at Tehran "capitalism and socialism had begun to find the means of peaceful coexistence and collaboration in the framework of one and the same world"[45] were two sides of the same ideological coin. The two camps were not two parts of one world; rather there was a firm "Augustinian" distinction characteristic of the Stalinist consolidation stage of Leninist regime and inter-regime development. The tension and separation of realms inherent in this juxtaposition was assured by limited contacts, vituperative rhet-

42. E. Weit, *At the Red Summit* (New York: Macmillan, 1973), pp. 190–91.

43. Shoup, "Communism, Nationalism," pp. 889–98 and Ken Jowitt, *Revolutionary Breakthroughs and National Development: The Case of Romania, 1944–65* (Berkeley: University of California Press, 1971), pp. 92–130.

44. Andrei Zhdanov, "Report on the International Situation," at the Founding Conference of the Communist Information Bureau in Poland, September 1947, in Robert V. Daniels, ed., *A Documentary History of Communism*, vol. 2 (New York: Vintage Books, 1960), p. 155.

45. Jacques Duclos, "On the Dissolution of the Communist Party of the United States," in Daniels, *History of Communism*, p. 139.

oric, and limited violence, all of which helped create the international "moat" around the Soviet bloc, which became known as the Iron Curtain. In this connection, the Korean War was the quintessential Stalinist consolidation undertaking. It clearly demarcated the two camps. In the short run, it also increased the loyalty and dependence of other Leninist regimes on the Soviet center. And in one instance, that of China, it satisfactorily "tested" Mao's ideological credentials[46] and practically subordinated his regime to the Soviet Union for the war's duration.

After World War II, Zhdanov argued that it was the United States, with its championship of "universal laws," that clearly opposed national sovereignty, and the Soviet Union that "indefatigably and consistently upheld the principle of real equality and protection of the sovereign rights of all nations big and small."[47] Leaving aside the issue of Western "bloc" organization, the Soviet bloc did not consist of "individual" sovereign nation-states, but of autarkic Soviet regime replicas, distanced from their own regime "kin" in the bloc, and distanced from non-Leninist "stranger" regimes in the broader international community. During Stalinist consolidation, the organization of Leninist regime relations resembled a traditional corporate group, with a dogmatic stress on group (or bloc) indivisibility expressed politically as either complete acceptance of Soviet decisions or excommunication, and ideologically as an absolute choice between charismatic association with the Soviet Union or political degeneration into an "ordinary" (bourgeois) regime. The Soviet-Yugoslav conflict illustrates both aspects. Santiago Carillo, the former head of the Spanish Communist Party, commenting on the Cominform's expulsion of Yugoslavia, has stated: "We either had to accept or reject [it], for whoever rejected it would also have ended up by being excommunicated. During that period excommunications were still the accepted thing, and I do not believe that any party was ready to run that risk."[48] The

46. "Speech at the Tenth Plenum of the Eighth Central Committee, the morning of 24 September 1962 in the Huai-jen Hall," in Schram, ed., *Chairman Mao Talks*, p. 191.
47. Zhdanov, "Report," p. 159.
48. Santiago Carillo, *"Eurocommunism" and the State* (London: Lawrence & Wishart, 1977), p. 131.

nature of the risk was quite explicit in the Cominform's message to the Yugoslavs: "The Central Committee of the Communist Party of Yugoslavia has placed itself . . . *outside the family* of the fraternal Communist Parties. . . . The Yugoslav leaders evidently do not understand . . . that such a nationalistic line can only lead to Yugoslavia's degeneration into an *ordinary* bourgeois republic."[49] To leave the corporate group, the Soviet bloc, and contact with its hierophanic center, was to lose one's extraordinary Leninist heroic identity, because that identity was corporately indivisible, not nationally "individual." To leave the quasi-sacral bloc was to become a profane, ordinary, ostracized entity.

Khrushchev's genuinely exceptional place in Soviet and Leninist history rests on his opposition to Stalin's dogmatic emphasis on bloc indivisibility, on his preference for a partisan emphasis on regime individuality under Soviet auspices, and on his transformation of the Soviet bloc into a Soviet-centered Leninist regime world. The Korean War dramatically asserted *and* undermined the Stalinist consolidation features of Leninist organization at the national, bloc, and international levels. It stimulated part of the Soviet leadership to reconsider the feasibility and appropriateness of Leninism's "Augustinian" definition. After Stalin's death, Khrushchev substantially redefined Leninist organization at all three levels: national, bloc, and international.

The "Aquinian" Reform

Ideological movements regularly produce two substantially different interpretations of how to define themselves politically. Among contemporary Afrikaaners, for example, there are *verkrampte* and *verligte* views and forces—that is, those who favor a rigidly dogmatic stance and those who favor a broader (but still intensely partisan) stance.[50] Historically, in Roman

49. "Resolution of the Communist Information Bureau, June 28, 1948, Concerning the Situation in the Communist Party of Yugoslavia," in Daniels, ed., *History of Communism*, p. 172. My emphasis.

50. For a discussion of the difference between *verligte* and *verkrampte*, see T. Dunbar Moodie, *The Rise of Afrikanerdom* (Berkeley: University of California Press, 1975), pp. 287–93.

Catholicism one can also identify two essentially similar but substantially different interpretations, Augustine's and Aquinas's. Khrushchev was Leninism's Aquinas. As with Aquinas, Khrushchev's innovations meant more than a shift in attitude; in both cases, substantial developmental shifts occurred in the institutional definition of the movement's ontology.

Khrushchev initiated a developmental shift in the Soviet regime from consolidation to inclusion, a development that more than anything signaled a reduction in the political and ideological tension between the quasi-sacral party regime and the society it ruled. In the Church's case, Aquinian inclusion was a modification to "meet a new situation . . . presented by the fact that Church and society were now identical in membership."[51] Soviet inclusion rests on a comparable recognition that Soviet society is no longer a "contaminating" force. Aquinians and Khrushchevians worry more that the social products of their respective organizations' developmental efforts might not identify themselves in terms consistent with the Church or Party's ideological self-image and political definition.[52] G. K. Chesterton captures the meaning of the developmental shift from Augustinian consolidation to Aquinian inclusion when he suggests that "there ought to be a real study called Anthropology corresponding to Theology. In this sense, St. Thomas Aquinas, perhaps more than he is anything else is a great anthropologist."[53] Why? Because due to Aquinas, it was "henceforth possible to look at a man either as a natural being or as a being designed for fellowship with God[,] whereas before the former could not be conceived separately from the latter."[54] Aquinas ameliorated the tension, diminished the alienation, and lessened the separation between Christian society and the Church. Khrushchev (and his inclusive successors) have done much the same in the Soviet Union.

51. Colin Morris, *The Discovery of the Individual, 1050–1200* (London: Camelot Press, 1972), p. 59.
52. See chapter 3.
53. G. K. Chesterton, *St. Thomas Aquinas* (Garden City, N.Y.: Image Books, 1956), p. 160.
54. Morris, *Discovery,* p. 161.

With his declaration that socialism's victory was complete *and final* in the Soviet Union,[55] Khrushchev removed the ideological underpinning of Stalin's dogmatic juxtaposition of a quasi-sacral regime and diffusely hostile contaminating society. "Augustinian" distrust and tension were replaced by "Aquinian" confidence that the Soviet regime could engage—not simply distance itself from—its several environments (national, bloc, and international) without automatically being "polluted." Khrushchev initiated a less tense and invidious relationship between regime and society, expressed most vividly (and controversially) in his notion "state of the whole people," a pointed assault on the Stalinist interpretation of "dictatorship of the proletariat." Khrushchev's developmental initiatives were not designed to destroy the Soviet castle regime's ruling "walls." They have drained its political terror "moat." The most significant consequence of Khrushchev's developmental revisions has been the Soviet regime's greater ability and willingness to recognize intermediate political realities in contrast to Stalin's dichotomic political and ideological distinctions.

Nationally, Khrushchev (unsuccessfully) attempted to create an intermediate political force of Party "citizens," the *obshchestvenniki*. The members of this force were drawn from the Party, but not from its official *apparatchiki* stratum. Khrushchev was attempting to revitalize the status of Party member per se. As Paul Cocks notes, "It is difficult to overestimate the gulf that had developed by the early 1950s between the party apparat and general party membership." By the 1930s, an "elaborate pass procedure had been established [for entry to the Central Committee building] and armed guards stood at the doors. Only in 1958–59 were the guards removed."[56] The castle metaphor has some merit.

Under Stalinist consolidation, Cocks writes, the Party *aktiv*,

55. See Khrushchev's speech at the 21st Congress of the CPSU in January 1959 in Daniels, *History of Communism*, p. 274. The addition of the term *final* was ideologically crucial. Stalin had asserted the possibility of "socialism in one country" being complete, but not final. Politically, this underwrote a stance of continual tension, vigilance, and terror.

56. See Paul Cocks, "The Rationalization of Party Control," in Chalmers Johnson, ed., *Change in Communist Systems* (Stanford: Stanford University Press, 1970), pp. 167–68.

that group of party members not holding paid official Party positions but having specific skills and available as a Party citizen pool, "dwindled and was not utilized, all business was handled by the *apparatchiki.*" In the *obshchestvenniki,* Khrushchev had identified a sociopolitical stratum of regular party "deacons" midway between the apparatchik "priests" and the nonparty "laity." His discovery and innovation reflected his faction's more empirical, less dogmatic, more confident, less anxious appraisal of the general Party membership and Soviet society, and their conviction that less "distance" between Party and society was possible and necessary.[57]

Within the bloc, Khrushchev replaced the norm of regime indivisibility with that of regime individuality. Regime indivisibility refers to an organization of Leninist regimes in which all accept the Soviet (or some other regime's) interest as their own, abnegate their particular political personality in favor of the USSR's, and view that act as enhancing and guaranteeing their own revolutionary authenticity. Between 1948 and Stalin's death, the Soviet bloc exemplified regime indivisibility. This doesn't mean that bloc members absolutely ignored local problems or thoroughly lacked nationally distinguishing features. Rather, it means that these problems and features were subordinated to obedience to and identification with the Soviet Union.

Khrushchev challenged Stalin's "monotheist" demand for an indivisible Soviet bloc, in which Soviet interests were identified as those of all Leninist regimes, and replaced it with a mode of organization that tolerated regime individuality in a Soviet-centered Leninist regime world. Regime individuality refers to an organization of Leninist regimes that imperatively asserts the substantive—not simply procedural—unity of a group *and* recognizes the existence of distinct and potentially conflicting interests within it. Khrushchev's notion of bloc unity closely resembled the theologian's notion of the Trinity. Raymond Williams tells us that the term *individual* originally meant "inseparable" in medieval thinking. He writes: "Its main use was in the context of theological argument about the nature of the

57. Ibid.; see also chapter 3.

Holy Trinity. The effort was to explain how a being could be thought of *as existing in his own nature yet existing by this nature as part of an indivisible whole.*"[58] Khrushchev's redefinition of Leninist regime relations did not allow for regime individual*ism* (i.e., independence); it did allow for regime individual*ity* or autonomy. It was a substantial, if not essential, development. But in recognizing and tolerating the emergence of regime "personalities" within a Soviet-led and -centered Leninist regime world, Khrushchev was directly attacking and revising the Stalinist "indivisible" bloc pattern so incisively and courageously criticized by Imre Nagy.

Writing in the midst of bloc turmoil in the mid 1950s, Nagy assaulted the dichotomic and mechanically solidary pattern of the Stalinist bloc. Nagy referred to the "discredited anti-Marxist, anti-Leninist viewpoint, according to which the only and exclusive method for building socialism was that used by the Soviet [Union]." He stressed the danger when a communist party "isolates itself from the majority of the nation," and the equal danger for international relations of preventing each Leninist regime from being guided by "its own particular circumstances" rather "than by dogmas." He called for the end of Hungary's "self-imposed seclusion, our isolation" and pointed out that Hungarians "never examined the international situation thoroughly in the light of our own country's interests nor from the viewpoint of its effects on our country." Hungary, he claimed, was a "member not only of the socialist camp but of the great community of nations."[59] Khrushchev had Nagy executed, but he accepted in good measure Nagy's "inclusive" critique of the dogmatically indivisible Stalinist pattern of bloc and international relations.

Khrushchev and his successors adopted a substantially different ideological and political approach to relations with other members of the Leninist regime world, one that tolerated their emergence as politically distinguishable entities, a set of regime "*obshchestvenniki.*" Zvi Gitelman has examined this development

58. Raymond Williams, *The Long Revolution* (Westport, Conn.: Greenwood Press, 1975), p. 73. My emphasis.
59. Imre Nagy, *On Communism* (New York: Praeger, 1957), pp. 13, 26, 35–36, 38, and 41.

in the context of Soviet–Eastern European relations. "East European policies which are at variance with those of the USSR are not necessarily policies directed against the USSR," he argues, conversely, "it is important to bear in mind that policies which are in conformity with Soviet policy are not necessarily determined by the USSR." This speaks to Soviet tolerance for regime individua*lity,* of some "diversity without deviance."[60] Gitelman studied Poland's position toward the Federal Republic of Germany and concluded that the Soviet Union "sets limits on Polish behavior . . . but did not determine the basic Polish outlook [or] set the Polish agenda in regard to the Federal Republic. There was and is a coincidence of Polish and Soviet interests but there was no dictation of Polish policy and the various shifts it has undergone."[61]

More recently, one can find a clear instance of an Eastern Europe policy coalition, made up of Hungary, East Germany, and Romania, opposing at least part of the Soviet leadership over the political right of Eastern European regimes to exercise limited, but real, foreign policy initiatives with the West, even when the Soviet leader was unable or unwilling to do so. The Hungarian Party's semipublic defense of East Germany's active approach to West Germany, in the form of articles by authoritative Hungarian Party figures, and in light of Soviet criticism of East Germany, was a significant political event. While East Germany was attempting to act autonomously on a definition of its own regime interest at a time of worsening Soviet-American relations, "the theoretical parameters of the dispute between Moscow and East Berlin . . . were staked out not in East Berlin but rather in Budapest. This in and of itself was rather remarkable, as conventional wisdom had seemed to dictate that the price that the Kádár regime paid for domestic economic reform was absolute foreign policy loyalty."[62] Honecker's very demonstrative presence at the Romanian 13th Party Congress was

---

60. Zvi Gitelman, "Toward A Comparative Foreign Policy of Eastern Europe," in Peter J. Potichny and Jane P. Shapiro, eds., *From the Cold War to Détente* (New York: Praeger, 1976), p. 158.

61. Ibid., p. 156.

62. See *East Berlin and Moscow: The Documentation of a Dispute* (Munich: Radio Free Europe, 1985), introduction by Ronald D. Asmus, p. 9.

another semipublic assertion of the East German position and the existence of a de facto coalition among the East Germans, Hungarians, and Romanians. Apparently, the coalition lost. Honecker's visit to West Germany was postponed. And for those whose epistemological loyalty is to the phrase "in the final analysis," that undoubtedly demonstrates essential continuity in the Soviet Union's domination of Eastern Europe. It does more than that. The episode revealed the ability of relatively weak members of the Soviet-centered Leninist regime world to differ semipublicly with and oppose a Soviet policy position; it showed the centrality of regime foreign policy autonomy or "individuality" as an issue in Soviet–Eastern European relations; and it demonstrated the possibility that shifting policy coalitions are a regular feature of that regime world.

All these features differ substantially from those of the Stalinist Soviet bloc. In that setting, conflicts were not semipublicly articulated; no ideological allowance was made for inter-regime policy conflicts within the context of overall loyalty to the Soviet regime; and neither the ideological nor organizational conditions existed that would permit such a coalition to come into existence. There seems to be a politically relevant content to the conceptual distinction between Stalinist bloc indivisibility and Khrushchevian bloc individuality—that is, between the developmental stages of Leninist consolidation and inclusion at both the national and bloc levels.

Evidence for regime "individuality" in a Soviet-centered Leninist regime world extends beyond the existence of semipublic, shifting policy coalitions. One can also locate more stable pairs of Leninist regimes with a positive or negative affinity for one another. Positive-affinity regime pairs include North Korea and Romania, and Cuba and Vietnam. I call these regime relations "stable affinity pairs" because they reflect more than a coincidence of interest over a specific issue, no matter how important. Relations between regime affinity pairs rest on a more diffuse and intense sense of mutual recognition or antipathy. Cuba and Vietnam mutually identify as small, ex-colonial countries that, assaulted by the same superpower, responded as revolutionary "heroes." Romania and North Korea's positive regime affinity rests in part on their exposed position vis-à-vis the Soviet Union, but more on their pariah history, as low-status communist parties in the Comintern, during World War II, and then as regimes after 1945.[63] The negative affinity between Cuba and Yugoslavia reflects their competition for status and influence within the "Third World," their opposing notions of the relationship that entity should have with the Soviet Union, and Cuba's resentment over Yugoslavia's alleged support of the Batista regime.[64] In studying these negative-affinity regime pairs, it is important to note the source of antipathy and conflict specific to their history as Leninist parties and regimes. For example, while Bulgaria and Yugoslavia do have crucial historical disagreements over Macedonia, the intensity of their current conflict also draws on the status conflict resulting from Bulgaria's Comintern preeminence being displaced by Tito's partisan-guerrilla preeminence. North Korea and Vietnam are another example of Leninist regimes with status conflicts. North Korea displaced Vietnam as the heroic front line in the early 1950s, was in turn displaced by Vietnam in the 1960s, and remains so in light of Vietnam's successful reunification. And Romania and Hungary's historical clash over Transylvania may well be intensified by the role anticommunist Romania played in overthrowing the Béla Kun regime and the role communist Romania played in replacing the Nagy regime.

In addition to semipublic, shifting issue coalitions and the more stable, but restricted, regime affinity pairs just discussed, one can identify two stable and broad regime coalitions within the Soviet-centered Leninist regime world. China, Romania, Yugoslavia, North Korea, and the nonruling parties of Italy and Spain form one. The Soviet Union, Vietnam, Cuba, Outer Mongolia, and the remaining Eastern European regimes form the other. (Albania escapes both these categories.) They differ on three issues. The first coalition or grouping refuses to accept in principle any fundamental distinction between those Leninist regimes that are members of the Warsaw Pact and CMEA

63. The relatively rapid defeat of the North Korean army by U.S. forces and the superseding of the North Korean military role by the Chinese quickly removed any sustained heroic role for the North Korean Party.

64. See Castro's bitter comments on Yugoslav support of Batista in *Granma*, August 25, 1968.

and those that are not. The thrust of this refusal is to deny the Soviet Union the ability to segment the components of the Leninist regime world and thereby monopolize the position of potential mediator between its various segments. The two coalitions also disagree on the relations of the "unaligned" movement to the Soviet Union, and the relative importance of the North-South dimension in international politics.

Its invasions of Hungary in 1956 and Czechoslovakia in 1968 prove that the Soviet Union does not ideologically tolerate regime individual*ism* and will politically destroy it when possible. Regime individualism refers to a mode of regime organization in which unity is defined procedurally, not substantively (that is, in a way that emphasizes national sovereignty over proletarian internationalism). The concept of individualism locates a single unit "without immediate reference . . . to the group of which one is a member."[65] Individualism is socially and "nationally" *the* modern challenge to Leninism's essentially traditional and charismatic political ontology. However, while the Soviet regime remains intolerant of regime individualism, the existence of semipublic and issue-specific coalitions, politically persistent positive and negative regime affinity pairs, and broadly based issue coalitions points to Soviet toleration of regime individuality, to a developmental change from a Soviet bloc to a Soviet-centered Leninist regime world.[66]

Internationally, Khrushchev's inclusive changes radically affected Soviet relations with the non-Leninist world by reducing the perceived and organized tension between what Stalin had identified and juxtaposed in Manichean fashion as "sacral" and

65. Williams, *Long Revolution*, p. 73.

66. Khrushchev's more tolerant stance toward (some) conflict(s) within the Leninist regime world parallels the emergence in sixteenth-century France of the *politiques*. The *politiques* were a group of statesmen who while adhering to their religious beliefs saw religious conflicts within Christianity as a threat both to particular Christian states (e.g., France) and to Christianity as an international political order. With Khrushchev, and particularly under Brezhnev, one can see the relative, but real, movement from dogmatic intolerance (à la Tavannes in France and Molotov in the Soviet Union) to partisan tolerance of a certain range of political differences in the Leninist world. The parallel with the emergence of the *politiques* is worth pursuing. See, in this connection, Henry Kamen's *The Rise of Toleration* (New York: McGraw-Hill, World University Library, 1967), pp. 131–45.

"profane" realms. The reduction in tension permitted the ideological and political identification, reclassification, and acceptance of intermediate entities and areas. No clearer or more striking instance of Khrushchev's "Aquinian" quality exists than his political recognition and ideological reclassification of the "Third World."

To return to the Middle Ages, the "Aquinian" revision of Augustinian Catholicism coincided with a more developed notion of Purgatory. According to Jacques Le Goff, the significance of this revised notion of Purgatory in the thirteenth century was that "it introduce[d] an intermediary category between two extremes [Heaven and Hell]. The new category was not made secondary or subordinate to the original two. Rather the center was raised up."[67] Something quite comparable and significant happened under Khrushchev's auspices.[68] The "Third World" was given a status like Purgatory, an autonomous place in the Soviet regime's political geography, and an indeterminate period of time before its occupants eventually reach socialist "heaven." The parallels between the cases are striking. In each instance, the new development had a genuine base in the organization's essential worldview. Augustine himself had provided the original terminology about Purgatory; and in 1918 it was Stalin who asserted: "Whoever desires the triumph of socialism must not forget the East."[69] If there was resistance to and suspicion within the Church over the new "Aquinian" understanding of Purgatory, there was a very similar response within the CPSU to the new status afforded the "Third World."

67. Jacques Le Goff, *The Birth of Purgatory* (Chicago: University of Chicago Press, 1984), p. 225.

68. I do not mean to argue that it was solely Khrushchev or Aquinas who conceived, initiated, and elaborated these changes. In fact, Le Goff argues that in contrast to his teacher Albertus Magnus, Aquinas assigned little direct importance to Purgatory. What I am arguing is that these developments in the Catholic Church and the Soviet Party bear the decisive imprint of the individuals who at the time exercised the greatest influence in their respective organizations and who favored a "reconciliation" with society and the recognition of intermediary entities and areas.

69. See Le Goff, *Purgatory*, p. 63; and see Joseph Stalin, *Works*, vol. 4 (Moscow: Foreign Languages Publishing House, 1953), cited in Alvin Z. Rubinstein, ed., *The Foreign Policy of the Soviet Union* (New York: Random House, 1960), p. 357.

In both cases, a profound and substantial developmental change within an essentially unchanged ontology was signaled by the introduction of new terms (e.g., *national democracy* and *revolutionary democracy*), terms "occurring at strategic points in social discourse and point[ing] to important historical phenomena."[70] And the introduction of such terms initiated a continuing debate over their ideological meaning and political implications.[71]

But most crucial of all, just as "Purgatory was one of a group of phenomena associated with the transformation of feudal Christendom of which one key expression was the creation of ternary logical modes through the introduction of an intermediate category,"[72] so Khrushchev's ideological and political designation of the "Third World" as an autonomous and substantial part of the Soviet Union's political geography was an integral part of the transformation of Stalinist consolidation to the distinctly new developmental phase of inclusion with its introduction of "intermediate (or ternary) categories."

Along with his anti-Stalinist upgrading of the "Third World" as a distinguishable and substantial political entity, Khrushchev also recast the meaning of "peaceful coexistence." For Western

70. Along with Le Goff, I believe that "these shifts in vocabulary [i.e., from "running dogs of the capitalists" to "national democratic states," "revolutionary democracies," or "states of socialist orientation"] and meaning are all the more significant when they occur within rigid ideological systems" (Le Goff, *Purgatory*, p. 227).

71. To get a firm sense of the difference between the Stalinist "Augustinian" and Khrushchevian "Aquinian" appreciation of the "Third World," and of the new and politically charged terminology that has been introduced and debated, contrast A. M. Diakov's, "The Crisis of British Domination in India and the New Stage of the Liberation Struggle of Her Peoples" (written in 1949) and E. Varga's comments on India in his *The Fundamental Questions of the Economics and Politics of Imperialism after the Second World War* (1957). Both are in Rubenstein, *Foreign Policy*, pp. 393–94, 397–99. Read Khrushchev's comments at the 20th Party Congress, also in Rubinstein, pp. 395–97, and their conceptual crystallization in the 1960 Moscow Statement in G. F. Hudson, Richard Lowenthal, and Roderick MacFarquhar, eds., *The Sino-Soviet Dispute* (New York: Praeger, 1961), pp. 192–96. See also Richard Lowenthal's "Russia, the One-Party Sytem, and the Third World," *Survey* 58 (January 1966): 43–59; Jerry Hough, *The Struggle for the Third World: Soviet Debates and American Options* (Washington, D.C.: Brookings Institution, 1986), pp. 149–59.

72. Le Goff, *Purgatory*, p. 227.

"monotheists," this term's existence prior to Khrushchev is evidence of essential continuity, not discontinuity. However, an ideological term's political meaning is mediated by its institutional environments. Khrushchev recognized that nuclear war had created one world with two parts. His political engagement of the West (including the Cuban episode), his recognition of the political autonomy of the "Third World," his toleration of regime individuality in a Soviet-centered Leninist regime world, his declaration of socialism's "complete and final" victory in the Soviet Union, and his reorganization of the Soviet Party's police and leadership features constituted a substantial developmental redefinition and reorganization of the Soviet Union's institutional formats and political relations with its societal, bloc, and international environments.

Khrushchev never challenged the special relationship between the Soviet regime and the October Revolution; he did broaden and partially demystify it. He never challenged the conception of the Soviet regime world as qualitatively different and superior to the West; he did revise the Soviet Union's perception of and political relations with the Western and non-European parts of the world.[73] Like Aquinas, he maintained his organization's essential ontology and changed its political epistemology. And like Aquinas he did not go unopposed.

The "Augustinian" Opposition

Molotov opposed Khrushchev's inclusive reforms within the Soviet regime, and Mao opposed them within the Leninist regime world. The Sino-Soviet conflict was more than anything one between regimes with opposing developmental-institutional interpretations of Leninism. It was not primarily a clash between nations with "ancient enmities." Nor was it primarily due to "the determination of Mao . . . that China should become a superpower and the determination of the Soviet leadership to prevent it."[74] These elements, like the contrasting levels of eco-

73. See, in particular, William Zimmerman's *Soviet Perspectives on International Relations, 1956–1967* (Princeton: Princeton University Press, 1969).
74. William E. Griffith, *Sino-Soviet Relations, 1964–1965* (Cambridge, Mass.: MIT Press, 1967), p. 4.

nomic development in China and the Soviet Union, had their place; they were important and secondary. The Sino-Soviet conflict was primarily a clash between opposing beliefs about, and institutional definitions of, the proper and imperative political identity for a Leninist regime. Fortunately, we have an extraordinary set of sophisticated Soviet and Chinese polemical documents that strongly support this interpretation.

According to the Chinese, their differences with the Soviet Union began with Khrushchev's de-Stalinization speech at the Soviet 20th Congress in 1956. It was not Khrushchev's attack on Stalin per se but rather Khrushchev's rejection of class struggle as the central tenet of Party rule that became the pivot of a widening, issue-filled dispute. The Chinese argued that "in completely negating Stalin . . . Khrushchev in effect negated the dictatorship of the proletariat and the fundamental theories of Marxism-Leninism which Stalin defended and developed."[75] The Khrushchevian notions of "state of the whole people," and "peaceful coexistence"[76] meant that the Soviet Union "was failing to draw a clear line of demarcation between the enemy and ourselves."[77] Repeatedly, the Chinese attacked the Soviet regime's inclusive measures with "Augustinian" warnings about political and ideological contamination from diffusely hostile national and international forces. The Chinese stressed that "in socialist society, the overthrown bourgeoisie and other reactionary classes remain strong . . . unreconciled to their defeat . . . working to undermine socialism . . . sneaking into governmental organs . . . constantly breeding political degenerates, and linked in a thousand and one ways with the international bourgeoisie."[78] Opposing Suslov, who asked, "Against whom do the Chinese theoreticians propose that we

75. "The Origin and Development of the Differences between the Leadership of the CPSU and Ourselves—Comment on the Open Letter of the Central Committee of the CPSU (1) September 6, 1963," in William E. Griffith, *The Sino-Soviet Rift* (Cambridge, Mass.: MIT Press, 1964), pp. 390, 391.

76. The Chinese had no doubt that these revisions were more than "attitudinal" or tactical shifts in Soviet regime format and policy.

77. Griffith, *Sino-Soviet Rift*, p. 420.

78. "On Khrushchev's Phoney Communism and Its Historical Lessons for the World: Comment on the Open Letter of the Central Committee of the CPSU (9), July 14, 1964," in Griffith, *Sino-Soviet Relations*, pp. 317–18.

implement this dictatorship [of the proletariat]?"[79] the Chinese asserted that "all socialist countries without exception, including the Soviet Union, are still far, far removed from fulfillment of the historical mission of the dictatorship of the proletariat," and the struggle between socialism and capitalism and the question of "who will win has not yet been *completely and finally* solved."[80] For Maoists, consolidation remained the imperative. In good "Augustinian" fashion, as Sheldon Wolin has put it, they continued to view the "political order as a kind of intermediate plane where the two antithetical symbolisms—*civitas terrena* and *civitas dei*—intersected." If for Augustine "the collective life of the political community was carried on amidst a deep tension between the naturalism of the daily activities of the community and super-naturalism of the City of God,"[81] for Chinese "Augustinians" a comparable tension characterized the relations between a quasi-sacral party dictatorship and a "polluting" societal and international environment.

The Chinese "developmental" opposition to the Soviet Union quickly became a political challenge to Soviet leadership of international Leninism. Arguments about the relative importance of nuclear or guerrilla war were arguments about the major locus of international political and military uncertainty, and had direct implications as to who should lead the Leninist world. When the Chinese argued that the "Third World" was "the storm center of world revolution . . . [and] the whole cause of the international proletarian revolution hinges on the outcome of the revolutionary struggles . . . of these areas,"[82] they were laying claim to the leadership of the international Leninist

79. "On the Struggle of the CPSU for the Solidarity of the International Communist Movement: Report by M. A. Suslov on February 14, 1964 at the Plenum of the CPSU Central Committee," in Griffith, *Sino-Soviet Relations*, p. 242.

80. "Speech at the Fourth Enlarged Session of the Committee of the Department of Philosophy and Social Science of the Chinese Academy of Sciences Held on October 26, 1963, by Chou Yang," in Griffith, *Sino-Soviet Relations*, p. 158. My emphasis.

81. Sheldon Wolin, *Politics and Vision* (Boston: Little, Brown, 1960), p. 125.

82. "The CCP's Proposal concerning the General Line of the International Communist Movement, June 14, 1963," in Griffith, *Sino-Soviet Rift*, p. 265.

movement. They were doing so on the basis of their guerrilla-war competence and "Third World" location. Not surprisingly, the Soviet rulers rejected this and offered nuclear competition with the West as the primary locus of international uncertainty, thereby assuring themselves continued leadership of Leninist regimes and parties.

Chinese criticism of Khrushchev's "insistence on establishing a kind of feudal patriarchal domination over the international communist movement and turning the relations between brother Parties into those between a Patriarchal father and his sons,"[83] and Chinese opposition to the Soviet leaders' tendency to offer their own Party Congress programs as authoritative programs for all Leninist regimes, were even more direct challenges to Soviet leadership. But the challenge was not over power per se. Rather leadership was necessary to check the "contaminating" spread of Khrushchevian ideological, political, and policy positions inside the Leninist world and to sustain the Chinese identification of Leninism's essential features with those of its consolidation stage.

In the 1960s an intensely conflictual pattern of inter-regime relations emerged within the Soviet-centered Leninist regime world. The pivot of this conflict was the Sino-Soviet clash over the imperative and appropriate institutional definition of Leninism, over two substantially different and opposed developmental interpretations of Leninism. Had this conflict remained within the international subsystem of Leninist regimes, it would have been of real, but limited, significance. It did not remain there. By the late 1970s, specifically in 1978–79, the Sino-Soviet developmental conflict was superimposed on the global conflict

83. "The Leaders of the CPSU are the Greatest Splitters of Our Times: Comment on the Open Letter of the Central Committee of the CPSU (7)," in Griffith, *Sino-Soviet Relations*, p. 163. The remarkable thing about the Chinese characterization of the Soviet position is its accuracy as a political anthropological reading of the Soviet attitude, one that was and remains quasi-patriarchal and familial. The Chinese emphasis on "brother parties" expresses a preference for a Leninist regime "war-band" of equal heroic units. This preference comes out very clearly in the Chinese designation of the socialist camp as a whole as the unit of charismatic worth, and in their demand for consultation within the camp prior to any programmatic decisions. But both regimes expressed a clear if differently organized preference for a traditional-charismatic mode of inter-regime organization in the Leninist world.

between the Soviet Union and the United States, producing the most dangerous situation since World War II.

THE INTERNATIONAL

The notion of a "strategic triangle" fundamentally hinders our ability to identify the most consequential phenomenon of the late 1970s, the superimposition of Sino-Soviet and Soviet-American hostilities.

The pivotal international political actor during this period was the Hua Guofeng regime in China. The most dangerous relationship was that fostered by Zbigniew Brzezinski of the Carter administration with the Chinese. The most violent expression of this phenomenon was the Soviet invasion of Afghanistan, an action directly related to and directed at China's successful amalgamation of Leninist regime world conflicts and East-West conflicts. Finally, the most significant challenge and corrective to this charged international situation has been the dramatic developmental stage shift within China from consolidation to inclusion.

Polycentrism and Geometry

On November 3, 1979, slightly more than a month before the Soviet invasion of Afghanistan, the *Economist* suggested that the "coming together of China and the West could be as hugely beneficial a shift in world politics as the Nazi-Soviet pact of 1939 was hugely maleficent: that unleashed a world war; this could prevent one."[84] I should say just the opposite about the "coming together" of China and the West. Yet one can find many statements like the *Economist*'s. Examining international relations during this general period, William Zimmerman concluded that whatever the formal configuration of power, "relations within the dominant international systems will be increasingly characterized by the flexibility of alignment and the proliferation of crosscutting linkages typical of pragmatic multiple systems. . . . Such chaotically configured interactions will

---

84. *Economist*, November 3, 1979, p. 13.

lack the neatness of the multipower quadrille . . . it remains nevertheless the case that it is complexity rather than esthetics which facilitates system stability."[85] The flaw in Zimmerman's argument comes from failing to complement an international with a developmental perspective and seriously to consider the developmental content and profile of the Leninist regimes in conflict during the 1970s. Yet, more than anything else, that developmental polarity favored the superimposition of conflicts within the Leninist regime world on those between the Soviet Union and the United States.

All too regularly, American and Soviet observers have chosen to understand Chinese behavior in one-dimensional terms, either ideological or national. In Edward Luttwak's rather crude view, one a number of observers share, the ideological element was never politically meaningful: "The textual contentions of the vulgar Marxists of Moscow and of Beijing cannot possibly be anything but the instruments of a hostility that has quite other causes. This is clearly demonstrated by the persistence of the dispute through the wildest gyrations of official theology on the Chinese side."[86] Similarly, for the Soviet observer Alexander Bovin, the Chinese, "having failed to get into Europe from the 'left' [by splitting communist parties] . . . have begun in the 1970s to see an entry from the right. . . . The reason is that the 'infantile disorder' of leftism has developed into a much graver ailment, whose symptoms are chauvinism and a great power posture . . . Beijing's strategic aim is to encircle the Soviet Union with a range of hostile states and political blocs."[87] Bovin juxtaposes the two Chinese modes of opposing the USSR too sharply. He is quite right about the Chinese desire to encircle (just as the USSR had been trying to encircle the Chinese since the late 1960s). But, like Luttwak, he

85. William Zimmerman, "The Transformation of the Modern Multi-State System: The Exhaustion of Communist Alternatives," *Journal of Conflict Resolution* 16, no. 3 (1972): 316.

86. Edward N. Luttwak, "The PRC in Soviet Grand Strategy," in Douglas T. Stuart and William T. Tow, eds., *China, the Soviet Union, and the West* (Boulder, Colo.: Westview Press, 1982), p. 265.

87. A. Bovin, "Beijing's European Flirtation," *Izvestiya*, November 11, 1979 (morning edition), p. 4.

doesn't grasp the full significance of China's adoption of a more national mode of opposition to the Soviet Union in the 1970s.

In adopting a more national idiom and arena to present its developmental challenge to the Soviet Union, China was not dropping an epiphenomenal ideological mask, and "exposing" a more "real" national conflict. China was choosing an arena and a unit of conflict—the nation state—that joined what had been two separate realms of conflict. In international politics, 1979 was a much more dangerous year than 1969. In 1969 the Soviet and Chinese conflict was militarily violent on their border, but was separate from the larger pattern of Soviet-American hostility. By 1979 the two realms of conflict were being joined in a manner that superimposed one on the other, thereby adding to the intensity and scope of each. By entering the broader realm of international politics while maintaining their dogmatic developmental inter-regime opposition and antipathy toward the Soviet Union, the Chinese were attempting to coopt the United States (and the West more generally) in China's "intrafamilial" conflict with the USSR. And in Brzezinski the Chinese found a person whose intense ideological antipathy toward the Soviet Union and whose influence in the U.S. government contributed markedly to a highly dangerous pattern of superimposed American-Soviet-Chinese national and ideological conflicts.

The most benign interpretation of Brzezinski's quite indiscriminate pursuit of alignment with the Hua regime is that he failed to recognize that the Sino-Soviet conflict and simultaneous Sino-American cooperation had more than a "global strategic" dimension;[88] that the Soviet Union would react to this alignment as not only a strategic challenge but also an ideolog-

88. Zbigniew Brzezinski's repeated reference to "global strategic concerns" almost always translated as a Chinese-like collapsing of all issues into a contest with the Soviet Union, a desire not merely to oppose or defeat but even to humiliate the Soviet regime. So when China invaded Vietnam, he felt "it revealed some limits to Soviet power by demonstrating that an ally of the Soviet Union [Vietnam] could be molested with relative impunity. . . . The Soviet reaction throughout was confined to threats and bluster." Until it invaded Afghanistan! See Brzezinski, *Power and Principle: Memoirs of the National Security Advisor, 1977–1981* (New York: Farrar, Straus & Giroux, 1983), p. 414.

ically insidious boundary blurring and threatening alliance
between a regime "stranger," the United States, and a "degenerate" regime "kin," China. To Cyrus Vance's great credit,
he always sensed the conflict-intensifying implications of this
"anthropologically" dangerous dimension, and consistently attempted to limit the Chinese-American relationship.[89] It is either to Brzezinski's intellectual discredit that he did not grasp
the reality and implications of superimposed conflict, or to his
political discredit that he did, and did not care.

Examining Brzezinski's conception of the Chinese-American
alignment against the Soviet Union, one is struck by its mechanical quality, expressed quite well in the following observation:
"Perhaps if the Soviets worry a little more about our policy
toward China we will have less cause to worry about our relations with the Soviets."[90] As for his feeling that the Chinese
regarded him as someone "whose strategic perspectives to some
extent they shared," it is an accurate but stingy observation.
To a shared strategic perspective, the Hua regime and Brzezinski added a common, if differently formulated, visceral antipathy toward the Soviet Union. The result was to infuse Sino-
American-Soviet relations with a tenor, scope, and intensity
that favored cumulation more than disaggregation of specific
issues between the United States and the Soviet Union, and an
exacerbation more than a diminution of their essential ideological opposition.

How far the Brzezinski policy favored the polarization and
superimposition of international issues comes out forcefully in
his confusion over and annoyance with Vance's differentiated
attempt to establish relations with Vietnam at the same time as
the United States was getting closer to China. According to
Brzezinski: "Before the new [Chinese] relationship could be
consummated, we had to deal with a policy diversion. For reasons which I could never quite understand from a policy stand-
point but perhaps may be better explained by the psychologically searing impact of the Vietnamese war tragedy, both

---

89. See Cyrus Vance's *Hard Choices: Critical Years in America's Foreign Policy* (New York: Simon & Schuster, 1983), pp. 79, 110–16, 120–22, 390–91.
90. Brzezinski, *Power and Principle,* p. 200.

Vance, and even more [Assistant Secretary of State Richard] Holbrooke seemed determined at this time to initiate a diplomatic relationship with Vietnam."[91] However, the case can be made that the Vance-Holbrooke position made good policy and political sense. It might have increased American autonomy and leverage in our relations with a China that had nowhere else to go internationally except toward the United States. And it could have contributed to a more differentiated, crosscutting pattern of U.S. relations with Leninist regimes in contrast to the one-dimensional superimposed international pattern assiduously, successful, and dangerously pursued by the Hua regime and Brzezinski.

By 1978–79, China had emerged as the common element in a whole series of increasingly related international conflicts; it had succeeded in good measure in superimposing two previously discrete realms of conflict, within the Leninist regime world and between the Soviet Union and the United States. It had thus created a global danger of very serious proportions.

Two Years of "Living Dangerously"

The Soviet invasion of Afghanistan in December 1979 was the culmination and most violent expression of a two-year global pattern of intensified and superimposed Sino-American and Soviet-American hostility. Viewed from the Carter-Brzezinski side, the common conflictual element in international life was Soviet imperialism in the Horn of Africa, Southeast Asia, and Central America. Viewed from the Brezhnev side, the common element was Chinese hostility within the Soviet-centered Leninist regime world and China's alignment with the United States. The Soviet assessment was more accurate.

Needless to say, each of the international events of 1978–79 has its individual significance. The Pahlavi regime's destruction in Iran, the Sandinistas' coming to power in Nicaragua, the development of the Saur Revolution in Afghanistan, Vietnam's invasion of Kampuchea, and Soviet-American SALT relations have their own history and import. However, at another level,

91. Ibid., p. 228.

these events are related. They can be synthesized, not merely summarized. China's "boundary" position and politically pivotal role stand out as the common, overlapping, and politically dangerous elements in most of these settings. China's military, symbolic, and political actions were designed to cumulate discrete regional conflicts and make them integral components of a superimposed Sino-Soviet/American-Soviet hostility.

China's response to Vietnam's invasion of Kampuchea was symbolically to identify Vietnam with Cuba (the U.S. bête noire) as a Soviet proxy. China would attempt to get ASEAN to align itself with the PRC and, through a careful sequencing of Deng Xiaoping's visit to the United States and China's subsequent attack on Vietnam, associate and implicate the United States in that action. In connection with the "Soviet brigade in Cuba" episode, an article in the *New York Times* by James Reston interpreted President Jimmy Carter's speeches to mean, "If the Soviet Union will not respect 'our interests and concerns' in the Western hemisphere, we will not respect their 'sensibilities' in Eastern Europe and elsewhere."[92] At approximately the same time, the announcement was made that the U.S. secretary of defense, Harold Brown, would visit China. Then, in October, Hua Guofeng traveled to Western Europe, where he pointedly assaulted Soviet "sensibilities" by emphasizing the "artificial" division of the two Germanies.[93] Hua's visit coincided in turn with U.S. military maneuvers at Guantánamo. It is very hard to find any crosscutting international cleavages in all this. Rather, what one sees is an overlapping set of crises unified by explicit efforts on the Hua regime's part to collapse them along one anti-Soviet dimension; an effort purposively supported by the Brzezinski wing of the Carter administration.[94]

92. James Reston, "The Hidden Prices," *New York Times*, September 23, 1979, p. E9.

93. See Michael Getler, "Hua Calls for Reunification of Germany during Visit to Bohn," *Washington Post*, October 23, 1979, p. A10.

94. The steps taken by National Security Advisor Brzezinski to integrate Chinese and U.S. policy included arranging, "on my own authority . . . for the Chinese to obtain a NATO briefing on the global strategic problem thereby initiating a tacit security relationship with them . . . holding regular consultative meetings with the acting head of the Chinese Liaison Mission," trying to "counter the image of the Carter Administration as being soft vis-à-vis the

This developing and intensifying pattern of superimposed American-Soviet-Chinese hostility culminated with the Afghan crisis in late 1979. By the end of that year, the regime of Hafizullah Amin was neither stable nor reliable from the Soviet point of view. Soviet "strategic" concerns led, in October, to an attempted coup against Amin. It failed. By November 1979, according to one observer, the Soviet leaders were worried that "Amin would turn to the United States, China, and Pakistan in order to counter Soviet pressures, checkmate insurgency, and consolidate his own power."[95] And Anthony Hyman notes that "Soviet policy makers appear to have been apprehensive by the end of 1979 not only about the imminent collapse of the Kabul regime, but even about Amin's pro-Moscow loyalties; the Soviet media were to make much of Amin's overtures to the Afghan opposition, to China, and to the USA."[96]

The Soviet invasion of Afghanistan in December 1979 may appear to be an overdetermined event related to many situations: Soviet uncertainty about American intentions regarding Iran, especially in light of talk in the United States about a Rapid Deployment Force; the instability and unreliability of the Amin regime, beginning with events in Herat in March 1979; the possible repercussions of developments in Iran and Afghanistan on Soviet Central Asia; the deterioration in Soviet–U.S. relations following the "discovery" of a Soviet brigade in Cuba;[97] and finally the consequent difficulties with the United States over SALT. It would be surprising if these events did

Soviet Union," urging the Japanese to go along with the "hegemony clause" in the Sino-Japanese accord, intensifying "the frequency and scope of my personal consultations with the head of the Chinese Liaison Mission," and using "each occasion to provide more and more detailed briefings regarding our foreign policy initiatives," as well as mentioning to Carter at the time of Deng's visit how important it was "not to convey to the Chinese any excessive U.S. alarm over possible Chinese actions" toward Vietnam. See Brzezinski, *Power and Principle*, pp. 203, 211, 218, 226, 409.

95. Selig Harrison, "Dateline Afghanistan: Exit through Finland?" *Foreign Policy* 41 (Winter 1980–81): 174.

96. Anthony Hyman, *Afghanistan under Soviet Domination, 1964–1981* (New York: St. Martin's Press, 1982), p. 166.

97. On the Soviet brigade in Cuba controversy, see Cyrus Vance, *Hard Choices*, pp. 358–62; "Crisis in U.S. Foreign Policy: Storm over Cuba," in Harry Kreisler, ed., *Foreign Policy News Clips* 11, no. 4 (October 17, 1979).

not "add up" for the Soviet leadership. However, the invasion of Afghanistan rested on something more integral and less "arithmetical," on what the Soviet leaders perceived as an attempted and potentially successful Sino-American encirclement. America, China, and Japan aligned in Asia; the possibility of American and Chinese aid to the Amin regime in Afghanistan; Chinese support of the American position in Iran; Chinese and American diplomatic gestures toward Romania and Yugoslavia (by Hua in the fall of 1978 and by Vance in the fall of 1979); China's demonstrative support for NATO; and Sino-American hostility toward Cuba and Vietnam made the Soviet fear of strategic encirclement plausible.

But Afghanistan had more than strategic significance for the USSR in the winter of 1979! The possibility of a second Chinese attack on Vietnam and the possible appearance of a Maoist-like Khalq regime in Afghanistan added distinct features to both the Soviet perception of international developments and the intensity of their responses. While not pro-Chinese in its foreign policy, Amin's Khalq regime definitely resembled the ultra-leftist China of the mid 1960s.[98] By the winter of 1979, the Soviet Union faced a revolutionary, but suspect, regime in Afghanistan resembling the "Maoist" regime in China it both feared and loathed, and the possibility that the Khalq leader might tactically align his regime with China and the United States, thereby combining and blurring acts of military and political-ideological encirclement. The Soviet leaders responded to the superimposed threats of strategic and ideological encirclement by invading Afghanistan. The invasion was directed at *two* audiences, one the Leninist regime world, the other the West.

Regarding the former, the Soviet invasion was probably intended in the first instance as a clear warning to China not to invade Vietnam again. As such, it was far removed from Brze-

---

98. In fact, like other contemporary movements of rage, such as Sendero Luminoso in Peru and the Khmer Rouge in Kampuchea, the Khalq, or "children of history," is more Fanonist than Leninist. On Sendero, see Cynthia McClintock, "Sendero Luminoso: Peru's Maoist Guerrillas," *Problems of Communism* 32, no. 5 (1983): 19–34; on the Khmer Rouge, see Michael Vickery, *Cambodia, 1975–1982* (Boston: South End Press, 1984).

zinski's conclusion that the Soviet leaders were only capable of bluster.[99] Quite the contrary, the Soviet invasion was a dramatic, visible, and impressive action, one designed to inhibit the Chinese and reassure other members of the Soviet-centered Leninist regime world, in particular the Vietnamese, the Cubans, and the Outer Mongolians.

To the United States, and the West more generally, the Soviet "message" should have also been clear. The Soviet Union viewed the deepening and broadening alignment between China and the United States as a "clear and present danger." In the context of Afghan developments, that had become intolerable. In such a circumstance, the Soviet Union was prepared to offer a violent (and somewhat desperate) response. So interpreted, the Soviet invasion of Afghanistan was not, as Carter suggested, the single most dangerous event in the postwar period; however, it was the most violent expression of what had become the most dangerous situation in the postwar period, the superimposition of Sino-Soviet and Soviet-American hostilities.[100]

But the Soviet invasion "message" was not clear in the West. How unclear comes out in Anthony Arnold's *Economist*-like interpretation of the Soviet invasion: "The fact that further development of U.S. rapprochement with China did not deter the USSR from proceeding as planned may be ascribed to Soviet miscalculations as to the strength of both Chinese and American reactions."[101] Just the opposite! It was Soviet "appreciation" and apprehension of the depth of the Sino-American align-

99. Brzezinski, *Power and Principle,* p. 414.

100. If we take as a good indicator of a critically dangerous event whether or not the United States goes to a nuclear alert, it is clear that the Cuban missile crisis and 1973 Israeli-Egyptian war were more dangerous events than the Soviet invasion of Afghanistan. However, if the 1977–79 period was, as I say, one in which structural, ideological, and political conflicts involving the United States, the Soviet Union, and China were conflated, creating a pattern of overlapping, superimposed American-Soviet-Chinese hostilities, then one could argue that certain international situations can be as dangerous as certain events in part because the threat they pose, being less concrete, is harder to identify and agree on, and harder to isolate, resting as it does on such a complex of mutually reinforcing considerations.

101. Anthony Arnold, *Afghanistan: The Soviet Invasion in Perspective* (Stanford: Hoover Institution Press, 1981), p. 98.

ment that triggered the invasion. The latter was not, as Seweryn Bialer suggests, a "major redefinition by the Soviets of what they considered a low risk and cost operation." Nor do I see any reason to conclude that the Soviet leaders "apparently consider[ed] that the relations of international forces and especially of military power [had] changed drastically in their favor."[102] Arguments like this that explain the Soviet invasion only in terms of relative Soviet and U.S. military strength and political "will" fail to grasp the major feature of those two dangerous years, the superimposition of the Soviet-Chinese Leninist regime world conflict and the Soviet-American global confrontation. The Soviet invasion of Afghanistan was a response to a perceived threat from two fronts and overlapping "worlds," an alliance between the most powerful "capitalist stranger" and hostile Leninist "kin."

Developmental Change in China

The Soviet invasion of Afghanistan in December 1979 could well have triggered a period of escalating military violence among the United States, the Soviet Union, and China had Solidarity appeared in Poland in 1979, not 1980; if Cuba in 1979 had been the Cuba of 1966; or if there had not been a substantial developmental change in China beginning in 1979 and decisively expanding in 1980. But China did change, and that change was more than a situational response to evidence of Soviet military power and capacity for aggression. After all, in 1968 the Chinese did not respond to the Soviet invasion of Czechoslovakia by inviting a major Soviet figure like Pyotr Kapitsa to China, or by declaring within several months of that invasion that the Soviet Union might, after all, be a socialist country.[103] Nor can one simply fall back on the "need" for economic modernization in China to explain the dramatic changes initiated by Deng in 1979. The "need" for economic modernization can be addressed in quite different ways. No,

---

102. Seweryn Bialer, "A Risk Carefully Taken," *Washington Post,* January 18, 1980, p. A17.

103. In this connection, see Richard C. Thornton, *China: A Political History, 1917–1980* (Boulder, Colo.: Westview Press, 1982), p. 431.

the changes in China are more developmental than situational; they are integral elements of a developmental change in the institutional configuration and political ethos of a Leninist regime, specifically, away from consolidation and toward inclusion.

Even a cursory examination of the institutional changes in China beginning in 1980 establishes their inclusive quality. Hsin-Chi Kuan's suggestion that "the Chinese Constitution of 1982 comes very close to the Inclusion type,"[104] may be said to apply to the entire "constitution" of Deng Xiaoping's regime. Deng's elevation of empirical reality, his emphasis on "learning from facts," is a typically inclusive rejection of a dogmatic regime epistemology, one that under Mao saw the Cultural Revolution's "sacral reality" as more genuine than any empirical statement of social and economic problems. Similarly, the move from a dogmatically concrete definition of leadership—the Maoist cult of personality—to a broader, more oligarchic notion is typically inclusive. But more than anything, the rejection of class struggle as the ideological pivot of Chinese political life marks Deng's regime as inclusive.

In every instance of a Leninist regime moving from its consolidation to inclusion stage, the primary object of ideological attack has been the notion of class struggle. The statement in the Czechoslovak Party's Action Program that "the Party resolutely condemns attempts to oppose the various classes, strata, and groups of the socialist society to each other and will eliminate everything that creates tension among them"[105] sounds very much like the position taken at the third plenary session of the 11th Central Committee by the Chinese Party, one that firmly discarded the slogan "Take class struggle as the key link," something the Deng leadership considered "unsuitable in a socialist society . . . where the focus of work should be socialist

104. Hsin-Chi Kuan, "New Departures in China's Constitution," *Studies in Comparative Communism* 17, no. 1 (1984): 54.
105. "The Action Program of the Communist Party of Czechoslovakia" (adopted at the Plenary Session of the Central Committee of the Communist Party of Czechoslovakia, April 5, 1968), in Robin Alison Remington, ed., *Winter in Prague: Documents on Czechoslovak Communism in Crisis* (Cambridge, Mass.: MIT Press, 1969), p. 94.

modernisation."[106] In the authoritative "Resolution of Certain Questions in the History of Our Party since the Founding of the People's Republic of China," the assault on class struggle, and more generally on the dogmatic consolidation stage of Leninism, is central and relentless. Mao is accused of having "widened and absolutized the class struggle" in 1962 and of making "theoretical and practical mistakes concerning class struggle in a socialist society [that] became increasingly serious."[107] Jeremy Paltiel is undoubtedly correct in designating the third plenum of the 11th Central Committee in China as the political equivalent of the 20th Party Congress in the Soviet Union.[108]

In every instance of a Leninist regime attempting to move from consolidation to inclusion, an intense conflict emerges within the Party elite; it is especially intense because the challenge to class struggle is more than a challenge to particular policies. It is a challenge to the regime's political configuration and ideological ethos. In China, the period from August 1977 to September 1979 was one of continual conflict between supporters of Hua-style consolidation and Deng-style inclusion. At the 11th Party Congress in August 1977, Hua Guofeng emphasized that "peace and unity does *not* mean there is no class struggle. The first Great Proletarian Cultural Revolution has come to a victorious conclusion, *but* class struggle has not reached its conclusion and continued revolution under proletarian dictatorship has *not* reached its conclusion."[109]

In the realms of international policy and politics, the conflict between these two developmentally opposed "lines" pitted Deng Xiaoping against Hua's supporter Geng Biao. Geng became a member of the Politburo during the period of Hua's

106. "Resolution on Certain Questions in the History of Our Party since the Founding of the People's Republic of China," *Beijing Review* 27 (1981), in *Communist Affairs* 1, no. 2 (1982): 474.

107. Ibid., pp. 464, 465.

108. Jeremy T. Paltiel, "De-Stalinization and De-Maoization: Leadership and Succession in the Institutionalizing Leninist Regime" (Ph.D. diss., University of California, Berkeley, 1984), p. 365, and more generally pp. 317–480.

109. Peter R. Moody, Jr., *Chinese Politics after Mao: Development and Liberalization, 1976–1983* (New York: Praeger, 1983), p. 47. My emphasis.

ascendancy (1977). His early career was in both the PLA and foreign affairs. At one point, he had been ambassador to Albania. In March 1978 he became vice premier of the State Council, and more important, in June, secretary general of the powerful Military Affairs Commission.[110] Geng Biao's report to the Politburo in January 1979 identifies him as a (perhaps the) most forceful exponent of superimposing the Sino-Soviet and American-Soviet conflicts in the service of China's developmental conflict with the Soviet Union. Though specifically directed toward the Indo-Chinese situation, Geng's report, as Michael Yahuda stresses, was very revealing about Chinese (or at least the Hua faction's) attitudes toward international politics. Geng Biao depicted the United States as the "secondary enemy," which has "been drawn into the united front against the Soviet Union." Relations with the United States are presented as proof that "American imperialism is in essence a paper tiger and not a sheet of iron," which because of present difficulties "is easy to win over to our side."[111] As for China's conflict with Vietnam, in Geng's view it was "in essence a struggle between social imperialism [read the Soviet Union] and socialist China."[112]

The crucial issues between Geng Biao and Deng Xiaoping were not whether China should accommodate itself to or oppose the Soviet Union, or whether it should seek a positive relationship with the United States or not. The conflict was over how opposition to the Soviet Union and association with the United States should be ideologically interpreted and politically expressed. Geng Biao attempted, somewhat successfully, to coopt international relations with the United States in pursuit of inter-regime conflicts with the "socially imperialist" Soviet Union. Deng Xiaoping also opposed the Soviet Union, but in different terms. For Deng, the Soviet threat to China was more national and military than ideological and political, more a threat to China's interests than to its Leninist identity. As a

110. My colleague Lowell Dittmer was kind enough to provide me with these details of Geng Biao's career.

111. Michael Yahuda, *China's Foreign Policy after Mao* (New York: St. Martin's Press, 1983), p. 204. My emphasis.

112. Ibid., p. 231.

result, his opposition to the Soviet Union was as forceful as Geng's but more sober, less hysterical.

The intense clash between China and the Soviet Union at a time when (under Mao and Hua) China was developmentally committed to consolidation and (under Khrushchev and Brezhnev) the Soviet Union was developmentally committed to inclusion; and the amelioration of that conflict once China (under Deng) became developmentally committed to inclusion suggests that regimes with the same ideology, but at different developmental stages, are likely, even highly likely, to conflict with one another, because developmental issues are matters of identity, not simply interest.

Deng's victory over Geng Biao and Hua Guofeng was signaled, predictably enough, by the Party's repudiation of class struggle as the pivot of national and international life. Delivering a speech at the Chinese Party's fourth plenum in September 1979, Yeh Chienying repudiated class struggle and continuous revolution as the ideological pillars of the PRC. And the day before the fourth plenum ended, "Chinese and Soviet representatives began preparatory talks for the coming normalization negotiations."[113] The fourth plenum in September 1979 should be seen as the occasion of Deng's, and his inclusive line's, political victory. It was the political inauguration of a major developmental, not merely policy, shift within the Chinese regime, one with direct implications for China's role in the Soviet-centered Leninist regime world and, more generally, in East-West relations.[114]

More than any single international event, China's internal developmental shift from consolidation to inclusion reduced the global tension and danger surrounding the Soviet invasion

113. Thornton, *China,* p. 427.
114. Using the developmental stage constructs of consolidation and inclusion, Jim McAdams has carefully examined the reciprocal impact of developmental regime change and change in foreign policy in the German Democratic Republic (from Ulbricht to Honecker), while Rick Spielman has done the same in a telling manner for the Gierek regime in Poland. See James A. McAdams, *East Germany and Détente: Building Authority after the Wall* (Cambridge: Cambridge University Press, 1985); Richard Spielman, "Claimed-Authority in a Leninist Context: The Case of Poland" (Ph.D. diss., University of California, Berkeley, 1985).

of Afghanistan in December 1979. With Deng's September victory, a noticeable shift in China's political stance, ideological appraisals, and policies became apparent. In December 1979, the Chinese stopped referring to the Soviet Union as a "revisionist" power. In January 1980 when U.S. Secretary of Defense Harold Brown visited Beijing—shortly after the Soviet invasion of Afghanistan—Brown "discovered that the Chinese leaders were wary of being used as a counterweight in the U.S.–Soviet geopolitical rivalry." In his description of the Brown trip, Cyrus Vance notes that before Brown left for Beijing, "the President decided to offer China nonlethal military equipment and reaffirmed an earlier decision to seek special treatment of China on high technology transfers. . . . In Peking, however, the *Chinese proved more wisely hesitant than we were.*"[115] In February 1980, the Vietnamese, who several months earlier had been nearly hysterical in their fear of a second Chinese "lesson," were saying, "maybe the Chinese are preparing for it, but their modernization is not finished." The Vietnamese vice foreign minister, Phan Hien, went on to suggest that "a resumption of Sino-Vietnamese fighting in the near future seemed unlikely."[116] Finally, in May 1980 during his visit to Washington, Deputy Premier Geng Biao, the loser at the September 1979 plenum, was in good Leninist fashion given the task of presenting Deng Xiaoping's new position on Sino-American relations to the U.S. government.[117] In his statements about Sino-American relations, Geng Biao "used the term 'friendship,' carefully avoiding the word 'alliance.'" And the U.S. assistant secretary of state for East Asia and the Pacific, Richard Holbrooke, "declared in a passage that particularly pleased the Chinese [more correctly the Deng faction] that the strategic triangle was no

115. Vance, *Hard Choices,* p. 391. My emphasis.
116. Justus M. van der Kroef, "The Indochina Tangle: The Elements of Conflict and Compromise," *Asian Survey* 20, no. 5 (1980): 489.
117. Just as Deng Xiaoping in his December 1978 visit to the United States "spoke for" the still dominant Hua-Geng faction, I don't mean by this that Deng opposed the invasion of Vietnam. I do want to argue that he saw the invasion quite differently than Geng and Hua—i.e., he did not want it to lead to an even more intense superimposition of Soviet-American-Chinese conflicts. In this connection, see Yahuda's analysis of Deng's comments during his visit to the United States (*China's Foreign Policy,* p. 232).

longer an adequate conceptual framework." Sino-American ties were "not a simple function of our relations with the Soviet Union."[118]

At the peak of American-Soviet-Chinese tension in late 1979 and early 1980, China did not simply disengage internationally in order to deal with the issue of economic growth; rather it undertook a shift in developmental task and stage with all the implications of such a shift for the Chinese regime's organization, ethos, and policies. As a developmental stage within the boundaries of Leninism's continuous features, inclusion has a "protestant" thrust. Inclusive Leninist regimes begin to locate and act on internal social and historical references. As with the emergence of a psychological self, inclusion regimes begin to establish a political identity distinct from any well-organized, authoritative external referent, precisely the thrust of Hu Yaobang's speech to the Party's 12th National Congress. He distinguished China's international position relative to Japan, the United States, and the Soviet Union by pointedly criticizing each of them, while not isolating China, Albania-style. Hu also declared China's membership in the "Third World," a highly permissive and unconstraining international grouping. Most significantly, Hu looked inward to China's history of the past 100 years as the regime's most significant referent. In light of China's decidedly "indivisible" attachment to the Soviet Union between 1949 and 1953, and its efforts to coopt American support for its "indivisible" developmental conflict with the Soviet Union in the late 1970s, Hu's assertion that "in the 33 years since the founding of our People's Republic, we have shown the world by deeds that China never attaches itself to any big power or group of powers" leaves much to be desired in the way of historical accuracy.[119] But what matters most in Hu's statement is the presentation of China's new developmental political identity, not historical accuracy.

China has become a "regime individual" with multiple political references and memberships (e.g., Leninist, Asian, "Third

118. Yahuda, *China's Foreign Policy*, p. 208.

119. Hu Yaobang, "Create a New Situation in All Fields of Socialist Modernisation," Report to the Twelfth Congress of the CCP, *Beijing Review* 37(1982), in *Communist Affairs* 2, no. 2 (1983): pp. 202–4.

World," and Chinese) organized along Chinese national priorities. China's inclusive definition of its political self in terms of multiple references ordered by internal priorities has enhanced its ability to take different positions on different international issues with different partners. This favors a pattern of cross-cutting, partial, and shifting international cleavages; it favors the disaggregation of international conflicts, in particular those involving the United States and the Soviet Union.

Soviet Bloc, Soviet Empire, or
Soviet-centered Leninist Regime World

In light of these regime and inter-regime developments, what can be said about the Soviet Union's current position within and relation to that set of regimes in the world ruled by Leninist parties? One can begin with the observation that the Stalinist Soviet bloc no longer exists as an adequate concept or as a political reality. Soviet influence and power now extend beyond the Hanoi-Prague axis, and Soviet political relations with other Leninist regimes (with the possible exception of Outer Mongolia) are no longer "indivisible."[120] But an observation of this order does not do much more than note the "diversity and complexity" of the Leninist regime world. We need a term or concept that does justice to the current pattern of relations among Leninist regimes and the Soviet Union's place in it.

Empire is the leading candidate, but one with serious problems. Take, for example, Charles Wolf's argument that "in the past dozen years or so the Soviet imperium has come to include Angola, Ethiopia, South Yemen, Vietnam, Laos, Cambodia, Benin, Mozambique, Afghanistan, Nicaragua, Syria, and Libya, in addition to its prior and continuing satellites, allies, and associates in Eastern Europe, Cuba, and more ambiguously North

---

120. There does appear to be some change in Soviet-Mongolian relations toward more "regime individuality" for the Mongolians even in light of the substantial efforts at regional economic integration (e.g., the Erdenets project) between the two regimes, and continued Russian cultural influence within the Mongolian elite. In this regard, see Demchigiyn Molomjamts, "A Leading Regularity: The Socialist Countries' Convergence and Mongolia's Experience," *World Marxist Review* 21, no. 2 (1978): 18–28.

Korea."[121] Wolf describes a grab-bag of significantly different relations between the Soviet Union and a highly heterogeneous set of regimes, implicitly raising the question Erich Gruen raises explicitly with respect to the Roman Empire. Gruen remarks fairly that *empire* is "a slippery concept" and asks: "Should the term be restricted only to direct control by a state over other states and peoples through annexation, occupation, and exploitation? Or can it be applied more widely to indirect suzerainty or 'hegemony,' in which ultimate authority rather than active rule belongs to the imperial power?" Gruen argues that Roman behavior in the East defies any neat label, because the Romans "threw their weight around in certain places and at certain times; on occasion they exercised firm authority, barked commands, carried off the wealth of a state. On other occasions and under other circumstances, they shunned involvement or decision, showed little interest in tangible gain, and shrank even from anything that can be characterized as 'hegemony.' A term for such behavior and attitude has yet to be concocted."[122] But we need such a term if we are accurately to characterize the Soviet regime's international influence and power over other Leninist and "revolutionary" regimes. I propose the term *centered regime world*. This term emphasizes the pivotal place a specific power occupies in relation to a clearly, if not absolutely, delineated set of regimes that support the positions, depend on the resources, and adopt the institutional facade of the central regime. And it avoids two major problems connected with the term *empire*.

In the postwar period, the Soviet Union has ruled over two quite different types of empire: the "indivisible" Stalinist bloc, and the more politically individuated and heterogeneous post-Stalin empire. Using *empire* to interpret both entities descriptively conceals as much as it reveals. It directs our attention to the geographical or spatial extension of the Soviet imperium but fails to alert us to the substantial, if not essential, change in

121. Charles Wolf, Jr., "Extended Containment," in Wildavsky, ed., *Beyond Containment*, p. 154.

122. Erich S. Gruen, *The Hellenistic World and the Coming of Rome* (Berkeley: University of California Press, 1984), 1:273.

relations between the imperial center and members of the imperium that has occurred over "developmental" time.

A second advantage the term *centered regime world* enjoys over *empire* is its less polemical connotation. Typically, those who favor and those who avoid the term *Soviet empire* have quite different political positions. While I recognize the value of polemics, it is more than likely that a polemically robust term will be analytically anemic. The very diffuseness that gives a polemical term power denies it analytical precision. That seems to be the case when the term *empire* is used to make sense of the Soviet regime's international power and influence. While less appealing stylistically, the term *centered regime world* offers a more accurate and less partisan appreciation of the Soviet Union's place in the current pattern of Leninist regime relations.

"MOSCOW CENTRE"

What substantiates or refutes a particular regime's claim to be the center of a regime world? Whether or not it is the only regime to control a major political uncertainty in all parts of that "world."

Within the Soviet bloc, other Leninist regimes had no control over any major Soviet uncertainty; they neither controlled nor manipulated any resource the Soviet Union considered necessary to sustain its political status, ideological self-conception, or military position. Their dependence on, support of, and adoption of Soviet features was practically absolute. The development, under Soviet auspices, of a more inclusive pattern of regime relations[123] has created a situation where members of

---

123. One indicated by the Soviet acceptance of "many roads to socialism" at the 20th Party Congress in February 1956, the dissolution of the Cominform in April 1956, the creation of a new department in the Soviet Central Committee for relations with "socialist" countries in 1957 (see in this connection Jerry Hough, "Soviet Policymaking towards Foreign Communists," *Studies in Comparative Communism* 15, no. 3 [1982]: 167–84), and the Moscow conference of Leninist parties in June 1969 that, according to Devlin, "marked the institutionalization of diversity and the right of dissent in the international communist movement" (Kevin Devlin, "New versus Old" [manuscript], p. 15).

the Soviet-centered Leninist regime world *do* control particular types of uncertainty that affect Soviet power and status.

Cuba has exercised a significant degree of control over the Soviet regime's conception of itself as an international revolutionary force. Cuban leverage varies with circumstance, but its international revolutionary activism has been a real source of status and influence in its relations with the Soviet regime. Particularly during the Sino-Soviet conflict, the Soviet Union's revolutionary "credentials" were sustained by its ties with Cuba. Vietnam enjoys comparable status owing to its revolutionary heroism during the war with the United States. Now as the Soviet Union's major political ally in Southeast Asia, it continues to control a limited, but real, strategic uncertainty with respect to both Soviet-Chinese and Soviet-American military relations. To some degree Romania, North Korea, and Yugoslavia control an important Soviet political uncertainty in their role as access points to the "Third World." To be sure, Cuba and Vietnam are the major entry points, but the "Third World" roles of the more rebellious North Korean and Romanian regimes, and of the independent Yugoslav regime, remain politically relevant to the Soviet leadership. The East German, Hungarian, Polish, Bulgarian, Czechoslovak, and Outer Mongolian regimes are the basis for a Soviet-centered effort at multinational integration, and thereby exercise some influence over a major Soviet ideological uncertainty, the USSR's proclaimed internationalism. And the non-ruling Western European (Italian, French, and Spanish) communist parties help ground the Soviet claim that the Soviet Union stands at the "center" of three worlds: the "Socialist," the "Third," and working-class movements in the capitalist "First" world. Each sector of the Leninist regime (and Party) world now controls a limited, specific, but significant uncertainty affecting the Soviet Union, be it ideological, political, or strategic.

However, only the Soviet regime controls a major uncertainty facing each of the other members of the regime world.

Only the Soviet Union can protect Cuba against the United States, and Vietnam and Outer Mongolia against China. Only the Soviet Union can provide the economic and consumer resources the Eastern European regimes require, along with in-

ternal and external military protection. And only the Soviet
Union is recognized by "Third World" regimes opposing the
United States as a credible potential military counter and economic supplier. In short, the Soviet Union occupies the central
position of ideological origin, military protector, and economic
storehouse. It remains the common and central referent for a
diverse, but bounded, set of regimes that exercise varying degrees of autonomy in their relations with it. Some, like the
Chinese and Yugoslav, are independent national regimes
whose orientation to the Soviet Union rests primarily on a core
of institutional affinities. Others, like Cuba and Vietnam, are
allies whose orientation rests on institutional affinities, material
dependence on military and economic resources, and an ideological "appreciation" of the Soviet regime as the ideological
center and political-military guarantor of a neotraditional regime world ("socialist internationalism"). Regimes like the Afghan and Ethiopian are Soviet subjects, regimes whose immediate survival depends on accepting direct Soviet control in
critical regime areas. Those of Nicaragua, Angola, South Yemen, Mozambique, Benin, and Congo-Brazzaville can be regarded as either candidates or "flirts," regimes whose survival
needs are pressing and who wish to make a claim of some sort
on the Soviet Union as protector and storehouse. But the
greater number of Soviet-centered Leninist regime world
members are European—Eastern European—and their relations with the Soviet Union are a dangerous amalgam of bloc
organization and "regime individuality."

The Eastern Part of Europe

Students of Soviet–Eastern European relations consider it axi-
omatic that the Soviet Union views Eastern Europe as an integral part of the Soviet political order. I think we are correct in
this. However, we should not treat this axiom as an analytical
security blanket. We need to question its utility, its accuracy,
and its meanings at different historical points.

In the past there may have been circumstances when the
Soviet elite's commitment to Eastern Europe was less than
unanimous or absolute. One should remember the unverified

rumor that part of the Soviet leadership was ready to sacrifice East Germany during the leadership succession struggle following Stalin's death. And there is the Chinese charge of September 1963 that "at the critical moment when the Hungarian counterrevolutionaries had occupied Budapest, for a time it [the Soviet leadership] intended to adopt a policy of capitulation and abandon Socialist Hungary to counterrevolution. . . . We insisted on the taking of all necessary measures to smash the counter-revolutionary rebellion in Hungary and firmly opposed the abandonment of Socialist Hungary."[124] Presently, we know that Eastern Europe has become a persistent economic drain, not benefit, to the Soviet economy. In light of the improvements in conventional as well as theater nuclear weapons, we also know the overall military value of the Eastern European "march" had been radically reduced. More specifically, the Jaruzelski coup in Poland has had a negative effect on the military contribution the Soviet Union can expect from the most significant Eastern European army. As for the future, William Zimmerman suggests, "in an international system in which the USSR has become a genuinely global power, it is much less certain that all future Soviet elites will attach unquestioned precedence to Eastern Europe."[125]

However, in the immediate future, the Soviet leaders will continue to give precedence to Eastern Europe. The strategic dimension to the Soviet–Eastern European relationship remains; and there is an important political sense in which "Eastern Europe [is] a living example of socialist internationalism and new international relations, indeed the most mature and sophisticated organizational effort on behalf of international communism to date."[126] But the Soviet attachment to Eastern Europe has other, perhaps more important, if less appreciated, bases. To begin with, the social-political transforma-

124. "The Origin and Development of the Differences between the Leadership of the CPSU and Ourselves—Comment on the Open Letter of the Central Committee of the CPSU (1) September 8, 1963," in Griffith, *Sino-Soviet Rift*, p. 395.

125. William Zimmerman, "What Do Scholars Know about Soviet Foreign Policy?" *International Journal* 37, no. 2 (1982): 203–4.

126. Nish Jamgotch, Jr., "Alliance Management in Eastern Europe: The New Type of International Relations," *World Politics* 27, no. 3 (1975): 428.

tion of Eastern Europe was *the* revolutionary accomplishment of the Brezhnev generation of Soviet leaders. The Soviet "generation of '38" made its revolutionary "bones" with the military conquest and political transformation of Eastern Europe. These experiences and achievements were to that generation what 1917–21 was to the Old Bolsheviks, and the period of industrialization-collectivization to the first generation of Stalinists—proof of its revolutionary heroism and internationalism. Eastern Europe isn't simply territorial "booty"; it is an integral and concrete expression of a political generation's revolutionary credentials and achievements, its revolutionary "patrimony." That explains Brezhnev's blunt assertion to the Czechoslovak leadership in the late 1960s that the Soviet Union would never give up Eastern Europe.[127]

Still, one must ask, might a new Soviet leadership generation, one that did not conquer and transform Eastern Europe, one with a position of global, not simply regional, power, identify less with the area? The probable answer, no. The reason, Eastern Europe is *European.* The Soviet leadership has always been intensely ambivalent about the Soviet Union's peripheral European status. The idea of "socialism in one country" was a response to the anomalous appearance of revolutionary socialism in "backward" Russia, but it never completely removed the ideological unease and cultural ambivalence Soviet leaders felt toward the area and development they "usurped," revolution in Western Europe. And from the very beginning, prominent Western European revolutionaries rejected Lenin's conclusion that the Russian Revolution was a development with universal application. No one did so more bluntly than the Dutch communist Hermann Gorter in reply to Lenin's *Left-Wing Communism.* After congratulating Lenin on his tactics, which "were brilliant for Russia," Gorter asked, "But what does that prove for West Europe? In my opinion, nothing, or very little. . . . How can a tactic be the same for East and West Europe?"[128]

127. See Zdeněk Mlynář, *Nightfrost in Prague* (New York: Karz Publishers, 1980), pp. 239–41.

128. Hermann Gorter, "Open Letter to Comrade Lenin: An Answer to Lenin's Pamphlet 'Left Wing Communism, an Infantile Disorder,'" in Hel-

Today the same partially invidious and completely accurate charge is made by Western Eurocommunists. In 1978, the French communist Jean Elleinstein could say that "for a developed and sophisticated Western society such as the French, the Bolshevik Revolution and Soviet society cannot serve as models."[129] Statements like this, and, even more, the Italian Communist Party's charge that "the phase . . . that began with the October Revolution, *has exhausted its driving force . . .* the advance of socialism in the present phase depends increasingly on the ideas and the democratic and socialist conquests in developed capitalist countries, particularly in Western Europe,"[130] threaten the Soviet regime with ideological marginality. Support by Eastern European regimes, the dependence of Eastern European regimes, and the adoption by Eastern European regimes of Soviet institutional features remains a vital component of the Soviet leadership's conception of itself as a European political and ideological, not simply military and economic, force. I suspect that its European status has become even more salient to the Soviet elite as its influence and power increases but remains limited to the non-European world (e.g., Afghanistan, South Yemen, Ethiopia, and Vietnam). The Soviet emphasis on the "eastern part of Europe" may well intensify in response to a Soviet apprehension that the growth of the USSR's international power that began with non-European Outer Mongolia may end with non-European Afghanistan. In retrospect the Soviet leaders may view their withdrawal from a part of European Austria as the greatest political, ideological, and status error in their foreign policy history. This line of reasoning suggests that the Gorbachev leadership's commitment to Eastern Europe will be exceptionally strong.

mut Gruber, ed., *International Communism in the Era of Lenin* (Garden City, N.Y.: Doubleday, Anchor Books, 1972), pp. 222–23.

129. See Jean Elleinstein's interview in G. R. Urban, ed., *Euro-Communism* (London: Maurice Temple Smith, 1978), p. 77.

130. "Resolution of the Executive Committee of the PCI," December 29, 1981, in *The Italian Communists* (Foreign Bulletin of the PCI [Rome], October–December 1981), pp. 138–39. My emphasis.

POSTSCRIPT, 1991

Gorbachev's sacrifice, or at least acceptance, of Eastern Europe's "defection" in 1989 is a decisive rebuttal to my contention in this essay (originally written in 1986) that its European quality made it his most important possession. Yet it was precisely Gorbachev's desire to make the Soviet Union a more integral part of Europe that led to the events of 1989, and their acceptance by the Soviet leadership. My premise was right; my prediction was wrong. The priority Gorbachev assigned to the Soviet Union's place as a European power—the premise behind my prediction that he would assign a very high priority to control of Eastern Europe—led him to do just the opposite of what I expected.

Why? Gorbachev's preference was for an Eastern Europe led by a group of reform communists (à la Jaruszelski in Poland, and Pozsgay in Hungary) who would openly engage, not further estrange, Western Europe. Their political failure and his perception in the summer of 1989 of a growing political threat from a coalition of Soviet and Eastern European opponents to both his rule and plan to make the Soviet Union an integral part of Europe explain his willingness to accept the defeat and demise of neotraditional Leninism in Eastern Europe.

6

GORBACHEV: BOLSHEVIK
OR MENSHEVIK?

WHAT IS TO BE UNDONE?

The relative status of Party cadres and Soviet citizens, the definition of political membership, and, more generally, the "constitution" of the Soviet polity are the signature issues of Gorbachev's rule. Can the Soviet regime under Gorbachev's leadership recast the until-now categoric status, the "nonbiodegradable" quality, of the Party apparat and cadres? The central question in the Soviet Union today is political, not economic, technological, or military. It is whether or not Lenin's "party of a new type," one of professional revolutionaries, can be converted into a party of politicians. This is the significance and implication, if not the motivation, of Gorbachev's reforms. The title of Gorbachev's next book should be *What Is to Be Undone!*

The historic quality of Gorbachev's political design is his effort to relativize both the place of the apparatus in the Party and the Party's place in the Soviet Union. The risk for a Leninist is that, should the efforts succeed, it will be at the expense of the Party's Bolshevik or Leninist identity. On the assumption that those who support Gorbachev are more or less aware of these risks, why do they entertain them?

DEVELOPMENTAL STAGES AND PHASES

Leninist regimes typically confront three (sequentially phased) developmental tasks: transformation, consolidation, and inclu-

This essay was originally published in 1990 under the same title in Stephen White, Alex Pravda, and Zvi Gitelman, eds., *Developments in Soviet Politics* (Durham, N.C.: Duke University Press, 1990), pp. 270–91. It appears here in slightly edited form.

sion. Each task has an identifiable and different political imperative, the Party's response to which creates distinguishable regime profiles.

Leninist transformation regimes are relatively decentralized in response to the imperative of coping with the turbulent environment created by the Party's effort to destroy its opposition's political and military power. During this stage, Leninist regimes have a *war camp* profile. Trotsky's armored train vividly captures the fluid clotting of power during this stage.

By way of direct contrast, Leninist consolidation regimes are exceptionally centralized in response to the imperative of minimizing access to the new regime by what the Party leadership sees as a socioculturally unreconstructed and contaminating society. Regimes of this order—Stalinist regimes—have a *castle-and-moat* profile. During this stage (often referred to as totalitarian), Stalin's observation that "the Party has become in all respects like a fortress, the gates of which are opened only to those who have been tested,"[1] forcefully expresses the tenor and organization of Leninism.

Leninist inclusion regimes reject this overriding fear of sociocultural contamination, with its hysterical emphasis on class war and anxious search for "enemies of the people," with an ambivalent, but substantial, attempt at political reconciliation with society. In response to the emergence of socially articulate audiences and incipient publics on the one hand, and the Party's "genetic" imperative to maintain a monopoly of political organization and membership on the other, most Leninist regimes have rejected their castle-and-moat profile, with its emphasis on ideological difference, political distance, and violent dominance of society. In its place, inclusion regimes with a *court profile* have developed; regimes still centralized in organization and concentrated in power, but less violent and more accessible. Leninist inclusion regimes were established in the Soviet Union between 1954 and 1961 and in most other Leninist states by the end of the 1960s (in China between 1978 and 1980). The cen-

---

1. Joseph Stalin, "The Proletarian Class and the Proletarian Party," in Bruce Franklin, ed., *The Essential Stalin* (New York: Doubleday, Anchor Books, 1972), p. 43.

tral dilemma for such regimes is to establish their political legitimacy—not simply sustain their punitive power and intimidating authority—without sacrificing the Party's political exclusiveness.

Since Malenkov and Khrushchev, all Soviet leaderships have oriented themselves primarily to the task of inclusion. For some thirty years, the CPSU's major political task has been to ensure that the social products of its developmental efforts identify themselves and act in terms consistent with the Party's ideological and organizational self-conception. Once it ideologically disabled itself with the announcement that the concept of the class enemy had been replaced by that of a "state of the whole people," the threat to the regime has been that the growing range of articulate social audiences in Soviet society might express itself as an articulated plurality of political and ideological publics. Since the 20th, 21st, and 22d Party Congresses, the CPSU has been faced with the reality that Soviet sociocultural developments threaten to create a new political frame of reference that jeopardizes the Party's status as THE political membership organization in the Soviet Union.

However, while all post-Stalin Soviet leaderships have been predominantly inclusive in orientation, their particular features have varied substantially and consequentially. All have rejected a "sultanist" leader's direct control of a police apparatus terrorizing a society feared as a threatening source of inner party contamination. But each—Khrushchev, Brezhnev, Andropov, Chernenko, and now Gorbachev—has made the inclusive word flesh in his own political fashion.

Needful to say, there is much more to this than the personal idiosyncracies of particular Soviet leaders (which, of course, play a role, but not the determining one). Each developmental stage in the history of the Soviet (and other Leninist) regimes can be analyzed in terms of charismatic, traditional, and modern phases. During its initial transformation *stage*, the Soviet regime moved from the Red Army–civil war charismatic *phase* of heroic confrontations to NEP, with its mixture of modern economic relations and growing traditional peasant social influence in local Party organizations (something the Smolensk files demonstrate quite clearly).

Similarly, since 1956, one can detect quite clear contrasts in the several inclusive Soviet leaderships that have succeeded one another in power. Khrushchev, the so-called "harebrained schemer," "adventurist," and "voluntarist," erratically and ineffectually attempted charismatic (not simply populist) modes of organizing and acting, as in his Virgin Lands campaign. Although undoubtedly a reflection of his personal predilections, Khrushchev's attempted *charismatic* variant of inclusion was more a political assault on an embedded Stalinist consolidation regime than a manifestation of political neurosis.

Khrushchev's attack on Party organization in 1962, his attempted elevation of the Party "laity" (the *obshchestvenniki*) and ideological emphasis on a "state and Party of the whole people" were traumatic challenges to the Party apparat's interpretation of inclusion—namely, symbolic ideological enfranchisement of Soviet society, and its own exclusive political enfranchisement.

The Brezhnev leadership accepted the post-Stalin inclusive argument that political rule must not be absolutized in the person of a patrimonial or "sultanist" leader like Stalin, but rejected Khrushchev's plebiscitarian argument that Party citizenship should be generalized to the entire Party. Brezhnev's rule absolutized apparat/cadre citizenship and answered Jerry Hough, who in light of the apparat's internal differentiation and complexity asked: "On what questions are the first secretaries dogmatically agreed on the nature of the answers?"[2] The answer was: on their superior and exclusive political status. The consequence of Brezhnev's rule was the creation of a *neotraditional* form of Leninist inclusion regime consisting of a booty economy, parasitical Party, and scavenger society.

THE BREZHNEV LEGACY

The remarkable thing about the Soviet economy is how premodern it is. All too often, form is confused with content, and a country that produces Sputniks, missiles, and steel "must"

---

2. Jerry Hough, "The Party Apparatchiki," in H. Gordon Skilling and Franklyn Griffiths, eds., *Interest Groups in Soviet Politics* (Princeton: Princeton University Press, 1971), p. 69.

have a powerful modern economy. In fact, it has three relatively unintegrated areas of economic action: military, consumer, and "black market." More important, the USSR has a neotraditional *political* economy, one radically different from those that currently impress political scientists. In crucial respects, the Soviet economy resembles an *oikos* more than a modern economy—that is, a social configuration in which the social, political, and economic arenas of society are not institutionally or conceptually delineated in private/public terms. While not literally organized as a "household," the Soviet political economy does formally approximate an *oikos*. As Aron Katsenelinboigen has noted, the Soviet leadership and even many Soviet economists have looked upon the economy "as a bazaar." The Soviet approach to planning has in Gregory Grossman's words "done little by way of consciously steering the economy's development or finding efficient patterns of resource allocation."[3] And, perhaps of most consequence, the economy has been approached by both Soviet cadres and subjects as a source of "booty" and plunder. Lacking any sense of ownership or attachment to social goods, Soviet subjects have viewed them as free goods, to be appropriated whenever possible. For their part, Soviet cadres regularly exact economic tribute from all areas under their rule and understand economic development in gross arithmetical, not economic, terms. Gorbachev's startling observation that without vodka and oil, the Soviet economy would not have experienced any real growth during the Brezhnev years is somewhat less surprising in the context of this peculiar "political economy."

However, it has been in the political and social realms, and the relation between the two, that the most serious developments occurred during Brezhnev's rule. Under his aegis, "trust in the cadres" led to the emergence of a parasitical Communist Party: not subject to effective central discipline, not able to distinguish between the particular interests of its elite members and the general interests of the Party or country, and insensi-

3. Aron Katsenelinboigen, "Conflicting Trends in Soviet Economics in the Post-Stalin Era," *Russian Review* 35, no. 4 (October 1976): 377; Gregory Grossman, "Notes for a Theory of the Command Economy," *Soviet Studies* 15, no. 2 (October 1963): 108–9.

tive to the distasteful social ethos and threatening political climate it was creating in the Soviet Union.

At the 27th Party Congress, Gorbachev pointed out that "at some stage individual republics, krays, oblasts and cities have been removed from the sphere of criticism; in places this has led to the appearance of untouchable rayons, collective and state farms, industrial enterprises, and so forth. From all this one must draw a hard conclusion: in the party there are not and must not be organizations outside control."[4] But obviously there were! In fact, by the early 1980s, the CPSU had degenerated from a Bolshevik combat party to what Albert Hirschman, writing about economic firms, once referred to as a "lazy monopoly"—"a little noticed type of monopoly tyranny . . . an oppression of the weak by the incompetent, an exploitation of the poor by the lazy."[5]

Gorbachev inherited a Leninist party riddled with Churbanov-like acts of individual corruption; cities like Moscow controlled by Grishin Mafias; and entire republics like Uzbekistan run by Party leaderships who confused Party rule with rule by persons drawn from their own ethnic clan. Rather than being unique, Romania, which I characterized in 1979 as "socialism in one family," was simply an extreme example of the party familialization occurring in a number of Leninist regimes from North Korea to Vietnam, Bulgaria, and the Soviet Union. By 1985, when Gorbachev was selected as general secretary, he might well have wondered how Lenin's "party of a new type" had come to resemble a Mafia of "the old type."

But from a Leninist point of view, there was no humor in any of this. The frustration of Boris Yeltsin (now president of the Russian Republic, then Party boss of Moscow) at the scope and depth of political and personal corruption in the Moscow Party sounds very much like the predicament of Saint Boniface in the eighth century that I referred to in an earlier essay. Boniface was compelled to restore adulterous priests to their positions

4. "Mikhail Gorbachev's Central Committee Report," Foreign Broadcast Information Service [FBIS], Daily Report, Sov-86-038, vol. 9, no. 38, supp. 41 (February 26, 1986), p. 36.

5. Albert Hirschman, *Exit, Voice, and Loyalty* (Cambridge, Mass.: Harvard University Press, 1970), p. 59.

"because if all the guilty ones were punished as the canons demanded there would be no one to administer baptism and perform other rites of the Church."[6]

The greatest irony in all this was that by the end of Brezhnev's rule, the CPSU, more than any nineteenth-century Western polity, approximated Marx's depiction of capitalist civil society in "On the Jewish Question."[7] Only in this instance, "civil society" (as conceived of by Marx) was located *inside the Communist Party*. Soviet party cadres placed their egoistic interests—their personally selfish and private familial commitments—above, and even equated them with, the Party's general interests. As for the mass of Party members, they were relegated to the political impotence Marx postulated for the mass of citizens in bourgeois polities. All of this may suggest that Soviet political development is more ironical than dialectical. Regardless of which, this development has been of enormous consequence, not only to the political and organizational integrity of the Soviet Party, but to the type of society that emerged under its auspices, a "scavenger society."[8]

One of the most misleading characterizations of the Brezhnev period has been the notion of a "social contract" between the regime and society in the Soviet Union, Gierek's Poland, and Husák's Czechoslovakia. Presumably this was based on an implicit trade-off: personal and social security for the subject, and political control by the Party elite—what George Breslauer calls the authoritarian welfare state.[9] In fact, none of these terms are

6. Quoted in Earl Evelyn Sperry, *An Outline of the History of Clerical Celibacy in Western Europe to the Council of Trent* (Syracuse, N.Y.: N.p. 1905), p. 18.

7. Karl Marx, "On the Jewish Question," is in Robert C. Tucker, ed., *The Marx-Engels Reader* (New York: Norton, 1972), pp. 24–52.

8. I use the term *scavenger society* metaphorically, but it appears that six years of Gorbachev's rule has led to widespread actual scavenging in the Soviet Union. See Esther B. Fein, "Recycling Is a Way of Life for Russians: To Survive, They Must Scavenge," *New York Times*, March 25, 1991. Viktor Filimonov, a Russian miner, charged: "Six years of perestroika and I have to buy my shorts on the black market. The Communists have made us beggars" (quoted by Serge Schmemann, "Strike by Soviet Miners Spreads, Challenging Gorbachev's Rule," ibid., March 28, 1991).

9. See George Breslauer's "On the Adaptability of Soviet Welfare-State Authoritarianism," in Karl W. Ryavec, ed., *Soviet Society and the Communist Party* (Amherst: University of Massachusetts Press, 1978).

apt. The only authoritarian Leninist regime has been the Polish one, because only in Poland does a powerful autonomous and autocephalous institution exist, the Catholic Church. Second, a politically distinctive feature of Leninist polities is the Party's denial of independent political stature to the state. In fact, the creation of state political autonomy is one of Gorbachev's major and most difficult tasks. And, finally, the notions of "welfare" and "welfare state" mean radically opposed, not simply different, things in a regime of subjects and one of citizens.

Most serious of all, the notion of social contract only focused on the instrumental nexus between the Soviet regime and society. It failed to grasp the expressive dimension of this relationship. Language does matter, and my use of the terms *parasitical* (Party) and *scavenger* (society) are quite deliberate. They are intended to dramatize the ethos and tenor of the relationship between regime and society, to sensitize the reader to these critical, but typically unexamined, dimensions of social and political life under the Soviet and other Leninist regimes.

Far from being a social contract, the nexus between the Brezhnev regime and Soviet society was that of a *protection racket*.[10] Members of Soviet society were rewarded for, and punished for not, acting like scavengers. Under Brezhnev, the CPSU lost its ability (and perhaps willingness) to locate and strategically define a social combat task, and consequently its ability to discipline its agents and prevent them from becoming what in preindustrial societies are known as "big men." Simultaneously that same Party enforced its monopoly on political enfranchisement, social privilege, and ideological insight into what was historically and absolutely "correct." The effect on Soviet society was neither neutral nor "contractual"; it was invidious.

Members of this society were forced to act in morally debilitating and personally insulting ways. Brezhnev's rule saw the degeneration of the Party, and the Party's denigration of society. Shoddy work, bribery, recourse to the "second economy," nepotism, hypocrisy, and servility were imperatives in the

---

10. Michael Mann uses precisely this term to describe a particular type of political power in *A History of Power from the Beginning to A.D. 1760* (New York: Cambridge University Press, 1986).

Brezhnev neotraditional polity. If not "role models," those who found scavenging agreeable were materially successful. For those members of Soviet society who were more educated, urban, and skilled, *but above all* more individuated, articulate, and ethical, this reality was embarrassing, alienating, and offensive—a source of increasing resentment, anger, and, potentially, political rage.

CATALYSTS FOR CHANGE

The political sociology of the Brezhnev neotraditional era consisted of a civil society (à la Marx) *within the CPSU* exacting political and economic tribute from a population forced to act like scavengers. This was Gorbachev's inheritance, next to which a "mess of pottage" might look appealing. However, the increasing urgency and sense of emergency that characterize his actions arise in no small measure from the stimulus-threat that appeared in a regime whose neotraditional features directly approximated those of the USSR. The regime was Poland; the threat, Solidarity.

As I pointed out earlier, during the Leninist stage of inclusion, the major imperative is to ensure that the new, more socially articulate audiences who appear in the context of industrialization, migration, education, and urbanization adopt a definition of their political status and role consistent with the ideological preferences and political exclusivity of the Party. The failure of the Polish Communist Party in 1980 must have been convincing, traumatic, AND prophetic for Soviet leaders like Gorbachev. Solidarity was *not* the emergence of civil society in Poland. It was the creation of what in another context Max Weber once called a *national citizen class*—in my terms, a public that challenged the strictly hierarchical relationship between rulers and ruled with the integrative role and domain of citizenship. Solidarity was the de facto emergence of a liberal definition and framework of political enfranchisement and organization. The dual power that appeared in Poland was stark and prophetic: citizen versus cadre.

Solidarity was the central external political catalyst for an increasingly forceful rejection of Brezhnevist neotraditionalism, but it was not the only one. The U.S. SDI initiative, the frustrating and embarrassing Soviet failure to keep up in the technological revolution, the ending of the Sino-Soviet conflict, and the appearance of radical reforms in what was once again seen as a bona fide Leninist regime were all important catalysts. Others were equally important, including, I suspect, the growing concern of part of the Soviet elite over the international fragmentation of the Leninist world into increasingly unrelated and unrecognizable components.

By the early 1980s, some Soviet leaders could and did see the appearance in the "Third World" of self-designated Leninist or "scientific socialist" regimes and movements. At best they were "facade Leninist regimes" à la Benin and South Yemen, and at worst Fanonist "movements of rage" like the Khalq in Afghanistan, the Khmer Rouge in Kampuchea, and Sendero Luminoso in Peru. These were (are) regimes and movements that find their raison d'être more in *The Wretched of the Earth* than in *What Is to Be Done.*

If Eurocommunism in Western Europe had very little impact on political life in Italy, France, and Spain, it very likely made a substantial and specific impression on certain members of the Soviet elite, including Gorbachev. Eurocommunism's message was that Western European communist parties found the Soviet neotraditional polity irrelevant, and more likely to converge with the "Third World" than the "First."

Finally, in Eastern Europe, the emergence in the 1970s of full-blown "socialism in one Romanian family" and incipient "socialism in one Bulgarian family" was supplemented by less extreme, but no more viable (and even less stable) forms of neotraditionalism in Poland, Czechoslovakia, and Hungary.

In the course of half a century, "Moscow Centre" had exchanged minimal military power and maximum political and ideological status (in the Leninist world) for maximum military power and near-pedestrian status. This could hardly have been viewed neutrally by the Soviet leadership as a whole.

More important, by the end of Brezhnev's rule, there was growing impatience and frustration over what some Soviet leaders must consider a curse—namely, the regime's apparent inability to develop a political format that can sustain social support, economic growth, and the Party's political integrity. This syndrome of impatience, frustration, and concern had a political locus in what one of Gorbachev's assistants has called the "daughters of the 20th Congress." In this connection, I. T. Frolov, the recently named editor of *Pravda*, has described how a number of cadres who now support and assist Gorbachev worked together in Prague on the editorial board of *Problems of Peace and Socialism* under Aleksey Rumyanstev, who even in the early 1960s voiced his sharp dissatisfaction with the decay in the Soviet regime.[11] Frolov's vignette has far-reaching significance. He is describing a *core site*, a setting in which a leader of stature in control of an organizational base gathers a group of political "companions," whom he engages in political discussion, criticism, and preparation.

One particularly decisive site emerged: its leader, Yuri Andropov; its base, the KGB; and a set of "companions" including Vitaly Vorotnikov, Nikolai Ryzhkov, and perhaps Gorbachev. These "sites" were perestroika's nuclei.

FROM NEOTRADITIONAL TO
SEMIMODERN LENINISM

Gorbachev's program of perestroika is an effort to create an inclusion regime in the Soviet Union whose modern elements match in strength and status the traditional and charismatic components of a Leninist regime. A modern society is one in which the dominant institutions are procedural, the dominant actor is the individual, and the dominant ethos is empirical.[12]

11. See Frolov's interview with Paolo Garimberti of *La Repubblica*, Foreign Broadcast Information Service [FBIS], Daily Report, Sov-89-074 (April 19, 1989), p. 83.

12. I do not equate liberal and modern society. Rather, I view liberal society as a particular and partisan institutional expression of modernity's generic features. The difficulty in differentiating the modern from the liberal is history's fault. So far, it has provided us with only one type of society, the liberal, whose partisan institutions—the market, electoral competition, and the scientific method—have a remarkable affinity with individualism, impersonalism, and empirically based abstractions—in other words, with modernity. However, there is no a priori reason to deny the possibility of a postliberal modern society, one with modern action orientations but postliberal institutions.

The thrust of Gorbachev's reforms consists of an effort to upgrade the role of the *individual* party member in opposition to the *corporate* stratum of apparatchiks; to upgrade the role of *impersonal* procedure in opposition to the *personal* arbitrary discretion of (former) Party "big men" like Vladimir Shcherbitsky, the first secretary of the Ukrainian Central Committee, and to upgrade the status of critical analysis (glasnost) in opposition to regime secrecy and ritual.

Whether one looks at the central place accorded election procedures, the notion of a "rule-of-law state," the introduction of economic practices in place of administrative command, or the remarkable ideological emphasis now placed on the individual, one is witnessing an extraordinary effort to reorient the Soviet regime in a modern direction. My use of the term *semimodern* in describing Gorbachev's reforms has two bases. To begin with, I take seriously Gorbachev's assertion that he will not knowingly "compromise on principles" like the leading role of the Party. Second, while Gorbachev's conception of the Party's leading role differs radically from any seen in the Soviet Union since the early 1920s, it still implicitly assumes *an identity of political preference on the part of Soviet society and the Communist Party.* Far from being corroborated, Gorbachev's assumption has been and will continue to be seriously challenged by many constituent elements in Soviet society. At some point, the likely response to these challenges will be a reaffirmation by the Party leadership of its "Bolshevik" credentials in an effort to retain political dominance, rather than mere governance. No such "Bolshevik" reaffirmation would either eliminate many of the modern practices currently being upgraded or allow them to set the political and economic terms of Soviet life; thus the term *semimodern.*

GORBACHEV'S NOVELTY

The novelty of Gorbachev's intended reforms seems so obvious that one doesn't have to spend a great deal of time making the point. There is the demand that "Party practice must become thoroughly democratic"; a demand backed up with the forceful observation that the Party apparatus "should be helping the

Party, [but] not infrequently puts itself between the Party masses and Party leaders and still further increases the alienation of the leaders from them." There is the acute criticism that "some comrades think people can only be checked up on from above [which] is not true. There is still another kind of verification, the check up from below in which . . . subordinates verify the leaders." In the same vein, the Party's general secretary has emphasized that "rank-and-file members verify their leaders at meetings by criticizing defects, and . . . by electing or not comrades to leading Party organs." There are admonitions to the effect that every communist "must change his very approach to the non-Party person. For this purpose the Communist must treat the non-Party person as an equal." At the center of all these observations and critiques is the hallmark demand for glasnost: "In the Soviet Union and the CPSU communists must honestly and openly admit their mistakes, honestly and openly indicate the way of correcting them. Not many of our comrades undertake this business with satisfaction. But they must!" Finally, one is struck by the Soviet leader's political sensitivity to the sociocultural change in Soviet society, to the "failure to understand that the workers now have a higher sense of dignity and a sense of being the ruling class [and] will not tolerate a bureaucratic attitude on the part of the Party."

The difficulty with these novel statements is that they are Stalin's, Molotov's, Zhdanov's, and Yaroslavskii's, and were made in 1925 and 1937.[13]

Gorbachev is not a Stalinist. Quite the contrary! While terminological similarities exist between Stalin's and Gorbachev's political language, their meanings radically oppose one another. The tenor of their pronouncements has nothing in common. Stalin's language in the 1930s has a decidedly hysterical tenor, while Gorbachev's is sober and procedural. The intent behind their formally similar language is equally dissimilar. Sta-

13. See J. Arch Getty, *Origins of the Great Purges: The Soviet Communist Party Reconsidered, 1933–1938* (New York: Cambridge University Press, 1985), pp. 92, 134, 142, 146, 155, for the statements from 1937. For Stalin's 1925 remarks, see his speech delivered at Sverdlov University in 1925 in J. V. Stalin, *Works*, vol. 7 (1925) (Moscow: Foreign Languages Publishing House, 1954; reprinted by Red Star Press, London, n.d.), pp. 158–215.

lin's call is for a political purge of the Party; Gorbachev's for a psychological recasting of the Party members' attitudes. Most consequentially, Stalin wanted to strengthen the Party as an exclusive "Bolshevik" political "fortress." According to Stalin, the Menshevik Martov wanted the Party to be more a banquet than fortress; so does Gorbachev.

ABSOLUTIZATION, GENERALIZATION, AND RELATIVIZATION

The novelty and difficulty of Gorbachev's semimodern efforts to recast the Party's role in the Soviet Union, and analogously the Soviet Union's role in international politics, can be understood in these terms.

Khrushchev restored the Party's organizational integrity with his de-Stalinization speech and actions. At the 20th, 21st, and 22d Party Congresses, he attacked the *absolutization* of the Party's political identity in the person of its *vozhd* Stalin. Khrushchev made the point bluntly: "After Stalin's death, the Central Committee of the Party began to implement a policy of explaining concisely and consistently that it is impermissible and foreign to the spirit of Marxism-Leninism to elevate one person, to transform him into a superman possessing supernatural characteristics akin to those of a god."[14]

Khrushchev's Leninist Magna Carta at the 20th Congress consisted of a covenant within the Party never to select a leader who might act "rudely" like Stalin. In effect, Khrushchev's Party platform was "Don't kill the cadres." For him, it was the Party that should be absolutized, not its leader, no matter how much the latter's power should be augmented in an effort to energize both society and Party.

Quite quickly and consistently (for a "harebrained adventurist") Khrushchev tried to *generalize* the Party's politically effective membership beyond the confines of the apparatchiks to include the *obshchestvenniki*—that is, the active Party members who were not part of the apparatus. Khrushchev attempted to create a form of plebiscitarian leadership in place of Stalin's patrimonial

14. *Special Report to the 20th Congress of the Communist Party of the Soviet Union* (published by the *New Leader*, New York, 1962), p. S7.

one. And all of Khrushchev's plebiscitarian efforts had the same rationale: to prevent the coagulation of power, initiative (or lack thereof), and status among the now unfrightened apparatchiks. In this regard, Khrushchev was a "Leninist Luther," but one with too few powerful "German princes" behind him. In fact, they surrounded, opposed, and deposed him.

In contrast to particular policy conflicts, the political issue behind Brezhnev's opposition to Khrushchev was over how inclusive, or generalized, the definition of Party "citizenship" was to be. Khrushchev quite clearly wished to upgrade the role and influence of the *obshchestvenniki*, the Party "laity," in relation to the apparat. His attempt to "dilute" the Central Committee's membership by inviting technical experts to its meetings; his bifurcation of the Party organization in 1962; his sponsorship of concepts like "state and party of the whole people" were all challenges to the Party cadre and apparat—and recognized as such.

If Khrushchev's "electoral platform" was "Don't kill the cadres," then surely Brezhnev's was "Don't fire the cadres." Almost all students of the Soviet Union have noted the remarkable stability of cadre assignment during Brezhnev's tenure. The slogan "Respect for the cadres" became in practice the *absolutization* of cadre power, the conflation of apparat and Party. Between 1953 and 1983—that is, between the deaths of Stalin and Brezhnev—Party power had been *generalized* to the party apparatus, *and then absolutized* in its hands. Functional, central-peripheral, and personal conflicts in the Party were on full display during this period, but Brezhnev's political genius lay in his ability to mediate such and preserve the apparat's corporate monopoly and privilege within the Party regime.

The intent behind Gorbachev's actions is to terminate the conflation of apparat and Party rule. In doing so, some of his actions are, like Khrushchev's, "Lutheran." The Protestant-like encouragement of initiative from all communists, captured in the phrase "Every communist is a leader"; the Protestant-like activation of the party "laity" in elections within the Party and for the Supreme Soviet; and the critical comments about the arrogance and command style of the apparatus are all reminiscent of Khrushchev's, but not identical. Khrushchev's modus operandi was mobilizational; Gorbachev's preference is procedural. He repeatedly warns against the temptation to substitute campaigns for sober procedural action. In fact, the measure of Gorbachev's novelty and risk as a Soviet leader is the centrality of "Madisonian" features in his vision of the Soviet Party and polity.

His efforts to create viable, electorally based Soviets and a "rule-of-law state," and his introduction of a new form of state presidency, are a vivid critique of Stalin's patrimonial rule, Khrushchev's plebiscitarian rule, and Brezhnev's patriarchal rule in favor of a more procedural one. Gorbachev proposes to rule, not through Gulag terror and purges, Virgin Lands–like campaigns, or corrupt largesse, but through a proposed pattern of internal checks and balances within the Party regime.

Question: What explains this radical effort, one that implicitly calls for a return to the pre–10th Congress (de facto) tolerance of factions in the Party?

Answer: Gorbachev and other "daughters of the 20th Congress" have become aware of, and come to beware, the fact that throughout its seventy-year reign the Communist Party of the Soviet Union has regularly succumbed to internal political corruption, with all its negative social and economic consequences; and just as regularly has adopted correctives that pose an equal threat to the Party's integrity in the short run and prove ineffectual in the long run.

An example: by the late 1920s, Party organization in various parts of the Soviet Union was riddled with venal political corruption. Recent studies by J. Arch Getty and Graeme Gill exaggerate the degree to which central control was threatened (largely because they equate central with regular bureaucratic control, thereby missing the importance of intermittent, but authoritative, plenipotentiary power from Moscow), but their evidence, along with that provided earlier by Merle Fainsod, does establish the de facto autonomy enjoyed by many regional and local Party secretaries.[15] Evidence also exists of Party cor-

15. See note 12 above; and Graeme Gill's "The Single Party as an Agent of Development: Lessons from the Soviet Experience," *World Politics* 39, no. 4 (July 1987), pp. 566–78.

ruption on the eve of collectivization. Fainsod's recounting of
the Smolensk scandal of 1928 includes one witness's observation that the "Guberniya Party conferences were just one big
drinking party."[16]

However, Stalin's correctives posed an equal, if different,
threat to the Party's integrity. Stalin's initial answer to the syndrome of inadequate central control and pervasive peripheral
corruption was to purge the Party. Having concluded by the
early 1930s that the tendency to corrupt routinization in the
Party was intrinsic, not organizational, he attempted in the late
1930s to maintain the Party's combat integrity by terrorizing it.
Still, even Stalin recognized that one cannot continually employ
an extraordinary measure like wholesale terror to a ruling elite
without paralyzing it. Consequently, by the early 1950s, one
sees renewed signs in the Party of local elites creating autonomous patronage cliques, becoming "big men" in their own
right, and confusing their personal and their families' well-
being with that of the Party's. In his classic work *Power and
Policy in the U.S.S.R.*, Robert Conquest describes the situation in
Georgia in precisely these terms. In explaining this recurrence
of Party corruption, Conquest quite plausibly notes that "even
Stalin could not fully control the emergence of local power
groups without a definite effort, so long as instructions went
through the leaders of the group itself, and reports came back,
in the main from them too."[17] Conquest goes on to make a
persuasive case that just prior to his death, Stalin was preparing
to respond to Party corruption as he had in the 1930s, with
terror.

With his death, and the developmental shift to inclusion,
efforts were made to eliminate the possibility of any future
Stalinist "corrective." The result: a Party "Magna Carta" that
for over thirty years has placed substantial political and ideological limits on any single leader's power. The ideological rejection of class struggle as the Party's central ideological orientation—the Party's recasting of Soviet society as a socially

16. Merle Fainsod, *Smolensk under Soviet Rule* (1958; New York: Vintage
Books, 1963), p. 49.

17. Robert Conquest, *Power and Policy in the U.S.S.R.* (New York: Macmillan, 1961), p. 138.

benign, though not politically equal, entity—has removed the strategic rationale for concentrating and concretizing power in the hands of a single leader charged with preventing the infiltration of the Party by an unreconstructed and hostile society.

The political limit is less explicit, but I think equally clear: only a Party leader who has convinced elite colleagues that he does not possess the (murderous) "rudeness" Lenin noted in Stalin (a "trifle as may acquire a decisive significance") can be elected general secretary.

But if the Party has succeeded in removing the purge and terror "correctives," no post-Stalin general secretary has been successful in preventing the growth of personal and organizational corruption in the Party. Khrushchev's various attempts at reform—in education, in his attempted reorganization of the ministries, and in his effort to create a powerful Party-State Control Commission—all failed; a testimony to the apparat's power to protect its exclusive interests. Brezhnev's novelty seems to have been to take the Party's organizational corruption and elevate it to the status of an organizational principle. The result by the early 1980s was "Rashidovshchina," not only in Uzbekistan but throughout the Party regime.

Gorbachev and his allies have come to power *determined to end the dilemma of either Party corruption or Party terror*. It would appear that during their tenure under Brezhnev, and association with Andropov, they pointed out, argued about, and worked out a radical response to this primordial feature of Leninist regimes.

PARTY-STATE VERSUS NATION-STATE

Gorbachev's political vision rejects Stalin's understanding of the Party's leading role; and in radical respects the post-Stalinist understanding as well. In fact, should Gorbachev succeed in "democratizing" the Party, the major *unintended* consequence will be to undo the Bolshevik-Leninist meaning of the Party's leading role.

Gorbachev has reached the conclusion that only by relativizing the place of the apparat in the Party AND relativizing the place of the Party in the Soviet Union can the syndrome of Party corruption, Party purges, and social alienation be broken through. This is a momentous political conclusion. If we recall David Easton's approach to a polity in which he distinguishes three possible entities—government, regime, and community— we can develop this argument.[18]

Stalin *was* the Soviet polity. Louis XIV's political aspiration was Stalin's achievement. If during the consolidation stage, the Soviet Union incarnated revolutionary socialism, and the Party incarnated the Soviet Union, then Stalin incarnated the Party. Stalin absolutized government, regime, and community in his person.

With de-Stalinization, Khrushchev attempted politically to generalize Party leadership of the Soviet Union from the government, represented by an absolute general secretary, to a regime comprised of Party cadres and *aktiv*. Khrushchev tried to generalize the boundaries of the Soviet polity to include the Party *as a whole*. The Party in all its diversity was to become government, regime, and community. (In fact, with his slogan "State and Party of the whole people," he even introduced a symbolic base for a Soviet political community beyond the Party's organizational confines.) Khrushchev was overthrown by a (Brezhnev-led) apparat that successfully equated the generalization of political power within a Party regime with its own absolute power.

Gorbachev and his supporters have concluded that to ensure the stable generalization of political membership and power throughout the Party regime, and prevent their absolutization in the hands of one leader, or one party sector, it is necessary to relativize the power of each apparatus within the Party, which can only be accomplished by relativizing the Party's power per se in an extended and empowered Soviet political community. Gorbachev is arguing and striving for a new Soviet and Party "constitution," one in which the relativization of apparat power in the Party, and Party power in society create a multidimensional polity with discernible, complementary, and mutually checking features at the levels of government, regime, and community. He has every right to declare what he is doing revolutionary. It is a revolution in the conception of the Lenin-

18. See David Easton, *A Systems Analysis of Political Life* (New York: Wiley, 1965).

ist Party and polity. And he can expect opposition that matches the scope of his intended revisions in intensity.

We already have two ideologically dramatic and politically expanding expressions of Gorbachev's political vision. In Hungary, a government spokesman recently announced that the time had come to substitute the Hungarian coat of arms for the red star—that is, to relativize the Party regime's political status vis-à-vis the national community. Other efforts at political reform in Hungary point in the same direction. The intended polity is to be the Hungarian (presumably socialist) national community, not the Party. In Poland, the suggestion has been made that the formal provision in the Polish constitution assigning the Party a leading role be removed. Exactly the same point; exactly the same significance. At its core, and wherever acted on, the Gorbachevian reform is an effort to relativize the Party's political position. Gorbachev's argument is that the Party must and can do so. It must in order to break the cycle of Party corruption, social alienation, and economic decay. It can because "socialism" has for a long time been secure from internal and external enemies, but has failed to act on those realities.

Gorbachev's analysis is as follows: the CPSU has succeeded in creating more than a Soviet Party regime; it has created a potential Soviet political community embracing both Party and nonparty members who accept the basic features of a Leninist regime. However, by absolutizing the Soviet polity in the hands either of a leader or of a sector of the Party, the Party has denied itself political viability, social legitimacy, and economic productivity.

The Gorbachevian reform rests on an attempted relocation of charismatic "correctness" from the Party to an enlarged and differentiated Soviet polity. Vadim Medvedev, the ideological secretary, said, in March 1989, that "the party does not lay claim to a monopoly in seeking the best paths of social progress; it does not believe that it possesses the ultimate truth. But Communists have something to defend firmly and adamantly. Namely our socialist values, our socialist choice."[19] By so saying,

19. See Foreign Broadcast Information Service [FBIS], Sov-89-041 (March 3, 1989), p. 57.

he was giving the Stalinist notion of "socialism in one country" a radically new political meaning. The "ultimate truth" has been generalized to the Soviet Union as a political community in which the Party's role is central but relative. The import of the relocation of charismatic correctness is that the Party is to be assigned a complementary, not dominant, place vis-à-vis the nation. Put differently, the implication, if not motivation, of Gorbachev's "restructuring" is to provide political substance to the notion of Soviet citizenship at the expense of Party membership. But is a Menshevik-like reform of that order compatible with the CPSU's Bolshevik organization and tradition?

There are three elements in Gorbachev's attempted reform that, if implemented, *will mean the end of Leninist regimes as we have known them.* First, the rejection at the 20th Congress of domestic class struggle—the political rationale for polarizing and juxtaposing the Party polity to Soviet society; second, the recent efforts to replace the Party's "correct line" with the idea of a politically correct Soviet society; which, third, finds its institutional expression in an ideally revived Soviet system led by a president whose political constituency is not exclusively the Party. To the extent that Gorbachev's vision of the presidency becomes a political achievement, not simply a political aspiration, the general secretary's and the Party's status become politically relative.

One thing should be clear: Gorbachev is out to revitalize, not destroy, the Bolshevik tradition. He may well be the last Leninist romantic, one who believes that relativizing the Party's power will allow a vital Soviet polity to emerge in which the Party's power and legitimacy will be secure. But the difference, even opposition, between his intentions and the consequences of his actions should also be clear.

POLITICAL CONCERN AND OPPOSITION

An accurate prediction can strengthen—but not prove—a theory, as when I argued in 1979 that Andropov would replace Brezhnev. An inaccurate prediction can serve the same purpose—in late 1985 I argued that Vitaly Vorotnikov would replace Gorbachev within a year—if one can discover the reason behind the error. The major one was my underestimation of the scope and intensity of the crises facing the post-Chernenko leadership, crises that called for increasingly radical leadership.

If one looks, there have been three Gorbachev leaderships in four years: Gorbachev I favored acceleration, Gorbachev II glasnost, and Gorbachev III supports "democratization" (which I interpret to mean the relativization of the apparat in the Party, and a comparable relativization of the Party in a newly emergent Soviet polity). Gorbachev's ability to pursue increasingly radical reform reflects the catastrophes (from corruption to Chernobyl) connected with Brezhnevian neotraditionalism, the short-lived quality of Andropov's efforts, and the unavailability *to date* of an acceptable alternative to his semimodern revision of the Party polity.

Opposition to Gorbachev exists, but characterizing it requires nuance. When Egor Ligachev denies that he opposes Gorbachev and says that all members of the Politburo agree with the charter for change announced in April 1985, I accept his claim, *and* remind myself that Li Peng and Zhao Ziyang agreed on the need for the Four Modernizations in China. Political conflict develops within a coalition as differing interpretations of generally agreed-on reforms manifest themselves. As the political implications of Gorbachev's interpretation of perestroika, and particularly "democratization," become apparent, one may predict that divergent, opposed, and even mutually exclusive political interpretations and positions will appear in the Politburo.

Evidence of politically divergent elite interpretations of perestroika already exists. One major expression occurred in November 1987 at the time of the October Revolution's seventieth anniversary. In his speech on that occasion, Gorbachev presented the most positive public appraisal of Stalin heard in years. Most (liberal) Sovietologists homed in on his blunt accusations against Stalin. "The guilt of Stalin and his immediate entourage before the Party and the people for the wholesale repressive measures and acts of lawlessness is enormous and unforgivable," he declared. But there was more, including the recognition that "a factor in the achievement of victory was the tremendous political will, purposefulness, and persistence, ability to organize and discipline people displayed in the war years by Josef Stalin"; and the need to recognize Stalin's incontestable contribution to the struggle for socialism, to remember that after Lenin's death, it was Stalin who headed the Party's leading nucleus and "safeguarded Leninism in an ideological struggle."[20]

A major question arises in connection with this speech: whose position was Gorbachev expressing, his own or that of some of his Politburo colleagues? The analysis I have presented suggests that Gorbachev was compelled to act as spokesman for positions he opposes. The full measure of opposition to Gorbachev came out in the speech's vituperative references to Trotsky, "who always vacillated and cheated"; Trotsky who denied Stalin's charter concept, the possibility of "socialism in one country"; and, of course, Trotsky who criticized the political monopoly of the apparat in the Party. I would argue strongly that Trotsky's, not Bukharin's, rehabilitation is central to Gorbachev's efforts to relativize the role of the apparat within the Party and recast the Soviet Union's role in international politics.

More than anything else, "new thinking" in Soviet foreign policy means rejecting the Stalinist notion of "socialism in one country," and no one did that more clearly than Trotsky, who emphatically argued for the need to include Russia, economically *and* culturally, in Europe. Trotsky noted prophetically that "the conditions for the arising of a dictatorship of the proletariat and the conditions for the creation of a socialist society are not identical, . . . [they are] in certain respects antagonistic. . . . Economic construction in an isolated workers' state, however important in itself, will remain abridged, limited, contradictory: it cannot reach the heights of a new harmonious society. . . . *The world wide division of labor stands over the dictatorship of the proletariat in a separate country and dictates its further road.*"[21] The visceral excoriation of Trotsky in the November

---

20. *New York Times*, November 3, 1987.
21. Leon Trotsky, *The History of the Russian Revolution*, trans. Max Eastman (Ann Arbor: University of Michigan Press, 1960), vol. 3, appendix II; see pp. 339, 401, and 418.

1987 speech was an attack on Gorbachev's incipient efforts to relativize the Party in the Soviet Union, *and* the Soviet Union in international relations (certainly not an attack on any preference by Gorbachev for "permanent revolution," domestically or internationally.)

Since 1987 there have been significant, but quite indecisive, signs of Trotsky's "reentry" into Soviet political life. However, nothing would relativize Lenin more than reintroducing and legitimating Trotsky's critical and integral association with him. If Stalin dealt a decisive blow to his opponents by murdering Kirov, Gorbachev would do the same to his by rehabilitating Trotsky.

More recently, the Party plenum in July 1989 revealed acute concern over Gorbachev's conception of perestroika. Many Western observers of the plenum too readily and indiscriminately interpreted statements by Politburo members as attacks on Gorbachev. It would be more accurate to say that the major thrust was one of acute concern over the Party's status and role, pointedly illustrated by Nikolai Ryzhkov's worried queries about the "Party's leading role in society's life," and the doubts about "its role as society's political core." The ideological secretary, Medvedev, captured the spirit of concern by declaring: "Most of us are in the grips of complex and contradictory reflections, experiences, and doubts: Are we going in the right direction . . . are we not weakening the very foundations of our socialist development?"

But the political concern of Ryzhkov and Vorotnikov became in Ligachev's hands a political criticism and attack on Gorbachev. Ligachev focused precisely and accurately on the "deviant" elements in Gorbachev's intended radical recasting of the Party. Ligachev declared that "it must be borne in mind that the CPSU is above all the party of the working class, and any restriction on it signifies a belittling and weakening of [its] role. A correct decision has been made to convene a worker's congress in the very near future."[22] One can find comparable statements by Eastern European leaders who are concerned with or

22. See Foreign Broadcast Information Service [FBIS], Sov-89-139 (July 21, 1989), pp. 52–79, for speeches at the plenum.

adamantly oppose the type of Party reform Gorbachev espouses. At the recent Hungarian Party congress, Karoly Grosz,
while endorsing a range of radical changes in the Party's ideological and organizational format warned against its "ignoring
the working class and the values and ideals of communism."
And in an interview given to *Pravda*, Nicolae Ceauşescu emphasized the Romanian Party's working-class character and the
professional revolutionary (Bolshevik not Menshevik) quality
of Party leaders.[23]

This ideological emphasis on the working-class character of
the Party is a direct political challenge to the creation of a
national polity in which the Party will play a relative, not absolute, role. And in presenting this challenge, Ligachev is not
speaking as a Stalinist, but as a Bolshevik-Leninist, for whom
the Party is THE polity. Ligachev made his Bolshevik position
crystal clear when, in the same speech, he pointedly asserted:
"There can be an increase in the soviets' role in society only if
the Party is strengthened, and not at the expense of its weakening, as certain people propose." Ligachev could quite justifi-
ably cry Menshevism, not Bolshevism, when Miklos Nemeth,
commenting on the Hungarian Party's recent reorganization,
said: "We don't want members, we want voters." Gorbachev's
reforms in the Soviet Union have not approached that point
but have the same implication: not the removal of the Party per
se, but rather its Menshevik-like reconstruction as a Party of
individual members acting through several regime institutions,
each with relative, and none with absolute, influence.

Gorbachev had defenders like Zaikov and Nazarbayev at the
plenum; and defended himself by reminding his colleagues
that they had all agreed to the unsettling and "revolutionary"
implications of perestroika! Remaining true to his conception
of Party "democratization," he renewed his call for less central
control and greater initiative and autonomy on the part of primary Party organizations. But this is precisely the issue generating political concern from leaders like (former Russian president) Vorotnikov, who until now have critically supported him.

23. Grosz's comments were noted in the *New York Times*, October 7, 1989,
and Ceauşescu's can be found in *Scînteia*, August 23, 1989.

REGIME ANALOGIES

In the midst of great uncertainty, historical analogies can help make sense of events in the Soviet Union (as well as in Eastern Europe and China). In the past I have used the analogy of the Ottoman Empire, and, unlike some others, I still find it valuable, because although not identical, the Soviet and Ottoman cases are indeed analogous.

The Soviet elite, like its historical Ottoman counterpart, characteristically favors a combat task and ethos—more social, less military, in the Soviet case—to sustain its integrity as a ruling organization. However, since Khrushchev, it has been unwilling and unable to find a combat task that subordinates the particular interests of its cadres to the Party's general interests. In Ottoman history, one periodically finds the same phenomenon, and in both cases the result has been political, social, and economic crisis. The Soviet and Ottoman responses to this condition are also analogous.

Nativists confront Westernizers: in the Soviet case those for "socialism in one country" confront those with a more ecumenical understanding of the Soviet Union's place in international politics. Proponents of plenipotentiary reform confront proponents of procedural reform: in the Soviet case, this takes the form of opposition between those who prefer the KGB (as the least corrupt, best-informed sector of the Party) and those who favor elections to soviets and Party committees as the central mechanism for reform. Finally, those with a more civic vision of the Soviet polity confront those with a more ethnic vision.

One can go a long way toward making sense of the historically remarkable events in the Soviet Union (and Eastern Europe) with a civic-ethnic framework. Analytically distinct, these orientations merge and conflict politically. One must be aware of their possible complementarity and polarity, and of their respective weighting within an elite and each of its members. Coincidentally, a former part of the Ottoman Empire, Yugoslavia, currently offers a telling contrast and conflict between a primarily civic-oriented Slovenian Party, and a more ethnically oriented Serbian Party.

In speculating about political outcomes in the Soviet Union, three regime types are conceivable; one is probable. Least likely is a semimodern civic regime that remains, in some identifiable sense, Leninist or Bolshevik. This is Gorbachev's intention. However, as I noted earlier, intentions and implications are quite different things; and the implications of his reforms are Menshevik, not Bolshevik. One has only to look at Hungary.

A more likely outcome is the emergence of an ethnically oriented Soviet regime. This could be relatively benign should a Vorotnikov become a Russian Atatürk (to extend the Ottoman analogy); or dangerous should a Ligachev become the leader of a nativist, xenophobic Soviet regime. Recent charges by the Party head of a Jewish *oblast* in the Soviet Union about Ligachev's possible support of anti-Semitic statements in the media indicate fears of such an outcome.

However, more likely than either of these decisive outcomes is a Soviet polity marked for a prolonged period of time by political turbulence and instability; one in which nativists confront Westernizers, Andropovites confront Gorbachevites, "civics" confront "ethnics," and neither the apparat nor terror provides the regime with its political linchpin.

A number of years ago, Melvin Croan asked whether Mexico might not be the future of Eastern Europe.[24] One might also look at Argentina, a regime and country split for decades between two forces—a nativist, xenophobic Peronist elite with ambivalent military and passionate working-class nationalist support, and a more civically and internationally oriented political leadership supported by an urban, professional middle class—which turbulently alternate in power. Argentina is a nation with a long-unrealized economic potential; a European society unable to create a Western European political culture; and a polity with sustained and largely contained political instability. But the point is not that Argentina or Mexico is the Soviet future. We should have learned long ago from Marx's mistake not to posit any regime's present as any other's future.

24. Melvin Croan, "Is Mexico the Future of East Europe: Institutional Adaptability and Political Change in Comparative Perspective," in Samuel P. Huntington and Clement H. Moore, eds., *Authoritarian Politics in Modern Society: The Dynamics of Established One-Party Systems* (New York: Basic Books, 1970), pp. 451–84.

The point is to dramatize the contours of the emerging polity in the Soviet Union (and Eastern Europe) and emphasize the international predominance of regimes whose primary political feature is contained instability.

The conflict within the CPSU between proponents of a semi-modern and proponents of a neotraditional organization of the Party will be exacerbated by the conflict *within and outside* the Party between "civics" and "ethnics"; between the supporters respectively of polities in which the more valued actor is, on the one hand, the critically articulate and active individual citizen, and, on the other, the corporate and solidary cultural group.

The most likely response (not solution) to these conflicts will be the emergence of a strong, not absolute, "Giolittian" president and presidency.[25] It will be this office and person who will carry the political weight of relativizing the Party's role without eliminating it; of addressing the Soviet Union's ethnic groups and demands without completely accepting ethnic sovereignty or xenophobia. At least one factor favors this outcome—its alternative, political chaos.

POSTSCRIPT, 1991

In 1990, a "fourth," more authoritarian, Gorbachev emerged. Two shocks explain Gorbachev's change of political persona and style. First, the Shatalin economic proposals—the famous 500-day program—undercut Gorbachev's belief that a noncapitalist market could be created. This assumption was at the heart of Gorbachev's effort to finesse inner-Party opposition and sustain some form of Leninist political economy. The Shatalin proposals made it very clear that while in the abstract the market exists independently of particular institutional forms, in practice that is not at all the case. Either the Soviet ministries (and the Soviet Union) or the Shatalin plan had to go. Shatalin went.

The second shock was even greater. In this essay, I argue

---

25. In connection with Giovanni Giolitti's leadership, see Richard Webster, *Industrial Imperialism in Italy, 1908–1915* (Berkeley: University of California Press, 1975), in particular the Prologue and notes on pp. 346–47.

that the premise behind Gorbachev's attempted political relativization of the Party was the presumed existence of a latent,
but real, Soviet citizenry. However, by 1990 it was clear that in
this regard the Soviet Union is like Gertrude Stein's Oakland:
"There is no there there." After seventy years of rule, the
CPSU had failed to create a supra-ethnic Soviet political community. There were Russians, Ukrainians, Georgians, and Lith-
uanians, but not very many "Soviets" in the Soviet Union. It is
not the dramatic presentation of ethnic demands per se that has
shocked Gorbachev. The absence of a more powerful counter-
vailing force of civic Soviet identification has done that.

In November 1987, Gorbachev could say the Party no longer
had a monopoly on truth, on the "correct line," because he
romantically presumed an identity between a "Soviet" national
myth and Party ideology. That presumption has been critically
assaulted by the intensity and scope of ethnic and social claims.
Gorbachev's response has been more "Bolshevik" than "Menshevik." If Gorbachev I emphasized administrative efficiency
(*uskorenie*), Gorbachev II psychological efficacy (glasnost), and
Gorbachev III political legitimacy (*democratsiia*); Gorbachev IV
emphasizes state authority.

In the absence of a sociopolitical constituency, a Soviet citizenry, Gorbachev has opted for support from a supra-ethnic
institutional constituency: the army, KGB, and Party/ministe-
rial apparat. Gorbachev's vision of a legitimate Party leading a
Soviet polity has had both its economic and political underpinnings removed. He possesses neither authority nor legitimacy.

7

THE LENINIST EXTINCTION

MASS EXTINCTION

World War II was the twentieth century's "big bang." Its end marked the defeat of the gravest threat in two hundred years to liberal Protestant capitalist democracy, and more fundamentally to modernity as a way of life based on the individual, impersonalism, association, and tolerance. Nazism was a unique assertion within Western Europe of an antimodern way of life based on the corporate ("racial") group, charismatic Führer, hierarchy of SS "heroes,"[1] and genocidal intolerance; a remarkable instance of charismatic leadership employing and subordinating traditional (German) nationalism and modern (German) science.

The outcomes of World War II have defined our political universe: its features, issues, and boundaries. The elimination of Nazism and Italian Fascism was the most immediate outcome. The appearance of nuclear weapons was a second. The social mobilization of African-Americans, and American women, along with the development of the American "West"— California—was a third. Decolonization, and the arithmetical addition of a "Third World," was yet another major outcome of the war. The emergence of the United States of America as the most powerful and prestigious reviver and guarantor of world liberal capitalist democracy was the most momentous outcome of World War II. But the emergence of the Soviet Union as a European continental power (soon allied with a Leninist regime

This essay was originally published in 1991 in Daniel Chirot, ed., *The Crisis of Leninism* (Seattle: University of Washington Press, 1991). It appears here in slightly edited form.

1. Charles W. Sydnor, Jr., *Soldiers of Destruction: The SS Death's Head Division, 1933–1945* (Princeton: Princeton University Press, 1977).

in China) and, in short order, as a nuclear, thermonuclear, and global power must rank as a close second.

The "promise" identified by many with the October Revolution in 1917, the view of the Soviet Union as a socialist hierophany and the nucleus of a superior successor to the world capitalist order—a view tarnished for many by the purges of the 1930s, Nazi–Soviet Pact, and initial Nazi victories—was reclaimed in 1945. A heroic Soviet Union emerged, soon to be multiplied by a set of geographically contiguous replica regimes from Czechoslovakia to Vietnam. Although physically devastated by the war, and still a largely peasant, "backward" country, the USSR was filled with self-confidence in its institutional performance and promise—a promise shared by some in the West who, like John Le Carré's character Bill Haydon, saw in the Soviet Union a crude, but Rousseauian, reality superior to the vulgarity of American material euphoria and nuclear power.[2]

With Stalin's death in 1953, the Soviet Union began to change substantially (if not essentially).[3] Coercion replaced terror. The Party once again ruled the secret police, not the other way around. Khrushchev lowered the Soviet foreign-policy drawbridge (or raised the "Iron Curtain") by recognizing the existence of an unaligned ex-colonial world and diplomatically engaging the West.[4] He also drained the terror "moat" between Soviet society and the Party by repudiating the Stalinist notion of the "enemy of the people" AND Lenin's internal class war tenet.[5]

In fact, Khrushchev's repudiation of class war in his 1956 de-Stalinization speech was an ideologically mortal blow to the integrity and vitality of Leninism as a Soviet and international phenomenon. With this action, Khrushchev removed the ideo-

2. In John Le Carré, *Tinker, Tailor, Soldier, Spy* (New York: Random House, 1964).

3. Ken Jowitt, "Moscow 'Centre,'" *East European Politics and Society*, no. 3 (Fall 1987): 296–349.

4. The Cuban Missile Crisis was a nearly fatal error on Khrushchev's part. However, the placement of missiles was intended as an act of military diplomacy, not as aggression.

5. See the *Special Report to the 20th Congress of the Communist Party of the Soviet Union* (published by the *New Leader*, New York, 1962).

logical and political rationale for juxtaposing the Party as the locus of a superior, more "real," way of life to an "unreconstructed culturally contaminating" Soviet society. With his ideas of "state of the whole people" and "Party of the whole people," Khrushchev diluted the ideological and political tension between the Party and its host, Soviet society. He weakened the Party's conviction that it had a still-unfulfilled mission requiring internal discipline. Khrushchev's revisions left a Party increasingly unable to distinguish between the Party "City of God" and the Soviet "City of Man"; between the cadres' particular interests and the Party's general interest.

Stalin was perverse, but a perverse giant, a malevolently mysterious Leninist Wizard of Oz. Under his rule, the Party, the Soviet Union, and his person were objects of fearful adoration—of awe. Khrushchev demystified the Party, the Soviet Union, and Leninism. Who can imagine Stalin thumping his shoe at the United Nations or wanting to visit Disneyland? This is not the place to analyze Khrushchev's decision to de-Stalinize, but to emphasize Khrushchev's belief that the Soviet regime should do more to engage and less to estrange the Soviet population, to be more "Aquinian" and less "Augustinian." However, his Party companions only supported those revisions that enhanced their collective and personal security, perquisites, and status. The Party elite favored Khrushchev's Party Magna Carta—that is, strictures against a Party sultan like Stalin and his possible use of a patrimonial secret police against the leadership itself. The Party elite also supported Khrushchev's repudiation of the ideological underpinnings of Stalinism: the concepts of the "enemy of the people," the dictatorship of the proletariat, and class war. However, it was predictably unwilling to lose its monopoly of political power, economic perquisites, and elite status. Khrushchev's "state and Party of the whole people" undermined the categorical and exclusive position of the Party's relation to society, and his attempt to create a plebiscitarian relationship with the Party "laity," its mass membership, directly threatened the politically superior role of the Party "bishops"—that is, the members of the central and regional Party/ministerial apparatus. Khrushchev's political revisions of Stalinism threatened both the corporate status of the

Party leadership *and* his own ability to withstand a threat to his power.

With Brezhnev, the Leninist "promise"—the confidence that a compelling, viable, "superior" way of life would appear in the Soviet Union—ended. What emerged instead was a Leninist polity with a parasitical Party, booty economy, and scavenger society.[6] Plekhanov's sarcastic comments about Lenin's Inca-like socialism found a morbid resonance in the persons of Brezhnev, Andropov, and Chernenko. In the 1980s, the Soviet leadership resembled the mummified Incan rulers of Cuzco.[7] In the thirty years between the deaths of Stalin and Brezhnev, the Soviet Party had created a "civil society" with exactly the features Marx identified in capitalism—unrestrained ego, selfishness, and greed—*within* the Soviet Communist Party.[8]

Soviet economic organization and culture resembled a traditional *oikos* as much, perhaps more, than a modern economy.[9] But of even greater import was the relation that developed during the Brezhnev era between the Party and Soviet society. It was more protection racket than social contract. Soviet (Polish, Romanian, Chinese, Hungarian, Cuban . . .) subjects were forced to act as supplicants and scavengers or be treated by the regime as psychotics.

As for the Soviet Union's international position and condition, it resembled the Soviet domestic situation. True, in the 1970s one could regularly hear Messrs. Brzezinski, Kissinger, Reagan, and others talking about the Soviet Union as the most aggressive, successfully expansive empire in history. Yet as one of only two global thermonuclear powers in world history, its imperial expansion in the post-Stalin era was limited to Cuba, Laos, Kampuchea, Ethiopia, Angola, Mozambique, Benin, Congo-Brazzaville, part of Yemen, and Afghanistan; all of which it would very likely have traded for the half of Austria it

6. See chapter 6 above.

7. Burr Cartwright Brundage's *Lords of Cuzco: A History and Description of the Inca People in Their Final Days* (Norman: University of Oklahoma Press, 1967) is a good introduction to the Incas and their "mummy bundles."

8. See Karl Marx, "On The Jewish Question," in Robert C. Tucker, ed. *The Marx-Engels Reader* (New York: Norton, 1972), pp. 24–52.

9. On the term *oikos*, see chapter 4, note 20, above.

gave up in the mid 1950s. For a Soviet leader looking at Soviet "internationalism" in the early 1980s, it must have come as a depressing shock to realize that the expansion begun in the early 1920s with "Third World" Outer Mongolia was repeating itself sixty years later with "Third World" Afghanistan—and less successfully. As I pointed out over ten years ago, the Soviet Union was converging domestically and internationally, but with the wrong world, the "Third" not the "First."

What explains Leninism's, in particular the Soviet Union's, "failed promise"? Let me suggest "four big and three little" reasons. I have already dealt with two.

The first was Khrushchev's ideological disarming of Lenin's "party of a new type," a combat party, as Philip Selznick correctly noted,[10] whose organizational integrity rested on its ability regularly to prevent the ritualization of its combat ethos and the transformation of deployable Party agents into undeployable Party principals. Khrushchev's ideological reconciliation with Soviet society, his definition of it as benign (although not politically equal) decisively undercut the Party's ability to identify and act on a social combat task.

The second was the Brezhnev leadership's adamant refusal to move from formal ideological reconciliation with Soviety society to its political integration. The Brezhnev regime rejected a political framework in which the Soviet subject could become a Soviet citizen; a framework in which the Party cadre would no longer be the sole political actor and the Party *the* polity. The result: a situation in which a "lazy Party monopoly"[11] ruled an increasingly articulate and alienated Soviet society. The Brezhnev pattern was paralleled by a comparable, but singular, development in Gierek's Poland, where Solidarity heralded the "end of Leninism."

Solidarity is the most powerful and consequential liberal democratic revolution since the French Revolution. A striking illustration of the ironical, not dialectical, nature of historical

10. Philip Selznick, *The Organizational Weapon* (New York: McGraw-Hill, 1952).
11. I am adapting Albert Hirschman's notion of a "lazy [economic] monopoly." See his *Exit, Voice, and Loyalty* (Cambridge: Mass.: Harvard University Press, 1970), p. 59.

development, Solidarity was a liberal democratic revolution carried out by a working, not a middle, class; a working class created by an antiliberal Leninist party and nurtured by an antiliberal Roman Catholic church.[12]

If part of a Leninist party's uniqueness rests in its political conflation of the state and public realms; in its effort to have the cadre fuse the roles of state official and citizen, then Solidarity's challenge is immediately apparent. Solidarity was more than a threat to Party power. Solidarity offered an opposing definition of political leadership and membership. It confronted the Party cadre with the national citizen. As a politically "self-limiting" movement,[13] Solidarity was an organized public whose membership consisted of voluntarily associated individual citizens opposed to a hierarchical, corporate Party polity. Solidarity and the Party were mutually exclusive *ways of life.*

If, to Solidarity's political "constitution," one adds the persistent inability after 1980 of the Polish United Workers' Party (*sic*) to find a variant of inclusion[14] capable of restoring Party discipline and confidence, and undermining Solidarity's national citizen appeal, then one can see why Polish developments in the 1980s were both traumatic and prophetic for some Soviet leaders. A part of the Soviet elite drew a profound conclusion from the Polish Party—*and* military's—inability successfully to fragment and coopt Solidarity—namely, *inclusion of social forces was no longer an adequate strategy to maintain the Party's monopoly.* The ongoing Polish drama in the 1980s heightened and crystallized the feeling of impatience and frustration at the Soviet regime's apparent inability to develop a political format that could sustain social support, economic growth, and the Party's political integrity. Soviet leaders concluded that the Party's political leadership and organizational rectitude required them to

---

12. I don't mean to ignore the socialist, anarchist, and Catholic components of Solidarity, only to identify its defining thrust. I characterize the novelty and historical significance of Solidarity in a work in progress, "The 'Correct Line' and the Spirit of Leninism."

13. See Jadwiga Staniszkis, *Poland's Self-Limiting Revolution* (Princeton: Princeton University Press, 1984).

14. See chapter 3 above.

risk "losing its life to save it." In good measure Solidarity was responsible for Gorbachev and perestroika.

In essence, perestroika is (was?) an effort to *relativize* the position of the *apparatchiki* within the Communist Party, of the Communist Party within Soviet society, and of the Soviet Union in the world. Previous Soviet leaders had adaptively reconfigured the Party's features to new internal and external task environments,[15] but each preserved the Party regime's absolutist constitution. Stalin absolutized the Party in the person of its leader, himself; Brezhnev absolutized the Party cadres; and Khrushchev attempted to absolutize the Party as a mass organization. *Gorbachev's novelty and tragedy as a Leninist lies in his effort to relativize the absolutist quality of the Party regime* by upgrading the soviets and relativizing the Party committees, by upgrading the presidency and relativizing the office of general secretary, by upgrading the Supreme Soviet and relativizing the Central Committee, and by upgrading the individual Party member and relativizing the power and status of the apparat. The problem with this adaptation is that a politically relativized Bolshevism is Menshevism.[16]

Organizations can be compared in terms of their "strength." Karl Deutsch has argued that "the social group . . . which can undergo the widest range of changes without losing its cohesion in a few essentials, so as to be able to include other patterns and structures within itself without losing its identity or its continued capacity for growth" has greater strength.[17] A Leninist party regime's strength depends on its ability to adapt without sacrificing its combat competence *or* its status as a self-contained (absolute) polity. Brezhnev's ritualization of the Party's role in society weakened the Party's "strength"; Gorbachev's relativization of the Party as THE Soviet polis has destroyed it.

Khrushchev's disavowal of class war, Brezhnev's neotraditionalization of the Soviet polity, the appearance of a revolu-

15. See chapter 5 above for an analysis of Leninism's developmental history.

16. See Bertram Wolfe, *Three Who Made a Revolution*, (New York: Dial Press, 1960) chs. 13–15.

17. See Karl Deutsch, *Nationalism and Social Communication* (Cambridge, Mass.: MIT Press, 1953), p. 49.

tionary national citizen class (Solidarity) in Poland, and Gorbachev's relativization of Lenin's absolute Party are the "four big reasons" for the end of Leninism. What are the "three little reasons"?

I have in mind, first, the Soviet Union's reconciliation with China. If the twenty-year conflict with China helped sustain the inertial political quality of the Brezhnev regime, then the end of that conflict allowed some members of the Soviet leadership to focus more intently on their own regime's internal debilitation.

SDI should be included among the "little reasons." Its fantastic quality, and the enormity of its policy implications for the Soviet order, undoubtedly interrupted the inertial quality of Soviet politics. So did the increasingly undeniable reality of scientific, technological, and industrial developments in the West and among the newly industrialized countries (NICs); dramatic reminders that after seventy years of murderous effort, the Soviet Union had created a "German industry of the 1880s" in the 1980s.[18]

This combination of "four big" and "three little" developments created a particular and peculiar environment for the USSR and other Leninist regimes. Some leaders and regimes approached the situation with caution, all viewed it with apprehension, a few saw it in terms of promise, many viewed it with urgency; and in the summer of 1989, one leader, Gorbachev, viewed the situation as an emergency. At that point, he acted preemptively. Gorbachev struck out against the emerging coalition of perestroika's Eastern European opponents (Jakes, Zhivkov, Honecker, and Ceauşescu) and those in his own Party. The significance of Gorbachev's actions in 1989 is that he was willing to accept the possible collapse of Leninist rule in Eastern Europe in order to maintain it in the Soviet Union; not that he intended or foresaw the political collapse of Leninism in Eastern Europe.

If in 1918 Lenin "offered" Imperial Germany the Ukraine to save Bolshevik Russia, in 1989 Gorbachev offered East Germany

18. See Daniel Chirot's essay in *The Crisis of Leninism*, ed. Chirot (Seattle: University of Washington Press, 1991). At one and the same time, SDI was a potential military threat to the Soviet Union, and an indication of just how far behind technologically the Soviet Union was.

to West Germany (and Eastern Europe to Western Europe) to save the Soviet Union. Lenin's Brest-Litovsk gamble succeeded; Gorbachev's will more likely fail. In the Soviet (Eastern European) environment I have described, Gorbachev's failure to respond to the flight of East German tourists was the catalyst that produced one of the most remarkable political events of the twentieth century, *the mass extinction of Leninist regimes.*

Intellectual perplexity and personal amazement are natural responses to the events of 1989 in Eastern Europe and the Soviet Union. Two rare types of historical development are involved.

As a rule history is "protestant," not "catholic." The primary feature of world history tends to be cultural, institutional, and ideological diversity. But episodically a "universal" ideological "word" becomes institutional "flesh," an authoritatively standardized and centered institutional format dominates a highly diverse set of cultures. Christianity with its standardized Mass, universal use of Latin, and international stratum of bishops, all centered for hundreds of years in Rome, is one instance. Liberalism with the gold *standard*, parliamentary democracy, and free trade, all centered for a century in "the City" of London, is a second. Leninism between 1947 and 1989, with a vanguard party, "correct line," collectivization, and combat industrialization, centered in Moscow, is a third. To witness the emergence in the twentieth century of what Toynbee called a "civilization" is extraordinary. To also witness its mass extinction is unique, for mass extinctions are even rarer than the appearance of "universal" states.[19]

Paleontologists devised the concept *mass extinction* to describe the abrupt and accelerated termination of species that are distributed globally, or near-globally. Their speed, comprehensiveness, and the absence of species "origination" distinguish mass extinctions from background extinctions. In light of the fantastic quality of events in the Leninist world during 1989, this concept is pertinent and valuable.[20]

19. See Arnold Toynbee, *A Study of History*, abridgement of vols. 1–6 by D. C. Somervell (New York: Oxford University Press, 1974), pp. 1–48.

20. On "mass extinction," see Stephen Jay Gould, *The Flamingo's Smile* (New York: Norton, 1985), pp. 417–51; id., *Hen's Teeth and Horse's Shoes* (New

In the natural world, there are two contending explanations for mass extinctions (e.g., of dinosaurs at the end of the Cretaceous period). One is physical, the other biological. The physical explanation is that an asteroid struck the earth and drastically changed the climatic environment, which in a short (geological) time destroyed the dinosaurs. In contrast, and sometimes opposition, to this perspective is a more gradualist biological one that emphasizes general deterioration over a long period of time, ending again with a unique pattern of mass extinction. Stephen Jay Gould combines the two by arguing that the extinction of the dinosaurs was a "complex combination of dramatic end superimposed upon general deterioration."[21]

I have argued here that "biological" reasons best explain the extinction of the Leninist regime in the Soviet Union. All "big four" reasons are internal to the Soviet polity or to developments within its regime world (e.g., Poland), while each of the "little three" are "physical" (i.e., are external to the Soviet order). In examining the "extinction" of Leninism in Eastern Europe, one might opt for a "physical" explanation. Gorbachev's relativization of the CPSU and all its attendant ideological and policy correlates were the equivalent of a political asteroid for the Czechoslovak, Bulgarian, East German, *and* Romanian regimes. More than anything, these regimes, like their Brezhnevian prototype, were politically and ideologically corrupt and inertial, lacked purpose and confidence, and relied for power on their Soviet patron. Their "extinction" perfectly fits Gould's notion of a "dramatic end superimposed upon general deterioration."

It's worth staying with paleontology a while longer. Paleontologists distinguish between mass mortality and mass extinction. "Mortality is the death of a single individual or individu-

York: Norton, 1983), pp. 320–52; Kevin Padian et al., "The Possible Influences of Sudden Events on Biological Radiations and Extinctions," in H. D. Holland and A. F. Trendall, eds., *Patterns of Change in Earth Evolution* (New York: Springer-Verlag, 1984), pp. 77–102; David M. Raup, "Approaches to the Extinction Problem," *Journal of Paleontology* 52, no. 3 (May 1978): 228–34. I thank my colleague Kevin Padian for trying his best to educate me on the subject.

21. Gould, *Hen's Teeth*, p. 324.

als; extinction implies the elimination of the last member of a species, and is, of course, 'forever.'"[22] In light of this distinction, my claim that Leninism—as an international political order with distinct boundaries and international membership—is extinct might be considered premature. Literally, yes; esentially, no. A Leninist regime has three character-defining features: the primacy of social combat, of class war, in relation to its social host; a monopoly of historical-political insight, whose incarnation at any given time is the "correct line"; and the exclusivity of the Party as the sole locus of political leadership and enfranchisement. Khrushchev attenuated the Party's identity by marginalizing the first, and Gorbachev has rejected the remaining two. Given the "founding" stature of the Soviet regime, and its historical role as origin, authoritative author, and model to varying, but always substantial, degrees for all other members of the Leninist regime world, its "death" signals extinction, not simply widespread mortality, for the entire family. Presently one can point to "Vendée Leninism" in Cuba, China, Southeast Asia, and North Korea. But without (even an ambivalent) point of (Soviet) reference, it will wither. The only question left is, which will be the "last Leninist dinosaur"?

Several former Leninist regimes, including some in Eastern Europe and among the Soviet republics, will experience *pseudoextinction*. Regimes of this type—for example, Romania and Bulgaria—will maintain features directly related to their Leninist predecessor, but will be recognizably distinct from them.[23] Point: even regimes whose new political profiles contain elements recognizably derived from their Leninist predecessors will no longer be Leninist or part of an international regime world. In 1989 the world became more "protestant."

A final feature of mass extinctions is crucial to my thesis: *they typically affect more than one species*. In this respect, the collapse of European Leninism may be seen more as a political volcano than asteroid. A volcano's eruption initially affects a circumscribed area, in this case limited to Leninist regimes, but, depending on its force, the effects of its eruption gradually, but

22. Padian et al., "Possible Influences," p. 86.
23. Ibid.

dramatically, affect biota globally. The Leninist volcano of 1989 will have a comparable effect on liberal and "Third World" biota around the globe.

The obvious and immediate consequence of Leninism's mass extinction is the dramatic "clearing away" process in the area previously known as the Soviet bloc, empire, or Leninist regime world. Extinctions "make room" for new regime types. Poland, Hungary, and Czechoslovakia are examples (whether they become liberal or authoritarian capitalist). So is Romania, even with the continued powerful, even predominant, presence of leaders groomed by their Leninist parents and in-laws in the preceding regime to succeed. "Leninist progeny" may exercise power but they do (and know they do) so in a decisively different national and international environment. Priests without THE Church aren't Catholic; cadres without THE Party aren't Leninists. Pseudoextinction does not mean a "faked regime death."

The "clearing away" effect of a mass regime extinction has an international, not only national, impact. Ask East Germans! But rather than fixating on the German boundary change, one should appreciate the possibility that it signals a number of boundary changes of extraordinary import. Yugoslavia and the Soviet Union have already begun attempts at federal-confederal reconfiguration that may readily turn into national disintegration.

Nor can we expect the "clearing away" effect of the Leninist extinction to be self-contained, to be a political storm that considerately loses its force as it approaches Western and "Third World" "coasts." Nothing could be farther from the truth. For practically a century—no time at all geologically, but a politically substantial and consequential period—international and national boundaries and identities have been shaped by a Leninist regime world led in different ways and to different degrees by the Soviet Union. For half a century, we have thought in terms of East and West, and now there is no East as such. The primary axis of international politics has "disappeared." Thermonuclear Russia hasn't, but the Soviet Union/Empire most certainly has. Its "extinction" radically revises the framework within which the West, the United States itself, the "Third World," and the countries of

Eastern Europe, the former Russian Empire, and many nations in Asia have bounded and defined themselves.

The Leninist extinction will force the United States to reexamine the meaning of its national identity. The persistent hysterical strain in American political culture has expressed itself for some seventy years now as an acute anxiety over communism, its latest expression being an SDI "condom" capable of keeping out the Evil Empire's nuclear and ideological "AIDS." One could read Zbigniew Brzezinski and Samuel Huntington on political power in the United States and USSR and never get an inkling of this quite unpragmatic dimension of American political culture.[24] Fortunately, the movies *Dr. Strangelove, or: How I Learned to Stop Worrying and Love the Bomb* (1964) and the *Invasion of the Body Snatchers* (1956) brilliantly capture the hysteria Brzezinski and Huntington miss. But, with the remarkable exception of the South African Communist Party, one is hard put to find a genuine Leninist party anywhere in the world on anything more than inertial glide toward political extinction. That leaves the three-hundred-year-old hysterical dimension (from "witches" to "reds" to "Evil Empire") of American political culture in search of an expression. In short, internationally and nationally, the Leninist extinction will have a direct impact on the political self-definition of the United States.

The "Third World" has also bounded and defined itself from its Bandung beginning by distinguishing itself from the West *and* the Leninist world. Whatever shared political identity the "unaligned" world of African, Asian, and Middle Eastern states have had has for the most part been a negative one—neither liberal nor Leninist. The "Third World's" ideological identity, its geographical borders, and its capacity to secure developmental aid have all depended on the conflict between two "universal states," the liberal United States and the Leninist USSR. The "field" within which the "Third World" of genuine and fictive nation-states bounded and defined itself has disappeared. A telling example will be found in Latin America, where the state-security ideology of the Brazilian, Peruvian,

24. Zbigniew Brzezinski and Samuel P. Huntington, *Political Power USA/ USSR* (New York: Viking Press, 1971), pp. 7–71.

and Argentinian armies was oriented to and dependent on the international communist threat and Soviet–U.S. hostility. Alfred Stepan has argued that a key theme in the Brazilian military's ideology was that the "underdeveloped (or 'Third World') countries were under great internal pressure . . . because of global ideological conflict, which had deep ramifications for the internal security of the country."[25] The Leninist extinction removes a powerful rationale for one of the most persistent phenomena in Latin America, military coups.

The Leninist extinction will directly affect political life, national identities, and international boundaries throughout the world. The world has entered a period of "tectonic" and traumatic, complicated and confusing changes, a period that would test even the skills of "Halitherses, keenest among the old at reading birdflight into accurate speech."[26] As Theodore Sorensen has recently pointed out, the Leninist extinction presents us with a "conceptual vacuum."[27] How we characterize the features of the emerging world will directly affect its future boundaries and identities.

GENESIS

According to the Bible, "In the beginning . . . the earth was without form and void."[28] To say that this describes the political condition of the world today would exaggerate reality and frighten those academics and political figures for whom a known and controlled world is a psychological and political necessity. However, the global impact on boundaries and identities begun by the Leninist extinction is more likely to resemble the world "J" outlines in Genesis than the stingy and static view

25. See Alfred Stepan, *The Military in Politics: Changing Patterns in Brazil* (Princeton: Princeton University Press, 1971), p. 179. I thank Matt Marostica for suggesting this change in the Latin American military's new environment.
26. Homer, *The Odyssey*, trans. Robert Fitzgerald (New York: Vintage Classics, 1990), p. 23.
27. Theodore C. Sorensen, "Rethinking National Security," *Foreign Affairs* 69, no. 3 (Summer 1990): 1–19.
28. *The New Oxford Annotated Bible with the Apocrypha*, expanded edition, (New York: Oxford University Press, 1977), p. 1.

of development Francis Fukuyama presents in "The End of History?"

In Fukuyama's view, "the triumph of the West, of the Western *idea*, is evident first of all in the total exhaustion of viable systematic alternatives to Western liberalism."[29] His allowance for the "sudden appearance of new ideologies or previously unrecognized contradictions in liberal societies" is a throwaway. For him, Hitler, the Nazi revolution, and World War II were a "diseased bypath in the general course of European development."[30] Similarly, his allowance that the "fascist alternative may not have been played out yet in the Soviet Union" is a liberal Goliath's view of a possible fascist David. (I leave it to the reader to develop the analogy.)

Fukuyama's homogenization thesis finds its complement in Jerry Hough's version of Soviet history, in which a "Khomeini" Lenin-Stalin world is replaced by a "Western" Gorbachev generation reared in an urban milieu, with wives dressed in Yves Saint Laurent clothes (and at least one, Raisa Gorbachev, writing a dissertation in sociology) all ready to undo the Bolshevik Revolution's "unnatural break with Russian history."[31] But historical "exceptions" of this order (the Nazi and Bolshevik revolutions) don't prove the "liberal rule"; one almost destroyed it; and the other had the nuclear power to do it.

I have no quarrel with Fukuyama's observation that liberal capitalism is now the only politically global "civilization"; or with his suggestion that "the present world seems to confirm that the fundamental principles of socio-political organization have not advanced terribly far since 1806." But I do reject his idealist, ahistorical assertion that liberal capitalist "civilization" is the "end of history," the last "civilization," and in the next section I shall show why liberal capitalist democracy will always generate opposing challengers. In the immediate future, the Leninist extinction is likely dramatically, and in some instances traumatically, to challenge the national boundaries and political

29. Francis Fukuyama, "The End of History?" *The National Interest*, no. 16 (Summer 1989): 3.
30. Ibid., p. 16.
31. Jerry Hough, *Russia and the West, Gorbachev and the Politics of Reform* (New York: Simon & Schuster, 1988), see pp. 7–44.

identities of both "Third World" and Western nations, and the character of the Western world itself, as well as to create obvious and serious obstacles to stable, viable elite and regime replacements in the Soviet Union, Eastern Europe, and Asia.

Jehovah's response to a world "void and without form" was twofold: *he created boundaries between and "named" the new entities.* His task was greater, but ours is comparable—to respond to a world that will be increasingly unfamiliar, perplexing, and threatening; in which existing boundaries are attacked and changed; in which the challenge will be to establish new national/international boundaries and "name"—identify—the new entities. Fukuyama's "End of History" and my Genesis images are exaggerations; but if a theorist's only choice is what type of error to make, I offer mine as more accurate and helpful in assigning meaning and attempting to influence the type of world we are entering.

In one respect, we are currently on the type of "full sea" Shakespeare had in mind when he had Brutus observe: "There is a tide in the affairs of men, / Which, taken at the flood, leads on to fortune; / Omitted, all the voyage of their life / Is bound in shallows and in miseries."[32] In more mundane terms, we may have reached what Alexander Gerschenkron liked to call a "nodal point," a situation of opportunity and the related risk of missed opportunity.[33] However, even Shakespeare's and Gerschenkron's more contingent sense of developmental possibilities in risky environments may be too optimistic. Both Shakespeare and Gerschenkron's formulations suggest a discernible point where action brings about successful and (pace Fukuyama) *novel* developments. But the current environment in the Soviet Union increasingly resembles the "earth without form and void." In September 1990, Premier Ryzhkov felt compelled to say: "I don't want to dramatize things. I don't want to frighten anyone. I have no right to do that. But laws are not obeyed, resolutions are not obeyed. There are massive viola-

32. William Shakespeare, *The Tragedy of Julius Caesar*, act 4, sc. 3, lines 17–20.

33. Alexander Gerschenkron, *Economic Backwardness in Historical Perspective* (Cambridge, Mass.: Belknap Press, Harvard University Press, 1966).

tions, to say nothing of criminal violations."[34] We must temper our Enlightenment optimism with the recognition that a crisis is not automatically a developmental opportunity. Today and for the near future, crises, not developmental opportunities, may be the rule. Nodal points may *or may not* appear in the Soviet Union. Similarly in Eastern Europe, the facile pacific notion of "transiting to democracy" (where, having entered at the "Lenin station," one gets off at the "liberal station") is challenged by the not-so-latent ethnic-economic maelstrom that extends from Bulgaria to Czechoslovakia.

If not Fukuyama, if not Gerschenkron, aren't we left with spreading chaos? Possibly! Certainly in coming to grips with the Leninist extinction's global impact, we must be prepared to witness and respond simultaneously to chaos in some areas, nodal points in others, and the unlikely, but persistent, possibility of new "civilizations" emerging *inside and/or outside of the liberal West*.

The first imperative is to anticipate national environments characterized by conflict (along both civic-ethnic and regional fault lines) and an international environment whose primary characteristic will be turbulence, not the stereotyped, fundamentally apolitical quality of international life during the Cold War.[35] Turbulent environments produce more than their share of simultaneous emergencies (e.g., reconceiving or abolishing NATO, the disintegration of the Soviet Union, and Iraq's invasion of Kuwait) for a significant number of national and subnational elites. An emergency environment calls for different political skills and leaders than the sterotyped bipolar environment of largely contained, and occasionally ritualized, emergency characteristic of the Cold War.[36] On balance, in a turbulent world environment, leaders will count for more than institutions, and charisma for more than political economy. It is precisely in epochs when existing boundaries and identities,

34. Nikolai Ryzhkov quoted in the *Oakland Tribune*, September 30, 1990.

35. See my *Images of Détente and the Soviet Political Order* (Berkeley: Institute of International Studies, University of California, 1977).

36. The regular "discovery" of gaps between overstated Soviet and understated American military capacity in presidential election years is one example of ritualized emergency.

international and national, institutional and psychological, are challenged and assaulted that "great men," or men who want to be considered great, offer themselves as points of certainty and promise. We can expect their appearance. William James said: "Societies . . . at any given moment offer ambiguous potentials of development. . . . Leaders give the form."[37] That is particularly true of Genesis environments.

Charismatic leaders in the former Leninist world, in the now politically and ideologically adrift "Third World," and/or in the liberal West itself who are constrained to act in the context of existing state institutions will be of real, but limited, consequence—that is, they can affect the distribution of power in a larger or smaller area, but are unable to act as the catalyst for *a new way of life*. The truly remarkable feature of turbulent, dislocating, traumatic Genesis environments is the dissolution of existing boundaries and related identities and the corresponding potential to generate novel ways of life.

A way of life consists of a new ideology radically rejecting and demanding avoidance of existing institutions (social, economic, religious, military, administrative, political, cultural—all), and calling for the creation of alternative—mutually exclusive—institutions with "superior" features (this invidious element is essential); a new political idiom, language, and vocabulary that in Genesis-like manner "names" and establishes the boundaries of the new way of life; a new, powerful, and prestigious institution (be it religious, economic, military, or political); the emergence of a social base from which members and leaders can be drawn to complement and substantiate the new ideology; the assignment and acceptance of a heroic historical task and related strategy, explicitly calling for risk and sacrifice; and, finally, a core area—geographical or institutional—that for

37. William James, *The Will to Believe* (New York: Dover Publications, 1956), pp. 227–28. In *The Eighteenth Brumaire of Louis Napoleon* Marx asserted that: "Men make their own history, but they do not make it just as they please; they . . . make it under circumstances directly encountered, given and transmitted from the past. The tradition of all the dead generations weighs like a nightmare on the brain of the living" (New York: International Publishers, 1963), p. 15. While this is always true, what distinguishes Genesis environments is the relative leeway charismatic leaders enjoy in defining boundaries and identities.

whatever set of accidental and social reasons generates a surplus of resources consistent with the task of creating a new way of life.

Some historical examples should make the argument more evocative. Liberal ideology asserted a new social ontology in which the individual, not the corporate group, was the basis of social identity and responsibility. In the first instance, liberal capitalism (as Karl Polanyi so brilliantly grasped) was the call for a new way of life, not the mere redistribution of power.[38] Nazism and Leninism made ideological demands of the same order (not of the same content).

All new ways of life depend on a new political vocabulary. Absolutism is unimaginable without Jean Bodin's radical reformulation of authority and sovereignty. Perry Anderson may exaggerate a little, but there is much in his contention that "the practice of Absolutism corresponded to Bodin's theory of it."[39] Leninism is unimaginable without its language of "dictatorship of the proletariat," "vanguard party," "correct line," and "democratic centralism."

Similarly, every new way of life whether social, economic, political, or cultural has a novel institution—a partisan pattern of authoritative behavior, associated with it. Absolutism had the Court (Versailles), liberalism the market and Parliament, Leninism THE Party and plan.

For each new way of life there must be a social base uprooted from its previous identity,[40] available for a new one, attracted to and validated by the features of the new ideology; a social base from which a new elite stratum emerges: courtiers in absolutist states, ascetic entrepreneurs in liberal capitalist states, Bolshevik cadres in Leninist regimes, and the SS in the Third Reich.

For a new way of life to assert itself, a social minority must

38. Karl Polanyi, *The Great Transformation: The Political and Economic Origins of Our Time* (Boston: Beacon Press, 1965), esp. chs. 3–10.

39. Perry Anderson, *Lineages of the Absolutist State* (London: Humanities Press, NLB, 1974), p. 51.

40. The classic statement about "social mobilization" is Karl Deutsch, "Social Mobilization and Political Development," *American Political Science Review* 55, no. 3 (December 1961): 493–514.

completely identify with and accept an imperative task—for example, establishing the superiority (not simply power) of the king; free trade and the market; "race" and Führer; Party and *kollektiv*—for a critical period of time during which new elites, practices, organizations, and beliefs institutionally coagulate.

Finally, the emergence of a new way of life requires the existence of a core site generating, concentrating, and then "exporting" a surplus of leadership talent and resources to the "unreconstructed" society it intends to transform: Versailles, Cluny, THE Party, London, Rome, Mecca-Medina, and Gdansk all played this creative role.

I am not prophesying the inevitable appearance of a new way of life in response to the Leninist extinction. I am saying the "clearing away" and traumatizing effect of this event will act as a stimulus and create potentials for such a development within the former Leninist world, the West, and the "Third World." In the next decade and beyond, an unusual number of leaders and movements will appear making claims about a new way of life or the restoration of a former period of glory. Saddam Hussein's call to the Arab/Muslim nation is only the first effort of this kind. Most aspirants will fail; perhaps all of them. But their appearance and actions will reflect and contribute to a world marked by increasing national and international disorder. We can expect conflict over geographical boundaries in the Soviet Union, Yugoslavia, Canada, and the Middle East (where Pakistani visions are as great a potential threat as the Iraqi). We can expect civic-ethnic violence in any number of countries around the world. The United Sates will have to deal with a growing number of "intermestic"[41] issues, issues like Israel, South Africa, Mexico, and Canada that are simultaneously national and international. All this does mean the "end of history," certainly that of the past forty-five years; and possibly that of the past two hundred years. It does not mean the inexorable assimilation of the world to the current liberal Western way of life, or even the continued adaptive "strength" of the liberal West.

41. See Bayless Manning, "The Congress, the Executive, and Intermestic Affairs: Three Proposals," *Foreign Affairs* 55, no. 2 (January 1977): 306–24.

THE WEST AND THE "REST"

The introduction of disorder and turbulence, appearance of charismatic leaders and movements, and possible evolution of new ways of life will occur in a political universe that at present is inertial and thus fairly well delineated nationally and internationally. History is more often "protestant" in its cultural and institutional diversity than "catholic" and uniform over cultural space, but that diversity is finite. As Miss Marple once observed: "You'd be surprised if you knew how very few distinct types there are in all."[42] Indeed in the past hundred years, liberal capitalist democracy, fascism/Nazism, Leninism, and variants of military rule exhaust the range of regime types. To predict the emergence and proliferation of Genesis environments, as I do in this essay, doesn't require developments to be either apocalyptic or unintelligible. Precisely because Genesis environments develop in, out of, and in opposition to more delineated and "named" environments, the theorist is positioned to grasp the connections and meanings of some developments. I completely agree with "William of Baskerville's" commentary: "At a time when as philosopher I doubt the world has an order, I am consoled to discover, if not an order, at least a series of connections in small areas of the world's affairs."[43] With the (initial) extinction of fascism/Nazism, and now the extinction of Leninism, the question is what types of political developments are likely in a world dominated by an uncontested liberal capitalist democratic "civilization," or way of life. I confidently predict one.

Liberal capitalist democracy has generated a heterogeneous set of opponents: Romantic poets, Persian ayatollahs, aristocrats, the Catholic Church, and fascists. However, for all the genuine and substantial differences separating these diverse oppositions, one can detect a shared critique. Liberal capitalist democracy is seen as one-sided in its emphasis on individualism, materialism, achievement, and rationality. The Roman

---

42. Agatha Christie, *The Murder at the Vicarage* (New York: Dell, 1958), p. 193.

43. Umberto Eco, *The Name of the Rose* (New York: Harcourt Brace Jovanovich, 1980), p. 394.

Catholic preference for the family over the individual and the Nazi preference for "race" in place of the individual are radically different critiques, but the general critique is the same: liberal capitalism fails adequately to provide for the essential group needs and dimension of human existence.

Similarly, liberal capitalism has regularly evoked passionate criticism and hostility in connection with its materialist bias and emphasis on achievement, its tendency to ignore or marginalize the human need for security, and its repression of expressive human action. But nothing has been more central to liberal capitalism, and more capable of sustaining and eliciting opposition over the past two hundred years, than its rational impersonalism. Liberal capitalist democracy's rejection of the heroic ethic, awe, and mystery that throughout most of history was seen as separating MAN from the world of animals and necessity has generated countermovements as diverse as those of the English Romantic poets and Roman Catholicism, and as perverse as Nazism and Stalinism.

My point is that liberal capitalist democracy's victories over the Catholic Church, then fascism and Nazism, and now Leninism are particularly momentous, but most of all *particular* victories. Precisely because liberal capitalist democracy has a bounded, distinctive, *partisan* identity, it cannot be all or do all things in equal measure. As long as the West retains its partisan liberal capitalist democratic identity, it will regularly generate movements—internally and externally—opposing or attacking, attempting to reform or destroy it; movements that in one form or another will emphasize the value of group membership, expressive behavior, solidary security, and heroic action. One locus for such is the "Third World."

Beginning with India's independence in 1947, the "Third World" has been regarded by many as a source of promise. For some in the West, it was the promise of actually extending and revitalizing liberal capitalist democracy. Elective village councils in India, colonially sponsored "gentry" in Nigeria, and the tradition of "consensual" decision making in East Africa were to enrich and extend the promise of the West. With Khrushchev, the Soviet Union added its political and ideological enthusiasm for (and thereby created a rivalry with the United States over) the "Third World." It was to be the Soviet Union's international "virgin lands." West African and Egyptian leaders became "Heroes of Lenin"; Fidel Castro a Leninist apostle.

But some "Third World" political leaders, intellectuals, and Western supporters went further and saw it as the source of revolutionary promise; the locus of a novel, compelling, better way of life, neither liberal nor Leninist. For Frantz Fanon, it was a question "of the Third World starting a new history of Man, a history which will have regard to the sometimes prodigious theses which Europe has put forward, but which will also not forget Europe's crimes, of which the most horrible was committed in the heart of man, and consisted of the pathological tearing apart of his functions and the crumbling away of his unity." "Third World" countries were "to do their utmost to find their own particular values and methods and a style which shall be peculiar to them."[44]

But the "promise" hasn't (yet) been realized. No new way of life has emerged anywhere in the "Third World." No new ideology has been embraced by leaders who go on to create a new political vocabulary for, and recruit a new leadership stratum from, a mobilized social base that "populates" innovative institutions, pursues historically extraordinary tasks, and draws from, as well as relies on, a powerful, prestigious core area. No London, Moscow, Mecca, or Rome has appeared in the "Third World." In stark contrast to a new international way of life, for the most part one finds depressingly familiar examples of tyranny, corruption, famine, and rage in *pre*national settings. Still, it is premature to write the "Third World" off as a potential source of a new way of life. After all, the ex-colonial world has been independent for less than half a century.

The core sites around which novel clusters of institutions comprising a new way of life develop are often marginal areas: the development of monotheism in Israel is one example; the emergence of liberal capitalism in a fragment of the Eurasian continent that for most of its existence was quite underdeveloped—one might even risk saying, backward—is another. Do

44. Frantz Fanon, *The Wretched of the Earth* (New York: Grove Press, 1966), pp. 255, 78.

such areas exist in the "Third World"? Perhaps South Africa![45]
It offers the analyst a striking tableau: intraracial violence between Inkatha and the ANC, interracial violence between Af-
rikaaner *verkramptes* and the nonwhite population; the sole militant communist party in the world (the SACP); and an African
leader, Nelson Mandela, who skillfully linked the African black
struggle to American politics and ideology with his suggestion
to the U.S. Congress that "one of the benefits that should accrue to both our peoples and to the rest of the world should
surely be that this complex South African society, which has
known nothing but racism for three centuries, should be transformed into an oasis of good race relations where the black
shall to the white be sister and brother . . . an equal human
being, both citizens of the world."[46] South Africa's industrial,
racially conflictual, tribal-urban, Christian, and revolutionary
society is a potential recipe for destructive brutality and/or constructive realities affecting a good part of the world.

However, even if there is (some) reason to consider South
Africa a "long-shot" core area for a new way of life, there are
"lesser" developments in the "Third World" (including South
Africa) with more immediate developmental implications in
light of, and in response to, the Leninist extinction and the
victory of the West.

I want to examine four: wars between "Third World" countries, the status of the NICs, and the related issues of democracy, immigration, and above all, Movements of Rage.

The Leninist extinction favors an increase in the number of
wars fought between "Third World" nations. The geographical
boundaries of many "Third World" countries are arbitrary,
and their national identities fictive.[47] The Soviet–U.S. rivalry
supported existing boundaries, insofar as any change would
indicate a possible shift of influence toward one and away from

45. To my mind, the best analysis of the current South African situation
is Robert Price's *South Africa: The Process of Political Transformation* (New York:
Oxford University Press, 1991).

46. Nelson Mandela, *Address to the U.S. Congress, June 26, 1990* (Washington, D.C.: Washington Office on Africa, 1990).

47. See Carl Rosberg and Robert Jackson's formulation of the "juridical
state" in "Why Africa's Weak States Persist: The Empirical and Juridical in
Statehood," *World Politics* 35, no. 1 (October 1982): 1–25.

the other superpower. Minus that rivalry, latent "Third World" irredenta will more readily and aggressively express themselves. Their significance will vary from the regionally contained Liberian variant, with its civil war and consequent invasion by several squabbling West African nations, to the Iraqi invasion of Kuwait and its consequent international repercussions. The Iraqi invasion of Kuwait is an example of a "Third World" leader attempting to create favorable new boundaries and political identities in what he sees as a disrupted, promising, and threatening environment.[48]

The emergence of the newly industrialized countries (NICs) in the "Third World" predates the mass extinction of Leninist regimes. I am not primarily concerned with the institutional strategies or the cultural and international settings that underlie their economic development. My focus is on their political identity. Not one is a stable liberal capitalist democracy. Nor do I see any reason to think democracy will fare well in any part of the "Third World." Like individualism, democracy is a historically rare and deviant phenomenon, requiring not only a certain level of economic and social development, talented leadership, and a dash of "fortuna," but also *intense cultural trauma.* As Ralf Dahrendorf has noted, it took a far from predictable sequence of Nazi revolution, American victory, and democratization to create liberal capitalist democracy in West Germany.[49] It took war, American victory, occupation, constitution-writing, and military protection to help create Japan's incomplete liberal democratization. The democratic movement in Poland, Solidarity, is unimaginable without the traumatic dislocation and migration of five million Poles to Poland's western territories in the context and aftermath of World War II. Nor did Spain and Greece simply "transit" to democracy; rather each experienced a wrenching civil war in the twentieth century that has a direct

48. The "promise": Saddam Hussein might have seen the end of the Cold War creating a larger zone of indifference for regional actors. The "threat": at the same time he may have concluded that the Cold War's end put a premium on staking one's claim in the Middle East before the full brunt of the American-Israeli military monopoly (with the Soviet withdrawal) was felt.

49. Ralf Dahrendorf, *Society and Democracy in Germany* (Garden City, N.Y.: Doubleday, Anchor Books, 1969), ch. 25.

sociocultural bearing on their ability to sustain liberal capitalist democratic constitutions.

In a world environment likely to become increasingly turbulent, a world in which political boundaries are challenged, political identities at stake, and the political rules of the game unclear, countries with democracy on their political agenda, like South Korea and South Africa, are likely to keep it on the agenda and out of power. I am amazed by the facility with which Latin Americanists, who quite recently were gloomily talking, conferencing, and writing about the "breakdown of democracy," are now enthusing about the "transition to democracy," not only in Latin America but, by acontextual extrapolation, in Eastern Europe and the Soviet Union. Economic and social development places democracy on a nation's political agenda; the *irreversible* transition to democracy depends on quite different sociocultural and institutional factors. Argentina's history bears perpetual witness to this. More economically distressed regimes, like the Philippine, whose democratic institutional facade finds little correspondence or support in the country's social and cultural "constitution" or the military's political cultures (seven coups have been attempted in the five or so years of Corazon Aquino's governance) are even more likely to find the *breakthrough, not transition,* to democracy beyond their current reach. Even India's circumscribed, faulted, but substantial democracy is threatened by a growing potential for national disintegration along regional, linguistic, and religious lines as it loses its Congress-based pan-Indian generation of bureaucrats, officers, and politicians.

For years, perhaps decades to come, one is more likely to see the emigration of people out of, rather than the immigration of democracy into, the "Third World." And emigration out of the "Third World" means immigration to the West. The most immediate and significant consequence of liberalism's "historic victory" is not the exporting of liberal capitalist democracy to the "Third World" and Eastern Europe; it is the importing of "Third World" *and* Eastern European populations into the West. This immigration directly challenges the balance of civic-ethnic identities within the West itself.

In the near future, the most extraordinary development

within the "Third World" may be the emergence and victory of movements of rage. These also predate the Leninist extinction, but it creates environments within which Nazi-like revolutionary substitutes for Leninism will appear.

I am thinking of movements that to date have not been theoretically connected: of the Mulele uprising in Kwilu province in what is now Zaire, of the Tupamaros in Uruguay, of the Khalq in Afghanistan, of the Khmer Rouge in Kampuchea, and of Sendero Luminoso in Peru. I am referring to revolutionary movements with a Leninist/Maoist vocabulary but a Fanonist ethos and character; movements whose motive force is nihilistic rage against the legacy of Western colonialism. These movements typically originate among provincial elites; men and women filled with hate for the culture of the capital city, and at the same time angered by their exclusion from it. Their murderous rage is directed against those "contaminated" by contact with Western culture—for example, those wearing ties, speaking French, or educated in a Western university.[50]

Movements of Rage are nihilistic political responses to failure; the failure of the "Third World" to create productive economies, equitable societies, ethical elites, and sovereign nations. They are desperate responses to the fact that nothing seems to work. The anticipated magical effect of adopting the label "one-party democracy," or "Leninist," or (as is becoming fashionable) "market capitalist democracy" has turned out (and will turn out) to be weak developmental magic for most "Third World" countries. Movements of Rage are violent nativist responses to failure, frustration, and perplexity. It is ironic that the man who called on the "Third World" to generate a superior way of life is the same man who claims that "violence is like a royal pardon. The colonised man finds his freedom in and through violence"; and "violence alone, violence committed by the people, violence organised and educated by its leaders,

---

50. The apparently murderous intensity of Iraqi behavior in occupied Kuwait can in good measure be characterized as booty and pillage behavior. I suspect that is inadequate. In addition, Hussein may well have viewed Kuwait as a parasitic, Western-corrupted, and contaminated society that not only had to be politically reintegrated into and economically exploited by Arabic Iraq but also ruthlessly purged of its Western cultural "decay."

makes it possible for the masses to understand social truths and gives the key to them."[51] True, Fanon was speaking to the colonized, but the Pol Pots, Hafizullah Amins, and Guzmans are quite ready to apply Fanon to the culturally "colonized" people of Kampuchea, Afghanistan, and Peru.

To my knowledge only one person has identified this phenomenon, V. S. Naipaul. While academia has had all of its attention monopolized by studies of state-building, rational choice, and the political economy of commodity regimes, in *The Return of Eva Peron*, and *Among the Believers*, Naipaul has insightfully described the potential in the "Third World" for fanatical nativist state-destroying movements that treat the economy as booty.[52]

One can question whether I have established a sufficient case for the existence of a new type of revolutionary movement, a variant of fascism/Nazism in the "Third World." In addition, one should critically observe that very few of these movements have come to power, and when, as in Afghanistan and Kampuchea, they have, they self-destruct. So did the Nazi regime— at the cost of fifty million lives. And, had the Nazis possessed nuclear weapons, Kenneth Waltz's thesis that proliferation of nuclear weapons reduces the chances of war (when the opponent has a protected second-strike capability) would have been put to the test—and come up short! Waltz fails to understand that there are different types of cultural-ideological rationality.[53] For him, anyone considering the destruction of their own regime is mad, psychotic. *But the issue isn't psychological; it is primarily cultural and ideological.* Pol Pot wasn't *mad*; rather he operates within a cultural and ideological framework that rejects the cultural premises underpinning a MAD strategy.[54]

51. Fanon, *Wretched of the Earth*, pp. 67, 117.

52. V. S. Naipaul, *The Return of Eva Peron* (New York: Vintage Books, 1981), and *Among the Believers: An Islamic Journey* (New York: Vintage Books, 1982). It would be interesting to see how many academics dealing with Latin America, the Middle East, South Asia and comparative politics assign any portion of these books.

53. As do the "enthusiasts" who belong to the school of rat(ional) choice theory.

54. See Kenneth N. Waltz, "Nuclear Myths and Political Realities," *American Political Science Review* 84, no. 3 (September 1990): 731–47.

I mentioned another potential criticism of my Movements of Rage thesis: very few have ever come to power. True, but that tells us very little about the potential for these movements in a post-Leninist world, unless one believes that the Leninist extinction is a self-contained event. The burden of my entire argument has been to challenge that assumption. In the new, more turbulent Genesis environments emerging in the aftermath of the Leninist extinction, species that didn't fare well earlier may do much better. After all, mammals did not appear *after* the dinosaurs. Rather, as long as dinosaurs existed, mammals were rather puny things with a restricted range of adaptive radiation. They did not grow in strength or "come to power" until the "clearing away" of the dinosaurs. In short, one cannot gauge the potential for future Movements of Rage by generalizing from their failure prior to the Leninist extinction.

Instead, one must imagine a "Third World" increasingly neglected by the United States and Soviet Union (as each attends to domestic crises) except when a very clear and present emergency occurs in a strategic location; a "Third World" where aggression occurs more and more frequently; a world where the technology of nuclear weapons becomes more widely dispersed; a world where the few democracies that have any standing (such as that of India) fail; and where checks on emigration to the West remove a vital escape valve. In that far from fantastic world, the "puny rage mammal" might indeed become a significantly disruptive international force, especially if it appears in a country like Mexico or Egypt.[55] This may be too speculative for many in academia, with its narrow perspective, one "with plenty of brain, but with a brain which, while seeing clearly and in detail all that is on the horizon, is incapable of conceiving that the horizon may change."[56] But that is what has already happened.

The Leninist extinction is not a historical surgical strike that will leave liberal and "Third World" "friendlies" unaffected. Everyone's horizons, including the West's, will be dramatically affected. But doesn't the worldwide rush to liberal capitalist

55. Another candidate, though at first glance of less international import, is Haiti under its new leader, Father Jean-Bertrand Aristide.

56. *The Recollections of Alexis de Tocqueville*, trans. Alexander Teixeira de Mattos (New York: Meridian Books, World Publishing Co., 1966), p. 18.

democratic idioms, policies, and institutional facades refute this claim? What of the shift by socialist parties to positions that differ insignificantly from those of their historic capitalist antagonists;[57] the tentative moves toward a multiparty system in African "socialist" regimes;[58] the belief by many Eastern Europeans in the market's miraculous quality? These are not illusory phenomena; they are real—but how substantial, consistent, or persistent? If one interprets these phenomena in developmental, rather than static, terms, their significance also rests in the expected surge of anger that will follow the failure (in most cases) of the market and electoral democracy to produce sovereign, productive, equitable nations in the greater part of Eastern Europe, the former Soviet Union, and the "Third World."

Those who currently presume a permanent identity and universal triumph for the liberal capitalist democratic way of life, should remember Eric Hobsbawm's observation that "the progress of democratic politics between 1880 and 1914 foreshadowed neither its permanence nor its universal triumph"[59] and read Max Weber's passage about the liberal capitalist "iron cage":

> No one knows who will live in this cage in the future [Weber writes], or whether at the end of this tremendous development, entirely new prophets will arise, or there will be a great rebirth of old ideas and ideals, or, if neither, mechanized petrification, embellished with a sort of convulsive self-importance. For of the last stage of this cultural development, it might well be truly said: "Specialists without spirit, sensualists without heart; this nullity imagines that it has attained a level of civilization never before achieved."[60]

57. See Seymour Martin Lipset's contribution to Chirot, ed., *Crisis of Leninism.*

58. On the rationale of African "socialism," see my "Scientific Socialist Regimes in Africa: Political Differentiation, Avoidance, and Unawareness," in Carl G. Rosberg and Thomas M. Callaghy, eds., *Socialism in Sub-Saharan Africa: A New Assessment* (Berkeley: Institute of International Studies, University of California, 1979), pp. 133–73.

59. Eric Hobsbawm, *The Age of Empire, 1875–1914* (New York: Pantheon Books, 1987), p. 111.

60. Max Weber, *The Protestant Ethic and the Spirit of Capitalism* (New York: Scribner's, 1958), p. 182.

Weber balances his pessimistic and damning comments about liberal capitalist nullities with an open appreciation of the possibility of "entirely new prophets," perhaps even the "rebirth of old ideas and ideals" (in the Western world.) Daniel Bell captures this openness (though not the associated risks) when he says: "We stand . . . with a clearing ahead of us. The exhaustion of Modernism, the aridity of Communist life, the tedium of the unrestrained self, and the meaninglessness of the monolithic political chants all indicate that a long era is coming to a close"[61]—an era whose general origin was the Enlightenment and the French Revolution, and whose particular origin was the "big bang" of World War II.

How the West responds to this "clearing" and what new boundaries and political identities emerge depend more than anything else on how the United States interprets and reacts to the Leninist extinction. To date, the reaction and interpretation have been *inertial and absolutist.* The Bush administration's fetishlike emphasis on maintaining NATO is a good example of inertia.

The American response to Iraq's invasion of Kuwait should be seen in two lights: first, as a warranted attack against an aggressive, Nazi-like Movement of Rage; second, as evidence of the United States's attempt to reassume the absolute global responsibility of the 1950s. With his Gulf policy, President Bush tried to force the world to stay within its postwar boundaries and identities. This effort is very consistent with what Louis Hartz insightfully called American liberal absolutism. According to Hartz, what has distinguished the Unites States, particularly since the Civil War, is the near-absolute quality of liberal capitalist (Protestant) democracy as the (ideological) American way of life. The consequence: an inability and unwillingness on the part of U.S. political elites to grasp or accept our cultural, ideological, and national relativity. As Hartz puts it, the issue for the United States is whether "a nation can compensate for the uniformity of its domestic life by contact with alien cultures outside it." He asks "whether American liberalism can acquire

---

61. Daniel Bell, *The Cultural Contradictions of Capitalism* (New York: Basic Books, 1978), p. xxix.

through external experience *that sense of relativity* . . . which European liberalism acquired through an internal experience of social diversity and social conflict."[62]

Throughout the twentieth century, the United States has oscillated between national messianism and isolationism, two sides of the same absolutist coin. How the political universe evolves depends in good measure on whether the United States stays within the stingy confines of absolutism: the belief that unless we are omnipotent, we must be impotent, currently expressed in the dead-end debate over decline (Paul Kennedy: "We are!" Joseph S. Nye, Jr., and Fukuyama: "We're not!").[63] I see two competing political futures: one dogmatic, the other tolerant.

Should the United States continue to cast itself primarily as military leader of the West, the domestic results will be increasing economic disorder, and consequent racial violence that will make the 1960s look benign. Internationally, conflict will increase, with a Japan that is more culturally absolutist than we are ideologically absolutist. Western Europe will explicitly reject the reactionary American conception of Western leadership. The U.S. response to these developments is likely to be a bitterly isolationist mentality, coupled domestically to a nativist backlash against the hostile ethnic/racial fragmentation (described by some as multicultural diversity) manifesting itself in the United States.

In that setting, with the West at odds with and in itself; the former Leninist world, far from having "transited" to liberal capitalist democracy, forced to cope with a growing civic versus ethnic maelstrom (exacerbated by latent boundary conflicts);[64]

62. Louis Hartz, *The Liberal Tradition in America* (New York: Harcourt, Brace & World, 1955), p. 14. The last chapter, "America and the World," remains as insightful and pertinent as ever about U.S. foreign policy.

63. Paul Kennedy, *The Rise and Fall of the Great Powers* (New York: Random House, 1987); for an example of Nye's position, see his "No, the U.S. Isn't in Decline," *New York Times*, editorial, October 3, 1990. (Actually, Nye is literally correct; for the time being it is merely in denial.)

64. I discuss this in "A Research Agenda for Eastern Europe," *East European Politics and Societies* 4, no. 2 (Spring 1990): 193–97, and more thoroughly in chapter 6 above. Adam Michnik has recently made the same point to a much wider audience in a typically compelling manner. See his "The Two Faces of Europe," *New York Review of Books*, July 19, 1990.

and a "Third World" reacting to economic, cultural, and political failure with increasing rage, one should not ignore the potential political role of the Roman Catholic Church. Like fascism, the Church may find new life in a post-Leninist world. Antiliberal, anticapitalist, antimodern, THE Church retains and espouses an identity, *a way of life*, that is corporate, solidary, charismatic, and international. Under Pope John Paul II, a Roman Catholic Church could serve as a focal point for a movement against liberal capitalist democracy embracing religio-ethnic movements in Eastern Europe, right-wing anti-immigration movements in the West, and some Movements of Rage in the "Third World" (after all, the Church did manage its relations with the Nazis quite well). A development of this order would surprise many, and shock others, but Genesis environments are full of surprises and shocks.

In shaping those environments, in delineating new boundaries and "naming" new political entities, at least one thing works in favor of Pope John Paul II, and even Gorbachev: unlike the U.S. president they know Fukuyama (and Hegel) are wrong. They know we stand on the threshold of a decisive reordering of world boundaries and identities, and, as the Pontifical Biblical Institute's "Father Jorge," Malachi Martin, says, they are actively attempting to shape the outcome of what he calls the "millennium endgame."[65] Both John Paul II and Gorbachev proceed from a dogmatically intolerant ideological base. Cardinal Siri "spoke" for Lenin when he asserted: "Tolerance . . . is not a virtue. It's a mere expedient, when you cannot do otherwise."[66] Roman Catholic dogma faces challenges within the Church, and Leninist dogma has been eroded to the point of extinction in Moscow. But dogma remains actively dominant in the Church, and inertially/latently dominant in what is left of the CPSU. It would be historically perverse if the West, specifically the United States, were to deny its greatest historical achievement—religious and political toleration—by dogmati-

---

65. Malachi Martin, *The Keys of This Blood: The Struggle for World Dominion between Pope John Paul II, Mikhail Gorbachev, & the Capitalist West* (New York: Simon & Schuster, 1990), passim.
66. Ibid., p. 607.

cally adhering to a liberal absolutist vision of its place in the
West and the world.

A *tolerant future* world depends on the United States recasting—not rejecting—its self-conception, its place in the West,
and its relation to the former Leninist and "Third" worlds. The
key to a more tolerant future is a relative sense of American
identity, domestically and internationally.

Domestically, this means rejecting the absolute emphasis
many now place on ethnic, racial, and gender identities with its
"tower of Babel" implications; *and* the backlash "white castle"
alternative. A nation that invented the inclusive political party
must now invent an ideological and institutional framework for
integrating privately diverse and publicly shared identities.

Internationally, the United States should reject George
Bush's assertion that the twenty-first century will be an American century. Such a view ignores and denies any number of
changes in international politics. It certainly ignores Chalmers
Johnson's sober observation that the Cold War is over and Japan and Germany won. Their inclusion as permanent members
of the U.N. Security Council would be a major recognition that
although central, the role of the United States in international
politics is relative. One unfortunate consequence of U.S. military success in Kuwait could be a reinforcement of the Bush
administration's absolute notion of the United States's international leadership; a notion that is part of our post–World War
II legacy and bears directly on the future of the West.

The West has survived and thrived because of its relatively
supple identity. Based on three revolutions that created the
grounds for liberal capitalist democracy: the British, American,
and French, the Western way of life has a "trinitarian" base
(unlike the monotheistic Leninist world, with its unique October Revolution). This helps explain the remarkable shift from
nineteenth-century British to twentieth-century American
leadership of the liberal world. The shift was not automatic, or
free of conflict and risk. In fact, it occurred in response to the
near-mortal assault on the West by the Nazis. The immediate
question is whether the United States will facilitate or obstruct
a twenty-first-century shift in Western leadership. Will it take a
trauma comparable to the Great Depression and Nazi assault to

recast the West's self-conception and leadership in response to the changes that will follow the Leninist extinction?

Japan is a most unlikely contender for Western leadership. So is unified Germany. A united Western Europe is a more likely candidate, but the most desirable outcome would be a more integral relationship between all three parts of the Western "trinity," with the United States more interested in joining the Common Market and less obsessed with maintaining an American NATO. A U.S. initiative deliberately and prudently to integrate the economies, cultures, and, in certain respects, military and governmental operations of the United States, Japan, and Western Europe would be difficult, but not as costly as a failure to imagine that "future."

A more humble, less smug, appreciation of Eastern Europe's discovery in 1989 of political ethics and individual dignity is called for. A more deliberate, even organized, approach to some "Third World" issues and countries, one that relativizes the political autonomy of all involved—Western and non-Western—should be considered. These new "First World"–"Third World" relations should at one and the same time be more intrusive and less callous than those now in place if they are not to contribute to the appearance of Movements of Rage.

A world without Leninism must decide whether fundamental social change always proceeds from traumatic, uncontrollably violent "big bangs," or whether reason and courage can limit violence, respect surprise and novelty, and "name" them in a tolerant spirit.

8

THE LENINIST LEGACY

CONCEPTUAL GEOGRAPHY

Eastern Europe's boundaries—political, ideological, economic, and military—have been radically redefined twice in less than a century. At the end of World War 1, "the disappearance of the Austro-Hungarian Empire (a truly momentous event in European history) left a huge gap in the conceptual geography of the continent. Of what did Central Europe now consist? What was East, what West in a landmass whose political divisions had been utterly and unrecognizably remade within a single lifetime"?[1] In 1989, the Soviet bloc became extinct; communist parties in every Eastern European country added the loss of political power to their earlier loss of ideological purpose during the phase of "real socialism"; and the Soviet Union, the "stern, . . . impersonal, perpetual Center"[2] of this imperium, not only tolerated but instigated its collapse. The result is a gap in Europe's "conceptual geography" no less significant than that of 1918.

In 1987, Dan Chirot and I pointed out that "because of its historical experience, the diversity of its cultural traditions, and its vulnerability to big power interference, Eastern Europe has had, and will continue to have, a uniquely creative role in producing ideas and experimental solutions for solving the major problems of the modern world. Not only a number of key artistic and literary movements, but also political ideologies

This essay is also to be published in Ivo Banac, ed., *Eastern Europe in Revolution* (Ithaca, N.Y.: Cornell University Press, 1992). It appears here in slightly different form.

1. Tony Judt, "The Rediscovery of Central Europe," *Dædalus* 119, no. 1 (Winter 1990), p. 25.

2. John Le Carré, *The Spy Who Came In from the Cold* (New York: Dell, 1963), p. 144.

such as fascism, socialism, and peasantism received major innovative contributions from Eastern and Central Europe in the first half of the twentieth century."[3] The mass extinction of Leninist regimes in Eastern Europe in 1989 is a dramatic, promising, and unsettling event, and its immediate consequence is a direct challenge to the boundaries and identities of the region and its constituent parts. Whether the transformation is looked at as an imperative, process, or outcome, Eastern Europe is in the midst of redefining its cultural frames of reference, political and economic institutions, and political-territorial boundaries. Once again, Eastern Europe has become a laboratory in which a set of experiments are being undertaken under less than controlled conditions. The likelihood is that most will fail, but some will succeed, and many of those will have predominantly anti–democratic capitalist features. Whatever the results of the current turmoil in Eastern Europe, one thing is clear: the new institutional patterns will be shaped by the "inheritance" and legacy of forty years of Leninist rule.

THE "INHERITANCE"

Confronted with a turbulent environment, there is a quite understandable, predictable, and observable tendency by intellectuals to restore certainty idiomatically. That certainly is the case with Eastern Europe. One of its most pronounced expressions is the fetishlike repetition of the phrase "transition to democracy," as if saying it often enough, and inviting enough Latin American scholars from the United States to enough conferences in Eastern Europe (and the Soviet Union), will magically guarantee a new democratic capitalist telos in place of the ethnic, economic, and territorial maelstrom that is the reality today. One is reminded of Mephisto's observation: "Men usually believe, if only they hear words, / That there must also be some sort of meaning."[4] From the "transition to democracy" perspective, Eastern Europe resembles a historical blackboard written

3. Daniel Chirot and Ken Jowitt, "Beginning E.E.P.S.," *Eastern European Politics and Societies* 1, no. 1 (Winter 1987): 2.
4. *Goethe's FAUST* (Garden City, N.Y.: Doubleday, Anchor Books, 1963), p. 253.

on with Leninist chalk for forty years, erased (largely) by Soviet actions in 1989, and waiting, tabula rasa, to be written on now in liberal capitalist script.

However, any substantial analysis of democracy's and market capitalism's chances in Eastern Europe must interpret the maelstrom itself, and that means coming to analytical grips with the cultural, political, and economic "inheritance" of forty years of Leninist rule. For Western analysts to treat the Leninist legacy the way Leninists after 1948 treated their own Eastern European inheritance—namely, as a collection of historically outmoded "survivals" bound to lose their cultural, social, and psychological significance—would be an intellectual mistake of the first order. All cultural and institutional legacies shape their successors. Peter Brown's creation of an age—late antiquity— rests on his rejection of a simplistic dichotomy of continuity versus discontinuity; on his appreciation of novel, not absolute, transformations of the Roman legacy.[5]

Some historical legacies positively contribute to the development of successor states. Karl van Wolferen presents a powerful (to me, compelling) case to support his argument that Japan's current economic success is directly related "to the authoritarian institutions and techniques dating from the first half of the twentieth century."[6]

The Leninist legacy is currently shaping, and will continue to shape, developmental efforts and outcomes in Eastern Europe—though not in a "Japanese" manner. Regarding the Leninist legacy, Timothy Garton Ash says: "Perhaps the beginning of wisdom is to recognize that what communism has left behind is an extraordinary mish-mash."[7] The comment is perceptive, suggestive, and self-defeating. The Leninist legacy is conflicting, confusing, *and,* fortunately, identifiable. Otherwise we are left with two inadequate and unacceptable alternatives: the simplistic application/imposition of (a very theoretically thin) "tran-

5. See Peter Brown, *The Making of Late Antiquity* (Cambridge, Mass.: Harvard University Press, 1978).

6. Karl van Wolferen, *The Enigma of Japanese Power* (New York: Random House, Vintage Books, 1990), ch. 14.

7. Timothy Garton Ash, "Eastern Europe: Après le Deluge: Nous," *New York Review of Books* 37, no. 13 (August 16, 1990): 52.

sition to democracy" literature to the Eastern European /Soviet setting, or acceptance, following the Mock Turtle, of current events in Eastern Europe as Modern Mystery (i.e., not History).[8]

PRIVATE VERSUS PUBLIC VIRTUES

In a curious, unintended, and highly consequential way, Leninist rule reinforced many of the most salient features of traditional culture throughout Eastern Europe (the Soviet Union and elsewhere). "Through their organization and ethos [Leninist regimes] have stimulated a series of informal adaptive social responses (behavioral and attitudinal) that are in many respects consistent with and supportive of certain basic elements of the traditional political culture in these societies," I argued in 1974. "In turn, these elements are antithetical to the appearance of a regime and society with an ethos and structure predicated on a complementary relationship between the public and private realms, on the viability of impersonal rules and norms, and on the value of egalitarianism expressed in the role of effective participant."[9] Today I would put it more succinctly, but no differently: the Leninist experience in Eastern Europe (and elsewhere) reinforced the exclusive distinction and dichotomic antagonism between the official and private realms.

For forty years, regardless of the quite substantial developmental changes in the Party's relation to its host societies,[10] ruling Leninist parties persistently defined and asserted themselves as the superior and dominant alternative to the nation-state, as the exclusive autarchic locus of political leadership and membership. The political consequence was to reinforce the traditional stark gap between a privileged, domineering official realm and a private realm characterized by mutual suspicion, resembling Montesquieu's description of despotic society.[11] No

8. Lewis Carroll, *Alice's Adventures in Wonderland* (London: Collins, 1973), p. 105.
9. See chapter 2 above.
10. See chapter 3 above.
11. I thank Veljko Vujovic for suggesting Montesquieu's observations to me. See *The Spirit of the Laws* (New York: Haftern Publishing Co., 1949), pp. 20–115.

politically integrating nationwide public realm existed in the greater part of Eastern Europe (or the Russian, then Soviet, Empire) before or during the period of Leninist rule. The Leninist experience intensely reinforced and added to the already-negative image of the political realm and the insular quality of the private realm. This reality expressed itself in a number of ways during the period of Leninist rule, and it persists more than inertially throughout Eastern Europe today.

To begin with, the Party's political monopoly and punitive relation to the population produced a "ghetto" political culture in Eastern Europe. The population at large viewed the political realm as something dangerous, something to avoid. Political involvement meant trouble. Regime-coerced political activity (not participation) sustained and heightened the population's psychological and political estrangement. At the same time, the Party could not be everywhere. So Leninist parties traded de facto privatization in nonpriority areas for active Party control and penetration of priority areas. This became particularly true during the Brezhnev period, when private egoism—*personalism* not individualism[12]—became the major sociocultural reality. As I argued eighteen years ago, *dissimulation* became the effective (and ethically as well as politically debilitating) bond between the domineering official and societal supplicant during the entire period of Leninist rule. For four decades, dissimulation became the central feature of the population's (misre)presentation of its public or, better, visible self. Dissimulation reflected the fear and avoidance responses of a subordinate population: the need to deflect the Party's attention from possible or real underfulfillment of tasks, and its unchecked penetration of one's private and social life. Dissimulation also provided the means for an estranged population regularly to interact with a powerful, entrenched, and illegitimate regime.[13]

The absence of a *shared public identity* as citizens, a role that would equalize rulers and ruled, and allow for truthful discus-

12. I distinguish individualism and personalism in the following manner: individualism is ego restrained both by impersonal norms and an internal discipline of deferred gratification. Personalism is ego unrestrained by anything except external obstacle or internal disability.

13. See chapter 2 above.

sion and debate, had a second consequence: the central place of rumor as covert political discourse. In the *Agricola,* Tacitus says rumor "is not always at fault: it may even prompt a selection."[14] Maybe in Rome; not in Eastern Europe (the Soviet Union, or China). There rumor had and continues to have a debilitating effect in political life. It divides, frightens, and angers those who participate in what amounts to a chronic mode of semihysterical (pre)political speech. To be sure, its impact is much greater in some countries than others. If Romania could export its rumors, it would be more developed than Germany. But the political-psychological impact exists in the entire region, and its substantive thrust is clear: it strengthens the insular, privatized quality of social life and obstructs public discussion of national issues. The neotraditional secrecy characteristic of a ruling Leninist party;[15] its corresponding distrust of an ideologically "unreconstructed" population; the invidious juxtaposition of an elite in possession of the real, but secret, truth about the polity, economy, world affairs . . . ; and a population living in the "cave" of political jokes and rumor are legacies that continue to shape the character of "civil society" in Eastern Europe and the Soviet Union. Civil society is more than economic and legal sociology; it is political culture.

In yet another way, the organization and operation of Leninist rule contributed to the difficulty Eastern European populations experience now in their efforts to create frameworks that relate their private, social, and political identities in a complementary, not fragmentary, fashion. Leninist regimes in Eastern Europe, the Soviet Union, and Asia organized their societies around a series of semi-autarchic institutions, the *danwei* in China, and *kollektiv* in the Soviet Union and Eastern Europe. Unlike liberal capitalist democracies, Leninist regimes "parcel" rather than "divide" labor. In Leninist regimes, the factory was (is) less a specialized institution and school of modernity than a functionally diffuse neopatriarchal provider: of houses, vacations, medical attention, food, and to some extent

14. Tacitus, *The Agricola* (Harmondsworth: Penguin Books, 1970), p. 59.
15. See chapter 4 above.

social activity for its workers.[16] The net effect was a division of labor that in important respects resembled Durkheim's *mechanical* division of labor, a "ringworm" division of labor in which each institution attempted to replicate the self-sufficiency of all the others.[17] Again the consequence was to juxtapose the polity and society antagonistically, and to fragment society itself. One corporate autarchic political entity, THE Party hierarchically dominated and connected a set of semi-autarchic socioeconomic entities whose only common bond was a distant, different, and dominant official realm—the Party, THEM.

The same pattern was created by the Soviet Union in its relations with Eastern European regimes. Remember Goumłka's interpreter's observation: "The men in power in the Eastern bloc talk constantly of 'internationalism,' but . . . no friendly neighbour relationship of the type that has developed since the end of the war between the French and the Germans has ever linked the Poles with the Russians or the Czechs or even the people of the DDR. They have remained 'stranger[s] to each other.'"[18] In the bloc, the Soviet regime occupied the same strategically dominant position the Party occupied in each society.[19] Regionally and nationally, the Eastern European polities were fragmented, not integrated: fragmented into mutually exclusive official and private realms bridged by mutually deceptive presentations of their respective "selves." In this respect, Leninist regimes fostered the generic features of all despotisms in which people are "far too much disposed to think exclusively of their own interests, to become self-seekers practicing a narrow individualism and caring nothing for the public good. Far from trying to counteract such tendencies despotism encourages them, depriving the governed of any sense of solidarity and interdependence; of good-neighborly feeling and a

16. Alex Inkeles and David Smith, *Becoming Modern* (Cambridge, Mass.: Harvard University Press, 1974). On China, see Andrew G. Walder, *Communist Neo-Traditionalism* (Berkeley: University of California Press, 1986), ch. 2. Soviet and Eastern European factories are not the "total institution" the Chinese factory appears to be, but are more similar than dissimilar.

17. Emile Durkheim, *The Division of Labor* (Toronto: Free Press Paperback, 1964), chs. 2 and 3.

18. E. Weit, *At the Red Summit* (New York: Macmillan, 1973), pp. 190–91.

19. See chapter 5.

desire to further the welfare of the community at large. It immures them, so to speak, each in his private life and, taking advantage of the tendency they already have to keep apart, it estranges them still more."[20]

The Party's charismatic modus operandi also shaped the actions and dispositions of Eastern Europe's populations. Leninist parties in this (and every) region were overwhelmingly concerned with targets and outcomes, with ends, not means; and they acted in a storming-heroic manner to achieve them. During the Brezhnev period, when they had exhausted their heroic-storming resources, capacity, and even inclination, they substituted a corrupt set of personal patron-client relations to achieve their substantive ends.[21] What no Leninist regime ever did was create *a culture of impersonal measured action.* The result is an Eastern European (Soviet, Chinese) population most of whose members have very little experience with regular, deliberate economic and political activity in a context of impersonal procedures; a population that in its authoritarian peasant and Leninist personas is more familiar with sharp disjunctions between periods of intense action and passivity than with what Weber termed the "methodical rational acquisition" (of goods or votes); a population that in its majority would find the tenor and operation of Ben Franklin's Protestant liberal capitalist way of life boring, demeaning, and, in good part, unintelligible.[22]

Ironically, even the remarkable discovery, articulation, and public expression of human dignity and public ethics by exemplary political figures like Adam Michnik and Václav Havel, and civic movements like Solidarity and Civic Forum partially reinforce the antagonistic juxtaposition of a suspect political

20. Alexis de Tocqueville, *The Old Regime and the French Revolution* (Garden City, N.Y.: Doubleday, Anchor Books, 1955), p. xiii. This book has a certain relevance to those interested in "transitions to democracy."

21. See chapter 4 above.

22. It is not enough to point out that most citizens in liberal capitalist democracies (certainly in the United States) themselves fail to vote and are poorly informed about issues and basic premises of democracy. The institutional framework, the practice and habits of elites, and the sociocultural constitutions in these countries assign critically different meanings to events in Western democracies and Eastern European countries.

world and one of private virtue and ethics. In 1989, in Eastern Europe, one saw the charismatic efflorescence of public ethics: demands for and expressions of individual dignity as the "base," not the superstructure, of political life. In 1989, in Eastern Europe, ethics moved from the purely personal realm to the public realm; not in the form of an intrusive private standard for public performance (as in the United States today), but as an autonomous political criterion for public action, one that judges leadership in terms of its impact on and contribution to human dignity.

However, liberal democratic polities do not rest primarily, for that matter cannot rest primarily, on the charismatic permanence of politically ethical leadership or the private ethics of its citizens. They rest on "public virtues." Dahrendorf rightly emphasizes that in a society where "private" virtue is exalted, "the human personality, becomes a creature without a public life, and the formation of the nation is left behind. Many may well be quite content with this state of affairs. Their greatest happiness is found in private life, in the heights and depths of friendship, and familial harmony, in the satisfaction of imprecise reveries, perhaps even in the nearly metasocial bonds with others in unstructured collectivities."[23] Now listen to the Russian poet Andrei Voznesensky: "In Russia, I think we have . . . spiritual life. We can talk all day and all night long about all kinds of questions, immortal questions. That is the Russian style of thinking. I want our economy to be the same as in the West. . . . But I am afraid to lose this Russian part of our soul."[24] Voznesensky's reflection, and for that matter the entire thrust of Hedrick Smith's recent description of Russian popular culture, speaks to the predominance of private over public virtues in the Russian population; and no great damage is done in generalizing his observations to the majority of people in practically every Eastern European nation.

Eastern Europe's pre-Leninist peasant culture and oligarchi-

23. Ralf Dahrendorf, *Society and Democracy in Germany* (Garden City, N.Y.: Doubleday, Anchor Books, 1969), p. 293.
24. Hedrick Smith, "The Russian Character," *New York Times Magazine,* October 28, 1990, p. 30. Practically every observation Smith makes about Russian culture in 1990 is analyzed in my 1974 article on political culture.

cal authoritarian elites (at times cosmetically outfitted with Western political facades), the neotraditional features of Stalinist and Brezhnevite rule,[25] *and* the ethical charisma of 1989, for all their qualitative difference, combine to provide a remarkably consistent and continuous support for a worldview in which political life is suspect, distasteful, and possibly dangerous; to be kept at bay by dissimulation, made tolerable by private intimacy, and transcended by private virtues or charismatic ethics. To return to Dahrendorf: the "inner-direction of those oriented to private virtues is incomplete. *It is inner-direction without its liberal element, the carrying over of interest to the market of politics and the economy.*"[26] To put it bluntly: the Leninist legacy, understood as the impact of Party organization, practice, and ethos, *and* the initial charismatic ethical opposition to it favor an authoritarian, not a liberal democratic capitalist, way of life; the obstacles to which are not simply how to privatize and marketize the economy, or organize an electoral campaign, but rather how to institutionalize public virtues. Eastern European elites and social audiences have inherited what is for the most part a suspicious culture of mutual envy fostered by a corrupt neotraditional Leninist despotism that in good measure unintentionally reinforced a set of "limited-good" peasant cultures.[27] The charismatically ethical antithesis provoked by "real socialism's" indignities—Solidarity being the paradigmatic instance—is by its very nature an unstable, inadequate base for a tolerant polity based on the complementarity of ethics and interests. Weber's observations are quite apt in examining the

25. On the Stalinist period, see Vera S. Dunham's *In Stalin's Time* (New York: Cambridge University Press, 1979); on the Brezhnev period, see chapter 4.

26. Dahrendorf, *Society and Democracy in Germany,* p. 291. My emphasis. When Dahrendorf contrasts public and private virtues, in effect he identifies the difference between political and apolitical cultures. In analyzing the "transition" from Leninist rule, it should be kept in mind that it is easier to change political organization and behavior than to create a culture (elite or mass) that sees politics as a worthy (not distasteful) arena of bargaining, compromise, and principled and public individual action. Without such a culture, rooted in the material and ideal interests of strategic social strata, democratic life is fragile.

27. See chapter 2 for a discussion of "limited good" cultures and the Leninist impact, and reference to the concept's author, George Foster.

current fate of Solidarity in Poland and Civic Forum in Czech-oslovakia: "When the tide that lifted a charismatically led group out of everyday life flows back into the channels of workaday routines, at least the 'pure' form of charismatic domination will wane and turn into an 'institution'; it is then either mechanized, as it were, or imperceptibly displaced by other structures, or fused with them in the most diverse forms, so that it becomes a mere component of a concrete historical structure. In this case it is often transformed beyond recognition, and identifiable only on an analytical level."[28]

THE FRAGMENTATION OF EASTERN EUROPE

A good place to begin specifying the type of developments likely to occur in Eastern Europe is with a look at a special flag. The most vivid symbol of the Romanian uprising in December 1989 was the sight of the Romanian flag with its Leninist center ripped out. Eastern Europe in 1990 and 1991 is like the Romanian flag: its Leninist center has been removed, but a good deal of its institutional and cultural inheritance is still in place. In all of Eastern Europe, the Leninist Extinction was as much a case of regime collapse as regime defeat, nicely captured by Garton Ash's term "refolution."[29]

And what one now sees taking place in Eastern Europe is more the breakup of existing identities and boundaries than a breakthrough to new ones. Before the latter happens, political conflict in Eastern Europe will have to get beyond the "many are called" to the "few are chosen" stage, to a point where the antagonists are politically organized, not simply viscerally iden-tified. Currently, the cleavages in Eastern Europe are neither crosscutting nor superimposed. They are diffuse, poorly artic-ulated, psychological as much as political, and, because of that, remarkably intense. One reason for the diffuse manifestation of sociopolitical cleavages is the absence of established successor

28. Max Weber, *Economy and Society*, ed. Guenther Roth and Claus Wittich (New York: Bedminster Press, 1968), 3:1120–21.
29. Timothy Garton Ash, "Refolution: The Springtime of Two Nations," *New York Review of Books*, July 15, 1989.

elites in these countries.[30] With the exception of Solidarity, prior to 1989, most opposition elites in Eastern Europe had minimal insulation from the intrusive punitive presence of their Leninist adversaries, minimal familiarity with one another and "politics as a vocation," and minimal success in bonding with a politically loyal social constituency. Only in Poland, over almost two decades, did a counterelite enjoy a Yenan-like protective/interactive experience; one that produced a contentious, but mutually tolerant and intelligible, elite that cohered, and even in its current divided and divisive state offers Poland something more important than either marketization or civil society: an "established" leadership. An "established elite" is one that recognizes the legitimate places of all of its members in the polity despite genuine and deeply felt party, policy, and ideological differences; has worked out civil and practical modes of interaction; and can identify and organize a sociopolitical constituency in a regular manner. Excepting Poland, no Eastern European country has an established (democratic or undemocratic) elite. That means they are fragile polities—highly fragile democratic polities.

We can begin with Hungary. According to Elemer Hankiss, among the new democratic forces "there is a certain confusion . . . they are rent by inner divisions; they have not yet built up their national networks and constituencies . . . they have not yet found their identities and their places in the political spectrum. They have not drawn up their detailed programs and have not clearly outlined the sociopolitical model they want to establish in this country."[31] In Czechoslovakia, the ethnic splits between Slovak and Czech leaders, the dramatic political entry of a religious authoritarian, the pope, in Slovakia (in April 1990) where one million (out of five million) Slovaks greeted him, and the recent selection of Václav Klaus—a man with little political connection to or affinity with the charismatically ethical Havel—as finance minister, pointedly underscores the absence

30. See Ralf Dahrendorf's contrast of "established" and "abstract" elites in *Society and Democracy in Germany*. Dahrendorf emphasizes the shared socialization of established elites and how this contributes to tacit cooperation.

31. See Elemer Hankiss, "In Search of a Paradigm," *Dædalus* 119, no. 1 (Winter 1990): 183–215.

of an established elite. The political flux of Civic Forum's disorganized partisan constituencies completes the picture of an attenuated, diffuse political "constitution" in what many consider one of the most promising candidates for "transition to democracy."

In Romania the governing elite does form an established elite. However, opposition elites (e.g., the Liberal Party, Peasant Party, Group for Social Dialogue, and Civic Alliance leaders in Romania) fundamentally reject the legitimacy of the incumbents. In Romania (and Bulgaria), one has Dutch-like sociopolitical "pillars" without a reconciling consociational political elite.[32] If that were not enough, there is evidence of serious fragmentation within the governing parties themselves in Bulgaria and Romania. The absence of democratic or undemocratic *established successor elites* in Eastern Europe favors and furthers the maelstrom quality of life throughout the area.

The difficulty in creating a democratic established political elite with a tolerant culture is exacerbated by the "refolutionary" change that occurred in 1989. Leninist personnel still play a prominent role in administrative, economic (and, in the Balkans, political) life. In Eastern Europe, one sees a novel evolutionary phenomenon: *survival of the first,* not simply the fittest.[33] Former party cadres are exceptionally well placed to successfully adapt themselves—and their families—to changes in the economic and administrative order. Evidence of this adaptive ability abounds in Poland, Hungary, and elsewhere in Eastern Europe.[34] Add to this the sizable portion of the population in Eastern Europe who in some significant way collaborated with

32. On Holland, see Arend Lijphart, *The Politics of Accommodation: Pluralism and Democracy in the Netherlands* (Berkeley: University of California Press, 1968).

33. My colleague in physics, Richard Muller, uses the phrase "survival of the first" in his discussion of evolutionary change in *Nemesis* (London: Heinemann, 1989), p. 14.

34. Bill Keller, "In Urals City, the Communist Apparatus Ends but Not the Communist Power," *New York Times,* December 13, 1990, illustrates very nicely how Party cadres take advantage of their positions to adapt to new environments. "In Sverdlovsk . . . the party is shoring up its positions by pumping its wealth into commercial joint ventures, small businesses and trading organizations," Keller points out. "The party owns the best hotel . . . has the best computers and printing services, and its 22 story office tower dominates the skyline."

the Party and you have the recipe for a nasty social climate, a climate of sustained, if so far largely contained, psychological bitterness, in some quarters rage—a bitterness that expresses the *emotional fragmentation* of populations who can't find an acceptable political solution to the issues of Leninist survivors and collaborators.[35] Fragmentation is the dominant Eastern European reality.

Daniel Bell's observation that "most societies have become more self-consciously plural societies (defined in ethnic terms)"[36] certainly applies to Eastern Europe today. The case of Yugoslavia is compelling. On balance, there is more reason to think Yugoslavia will not exist as a sovereign entity in five years than that it will. Civil war is a probability in good part because ethnic hate is a reality. The mutual hatred of Serbians and Albanians in Kossovo, between Slobodan Milosevic's Serbia and Franjo Tudjman's Croatia (and, for that matter between Serbs and Croats in Croatia), when combined with economic issues and the effective demise of the League of Yugoslav Communists favors civil war more than civic culture. The same might be said of the Soviet Union, where in one "Eastern European" republic, Moldavia, the political elite are "flirting" with Romania, while trying to suppress a secession movement by the Gagauz Turkic minority in the southern part of the republic and the efforts by its Russian population around Tiraspol to maintain Moldavia's ties with the Soviet Union. But the problem of *ethnic and territorial fragmentation* exists also in the northern tier of Eastern Europe—in Czechoslovakia where many Slovaks are demanding that Slovak be the official language in Slovakia, something quite unacceptable to the hundreds of thousands of Hungarians living there. The Slovak National

35. If one takes Czechoslovakia, it has been estimated that some five of the fifteen million inhabitants have had some relation to the former Communist Party. So if one adds survivors and collaborators, one out of three Czechoslovaks are suspect to the remaining two. See Serge Schmemann, "For Eastern Europe Now, a New Disillusion," *New York Times*, November 9, 1990; Burton Bollag, "In Czechoslovakia, Hunt for Villains," ibid., February 3, 1991; and Stephen Kinzer, "German Custodian of Stasi Files Insists on Justice," ibid., January 20, 1991.

36. Daniel Bell, *The Winding Passage* (New York: Basic Books, 1980), p. 224.

Party demands full independence for Slovakia, and the rowdy
reception given President Havel during his visit there in March
1991 is further evidence of the hostility felt by the active Slovak
minority who favor independence.[37] Finally, should anyone
need reminding, the territorial issues between Yugoslavia and
Albania, Romania and Hungary, and Poland and its eastern
neighbor are latent not extinct. Today Eastern Europe is a
brittle region. Suspicion, division, and fragmentation predominate, not coalition and integration. Sooner rather than later,
attitudes, programs, and forces will appear demanding and
promising unity.

In response to enduring economic disorder, popular desperation will—and already has—led to large-scale emigration that
includes many of the youngest, most skilled, and most talented
of the population. According to the *New York Times,* 1.2 million
people left "what used to be the Soviet Bloc," in 1989. Seven
hundred thousand were East German. Serge Schmemann quite
correctly emphasizes that "nobody can predict . . . how the
growing hardships in the East, and especially in Romania, Bulgaria, and Yugoslavia, will develop. What is known is that all
economists agree that things in Eastern Europe will become far
worse before they become better."[38] Like ethnic separatism and
antagonism, emigration fragments a nation and will generate
nationalist calls to end *demographic fragmentation.*

Unstable governance by recently formed ruling parties and
coalitions—*political fragmentation*—also favors authoritarian developments. Poland, "tired but exhilarated after 14 months of
a Solidarity Government, is bracing for a presidential election
campaign that threatens to divide the nation and jeopardize
economic and political change." The bitter conflict between
Lech Walesa, Stanislaw Tyminski, and Tadeusz Mazowiecki took
place in a country where "the standard of living has dropped
35%, unemployment is expected to climb to 1.5 million by year's

37. See Vladimir V. Kusin, "Czechs and Slovaks: The Road to the Current
Debate," *Report on Eastern Europe* 1, no. 40 (October 5, 1990): 4–14.
38. Serge Schmemann, "East Europe's Emigres Stall Just Short of West,"
New York Times, November 1, 1990.

end and there is a recession in industrial production."[39] In Hungary, "the ruling center-right coalition, in power for less than six months, took a beating in local elections. . . . The most severe blow was felt in Budapest, where opposition parties won 20 of the city's 22 electoral districts. . . . With inflation creeping past 30 percent, unemployment on the rise *and the political debate again mired in a barrage of accusations,* the mood in Hungary is grim."[40]

PAST, PRESENT, FUTURE

I have presented a "catholic" not "protestant" argument regarding Eastern Europe's Leninist legacy and current fragmentation(s). I have obviously, if not explicitly, argued that the historical differences between countries and their current modes of transition from Leninism are not as important as the similarities. Poland is the one genuine exception, because of its "failure" to carry out a Stalinist anti-peasant and anti-Church revolution; the historically momentous emergence of a counterpolity, Solidarity; and its current ability to entertain passionate intra-elite conflict *and* sustained governmental action with social support. However, all but one of the other Eastern Europe regime "transitions" were instances of rapid and peaceful "decolonization" and consequently face the same problems as "Third World" successor elites, who transited to independence rapidly and for the most part peacefully: a very undeveloped capacity to cohere and govern after taking power.[41]

Now for the necessary genuflection to national differences: they exist. It is clear that different types of fragmentation will predominate in different countries, and that some will have

39. John Tagliabue, "Poland's Elections Threaten to Jeopardize Change," *New York Times,* September 23, 1990.

40. Celestine Bohlen, "Hungarian Coalition Is Badly Beaten at Polls," *New York Times,* October 6, 1990. My emphasis.

41. In the "Third World," guerrilla counterelites who fought (the longer the better) against the colonizer constituted themselves as more cohesive successor elites. In this respect, Poland's Solidarity is more like the Algerian FLN, KANU in Kenya, and the Indian Congress Party than the "Ghanaian" rest of Eastern Europe. In Romania, where there was violence, it did not last long enough and was too anomic to generate a counterelite, let alone a cohesive one.

lower thresholds of violence. But is should be equally clear that today the *dominant and shared* Eastern European reality is severe and multiple fragmentation.

Allow me to continue with my "catholic heresy" and suggest that in this setting it will be demogogues, priests, and colonels more than democrats and capitalists who will shape Eastern Europe's general institutional identity. Most of the Eastern Europe of the future is likely to resemble the Latin America of the recent past more than the Western Europe of the present. Irony of ironies, it may be earlier writings by American academics on the "breakdown of democracy" in Latin America rather than the recent literature on "transition to democracy" that speak most directly to the situation in Eastern Europe.[42]

Eastern European fragmentation offers a firmer foundation for transiting to some form of authoritarian oligarchy (in response to perceptions of anarchy) than to democracy. One likely area-wide response to fragmentation will be a growing political role for the Catholic Church. The pope and national churches are major actors, not only in Poland, where Walesa and his "Center," as well as the Peasant Party, offer firm political support, but in Hungary, Slovakia, Croatia, and Slovenia. The Church offers a hierarchically ordered community quite proximate in organization *and ethos* to the patriarchal peasant and neotraditional Leninist Eastern European experience prior to 1989; an international presence, something Eastern European populations and elites need now that their claim on Western European and American democrats and capitalists is losing some of its initial attractiveness; and a legitimating myth for authoritarian political rule in conjunction with a nationally unifying military. I should emphasize that, just as the Latin American case might be relevant after all to Eastern Europe—in its breakdown of rather than transition to democracy experience, in its Peronist more than its Alfonsin/Menem incarnation,[43] so

42. See Juan Linz and Alfred Stepan, eds., *The Breakdown of Democratic Regimes* (Baltimore: Johns Hopkins University Press, 1978); and Guillermo O'Donnell, Philippe Schmitter, and Laurence Whitehead, eds., *Transitions from Authoritarian Rule* (Baltimore: Johns Hopkins University Press, 1986).
43. I find K. H. Silvert's "The Cost of Anti-Nationalism: Argentina," in Silvert, ed., *Expectant Peoples: Nationalism and Development* (New York: Random

the Spanish case might prove to be equally relevant—in its Franco even more than its Gonzalez stage of development.

One must be prepared to see Eastern European armies and their leaders become more self-aware, confident, and assertive as the maelstrom develops. The military will offer and receive support IF, as is likely, these economies continue to deteriorate; IF, as is likely, a clear pattern of "hustler" rather than market capitalism produces an ostentatiously wealthy consuming elite in societies that resent disparities in wealth and remain perplexed as to how one succeeds independently of a benevolent state—precisely the underpinnings of Peronism;[44] IF, as is likely, Western Europe fails to provide a massive "democratic subsidy"; and IF, as is likely, frontier and border issues become salient in a context of civil violence, even war, in Yugoslavia and/or in the Soviet Union. Already, the Romanian army provides whatever glue exists in holding that country together. The same is true of Yugoslavia. And recently, in Bulgaria, a "regional judge in Haskovo registered the Bulgarian Legion 'Georgi Stoikov Rakovski' as an official organization. The group . . . was founded to promote professionalism in the army and to campaign for soldiers' rights."[45]

However, in contrast to the shared quality of the Leninist legacy and fragmentation of Eastern Europe's successor regimes, the impact of the military and Church may vary decisively from country to country. Here we must be more "protestant." To begin with, even those countries with a pre–World War II history of political activity by the army, like Serbia, Bulgaria, Romania, and Poland, have now had regimes for

House, 1963), pp. 345–73, the most insightful analysis of Argentina's remarkable sixty-year failure to combine political modernity (i.e., civic nationalism) with an industrial economy.

44. In explaining Peronism, Naipaul quotes Eva Peron: "The strange thing is that the existence of the poor did not cause me as much pain as the knowledge that at the same time there were people who were rich"; and goes on himself to note that "that pain about the rich—the pain about other people remained the basis of the popular appeal of Peronism. That was the simple passion—rather than 'nationalism' or Peron's 'third position'—that set Argentina alight." (V. S. Naipaul, *The Return of Eva Peron* [New York: Vintage Books, 1981], pp. 176–77).

45. See Duncan M. Perry, "A New Military Lobby," *Report on Eastern Europe* 1, no. 40 (October 5, 1990): 1–4.

close to half a century that have subordinated the army politically and denied it both a distinctive national mission and institutional elan. Second, at the moment neither the Czechoslovak nor the Hungarian army appears to have any significant
place in the polity. As for the Catholic Church, it is not strong
in the Czech lands or the Balkans.

The reality appears, then, to be decisively "protestant," diverse. However, if one adds a factor I have not yet touched on,
the economic, the situation and interpretation of the area-wide
role of armies and Church might change substantially. Currently, there is a debate in and outside Eastern Europe as to
what type of governance is best suited to deal with Eastern
Europe's economic emergency.

"The immediate question . . . is: What variant of democratic
politics can, on the one hand, provide sufficiently strong stable,
consistent government to sustain the necessary rigors of fiscal,
monetary, and economic policy over a period of several years,
while, on the other hand, being sufficiently flexible and respon-
sive to absorb the larger part of the inevitable popular discon-
tents through parliamentary, or at least, legal channels, thus
preventing the resort to . . . ultimately extraparliamentary
means[?]" writes Timothy Garton Ash. He agrees with Al
Stepan—one of the leading figures in the "transition to democracy" school—that "an unambiguously parliamentary system
has a better chance of striking the necessary balance [between
economic development and democratic participation] than a
presidential one." I don't. The choices are not presidential authoritarianism, with the president either becoming a "weak president, because he bows to the majority, or a strong but anti-
democratic one, because he does not," or Ash's "strong freely
elected coalitions."[46] (In fact, given the current maelstrom of
ethnic, economic, ecological, and political emergencies, any ex-
pectation of "strong freely elected coalitions" might be called
utopian liberalism.) A third "option" exists—liberal authoritarianism.

In Eastern Europe, the immediate political imperative is economic. Any successful response to this imperative is likely to

46. Garton Ash, "Eastern Europe," pp. 54–55.

have an authoritarian cast. Take a "good" case for democratic capitalism, Czechoslovakia, a country that dismissed its communist defense minister. General Vacek, and where the Church is a political force only ͏ᴨ the minority Slovak area. The economic emergency has led to Václav Klaus's dramatic political emergence. Klaus has a daunting charge, with traumatic implications, comparable to what was attempted in England when the Speenhamland public welfare system was abolished by the Poor Law of 1834.[47] And he must act on this charge without the advantage of (m)any shared substantive agreements or stylistic affinities within the Czechoslovak governing elite(s) or any well-delineated sociopolitical constituency to offer regular partisan support for his program!

What is likely to happen? Klaus's economic reforms will fail. What would it take to succeed? A Giovanni Giolitti, not a Havel, as president;[48] a Giolitti with a *dominant* parliamentary faction able to draw on a strategically placed and privileged voting constituency, with tacit but evident support from the Czechoslovak military and Catholic Church. In short, it will take the type of liberal authoritarianism that existed in nineteenth-century *Western* Europe. Both unambiguously freely elected parliamentary coalitions and presidents who rely primarily or exclusively on the military and the Church will be overwhelmed by emergency environments. I suggest that a form of liberal authoritarianism like the bourgeois regimes of nineteenth-century Western Europe[49] is a desirable alternative to the

47. All of Eastern Europe (and the Soviet Union) are in a "Speenhamland" situation. (On the Speenhamland system in nineteenth-century England, see Karl Polanyi, *The Great Transformation: The Political and Economic Origins of Our Time* [Boston: Beacon Press, 1965], esp. pp. 77–102, which emphasizes the social trauma associated with the introduction of a capitalist self-regulating market system.) In connection with Klaus and his reforms, see Henry Kamm, "Prague Reformers Reject Havel Bid," and Stephen Engelberg, "Czech Conversion to a Free Market Brings the Expected Pain and More" and "With No Controls and Little Competition, Prices Soar in Czechoslovakia," *New York Times*, October 16, 1990, January 4 and 30, 1991.

48. On Giolitti, see Richard Webster, *Industrial Imperialism in Italy, 1908–1915* (Berkeley: University of California Press, 1975), in particular the Prologue and notes on pp. 346–47.

49. In this connection, see Theodore S. Hamerow, *The Birth of a New Europe: State and Society in the Nineteenth Century* (Chapel Hill: University of

religio-ethnic, militant nationalist, even fascist regimes that might emerge from the maelstrom; and a more practical response than the utopian wish for immediate mass democracy in Eastern Europe.

The economic emergency in Eastern Europe is a social emergency, and the political responses to it are likely to draw on institutions, elites, policies, and orientations that in varying, but also shared, ways define themselves in terms of hierarchy and solidary and exclusionary practices—like the military and Church. The issue is not their participation, but on what terms!

THE "TWAIN" HAD BETTER MEET

The Leninist legacy in Eastern Europe consists largely—not exclusively—of fragmented, mutually suspicious, societies with little religio-cultural support for tolerant and individually self-reliant behavior; and of a fragmented region made up of countries that view each other with animosity. The way Leninists ruled and the way Leninism collapsed contributed to this inheritance. However, the emergence and composition of movements like Civic Forum in the Czech lands, Public against Violence in Slovakia, the Alliance of Free Democrats in Hungary, the Union of Democratic Forces in Bulgaria, and the Civic Alliance in Romania bear witness to the reality of a modern citizenry in Eastern Europe. But it is one that must compete with anti-civic, anti-secular, anti-individual forces outside and inside itself. With the possible exception of Poland, no Eastern European country has a predominantly civic established elite and constituency. Question: Is there any point of leverage, critical mass of civic effort—political, cultural, and economic—that can add its weight to civic forces in Eastern Europe and check the increasing frustration, depression, fragmentation, and anger that will lead to country- and regionwide violence of a communal type in Eastern Europe? Yes! Western Europe.

The necessary, though not necessarily forthcoming, Western European response to the syndrome of Eastern European frag-

---

North Carolina Press, 1983), pt. 3; and Eric Hobsbawm, *The Age of Empire, 1875–1914* (New York: Pantheon Books, 1987).

mentation(s) is *adoption:* of Eastern Europe by Western Europe. The fragmentation of Eastern Europe and the Soviet Union (where recently a district of Moscow attempted to claim sovereignty over the Bolshoi Ballet) is not a neutral, peripheral, self-contained event.[50] It is already affecting political identities and relations in and between the Western and "Third" worlds. The disintegration of the former Leninist world and the ongoing fragmentation of its successor regimes can either be the stimulus for a parallel ethnic/civic confrontation in Western Europe (and the United States), or a stimulus for the West to attempt in Eastern Europe and parts of the Soviet Union what West Germany is attempting in East Germany: adoption.

This would require enormous imagination, coordination, and intrusion on Western Europe's (and, in a significant way, the United States's) part: a massive economic presence, provision for major population shifts on the European continent, and intracontinental party cooperation and action; all of which would substantially affect the current definition and operation of national sovereignty. One alternative is for Western Europe to become liberal fortress Europe and deny its "brother's keeper" responsibility. In that case, developments in Eastern Europe will degenerate in a frightening fashion.

50. See chapter 7 above.

9

A WORLD WITHOUT LENINISM

FROM JOSHUA TO GENESIS

For nearly half a century, the boundaries of international politics and the identities of its national participants have been directly shaped by the presence of a Leninist regime world centered in the Soviet Union.[1] The Leninist extinction of 1989 poses a fundamental challenge to those boundaries and identities.

Boundaries are an essential component of a recognizable and coherent identity. Whether territorial, ideological, religious, economic, social, cultural, or amalgams thereof, the attentuation of or dissolution of boundaries is more often than not a traumatic event—all the more so when boundaries have been organized and understood in highly categorical terms.

By the end of the 1940s, world politics was largely antipolitics. The Cold War provides a striking instance of a stereotyped political division of labor. In each of the parallel worlds (West and East), one country patriarchally monopolized political decisions. For the most part, the behavior of any member of either world (liberal or Leninist) could be predicted by knowing which camp it belonged to. Mutual fear of ideological contamination manifested itself as murderous hysteria in the Soviet Union and gratuitous hysteria in the United States, and was supplemented by efforts to disrupt each other's camps. Ideally, the members of each world, camp, or bloc were one-dimensional entities who defined themselves exclusively in terms of membership in their respective political and military organizations; had one domi-

This essay is also to be published in Robert O. Slater, Barry M. Schutz, and Stephen R. Dorr, eds., *Global Restructuring and the Third World* (Boulder, Colo.: Lynne Rienner Press, 1992). It appears here in slightly different form.

1. See chapter 5 above.

nant referent, the leader of their respective camps; and one identity, the ideology that formally distinguished the members of one camp from the other. Thus, entities as different as Albania and East Germany were viewed almost exclusively as communist, while Turkey and Norway were viewed one-dimensionally as free world countries.[2] Exceptions were real, rare, and most of all indecisive challenges to the rigid boundaries and identities that defined world politics for forty years. Yugoslavia's defection from the Soviet bloc in 1948; France and England's invasion of Egypt in 1956; Romania and France's assertion of national military autonomy; U.S. and Soviet recognition of a "Third World"; and the substitution of "peaceful coexistence" and détente for the frigid war that followed World War II were substantial developments. But neither alone nor together did they break through the categorical political and ideological boundaries, or corresponding rigid political identities, of the postwar period.

The Cold War was a "Joshua" period; one of dogmatically centralized boundaries and identities. In contrast to the biblical sequence, the Leninist extinction of 1989 has moved the world from a Joshua to a Genesis environment: from one centrally organized, rigidly bounded, and hysterically concerned with impenetrable boundaries to one in which territorial, ideological, and issue boundaries are attenuated, unclear, and confusing. We now inhabit a world that, while not "without form and void," is one in which the major imperatives are the same as in Genesis, "naming and bounding."[3]

In one important respect, 1989 resembles 1066. In that year, England did not move a geographical inch, but the "conceptual geography" of all Europe changed decisively. As David Douglas has lucidly argued: "Beyond doubt, the latter half of the eleventh century witnessed a turning-point in the history of western Christendom. . . . By the conquest of a great kingdom [the Normans] effected a political regrouping of north-western Eu-

2. See my *Images of Détente and the Soviet Political Order* (Berkeley: Institute of International Studies, University of California, 1977), pp. 1–26.

3. On Joshua and Genesis "environments," see *The New English Bible with the Apocrypha* (Oxford University Press, Cambridge University Press, 1970), pp. 1–60, 241–69.

rope with lasting consequences both to France and England. . . . They contributed also to a radical modification of the relations between eastern and western Europe with results that still survive." A reconfigured, differently named and bounded world emerged, one "centred upon France [and including] not only . . . England . . . but the Italy which the Normans helped to transform."[4]

In the mid eleventh century, the political tectonic plates radically shifted. In the late twentieth century, it has happened again. There is also a radical difference between 1066 and 1989. Today it is hard to find the "Normans"—namely, a self-confident elite and institutions with the power to break up existing boundaries and identities *and* effectively export/impose a viable substitute. If we take Ladis Kristof's distinction between frontiers and boundaries, the political, economic, and ideological collapse of Leninist regimes in Europe (and their inertial persistence in parts of Asia, and in Cuba) has destroyed existing political/ ideological boundaries and created a nebulous frontier condition in international politics. According to Kristof, "the nature of frontiers differs greatly from the nature of boundaries. Frontiers are a characteristic of rudimentary socio-political relations and/or absence of laws. The presence of boundaries is a sign that the political community has reached a relative degree of maturity and orderliness. . . . [Frontiers] are the result of rather spontaneous, or at least ad hoc solutions and movements, [boundaries] are fixed and enforced through a more rational and centrally coordinated effort after a conscious choice is made among the several preferences and opportunities at hand."[5] In the aftermath of the Leninist extinction, frontiers are likely to replace boundaries in a number of settings.

In light of this contention, it is interesting to see how quickly some academics and political figures have discovered a "Norman reality" able to stave off the threatening turbulence associated with the Leninist extinction and create new and more desirable boundaries and identities. Both Fukuyama's "end of

4. David C. Douglas, *William the Conqueror: The Norman Inpact upon England* (Berkeley: University of California Press, 1964), pp. 6–7.
5. Ladis D. Kristof, "The Nature of Frontiers and Boundaries," *Annals of the Association of American Geographers* 49, no. 3 (1959): 269–82.

history" thesis, and the "transition to democracy" school either explicitly or implicitly see the liberal democratic West as a constructive "Norman" entity ready and able to take advantage of the boundary and identity "clearing away" effects of the Leninist extinction and shape the world in its own image.[6] This prevalent optimism rests on several assumptions. First, that though not negligible, the Leninist legacy—the cultural, social, political, and economic inheritance left to successor regimes in Eastern Europe (and what was the Soviet Union)—is not debilitating enough to overwhelm indigenous efforts at democratization. Second, that the Leninist extinction was a self-contained event that will not significantly disrupt the boundaries and identities of the Western and "Third" worlds. Third, that the Western world is one of ideological, institutional, and national self-confidence and promise, not simply power and wealth. I question all these assumptions.

THE LENINIST EXTINCTION

I have argued elsewhere that one can identify at least two relevant rare historical events: (1) the emergence of an authoritatively standardized and centered institutional format dominating a highly diverse set of cultures—examples being Roman Christianity, Arabic Islam, British liberalism, and Soviet Leninism; and (2) the "mass extinction" of species—precisely what happened to Leninism in 1989.[7] *Mass extinction* refers to the abrupt and accelerated termination of species that are distributed globally or nearly so. What separates it from other forms of extinction is its speed and comprehensiveness. Developments in the Leninist world in 1989 can be understood as a mass extinction. Leninism's "genetic" or identity-defining features, those that provided Leninist regimes and the Leninist regime world with a continuously recognizable identity over time and across space were destroyed. The concepts of class

6. See Francis Fukuyama, "The End of History?" *The National Interest*, no. 16 (Summer 1989): 3–18. And see Guillermo O'Donnell, Philippe Schmitter, and Laurence Whitehead, eds. *Transitions fron Authoritarian Rule* (Baltimore: Johns Hopkins University Press, 1986).

7. See chapter 7 above.

war, the correct line, the Party as a superior and exclusive locus of political leadership and membership, and the Soviet Union as THE incarnation of revolutionary socialism have been ideologically rejected and politically attacked in the Soviet Union, and Soviet support has been withdrawn from Leninist replica regimes in Eastern Europe. The momentous result has been the collapse of those regimes and the emergence of successor governments aspiring to democracy and capitalism, but faced with a distinct and unfavorable Leninist legacy.

That legacy includes a "ghetto" political culture that views the governmental and political realm suspiciously, as a source of trouble, even of danger; a distrustful society habituated to hoarding information, goods, and goodwill, which shares them only with intimates and is filled with Hobbesian competition; rumor as a mode of discourse that works against sober public discussion of issues; a segmentary, not complementary, socioeconomic division of labor in which the semi-autarchic workplace favors social insulation; a political leadership whose charismatic-storming approach to problems did very little culturally or psychologically to familiarize these societies with "methodically rational" action; and Soviet-enforced isolation between the nations of Eastern Europe, something that reinforced and added to their mutual ignorance, distrust, and disdain. All in all, it is not a legacy that favors liberal capitalist democracy.[8]

However, the Leninist extinction's impact will not be limited to the former Leninist world. Any argument that the collapse of Leninist regimes is some sort of historical surgical strike leaving the rest of the world largely unaffected qualifies as a striking example of political and intellectual denial. The Leninist extinction should be likened to a catastrophic volcanic eruption, one that initially and immediately affects only the surrounding political "biota" (i.e., other Leninist regimes), but whose effects most likely will have a *global impact* on the boundaries and identities that for half a century have politically, economically, and militarily defined and ordered the world.

Like the Norman victory, the Leninist defeat will lead to a reconfigured world. But the Leninist extinction differs funda-

8. See chapter 8 above.

mentally from the Norman Conquest. Extinctions create turbulent (not pacific) environments, characterized by shifting and contested boundaries (of all types—territorial, ideological, cultural, economic, and political) and by insecure identities. Political assertions and intellectual schemes whose explicit or implicit intent is to alleviate the anxiety inevitably accompanying the unexpected and dramatic removal of existing boundaries are predictable. So are attempts to maintain beneficial and familiar boundaries and identities. The fear of chaos seems to be a culturally and historically shared human instinct. Political and intellectual efforts at reassurance are an amalgam of rational, superstitious, denial, and inertial behavior (with greater weight assigned to each succeeding element). A good example is the fetishlike emphasis the Bush administration places on the NATO boundary identity. But reassurance and optimism are not substitutes for examining what is in its nature difficult to examine: in this case the potential maelstrom emerging in the aftermath of the Leninist extinction.

WHERE TO DRAW THE LINE

Ellis Goldberg has contrasted the bounded territorial closure so typical of medieval Europe with the absence of such in medieval Islam. His point is that bounded economic and cultural communities existed in the medieval Islamic world without a politically predominant territorial state.[9] Be that as it may, since the nineteenth century, territorial boundaries have become a more salient concern in the Arab world. In fact, with the ascendance of the Western nation-state as the internationally dominant mode of political loyalty and economic organization, the nation-state as reality, fiction, and aspiration has become the obligatory mode of political organization and loyalty in the world. And territorial boundaries are intimate and crucial components of nation-state identity.[10] The Leninist extinction threatens

9. Ellis Goldberg, "Border, Boundaries, Taxes and States in the Medieval Islamic World" (paper delivered at SSRC conference, University of Washington, Seattle, April 1990).

10. On the relationship between the two in very different historical settings, see Peter Sahlins, *Boundaries: The Making of France and Spain in the*

some and will challenge many other existing territorial boundaries.

The immediate and obvious challenge to territorial boundaries is within the Soviet Union and parts of Eastern Europe.
Demands for sovereignty in Georgia, the Ukraine, the Baltic
states, and Russia itself have created a turbulent, tense, unre-
solved situation in one of the world's two thermonuclear super-
powers.[11] In Eastern Europe, Yugoslavia is on the verge of
disintegrating. And the recent effort to save Czechoslovak
unity with a hyphen (Czecho-Slovak) emphasizes how widespread the potential for territorial boundary and corresponding political identity change is within the former Leninist regime world. In fact, it may turn out that it was a great deal
easier to contain a well-bounded and identified Soviet bloc than
to prevent the current boundary and identity breakdown in the
same area from spilling over into adjacent areas.

Central Asia

The Soviet Union's Central Asian republics are demanding sovereignty. "Central Asia is an old idea taking on new life not only
in Pakistan but also in the Asian Muslim world beyond the
Middle East—as far east as China's Xinjiang region" writes Barbara Crossette, who is certainly right when she says, "No one
expects a new Central Asian empire to stir the ghost of Tamer-
lane, certainly not in an age when nationalisms are fragmenting
rather than enlarging geographical domains. But a process,
however tenuous and exploratory, of rediscovering old cultural, historical, religious, and commercial bonds is under way,
perhaps most of all in Pakistan, the nation in the middle."
Equally important is the fact that "not all the interest in Central
Asia is benign or cultural. William Maley of the Australian De-
fence Force Academy . . . says some Pakistani generals would

Pyrenees (Berkeley: University of California Press, 1989), and W. D. Davies,
The Territorial Dimension of Judaism (Berkeley: University of California Press,
1982).

11. On the status as of December 1990 of claims to sovereignty, see Ann
Sheehy, "Fact Sheet on Declarations of Sovereignty," *Report on the USSR*
(Radio Liberty), pp. 23–25.

like to extend their strategic borders into Soviet territory through Afghanistan. . . . And thoughts of a new community of interests unsettle India, which fears it may one day confront a bloc of conservative Islamic lands from its western borders to the horizons of Europe."[12]

Eastern Europe

In the Soviet republic of Moldavia (now called Moldova), there are clear signs that the majority Romanian population want an integral political relation with Romania.[13] At the same time, Arpad Goncz, Hungary's president, was the first head of state to visit the Ukraine since its declaration of sovereignty this summer.[14] The significance of the Ukraine becoming a sovereign state includes its potential emergence as a major regional actor in a set of complementary and conflicting coalitions with Hungary, Czechoslovakia, Romania, and Poland.[15] And the Hungarian president's visit has obvious significance for the Romanian-Hungarian ethnic/territorial dispute over Transylvania.

The Balkans

The potential disintegration of Yugoslavia should alert us to the possibility of a new boundary-identity configuration in southeastern Europe. The Macedonian issue is latent, not extinct, and will involve Serbia, Bulgaria, and, most likely, Greece and Turkey. In fact, given the current Iraqi crisis, the crisis in Soviet Central Asia, and the crisis in both Bulgaria and Yugoslavia, Turkey may emerge as a pivotal, not peripheral, nation in a radically reconfigured political region that partially blurs, overlaps, and displaces the boundaries between the Middle

12. Barbara Crossette, "Central Asia Rediscovers Its Identity," *New York Times*, June 24, 1990, p. E3.
13. On the growing ties between Soviet Moldova and Romania, see Vladimir Socor, "Moldavia President Breaks New Ground in Romania," *Report on the USSR* 3, no. 8 (February 22, 1991): 20–23.
14. See Alfred Reisch, "Hungary and Ukraine Agree to Upgrade Bilateral Relations," *Report on Eastern Europe* 1, no. 44 (November 2, 1990): 6–13.
15. See Roman Szporluk, "The Burden of History—Made Lighter by Geography?" *Problems of Communism* 5, no. 39 (July–August 1990): 45–48, on Poland's geopolitical orientation.

East, Balkans, and Soviet Central Asia. The disintegration of territorial boundaries and political/ideological identities in the former Leninist world is not likely to respect territorially proximate boundaries and identities.

Western Europe

Developments in Czechoslovakia, particularly the bitter relations between its two ethnic components, heighten the prospect of a political-territorial revision of boundaries and identities in favor of confederation. Add to that Slovenia's desire to be free of "backward" Yugoslavia, and the existence of an "increasingly potent regional party [in North Italy] called the Lombard League [demanding] full autonomy to Lombardy and other regions in [Italy's] affluent North,"[16] and you have yet another potential for a reconfiguration of Europe's territorial, commercial, and political boundaries. Such a reconfiguration would favor what Tadeusz Mazowiecki, the former Polish prime minister, recently bemoaned—the tendency to split Eastern Europe and all of Europe into an A and B category.[17]

Asia

Nor should we exclude the Asian Leninist world from our consideration of potential territorial boundary and political identity changes. The persistence of Leninist rule in China rests on the continued presence of Old Bolsheviks, to the longevity of its founding cadres, leaders who have the one thing that Eastern European Leninist rulers lacked in 1989, self-confidence in their political and ideological purpose. But even the Chinese, North Korean, and Vietnamese regimes find it impossible to define that purpose in practical "combat" terms. They suffer from the same combination of revolutionary ritualization and ad hoc modernization that characterized Leninist neotraditionalism in Europe.[18] In the absence of even an ambivalently

16. Clyde Haberman, "Rising Party in Italy's North Wants to Get Rome and the South off Its Back," *New York Times,* June 24, 1990.

17. See Ken Jowitt, "A Research Agenda for Eastern Europe," *East European Politics and Societies* 4, no. 2 (Spring 1990): 193–97.

18. See chapter 4 above.

viewed Soviet center, and given their ideological acceptance of the politically benign—not equal—nature of their societies, these regimes are on an inertial path to extinction. In North Korea, the death of Kim Il Sung will immediately and threateningly raise the issue of unification with South Korea—of territorial boundary and political identity change. (The nuclear reactor at Yongbyon in North Korea could well become a source of extraordinary concern and danger should there be turmoil in North Korea.) In China, the eventual physical demise of its leadership stratum will immediately raise the threat of regionalism. It is true that "one of the Chinese Communist Party's proudest accomplishments is that it reunited a nation torn apart by warlords and recreated a central government that could lead the country." It is also true that "that achievement stands, but in these days of economic slowdown, it is somewhat undermined by provinces that are quietly carving up the vast national market into protectionist fiefs. . . . The new restrictions on [internal] trade . . . underscore the strength of the centrifugal forces that some Chinese fear could lead eventually to the fragmentation of their motherland."[19] Regionalism in China is no more likely to be self-contained than boundary-identity changes in the Soviet Union or Eastern Europe. Peaceful, violent, decisive, or indecisive reconfigurations within China will necessarily involve both Taiwan and Hong Kong.

If identifiable potential exists for territorial boundary and political identity changes in the former Leninist world, and for direct spillover into neighboring areas in Asia, the Middle East, and Western Europe, the collapse of Leninism as an internationally identified and bounded entity will also affect boundaries and identities in the rest of the world, particularly the "Third World."

Just as the British Navy gave substance to the Monroe Doctrine boundary declaration, the compelling reality of the Soviet–U.S. conflict gave substance and stability to the formal declaration of territorial boundaries in the "Third World." The influence exercised by superpower patrons on "Third World"

19. Nicholas D. Kristof, "In China, Too, Centrifugal Forces Are Growing Stronger," *New York Times,* August 26, 1990.

clients in their role as political models, economic warehouses, and armories, when added to each superpower's fear that a change in boundaries could add to its rival's power, helped stabilize "Third World" territorial boundaries.[20] The Leninist extinction and the declaration by the United States that the Cold War is over have altered those environmental constraints.[21] Furthermore, the fact that those constraints were largely coercive meant that they repressed, rather than removed, a number of underlying historical issues and frames of references that continue to have a latent claim on many "Third World" elites. Consequently, many of those issues and frames of reference should now begin to reemerge. In this connection, Kenneth Stein's comments about the Middle East are quite apt. "For the last 200 years, Middle Eastern peoples and their leaders have been reacting to outsiders' notions of political organization—nationalism, modernization, secularization—and to the evolving rules of international behavior. But now they have greater control over their own affairs." Syria's Hafiz al-Assad has a mural in his office depicting the battle of al-Hittin in 1187, where Saladin won a crucial victory over the Crusaders, and values it because it was "where the Arabs defeated the West."[22] This speaks to one frame of reference that may become more salient and consequential in a world without Leninism.

Finally, there are developments in the West with territorial boundary and identity implications. These developments are

20. The relatively weak transportation infrastructure and state power of many "Third World" regimes also play a major role in the passive integrity of their territorial boundaries. See, e.g., Immanuel Wallerstein, "The Range of Choice: Constraints on the Policies of Governments of Contemporary African Independent States," in Michael Lofchie, ed., *The State of the Nations: Constraints on Development in Independent Africa* (Berkeley: University of California Press, 1971), pp. 19–37; and I. William Zartman, *Ripe for Resolution: Conflict and Intervention in Africa* (New York: Oxford University Press, 1989), pp. 19–20.

21. Made most recently by President Bush at the signing of the Charter of Paris. See the column by R. W. Apple, Jr., in the *New York Times*, November 22, 1990. The massive American presence in Saudi Arabia contradicts this statement. I shall discuss the Bush administration's response to the end of the Cold War shortly.

22. Kenneth W. Stein, "A Tradition of Intrusion Collides with Western Rules," *New York Times*, September 16, 1990.

neither a direct nor an indirect response to the Leninist extinction, but their course will be affected by and affect the turbulent boundary- and identity-challenging environments created by that event. I have in mind two Western developments: the Chunnel and Quebec. It's remarkable that British workers have met "their French counterparts somewhere under the middle of the Channel—La Manche, to the French—and for the first time in 8,000 years England will again be linked to the Continent." William Grimes goes on to note that "as the most dramatic example of shrinking European frontiers, [the Channel tunnel is] already carrying heavy symbolic freight."[23] More than that, when combined with the evolving transportation infrastructure in Western Europe, and the moves toward a common currency, the Chunnel has quite understandably led some "to fear it will blur their national identities." In the Chunnel era, boundaries and identities in Western Europe will differ radically from that day in 1930 when a headline appeared in the British press saying: "Fog in Channel: Continent [not Britian] Cut Off."

The British-French connection plays a major role in another instance of potential boundary-identity change in the West, in Quebec. "After the collapse of a constitutional accord that would have granted protection to Quebec's distinct culture, the province's Government made it clear that it will no longer deal with the national Government as a superior entity, but as an equal partner in managing common interests."[24] The possibility that Quebec might secede from Canada is real. Should that occur, one may assume that several other Canadian provinces will reconsider their existing relationships with Canada *and* the United States.

"MANY ARE CALLED BUT FEW ARE CHOSEN"

Simply outlining these potential changes will irritate many social "scientists," and (should they ever read this) make policy-

23. William Grimes, "Chunnel," *New York Times Magazine*, September 16, 1990.
24. John F. Burns, "Ottawa and Quebec Search for a New Relationship," *New York Times*, June 26, 1990; and "Quebec Demands Greater Powers If It Is to Remain in Canada," ibid., January 30, 1991.

makers apprehensive. Because if I am right, policymakers had better hire political cartographers to draw new "maps" that more accurately reflect changing territorial boundaries and political identities. Even more unsettling, the policymaker will have to entertain the real possibility that national, regional, and international boundaries and identities will be contested for a long time to come. As for social "scientists," some would say I have indulged in sheer speculation. I object to the adjective *sheer*. What have I done?

I have deductively concluded that the extinction of a defining and bounding element of the international order is likely to create disorder both within its own boundaries and in adjacent areas. I have inductively argued that one can identify *potential* spillover effects of the Leninist extinction in Central Asia, the Balkans, Asia, and Western Europe in the form of new political orientations, concerns, and aspirations. I have also argued that one should be alert to the possibility of new regional political actors such as the Ukraine and Turkey; and equally alert to the possibility of new territorial entities—for instance, an independent Quebec, a confederal Czecho-Slovakia, an expanding Pakistan, a united Korea, and center-region conflict in China (also involving Taiwan and Hong Kong).

However, when I say, "Many are called but few are chosen," I also recognize that potentials may not—in fact, some are highly unlikely to—materialize, and even if they do, they may be defeated by opposing developments or realities. An example: regionalism may become a genuine threat to China's integrity and be contained or defeated by a national Chinese army. Pakistan may try to expand at the expense of a disintegrating Soviet Union and be defeated by a Russian (not Soviet) army. The threat of economic disorder and a murderous civil war may deter Milosevic and Tudjman from pursuing their confrontational course in Yugoslavia. One has to be either dull or lazy not to try and identify potential boundary-identity changes in a world struck by the extinction of one of its defining components; and foolish to assume that all potential boundary/identity revisions have equal chances to succeed. In any case, my primary concern is not the success or failure of potential boundary/identity changes—*that* would be sheer speculation, in fact prophecy. My point is that the Leninist extinction poses a dramatic, worldwide challenge to existing territorial boundaries and political identities. The outcomes may encompass a change in Korean political geography, the proliferation of military boundary conflicts in the "Third World" like that between Iraq and Kuwait, and the emergence of what David Calleo has so suggestively termed, a "multinational continental system" in Western Europe better able to "regulate the affairs of a whole continent than the more rigidly centralized national structures of the earlier continental systems, the United States and the Soviet Union."[25] I suggested earlier that analyzing a maelstrom is intrinsically difficult, but not impossible if we begin with challenges and threats to territorial *boundaries and identities* within the former Leninist world; with the spillover effect the disintegration of established territorial boundaries and identities in the Leninist world will have / is having on adjacent areas; and with discovering the location of new territorially bounded political entities—that is, locating and analyzing new pivotal nations or core areas around which reconfigured political regions and coalitions may form.

CIVIC VERSUS ETHNIC: BOUNDARIES AND IDENTITIES

The Leninist extinction's impact on global, regional, and national boundaries and identities will *not* be limited to territorial boundaries. Its influence on the redefinition of *issue* boundaries and consequent reshaping of political identities will be as, perhaps more, profound. The civic/ethnic identity issue is a defining one for all the Soviet empire's successor states. This cleavage expresses itself in three ways: first, as ongoing discussions about, declarations of, and possible efforts to secede. Second, as possible irredentas. The visit of the Hungarian president to the Ukraine mentioned earlier focused largely on the Transcarpathian *oblast* in the western Ukraine, with its nearly

25. David P. Calleo, "American National Interest and the New Europe: Some Early Thoughts," in Daniel Chirot, ed., *The Crisis of Leninism 1989* (Seattle: University of Washington Press, 1991).

200,000 ethnic Hungarians. It is a fair assumption this visit was noted in Slovakia, with its half a million Hungarians, and in Romania, with its nearly two million Hungarians. No "logic" inexorably leads Hungary to reclaim its ethnic kinsmen in Slovakia, Yugoslavia, the Ukraine, and Romania. In fact, as Donald Horowitz argues, "the decision to embark upon an irredentist course is freighted with elements that counsel restraint. Unlike aid to secessionists, it probably means direct involvement in actual warfare."[26] But turbulent and fragmented Eastern European and Soviet environments do support the appearance of groups and programs favoring a dominantly ethnic-territorial definition of political identity.[27]

The third expression of the civic/ethnic issue is internal conflict over the predominant definition of national identity. *The nation-state is a partially antagonistic amalgam of state, civic, and ethnic orientations and organization.* Metaphorically, these national components can be matched with the French Revolution's slogan: Liberty (the civic), Equality (the state), Fraternity (the ethnic). In a nation-state, the impersonal secular state creates a domain in which ideally all are treated equally. However, the state's emphasis on impersonalism and standardization jars with the *Gemeinschaft* qualities of ethnic affective identifications; and while supportive of civic equality, the state's ethos and structure are at odds with the critical scrutiny that is the civic or public realm's distinctive feature. In a related manner, the civic and ethnic components of national identification and organization are partially antagonistic. The civic component emphasizes the individual, the ethnic component emphasizes the group; the civic orientation is critical, the ethnic, solidary. At issue, then, in every nation-state is how the "three persons" of the state, civic, and ethnic trinity are weighted and defined.

If, under Leninist rule, *kto-kovo?* asked whether or not the Party was dominant, the question today in the nations of the extinct Soviet bloc is whether civic or ethnic forces dominate their political life: 1989 was the year of the civics; 1990 saw the

26. Donald L. Horowitz, *Ethnic Groups in Conflict* (Berkeley: University of California Press, 1985), p. 282; and see all of ibid., ch. 6, "The Logic of Secessions and Irredentas."
27. See chapter 8 above.

forceful emergence of ethnic political foces (in Croatia, Serbia, Slovakia, Hungary, Romania, the Ukraine, and Poland). The boundary between those representing one or the other iden-tity—civic or ethnic—tends to be stark, and the psychological, cultural, and political confrontation intense. Far from being complementary, these groups, programs, and orientations are competing for dominance and threaten to divide their so-cieties and destabilize their governments. Should ethnic politi-cal forces prevail, as they already have in Serbia, Croatia, and Romania, the potential for violence in and between countries in Eastern Europe and the involvement of Western Europe and Russia increases.

The civic/ethnic issue is also increasingly salient in Western Europe. In part this is because of the Leninist extinction of 1989 and resulting immigration. The recent electoral success in Austria of a nativist party can be directly attributed to the fear of Balkan immigrants. The prospect of some two million refu-gees from the Soviet Union and Eastern Europe in 1991 has led to political apprehension and ethnic rejection of "foreigners." The combined fear of migrants from North Africa[28] and ref-ugees from the "East" has made the civic/ethnic issue in West-ern Europe a source of divisive instability in a region that pres-ently appears more confident and purposive than any in the world.

The civic/ethnic divide is not limited to the former Leninist world or Western Europe. The conflicts between Afrikaaners and blacks in South Africa, and between the more civic ANC and the ethnic Zulu Inkatha in the same country; the conflict in Canada between British and French descendants; and the growing conflict over the status of the English language in In-dia all speak to the increasing international salience of this par-ticular identity cleavage.[29] So does the growing claim ethnicity and race make on citizens in the United States. Different as the expressions are: affirmative action, multicultural education,

28. See Alan Riding, "4 European Nations Planning A New Focus on North Africa," *New York Times,* September 30, 1990.

29. See Barbara Crossette, "Western Wedge in the Indian Subcontinent," *New York Times,* December 23, 1990, for a discussion of language politics in India today.

Rainbow Coalition, Spike Lee's movies, Louis Farrakhan's Nation of Islam, David Duke's Klan politics, and Bush's flag mania; they all contribute to the ethnically bounded polarization of a civic polity.

Civic/ethnic identity issues inside, adjacent to, and distant from the former Leninist world will interact with one another in a more or less direct and consequential way. The language and reality of this conflict is becoming a universal regardless of existing boundaries and identities.

In the aftermath of the Leninist extinction, one can identify a number of issues that don't "respect" existing territorial, ideological, and issues boundaries and identities. For example, *the status of women.*

Antifeminism is palpable throughout Eastern Europe. The Roman Catholic Church's anti-abortion stance is a striking, but not the only, example, as the literature in Hungary blaming women for the social disorder in that country testifies.[30] The presence of American troops has helped trigger a demonstration against the categoric gender division of labor in Saudi Arabia. In South America, the phenomenal growth of evangelical Protestantism has at its core the disportionate role of women as members and leaders.[31] This is not to say the gender issue means the same thing in each of these settings. Nor should that cautionary note prevent one from grasping the emergence of a new issue with potential national, regional, and international boundary and identity implications.

The same holds for *religion.* Since the Iranian revolution, radical Islam has been recognized as a resurgent boundary-making and identity-claiming force. Fundamentalist Muslims in Tunisia, Algeria, and Saudi Arabia are serious and influen-

30. Joann Goven, "On the 'Men's Mutiny'" (manuscript, 1990), discusses this. And see Celestine Bohlen, "East Europe's Women Struggle with New Rules, and Old Ones," *New York Times,* "This Week in Review," November 25, 1990.

31. On this movement, see John Marcom, Jr., "The Fire Down South," *Forbes,* October 15, 1990; David Stoll, *Is Latin America Turning Protestant?* (Berkeley: University of California Press, 1990), and David Martin, *Tongues of Fire: The Explosion of Protestantism in Latin America* (Cambridge, Mass.: Basil Blackwell, 1990). To Marcom's observation that "in Brazil as elsewhere the media have tended to ignore this religious revival," one might add, so has academia.

tial political "players," who if they come to power, particularly in Saudi Arabia, will have a crucial impact on relations between the West and Middle East. So when Safar al-Hawali, dean of Islamic studies at Umm al-Qura University in Mecca interprets the Iraqi crisis, not as "the world against Iraq," but as "the West against Islam," one should take note. According to Mamoun Fandy, "Dr. Hawali is one of Islam's most respected theologians and the primary spokesman for the Wahabi sect." The house of Saud adheres to the Wahabi sect. While stopping "short of calling for the overthrow of the Saud family [Hawali does emphasize that it is] contrary to the laws of Islam . . . to join with non-Moslems in a battle against Moslems." The Prophet warned, "Rome will attack you in many forms," Hawali reminded his listeners. "The Crusaders, the British and French colonialists, and now the Americans are all forms of Rome."[32] Islamic fundamentalism didn't disappear with Khomeini.

Nor is the religious factor limited to Islam. Roman Catholicism is on the political offensive in Eastern Europe, the Soviet Union, and Western Europe; on the political defensive in Latin and North America; and politically active everywhere. Whether calling for obligatory religious education in Hungarian and Polish schools, opposing abortion in Poland and the United States, aligning itself with the Soviet position on Iraq through the public statements of American bishops and in discussions between Gorbachev and the pope at the Vatican, or sponsoring "base communities" in Latin America, the Catholic Church has reemerged as a newly invigorated global political actor.[33] The Orthodox Church could emerge as a regional actor in Russia and the Balkans offering support to armies and ethnic nationalists in their possible effort to create a stable authoritarian order.[34] The Leninist extinction and the resulting psychological, economic, and cultural dislocation in the Soviet Union and

32. Mamoun Fandy, "The Hawali Tapes," *New York Times*, November 24, 1990.

33. In this connection, see Malachi Martin, *The Keys of This Blood: The Struggle for World Dominion between Pope John Paul II, Mikhail Gorbachev & the Capitalist West* (New York: Simon & Schuster, 1990).

34. This has already happened in Russia, where in December 1990 the Orthodox patriarch identified himself with demands for preservation of the Union and order.

Eastern Europe favors the growth of the Catholic and Orthodox Churches; while the collapse of the dominant West-East
boundary offers greater scope for the identity-claiming power
of Islam.

Cities have become gathering places of pollution, poverty,
invidious contrasts of cosmopolitan and lumpen life-styles, religious conflict, and ungovernability. Cities as different as Detroit, Cairo, Lagos, Mexico City, and Bucharest may become the
sites of urban jacqueries.

AIDS is another example of a new national/international issue; one that directly affects political alignments and conflicts.
In the United States, AIDS is a medical, sexual, and racial issue,
bounding and defining issues and actors in new ways, while
reinforcing existing racial and sexual polarities. In Africa,
AIDS is a medical epidemic that threatens the lives of millions;
in Uganda maybe a third of the population is infected.[35] In
Romania, the incidence of the HIV virus among infant orphans
in hospitals and latent hysteria in the population are both high.
China, which not long ago was blaming AIDS on the "rotten
mentality and lifestyle of capitalist society . . . is seeking Western
help." China's minister of public health, Chen Minzhang, has
recently said, "We have an AIDS problem that has a very dangerous potential to expand."[36]

And all of these issues: gender, religion, cities, and AIDS are
linked to the civic/ethnic divide. In the United States, a *New
York Times* / WCBS-TV News poll found that "10 percent of
blacks said the AIDS virus was deliberately created in a laboratory in order to infect black people. . . . Another 19 percent
said that theory might possibly be true and 63 percent said it
was almost certainly not true. . . . Of the whites polled 1 percent
said it was true, 4 percent said it was possibly true, and 91

35. See Jane Perlez, "Spread of AIDS Is Worrying Uganda," *New York
Times,* January 30, 1991. According to research undertaken by the Futures
Group, the predicted loss of twelve million people between now and 2015
"was a combination of people who would die of AIDS and those who would
never be born." President Musaveni stated that "the same study projects five
to six million Ugandan children would be orphans by 2010 because their
parents would have died of AIDS."
36. *Oakland Tribune,* November 21, 1990.

percent said it was almost certainly not true."[37] AIDS has become a medical and sociocultural base for potential hysteria in the United States, and a powerful issue reinforcing polarized racial identities and boundaries.

Religious identity claims challenge civic and secular identities in the Middle East and the former Leninist world in the Soviet Union and Eastern Europe. The decay of cities pits the more affluent, educated, cosmopolitan, civic (and often culturally invidious) dwellers against the poorer, less educated, more parochial (and often more violent) occupants. Cities are the site of increasing ethnic violence, as Italian/African-American and Korean/African-American conflicts in New York City demonstrate. Journalists increasingly report on urban racial turmoil— for example, in Chicago over a proposed resolution honoring Fred Hampton, a Black Panther shot by Chicago police in 1969.[38] The novelist Tom Wolfe has brilliantly and evocatively captured the tense, nasty tenor of race relations in New York.[39] And even the cautiously balanced academic treatment of race in the National Research Council's *A Common Destiny: Blacks and American Society* recognizes the substantial potential for racial violence in American cities.[40] As for gender contrast, it has enormous potential for categoric we-they divisiveness, the hallmark of ethnic division.

The Leninist extinction destroyed the dominant West-East international boundary and identity distinction. In the turbulent environments emerging today, the civic/ethnic distinction (while not centrally organized like the West-East conflict), is a central boundary/identity distinction in two respects: it can serve as a conceptual base for making sense of a disordered

37. Jason DeParle, "Talk Grows of Government Being Out to Get Blacks," *New York Times,* October 29, 1990.

38. See Dirk Johnson, "Seeking New Harmony, but Finding a Racial Rift," *New York Times,* November 25, 1990.

39. Tom Wolfe, *The Bonfire of the Vanities* (New York: Bantam Books, 1988).

40. See Gerald David Jaynes and Robin M. Williams, Jr., eds., *A Common Destiny: Blacks and American Society* (Washington, D.C.: National Academy Press, 1989). And see Steven A. Holmes, "Miami Melting Pot Proves Explosive," *New York Times,* December 9, 1990; Clifford Kraus, "Latin Immigrants in Capital Find Unrest a Sad Tie to Past," ibid., May 8, 1991.

world, and it already serves as an increasingly powerful political base for national and international conflicts.

"INTERMESTIC" ISSUES

While no boundary or identity is absolute, at least the one between domestic and international issues has been clear. Developments in the past two decades have challenged that clarity; so will the Leninist extinction.

In the 1970s, the proliferation of multinational corporations led many to question the clarity of national-international boundaries. The point was dulled for many American academics by the observation that most multinationals were U.S. companies operating in other nations. In the 1990s, the likelihood that an important number of the United States's most pressing problems will *simultaneously be national and international* should make it increasingly difficult to maintain this boundary distinction. There is nothing unique or new about international and national issues overlapping. In fact, with the exception of nuclear weapons, there is precedent for practically everything. However, only the sun isn't new; there are new things under it. If in World Wars I and II, a number of German-, Italian-, Irish-, and Japanese-Americans were concerned, some ambivalent, and a few opposed to the alignment and actions of the United States, one could still readily distinguish international issues and domestic responses. That task is more difficult in an "intermestic" situation.[41] Viewed ideal-typically, an intermestic relation is one in which nations simultaneously adhere to their respective sovereignties, while elites and publics from each nation regularly and reciprocally involve themselves, "mix," in the other's domestic affairs. "Intermestic" conflict superimposes conflicts within nations on conflicts between nations.

To date, Israel has been the United States's sole "intermestic"

41. I take the term *intermestic* from Bayless Manning, "The Congress, the Executive, and Intermestic Affairs: Three Proposals," *Foreign Affairs* 55, no. 2 (January 1977): 306–24. Manning refers to international issues that become national ones. I refer to issues where that distinction loses a good deal of its meaning.

issue. South Africa, Mexico, Canada, and Japan (the first being more likely than the second, the second more likely than the third . . .) are likely to join Israel. The crystallization of an African-American middle class and a college generation of American blacks for whom the status of black South Africans, affirmative action, and multicultural education are all domestic American issues; the visit of Nelson Mandela, his political adoption by liberal whites and African-Americans, his brilliant identification of race relations in the United States and South Africa in his speech before the U.S. (not African National) Congress, and his support of Native Americans blur domestic/international boundaries.

Canadian–U.S. economic ties, Quebec's possible secession, and the influence of U.S. culture in Canada have created a unique relation between two sovereign neighboring countries. And then there is Japan. U.S. sponsorship of the postwar Japanese polity and economy; Japanese investment in and ownership of American properties; Japan's continuing economic strength and decreasing need of U.S. military support, combined with increasing American envy and irritation at Japan's success, have created a situation very different from past national military, ideological, and economic rivalries.

In the "intermestic" cases I have identified, existing national boundaries and political identities have not been removed or even devalued. They have been added to, bypassed, and implicitly challenged. American Jews emigrate to Israel, and Israeli Jews immigrate to New York. African-American elites evaluate administrations in terms of their civil rights actions in the United States and policies toward South Africa. Nelson Mandela is as popular a figure for many African-Americans as Jesse Jackson. Meir Kahane was a political figure in both New York and Jerusalem. Relations between the United States and Mexico offer a particularly striking example of an "intermestic" situation, including as they do immigration from Mexico (and resulting ethnic turmoil and tension in a city like San Diego), potential political disorder in Mexico,[42] the explosive growth

42. See Mark A. Uhlig, "Mexico's Salinas Rains on His Own Parade," *New York Times*, November 25, 1990.

of *maquiladoras*[43]—U.S.-owned companies along the Arizona-Mexican border (some 1,800 American factories and 500,000 Mexican workers), and a more politically articulate and organized Chicano population in the United States.

War in the Middle East with Israel and Saudi Arabia on opposite sides, a civil war in South Africa, and/or in Mexico, Quebec seceding from Canada, or a halt to Japan's investing in and operating plants in the United States—any one of these developments would shape U.S. national debates and internal conflicts in a novel way, one our inertial definition of international boundaries and national identity would leave us ill-prepared to deal with.[44]

JEREMIAH OR HANANIAH?

The Leninist extinction is a "world-historical event." It challenges and threatens existing identity-shaping and identity-reflecting boundaries. The thrust of my argument has been threefold: to argue the "universal" rather than self-contained quality of the Leninist extinction; to do so in terms of its impact on existing boundaries and identities; and to use the framework of boundaries and identities to underscore the likely changes, anxiety, and issues that will shape our political future. Analyzing the likely consequences of the Leninist extinction leads me to conclude that we face a period of global, regional, and national turmoil over boundaries and identities. In this regard, I am more of a Jeremiah than a Hananiah.[45] Lest anyone worry, there is no shortage of academics who are optimistic about developments in a world without Leninism: "Hananiah" Hough's recent work on Gorbachev's "controlled chaos" in the

43. See the article by Sandy Tolan, "The Border Boom: Hope and Heartbreak," *New York Times Magazine,* July 1, 1990.

44. It should be clear that the U.S.–Japanese relationship has fewer intermestic features than any of the other cases.

45. On Jeremiah's pessimism and Hananiah's optimism, see "The Book of the Prophet Jeremiah," *New English Bible,* p. 950. At a recent conference at Yale, Juan Linz, in the course of his optimistic evaluation of democracy's chances in Eastern Europe, characterized my analysis of the Leninist legacy as Jeremiah-like. I am in his debt. It lead me to rediscover Jeremiah and discover Hananiah.

Soviet Union, Juan Linz's and Giuseppe Di Palma's prognosis for Eastern Europe, Fukuyama's belief in liberalism's historically definitive triumph, and Ben Wattenberg's view of developments in America all are characterized by a willful optimism I don't share.[46]

One reason is the inertial "state of the (American) union."

A striking example of inertial policy is the Bush administration's hypnotic commitment to NATO.[47] To be sure, inertia can be (and is) readily portrayed as prudence. But in turbulent environments, it is prudent to be imaginative and innovative. There is no evidence of either imagination or innovation in U.S. foreign policy; there is evidence of inertial reaction. If U.S. attitudes toward NATO are inertial, the U.S. response to Iraq's aggression is one of denial, in this case that it is 1990 not 1950; that it is Iraq and Kuwait, not North and South Korea; that it is North versus South, not West versus East; that in the aftermath of the Leninist extinction, any number of Iraq-Kuwait situations may arise, and that *the current administration has no criterion for deciding when and how to intervene.* I doubt the president or his advisers have any criteria to differentiate types of boundary change (e.g., Syria's actions in Lebanon, Israel's ac-

---

46. In 1987, Jerry Hough claimed that Western observers were "exaggerating the difficulty of reform" in the Soviet Union and had "exaggerated Gorbachev's problems at home." In 1989, Hough spoke of Gorbachev's "controlled chaos [which was] not simply directed at strengthening his political control for the sake of power. It is to maintain his control while he transforms Russia." That's optimism. But according to Professor Hough, his predictions about Soviet developments have been consistently accurate for ten years. Which ten years? See Jerry Hough, "The End of Russia's 'Khomeini' Period," *World Policy Journal* 4, no. 4 (Fall 1987): 583–605; "Gorbachev's Politics," *Foreign Affairs* 68, no. 5 (Winter 1989–90): 26–42; and "Gorbachev's Endgame," *World Policy Journal* 7, no. 4 (Fall 1990): 639–73 (see n. 29 for the claim to "ten years of successful prediction"). Giuseppe Di Palma's optimistic arguments can be found in *To Craft Democracies: Reflections on Democratic Transitions and Beyond* (Berkeley: University of California Press, 1990). And see Ben Wattenberg's *The First Universal Nation* (New York: Free Press, 1990).

47. See Craig R. Whitney, "NATO Leaders Gather, in Search of a Purpose," *New York Times,* July 4, 1990; and Alan Riding, "NATO Struggling to Redefine Itself," ibid., September 24, 1990. I don't find the argument that it would have taken longer than a year for elites to respond innovatively to the boundary and identity changes of 1989 satisfactory. Time is a factor, but not the critical one. The need for new concepts is greater than the need for more time; and the relationship between the two is by no means direct.

tions on the West Bank, and Iraq's actions in Kuwait). And I worry that success in Kuwait will reinforce the absolute assumption by the United States of global responsibility for unchanged territorial boundaries.

For fifty years the United States has defined every international issue as THE issue. U.S. foreign policy has been absolutist, not imperialist. It is ironic that a nation so adept at national compromise and bargaining should be so resistant to and unwilling to develop those talents in international relations. Obviously, some conflicts are not amenable to compromise; it should be equally obvious that some are, and that the United States cannot sustain its absolutist position, if for no other reason (and there are other reasons) than it can't afford it. As David Calleo notes: "America is today in no position to return to its hegemonic dreams of 1945. Financially, the U.S. has grown dependent on the inflow of foreign capital and can reduce its dependency only by reducing its fiscal deficit—a difficult course quite incompatible with sustaining its present military establishment, let alone transforming it into a world police force."[48]

Things don't get better for the United States when one looks at its world economic position. Relatively speaking, the United States would be better served by closer economic ties with Western Europe than with an unstable Mexico. But, "over the years, American efforts to insert the United States inside the structures of the European Community have been contentious [and] unsuccessful. So long as the EC is primarily an economic coalition, these efforts are not likely to succeed in any serious way in the future. Inevitably, the U.S. is seen not only as a political ally, but also as a major economic rival."[49] Nor do future economic relations with an economically and culturally nonbiodegradable Japan offer much ground for optimism. Add to that the growing civic/ethnic divide within the United States and the world and one finds little support for Hananiah, *except* in one segment of the liberal capitalist democratic world, Western Europe. If in the nineteenth century Great Britain was liberal

48. Calleo, "American National Interest and the New Europe," p. 168.
49. Ibid., p. 173.

capitalist democracy's core, and the United States in the twentieth, in the twenty-first century Western Europe may become the pivot of a reconfigured liberal world and way of life, a source of political promise and ideological self-confidence, not only military power and economic wealth.[50] However, here also we are dealing with a potential development whose future will be shaped by the turbulently bounded environments that are the legacy of the Leninist extinction.

50. At the close of the Charter of Paris meetings, French President Mitterand offered a sober insight: "We Europeans have 10 years in which to win our race against history" (Alan Riding, "Fog over the New Europe: How to Achieve Aims," *New York Times*, November 22, 1990).

Index